AMERICA
IN QUOTATIONS

A Kaleidoscopic View
of American History

Compiled and Edited by Howard J. Langer

GREENWOOD PRESS
Westport, Connecticut • London

Library of Congress Cataloging-in-Publication Data

America in quotations : a kaleidoscopic view of American history / compiled and [edited] by
Howard J. Langer.
    p. cm.
    Includes bibliographical references (p.) and index.
    ISBN 0–313–30883–7 (alk. paper)
    1. United States—History—Quotations, maxims, etc.   2. United States—Biography.   3.
Quotations, American.   I. Langer, Howard.
    E173.A525   2002
    973—dc21   2001033694

British Library Cataloguing in Publication Data is available.

Copyright © 2002 by Howard J. Langer

Library of Congress Catalog Card Number: 2001033694
ISBN: 0–313–30883–7

First published in 2002

Greenwood Press, 88 Post Road West, Westport, CT 06881
An imprint of Greenwood Publishing Group, Inc.
www.greenwood.com

Printed in the United States of America

The paper used in this book complies with the
Permanent Paper Standard issued by the National
Information Standards Organization (Z39.48–1984).

10 9 8 7 6 5 4 3 2 1

Copyright Acknowledgments

Photo of World Trade Center disaster (p. 372) courtesy of Corbis Sigma. Copyright by Jason Szenes/
Corbis Sigma.

Every reasonable effort has been made to trace the owners of copyright materials in this book, but
in some instances this has proven impossible. The author and publisher will be glad to receive
information leading to more complete acknowledgments in subsequent printings of the book and in
the meantime extend their apologies for any omissions.

For Florence,
to whom I owe
everything

Contents

Acknowledgments

To begin with, this project has been as frustrating as it has been fascinating. Compiling quotations about what has been written and spoken in the history of America is to be let loose in the biggest candy store in the world. And that is where the problem lies.

No history is richer or more colorful than American history. The problem is that a quote or two are no more than a tease or—in more modern terms—a sound bite about an incident, a situation, an investigation, a battle, a war, or an individual decision that may affect the lives of millions.

Let me give you a few examples of editing problems.

When President Jefferson wrote his instructions to Meriwether Lewis on exploring the Louisiana Purchase, he specified in great detail what to look for, how to act with Indian tribes, what kinds of equipment and personnel he would need, and so on. For reasons of space, I kept the quote pretty much to the objective of finding the Northwest Passage to the Pacific. Readers are urged to go back and read Jefferson's complete instructions.

The same thing goes for Jefferson's handling of the Burr conspiracy. The president had no Federal Bureau of Investigation (FBI), no Central Intelligence Agency (CIA), no Joint Chiefs of Staff, no National Security Council, no telephone, telegraph, CNN, ham radio, or even Pony Express. Yet he handled the threat with a meticulous regard to details, only a part of which is included in this book. Again, go back to the original—and marvel.

Another wholly inadequate look at a particular historical chapter in American history is the story of Alger Hiss and Whittaker Chambers. That case, involving a confessed former Communist fingering a former high State Department official for espionage, dominated the media for many months and led to the meteoric rise of Congressman Richard Nixon in American politics. A fine summary of that affair is to be found in *Friendship and Fratricide: An Analysis of Whittaker*

Chambers and Alger Hiss, by Meyer A. Zeligs. Both Hiss and Chambers gave their own accounts in separate books.

When President Ford granted a full pardon to former president Richard Nixon following the Watergate affair, Ford was roundly criticized by many observers. Ford's side of the issue, however, was never really told. In his book *A Time to Heal,* an extraordinary section is devoted to the entire pardoning process. It includes a wistful account of a meeting by a Justice Department official with the disgraced ex-president at San Clemente, California. It is a moving story that could not be adequately told in brief quotations. Speaking of Watergate, I urge everyone researching the subject to look into Leon Jaworski's book *The Right and the Power.* The book's appendix provides lists of both individuals and corporations that were found guilty, pleaded guilty, or pleaded no contest to a wide range of illegal activities—from breaking into the offices of a psychiatrist, to illegal campaign contributions. The list of individuals is fairly well known, but the list of corporations will raise many eyebrows.

Similarly, many books give full accounts of such historical events as the two presidential impeachments, the acquisition of the Panama Canal, Watergate, and Iran-Contra. You are encouraged to make extensive use of this book's bibliography to fill in the details about the historical subjects that interest you.

I have tried to incorporate editorial notes wherever possible to indicate what may have preceded—or followed—a particular quote. For many of these added details, I have drawn from the usual encyclopedic sources, as well as such references as *Encyclopedia of American History,* edited by Richard B. Morris and Jeffrey B. Morris; *Concise Dictionary of American History,* edited by Wayne Andrews; *Benet's Reader's Encyclopedia,* originally edited by William Rose Benet; and *A Chronological Encyclopedia of American History,* by Irving S. Kull and Nell M. Kull.

Because sources do not always agree, I have made choices and assume full responsibility for any errors in this work.

As far as formal acknowledgment is concerned, I begin with the various libraries. First, the staff of the New City (Rockland County, New York) Public Library has been an active part of the research process, particularly in the acquisition of materials not available from its own shelves. Additional libraries include Finklestein Memorial Library in Spring Valley, and the public libraries of Nanuet, Pearl River, and Orangeburg, New York. I appreciate the assistance given by both public and college libraries in the Catskill system. I must also mention the New York City Public Library and the West Point library.

I would also like to acknowledge the cooperation of the various presidential libraries, particularly the Hoover, Carter, Reagan, and Bush libraries, for providing specific documents.

On a personal note, I want to thank my friends and relatives for encouragement, support, and ideas.

For allowing me the opportunity to pursue this project, I would like to thank my friends at Greenwood Publishing Group, particularly Bob Hagelstein, Jim Sabin, and Cynthia Harris.

Wherever possible, the original source of a quotation is given, rather than a secondary source.

Where a document is generally available—a specific presidential speech, for example, or a well-known quotation available in many sources—I have given just the name of the speaker, date, place, and occasion of the quote. Quotes from important Supreme Court decisions have been drawn largely from secondary sources that do not run the opinions in full. Readers who want the full texts should go directly to the authoritative legal references.

I used the *New York Times* on a daily basis, not merely for quotations but to get a context for what was worth including. It was—and is—indispensable.

Introduction

A kaleidoscope is a wondrous thing. Hold it up to the light and look through the tiny peephole. What a lovely design of shapes and colors! Now turn the little wheel at the far end. Even the slightest turn of the wheel changes the design dramatically. A whole new pattern of shapes and colors appears, formed by the changing reflection of the mirrors inside. With each turn, every piece of colored glass is given a different position and configuration. Sometimes one color dominates the pattern, sometimes another. The pattern is ever-changing.

The recorded history of America has been a lot like that.

For most of our history, the wheel of the kaleidoscope rarely moved—and white men dominated.

Largely overlooked were women, people of color, ethnics, and members of a wide spectrum of groups other than those in "polite society." Our history was often just the story of those in politics and the military.

This work is an attempt to help turn the wheel and show a kaleidoscopic view of our heritage. It is a historical anthology, presented as a series of quotations in chronological sequence. It constantly changes the focus from the famous to the forgotten, from the great billboard to the small snapshot.

The quotations deal with the multifaceted nature of America's many cultures, its values, and its thoughts. Most—but not all—of the quotations are by Americans. The early quotations, of necessity, are by European explorers and "discoverers." Later in our history, outsiders are quoted because they saw us in ways that we could not see ourselves.

Most of the book is divided into traditional segments of American history. The book may therefore be read in different ways.

First, one may wish to see what specific individuals wrote or said or to look into a particular subject area.

Second, one may get a feel for what was happening during different periods of

American history, such as the pre–Civil War period called "House Divided" or the period of industrialism during the latter part of the 19th century.

Third, one may trace an individual's changing views about different issues, such as slavery, intervention, or civil rights.

Finally, because of its chronological format, this book may be read from cover to cover as a very different kind of American history book—one that enriches a traditional narrative history.

Each section of the book provides a brief context for the material that follows. In addition, editorial notes accompanying many of the quotations may offer background material that tells what happened before—or after—the date of the quote.

This story of America is told through the words of its people. There are excerpts from speeches, letters, conversations, diaries, editorials, interviews, news stories, advertisements, songs, poems, jokes, short stories and novels that had some impact on American life and thought, and analyses by historians and other scholars. There are quotations from official pronouncements by government agencies, labor unions, political parties, and the military. There are excerpts from court decisions, lawyers' arguments, captions from cartoons, movie lines, slogans, and accounts broadcast over radio and television.

It is traditional to have winners in a collection such as this—usually those in politics and in the military. But here the reader will find losers as well.

The winners and losers come from all walks of American life: labor leaders and civil rights activists, heroes and villains, poets and humorists, farmworkers and slaves, members of the clergy and Native Americans.

This book offers a retrospective of the great changes in America's past—the good and the bad, the beautiful and the ugly. Here are joyful expressions of freedom and mournful cries of slavery, the spirit of brotherhood and the savagery of racial violence, the splendor of great industrial enterprises and the ugliness of labor strife, military bravery as well as butchery. It is all part of our history and heritage.

There is a real advantage to the chronological format of this book. One may look at a statement by an individual in context. As circumstances changed, so did the ideas expressed.

Thus, the statement of any individual must be weighed in terms of the time that it was made. People change their minds, and an opinion expressed during the fever pitch of a crisis may well change after the issue has been resolved.

This has happened after every crisis in the nation's history. I have tried to choose those quotes that shed some light on the issue. This is particularly true about the civil rights movement. At the height of the struggle, there were bitter statements on both sides. After the crisis ended, extremists became moderates. Intemperate words may raise eyebrows in retrospect. Consider the time when the statement was made.

Quotations made at about the same time are often jarring. Consider the juxtaposition of Martin Luther King Jr.'s speech with that of civil rights activist

James Farmer. On the same day that King gave his "I have a dream" speech, Farmer was in a southern jail. His speech was read for him on the same platform in Washington. Farmer's remarks were defiant: "We will not stop until the dogs stop biting us in the South and the rats stop biting us in the North."

A word about editing. Quotations have been trimmed for reasons of space. A few extremely long, run-on sentences may have been broken down into several shorter ones. In some of the earliest quotations, spellings may have been modified for clarity. Words in brackets within a quotation have been inserted to clarify or explain. Though bracketed words are not the precise words of the person being quoted, they are used to make clear the sum and substance of the speaker's viewpoint.

Words used to describe African Americans have changed over the years, and the exact wording has been kept. Thus, one will find references to blacks, colored, Negro, negro, and—I am afraid—nigger. When President Andrew Johnson referred to Frederick Douglass with that term, it had to be left in. It is an important part of understanding where we came from and where we are now.

As I have said before, the book is divided, for the most part, into traditional historical periods. Some of these periods have specific time slots, such as the American Revolution, Civil War, Reconstruction, and Boom and Bust.

Other sections were far more difficult to lock into strict time frames. In this book, the civil rights movement starts with the Supreme Court decision on school desegregation. But the movement probably began more than a century earlier, with the first battles for abolition of slavery and the movement for woman's rights, and that movement has never really ended. The same with the section on the Cold War, which did not really end until the breakup of the Soviet Union. In these and other cases, the particular section merely indicates a period when that particular issue was most prominent.

It has been said that history is written by the victors. Here, as I have said before, the reader will also find the vanquished. In short, this is a picture of America, warts and all. Turn the wheel of the kaleidoscope.

I believe that this is the greatest country in the history of the world. There have been injustices committed in our past, but I think that we are strong enough to face up to them and, by doing so, to become stronger, wiser, and greater.

Before the arrival of Columbus, a typical Indian village in the southeast would have looked very similar to this. Painting of Secotan on the Pamlico River was made in the 16th century.

1

Before Columbus

The first discoverers of America were not Europeans but Asians. Some came across what is believed to have been a land bridge between what we now call Siberia and Alaska. That could have been as long as 35,000 years ago—or even longer. Over the years that followed, other Asians made their way here across the Pacific, island by island, in small boats. The children of these first aliens, born here, became the first Native Americans.

Because they had no written language, few real quotations are available for this period of time. Material from two documents follows. One is a remarkable prophecy passed down in the oral tradition from father to son. It tells of strange men coming to hunt for a certain stone.

The other document is from a book written by Marco Polo, with tales of a land filled with gold and precious stones. Marco Polo was referring to Asia, but the explorers who came to America were drawn by the vision of great riches. The two items are thus related, for the dreams of one group are about to become the nightmare of another.

A LOOK INTO THE FUTURE

1. There is a time coming . . . when many things will change. Strangers called Earth Men will appear among you. Their skins are light-colored, and their ways are powerful. They speak no Indian tongue. Follow nothing that these Earth Men do, but keep your own ways that I have taught you as long as you can. (Sweet Medicine, from *Cheyenne Memories*, by John Stands in Timber and Margot Liberty.)

2. The buffalo will disappear, at last, and another animal will take its place, a slick animal with a long tail and split hoofs, whose flesh you will learn to eat. But first there will be another animal you must learn to use. It has a shaggy neck and a tail almost touching the ground. Its hoofs are round. This animal will carry you on his back and help you in many ways. (Ibid.)

3. Those people will wander this way . . . they will be looking for a certain stone. . . . They will be people who do not get tired, but who will keep pushing forward, going all the time. They will keep coming, coming. . . . They will travel everywhere looking for this stone which our great-grandfather put on the earth in many places. . . . These people will not listen to what you say; what they are going to do they will do. You people will change: in the end of your life in those days you will not get up early in the morning, you will not know when day comes. . . . They will try to change you from your way of living to theirs. . . . They will tear up the earth, and at last you will do it with them. When you do, you will become crazy, and will forget all that I am teaching you. (Sweet Medicine from *In the Spirit of Crazy Horse*, by Peter Matthiessen.)

TALE OF THE FAR EAST

4. The king of the Island [Japan] hath a mighty palace all roofed with finest gold, just as our churches are roofed with lead. The windows of that palace are all decorated with gold, the floors of the halls and of many chambers are paved with golden plates, each plate a good two fingers thick. There are pearls in the greatest abundance. (Marco Polo, from *The Book of Marco Polo*, dictated in prison in 1298, cited in *Admiral of the Ocean Sea*, by Samuel Eliot Morison.)

[Morison describes this passage as coming from Columbus' own copy of the Polo work. It is included here as the stimulating factor for European interest in finding a water route to the Far East.]

2

Beginnings

Starting with Columbus, the European explorers and colonizers came to the New World with the arrogance of self-righteous, "superior" beings. Some of the newcomers marveled at the trusting nature of the inhabitants. Other newcomers brought with them documents that allowed them to distribute lands that belonged to the people whose ancestors had lived there for thousands of years.

Misunderstandings became mistrust. Small enclaves of colonists found it difficult to survive.

COLUMBUS COMES ASHORE

5. Presently they saw naked people, and the Admiral went ashore in the armed ship's boat with the royal standard displayed. So did the captains of *Pinta* and *Nina* . . . in their boats, with the banners of the Expedition, on which were depicted a green cross with an F on one arm and a Y on the other, and over each his or her crown. . . . [A]ll having rendered thanks to Our Lord kneeling on the ground, embracing it with tears of joy for the immeasurable mercy of having reached it, the Admiral arose and gave this island the name San Salvador. Thereupon he summoned to him the two captains [and the] secretary of the armada . . . and all others who came ashore, as witnesses; and in the presence of many natives of that land assembled together, took possession of that island in the name of the Catholic Sovereigns with appropriate words and ceremony. (Description of landing in the New World, October 13, 1492, based

Arriving in the New World, Columbus claims the land for Spain, October 12, 1492. In the background, the ships *Pinta, Nina,* and *Santa Maria.*

on the journal of Columbus, from *Admiral of the Ocean Sea,* by Samuel Eliot Morison.)

SIZING UP THE POPULATION

6. In order that we might win good friendship, because I knew that they were a people who could better be freed and converted to our Holy Faith by love than by force, I gave to some of them red caps and to some glass beads, which they hung on their necks and many other things of slight value, which they took much pleasure. . . .

Later they came swimming to the ship's boats . . . and brought us parrots and cotton thread in skeins and darts and many other things, and we swopped them for other things that we gave them, such as little glass beads and hawk's bells.

Finally they swopped and gave everything they had, with good will. But it appeared to us that these people were very poor in everything. They go quite naked as their mothers bore them, and also the women. . . .

[They were] very well made, of very handsome bodies and very good faces; the hair coarse almost as the hair of a horse's tail and short; the hair they wear over their eyebrows, except for a hank behind that they wear long and never cut. Some of them paint themselves black and they are of the color of the Canary Islanders, neither black nor white. . . . [S]ome paint themselves white . . . , others red, and others with what they have. Some paint their faces, others the whole body, others the eyes only, others only the nose.

They bear no arms, nor know thereof; for I showed them swords and they grasped them by the blade and cut themselves through ignorance; they have no iron. Their darts are a kind of rod without iron, and some have at the end a fish's tooth and others, other things. . . .

I now believe that people do come here from the mainland to take them as slaves. They ought to be good servants and of good skill, for I see that they repeat very quickly all that is said to them; and I believe they would easily be made Christians, because it seemed to me that they belonged to no religion. I, please Our Lord, will carry off six of them at my departure to Your Highnesses, so that they may learn to speak. (Christopher Columbus, letter to King Ferdinand and Queen Isabella, 1493, cited in *Admiral of the Ocean Sea*, by Samuel Eliot Morison.)

HISTORIAN'S VIEW

7. Unfortunately this guilelessness and generosity of the simple savage aroused the worst traits of cupidity and brutality in the average European. Even the Admiral's humanity seems to have been merely political, as a means to eventual enslavement and exploitation. But to the intellectuals of Europe it seemed that Columbus had stepped back several millennia, and encountered people living in the Golden Age, that bright morning of humanity which existed only in the imagination of poets. Columbus's discovery enabled Europeans to see their own ancestors, as it were, in a "state of nature," before Pandora's box was opened. (Samuel Eliot Morison, assessing Columbus and the discovery of the New World, from *Admiral of the Ocean Sea*, by Samuel Eliot Morison.)

ENCOUNTER ON THE MISSISSIPPI

8. [Hernando de Soto, governor of Cuba, persuades the Spanish king to allow him to explore Florida for gold. His search takes him through much of what is now the southeastern United States. In May 1541, he and his military force of 600 find themselves at a great river. They are at the Mississippi, about 30 miles south of what is now Memphis, Tennessee.]

The next day the cacique [Indian chief] arrived, with two hundred canoes filled with men, having weapons. They were painted with ochre, wearing great bunches of white and other plumes of many colors. . . . [They had] leathered shields in their hands, with which they sheltered the oarsmen on either side. The warriors [were] standing erect from bow to stern, holding bows and arrows. The barge in which the cacique came had an awning at the poop, under which he sat. . . .

All came down together, and arrived within a stone's cast of the ravine, whence the cacique said to the Governor [Hernando de Soto], who was walking along the riverbank, with others who bore him company, that he had come to visit, to serve, and obey him; for he had heard that he was the greatest of lords, the most powerful on all the earth, and that he must see what he would have him do. The Governor expressed his pleasure, and besought him to land, that they might the better confer; but the chief gave no reply, ordering three barges to draw near, wherein was great quantity of fish, and loaves like bricks, made of the pulp of plants, which Soto receiving, gave him thanks and again entreated him to land.

Making the gift had been a pretext, to discover if any harm might be done; but, finding the Governor and his people on their guard, the cacique began to draw off from the shore, when the [Spanish] crossbowmen who were in readiness, with loud cries shot at the Indians, and struck down five or six of them. They retired with great order, not one leaving the oar, even though the one next to him might have fallen, and covering themselves, they withdrew. ("The Gentleman of Elvas," a member of the de Soto expedition, on the Mississippi River, May 1541, from *Spanish Explorers in the Southern United States*, cited in *The American Reader*, edited by Paul M. Angle.)

[From here on, de Soto wages a war of conquest against the inhabitants of the region. In May 1542, he dies of disease. About half his force survives the expedition. No gold is found.]

LETTER OF PATENT

9. Elizabeth by the grace of God of England, France and Ireland Queen, defender of the faith, &c. To all people to whom these presents shall come, greeting.

Know ye that of our especial grace, . . . we have given and granted . . . to our trusty and well beloved servant Walter Ralegh Esquire . . . free liberty & license . . . for ever hereafter, to discover, search, find out, and view such remote, heathen and barbarous lands, countries, and territories, not actually possessed of any Christian prince, nor inhabited by Christian people . . . to have, hold, occupy & enjoy to him, his heirs and assigns for ever, with all prerogatives, commodities, jurisdictions, royalties, privileges, franchises and pre-eminences, thereto or thereabouts both by sea and land. . . . (Queen Elizabeth I, letter of patent to Walter Ralegh, March 25, 1584, cited in *The Principal Navigations, Voyages, Traffiques, and Discoveries of the English Nation*, by Richard Hakluyt.)

10. And we do grant to the said Walter Ralegh, his heirs, and assigns, and to all, and every other person . . . being of our allegiance, whose names shall be noted or entered in some of our courts of record, within our Realm of England, that with the assent of the said Walter Ralegh, his heirs and assigns, shall in his journeys for discovery, or in the journeys for conquest hereafter travail to such lands, countries and territories . . . and to them, and to every one of their heirs . . . being either born within our said Realm of England or Ireland, or in any other place within our allegiance, and which hereafter shall be inhabiting within any [of] the lands, countries, and territories, with such license . . . shall and may have all the privileges of free denizens, and persons native of England . . . as if they were born and personally resident within our said Realm of England. . . .

And forasmuch as upon the finding out, discovering, or inhabiting of such remote lands, countries, and territories as aforesaid, it shall be necessary for the safety of all men, that shall adventure themselves in those journeys or voyages, to determine to live together in Christian peace, and civil quietness each with other, whereby every one may with more pleasure and profit enjoy that whereunto they shall attain with great pain and peril. (Ibid.)

[The spelling of Ralegh used here is as it appears in the document. Ralegh attempted to colonize an area of North America that he called "Virginia," in honor of the Virgin Queen, Elizabeth. His attempts failed.]

MYSTERY OF ROANOKE ISLAND

Three years after leaving the English colony at Roanoke island, colonial leader John White returns from England. His ship is loaded
with badly needed provisions for the colonists.

11. Towards evening we came to an anchor at Hatorask. We saw a great
smoke rise in the Roanoke near the place where I left our colony in the year
1587, which smoke put us in good hope that some of the colony were there
expecting my return out of England. . . .

[Next morning] we sounded with a trumpet a call, and afterward many familiar
English tunes of songs, and called to them friendly. But we had no answer. . . .

[A]t my departure from them in 1587 I willed them that if they should happen
to be distressed in any of the places, that they should carve over the letters or
name a cross; but we found no such sign of distress. And having well considered
of this, we passed towards the place where they were left in sundry houses, but
we found the houses and the place very strongly enclosed with a high palisade
of great trees . . . very fort-like.

[O]ne of the chief trees or posts at the right side of the entrance had the bark
taken off, and five foot from the ground in fair capital letters was graven CROA-
TOAN without any cross or sign of distress. . . .

[W]e entered into the palisade, where we found many bars of iron, two pigs of
lead, four iron fowlers, iron sacker-shot (for large cannon) and such like heavy
things, thrown here and there, almost overgrown with grass and weeds. . . .

[W]e found five chests that had been carefully hidden of the planters, and of
the same chests three were my own, and about this place many of my things
spoiled and broken, and my books torn from the covers, the frames of some of
my pictures and maps rotten and spoiled with rain, and my armor almost eaten
through with rust.

This could be no other but the deed of the savages our enemies. (John White,
Roanoke island, "Virginia" [actually North Carolina], August 1590, cited in *Diary
of America*, edited by Josef Berger and Dorothy Berger.)

[Historians have puzzled over the lost colony mystery for centuries. Many now believe
that survivors may have joined friendly Native Americans on the nearby island of Croa-
toan.]

LIFE ALONG THE RIVER

12. When I came on shore, the swarthy natives all stood and sang in their fashion. Their clothing consists of the skins of foxes and other animals, which they dress and make the garments from skins of various sorts. Their food is Turkish wheat [maize], which they cook by baking, and it is excellent eating. They soon came on board, one after another, in their canoes, which are made of a single piece of wood. Their weapons are bows and arrows, pointed with sharp stones, which they fasten with hard resin. They had no houses, but slept under the blue heavens, some on mats of bulrushes interwoven, and some on the leaves of trees. They always carry with them all their goods, as well as their food and green tobacco, which is strong and good for use. They appear to be a friendly people, but are much inclined to steal, and are adroit in carrying away whatever they take a fancy to. . . .

It is as pleasant a land as one can tread upon, very abundant in all kinds of timber suitable for ship-building, and for making large casks. The people had copper tobacco pipes, from which I inferred that copper must exist there. (Henry Hudson, "along the Hudson River," 1609, cited in *Narratives of New Netherland: 1609–1664*, edited by J. Franklin Jameson.)

[This material originated in *New World*, by Johan de Laet, first published in Holland in 1625. As a director of the Dutch West India Company, de Laet received letters and reports from the various explorers.]

13. I sailed to the shore in one of their canoes, with an old man, who was the chief of a tribe, consisting of 40 men and 17 women; these I saw there in a house well constructed of oakbark, and circular in shape, with the appearance of having a vaulted ceiling. It contained a great quantity of maize, and beans of the last year's growth, and there lay near the house for the purpose of drying enough to load three ships, besides what was growing in the fields. On our coming near the house, two mats were spread out to sit upon, and immediately some food was served in well made red wooden bowls; two men were also despatched at once with bows and arrows in quest of game, who soon after brought in a pair of pigeons which they had just shot. They likewise killed at once a fat dog, and skinned it in great haste, with shells which they get out of the water. They supposed that I would remain with them for the night, but I returned after a short time on board the ship. The land is the finest for cultivation that ever in my life set foot upon, and it also abounds in trees of every description. The natives are a very good people; for, when they saw that I would not remain, they supposed that I was afraid of their bows, and taking the arrows, they broke them in pieces, and threw them into the fire, etc. (Ibid.)

14. They found there also vines and grapes, pumpkins, and other fruits. From all these things there is sufficient reason to conclude that it is a pleasant and fruitful country, and that the natives are well disposed, if they are only well treated, although they are very changeable, and of the same general character as all the savages in the north. They have no religion whatever, nor any divine worship. . . . Much less have they any political government, except that they have their chiefs. . . . On different occasions some of our people have been surprised by them and slain; for they are revengeful and very suspicious, and because often engaged in wars among themselves, they are very fearful and timid. But with mild and proper treatment, and especially by intercourse with Christians, this people might be civilized and brought under better regulation; particularly if a sober and discreet population were brought over and good order preserved. They are, besides, very serviceable, and allow themselves to be employed in many things for a small compensation; even to performing a long day's journey, in which they discover greater fidelity than could be expected of such a people. (Ibid.)

3

Colonial Period

The English colonists brought self-government to New England, as well as strong beliefs about education, religion, and how people should behave. Dissent was frowned upon. The lucky dissenters were banished and started colonies of their own. "Witches" were not so lucky. In Europe they were being burned at the stake. In America they were usually hanged.

Meanwhile, the slave population was growing quickly, particularly in the South.

MAYFLOWER COMPACT

15. In the Name of God, Amen. We, . . . the Loyal Subjects of our dread Sovereign, Lord King James, . . . Having undertaken for the Glory of God, and Advancement of the Christian Faith, and the Honour of our King and Country, a voyage to plant the first colony in the northern Parts of Virginia, Do by these Prevents, solemnly and mutually in the Presence of God and one another, covenant and combine ourselves together into a civil Body Politick, for our better Ordering and Preservation. . . . And by Virtue hereof do enact, constitute, and frame such just and equal Laws, Ordinances, Acts, Constitutions, and Offices, from time to time, as shall be thought most meet . . . the general Good of the Colony. (Mayflower Compact, Cape Cod, November 11, 1620.)

Witchcraft trial at Salem, Massachusetts, 1692.

DELIVERANCE

16. Being thus arrived in a good harbor and brought safe to land, they fell upon their knees and blessed the God of heaven, who had brought them over the vast and furious ocean, and delivered them from all the perils and miseries thereof, again to set their feet on the firm and stable earth, their proper element. (William Bradford, Plymouth, Massachusetts, events of December 16, 1620, from *History of the Plymouth Plantation.*)

SONGS TO ENTICE SETTLERS

17.

The soil it is Fertii, as I have been told,
The Climate so warm that you need not fear cold;
The Wealthy and Great, to their honour I say,
Will all the expence of your passage defray.

(Song lyrics, "A Trip to the New Found Out Land," early 17th century, from *American Colonial Documents to 1776*, edited by Merrill Jensen.)

18.

All you that want business, and willing to goe,
They'll find you Utensils, sithe, Mattock and hoe;
A pick Ax and shovel, a baskit and spade,
And all things convenient for every Trade.
Tho you are but journey men Artisans here,
You'll all become Masters as soon as you're there.

(Ibid.)

PATROONSHIPS AVAILABLE

19. Privileges and Exemptions for Patroons, Masters and Private Individuals, who will settle any Colonies . . . in New Netherland. . . .

Such participants shall be permitted to send in the ships of this Company going thither, three or four persons to inspect the situation of the country, provided that they, with the officers and ship's company, swear to the articles, so far as they relate to them, and pay for provisions and for passage, going and coming, six stivers' [about twelve cents] per diem. . . .

[After selection by the company] such persons shall be acknowledged patroons of New Netherland who shall undertake, within the space of four years next after they have given notice . . . to plant a colony there of 50 souls, upwards of 15 years old; one-fourth part within one year, and within three years after . . . the remainder, to the full number of 50 persons. . . .

They [the patroons] shall forever possess and enjoy all the lands lying within the . . . limits, together with the fruits, crops, minerals, rivers and fountains thereof. . . .

There shall likewise be granted to all patroons . . . liberty to dispose of their aforesaid heritage. . . .

The patroons may make use of all lands, rivers and woods lying contiguous to their property, until this Company, or other patroons or private persons, shall take possession of them. . . .

Those who shall send persons over to settle colonies shall furnish them with proper instructions in order that they may be ruled and governed comfortably to the rule of government. . . .

The patroons and colonists shall be privileged to send all their people and effects thither in ships belonging to the Company, provided they take the oath and pay the Company. . . .

[The company] will not take from the service of the patroons any of their colonists, either man or woman, son or daughter, man-servant or woman-servant, and, though any of these should desire the same, they will not receive them, much less permit them to leave their patroon, and enter into the service of another, unless on consent obtained from their patroons in writing, and this for and during so many years as they are bound to their patroons. After the expiration whereof, it shall be in the power of the patroons to send hither all such colonists as will not continue in their service, and not to set them at liberty until then. (General West India Trading Company pamphlet, March 1630, cited in *Narratives of New Netherland: 1609–1664*, edited by J. Franklin Jameson.)

[The preceding is only a partial list of the almost-feudal privileges and exemptions. Patroons, for example, could set up their own courts and had tax exemption for eight years. Patroonships were established along the Hudson, Connecticut, and Delaware rivers.]

PUNISHMENT FOR DISSENT

20. Mr. [Roger] Williams . . . proceeded more vigorously to vent many dangerous opinions, as amongst many others these were some . . . that there should be a general and unlimited toleration of all religions, and for any man to be punished for any matters of his conscience was persecution.

He not only persisted, but grew more violent in his way, insomuch as he staying at home in his own house, sent a letter, which was delivered and read in the public Church Assembly, the scope of which was to give them notice, that if the Church of Salem would not separate not only from the Churches of Old-England, but the Churches of New-England too, he would separate from them. The more prudent and sober part of the Church being amazed at his way, could not yield unto him. Whereupon he never came to the Church Assembly more, professing separation from them as Antichristian, and not only so, but he withdrew all private religious Communion from any that would hold Communion with the Church there, insomuch as he would not pray nor give thanks at meals with his own wife nor any of his family, because they went to the Church Assemblies.

The prudent Magistrates understanding, and seeing things grow more and more toward a general division and disturbance, after all other means used in vain, they passed a sentence of Banishment against him out of the Massachusetts colony, as against a disturber of the peace, both of the Church and Commonwealth. (Nathaniel Morton, secretary, Massachusetts Bay Colony, Salem, Massachusetts, 1634–1636, cited in *Eyewitness to America*, edited by David Colbert.)

[Williams settled in nearby Rhode Island, where he founded the city of Providence. Many of his followers joined him there.]

ESCAPE FROM THE IROQUOIS

With the help of friendly mariners, a Jesuit priest flees from his captors.

21. Being outside of the barn, without having made any noise or awakened any guards, I cross over a fence which confined the enclosure about the house; I run straight to the river where the ship was—this is all the service that my leg, much wounded [by a dog's bite], could render me; for there was surely a good quarter of a league of road to make.

I found the [small] boat . . . , but the water having subsided, it was aground. I push it, in order to set it afloat. Not being able to effect this, on account of its weight, I call to the ship, that they bring the skiff to ferry me, but no news. I know not whether they heard me; at all events no one appeared. The daylight meanwhile was beginning to discover to the Iroquois the theft, that I was making of myself. I feared that they might surprise me in this innocent misdemeanor. Weary of shouting, I return to the boat. I pray God to increase my strength; I do so well, turning it end for end, and push it so hard that I get it to the water. Having made it float, I jump into it, and go all alone to the ship, where I go on board without being discovered by any Iroquois.

They [ship's crew] lodge me forthwith down in the hold and in order to conceal me they put a great chest over the hatchway. I was two days and two nights in the belly of that vessel, with such discomfort that I thought I would suffocate and die with the stench. . . .

The second night of my voluntary prison, the minister of the Dutch came to tell me that the Iroquois had indeed made some disturbance, and that the Dutch inhabitants of the country were afraid that they would set fire to houses or kill their cattle. They have reason to fear them, since they have armed them with good arquebuses [matchlock guns]. To that I answer: "If the storm has risen on my account, I am ready to appease it by losing my life." [This was a reference to the biblical story of Jonah.] I had never the wish to escape to the prejudice of the least man of their settlement.

Finally, it was necessary to leave my cavern; all the mariners were offended at this, saying that the promise of security had been given me in case I could set foot in the ship, and that . . . I had put myself in peril of life by escaping upon their words, that it must needs be kept, whatever the cost. I begged I be allowed to go forth, since the captain who had disclosed to me the way of my flight was asking for me. I went to find him in his house, where he kept me concealed. . . .

Finally, the captain told me that it was necessary to yield quickly to the storm, and wait until the minds of the savages should be pacified. . . . So there I was, a voluntary prisoner in his house, from which I am writing back to you the present letter. (Father Isaac Jogues, a Jesuit missionary from France, letter to Father Charles Lalemant, his superior in Canada, New Netherland, August 30, 1643, cited in *Narratives of New Netherland: 1609–1664*, edited by J. Franklin Jameson.)

[Father Jogues made good his escape. He later returned to continue his missionary work and was slain.]

OUTWITTING SATAN

22. It being one chief project of ye old deluder, Satan, to keep men from knowledge of ye Scriptures. . . . It is therefore ordered, that every township in this jurisdiction, after ye Lord hath increased their number to 50 households, shall then forthwith appoint one within their town to teach all such children as shall resort to him to write & read, whose wages shall be paid either by ye parents or masters of such children, or by ye inhabitants in general. (School law, Massachusetts Bay Colony, 1647, from *Records of the Governor and Company of the Massachusetts Bay in New England.*)

POEM OF LOVE

23.

If ever two were one, then surely we.
If ever man were loved by wife, then thee,
If ever wife was happy in a man,
Compare with me ye women if you can. . . .
Thy love is such I can no way repay,
The heavens reward thee manifold, I pray!
Then while we live, in love lets so persever,
That when we live no more, we may live ever.

(Anne Bradstreet, New England housewife, ca. 1650, from *The Intellectual Life of Colonial New England*, by Samuel Eliot Morison.)

WHY NEW NETHERLAND SURRENDERED

24. Illustrious, High and Mighty Lords. . . .
[T]his loss could not be avoided by human means, nor be imputed to me. . . .
I dare not interrupt your . . . most important business by a lengthy narrative of the poor condition in which I found New Netherland on my assuming its government. The open country was stripped of inhabitants to such a degree that, with the exception of the three English villages of Heemstede, New Flushing and Gravesend, there were not fifty bouweries [farms] and plantations on it, and the whole province could not muster 250, at most 350 men capable of bearing arms.
[This situation] . . . was caused, first, in default of a settlement of the boundary so repeatedly requested by the troublesome neighbors of New England, who numbered full fifty to our one, continually encroaching on lands within established bounds, possessed and cultivated in fact by your . . . subjects.
Secondly, by the exceedingly detrimental, land-destroying and people-expelling wars with the cruel barbarians, which endured two years before my arrival here, whereby many subjects who possessed means were necessitated to depart, others to retreat under the crumbling fortress of New Amsterdam, which,

on my arrival, I found resembling more a mole-hill than a fortress, without gates, the walls and bastions trodden under foot by men and cattle. . . .

[W]e were plunged three times into perilous wars, through want of sufficient garrisons. . . .

[O]ur above-mentioned too powerful neighbors and enemies found themselves reinforced by four royal ships, crammed full with an extraordinary amount of men and warlike stores. Our ancient enemies throughout the whole of Long Island, both from the east end and from the villages belonging to us united with them, hemmed us by water and by land, and cut off all supplies. Powder and provisions faulting, and no relief nor reinforcement being expected, we were necessitated to come to terms with the enemy, not through neglect of duty or cowardice, as many, more from passion than knowledge of the facts, have decided, but in consequence of an absolute impossibility to defend the fort, much less the city of New Amsterdam, and still less the country. (Peter Stuyvesant, recently deposed governor of New Netherland, report to the directors of the West India Company, Holland, October 16, 1665, cited in *Narratives of New Netherland: 1609–1664*, edited by J. Franklin Jameson.)

[Stuyvesant had surrendered New Netherland to the British in 1664. The name of the city of New Amsterdam was changed to New York.]

A MATTER OF RANK

25. Your governor is but a subject of King Charles of England. I shall not treat with a subject. I shall treat of peace only with the King, my brother. When he comes, I am ready. (King Philip, to a messenger sent by Governor Winslow to discuss a treaty, ca. 1674.)

HAND OF FRIENDSHIP

26. I am very sensible of the unkindness and injustice that hath been too much exercised toward you by the people of these parts of the world, who . . . sought . . . to make great advantages by you. I am not such a man, as is well

known in my own country, I have great love and regard towards you, and I desire to win and gain your love and friendship by a kind, just and peaceable life. (William Penn, message to the Indians of Pennsylvania, October 18, 1681, from *William Penn*, by Catherine Owens Peare.)

THE WITCHCRAFT PROBLEM

27. Our good God is working of miracles. Five witches were lately executed, impudently demanding of God a miraculous vindication of their innocency. Immediately upon this, our God miraculously sent in five Andover witches, who made a most ample, surprising, amazing confession of all their villainies, and declared the five newly executed to have been of their company, discovering many more, but all agreeing in Burroughs being their ringleader, who, I suppose, this day receives his trial at Salem, whither a vast concourse of people is gone, my father this morning among the rest. Since those, there have come in other confessors; yea, they come in daily. (Rev. Cotton Mather, letter to John Cotton Jr., Boston, 1692, cited in *Letters of a Nation*, edited by Andrew Carroll.)

[The Salem witchcraft trials of 1692–1693 would result in some 20 "witches" executed and 150 imprisoned.]

A QUESTION OF LIBEL

28. Mr. Hamilton has confessed [on behalf of his client] the printing and publishing, and I think nothing is plainer than that the words in the information are scandalous, and tend to sedition, and to disquiet the minds of the people of this province. And if such papers are not libels, I think it may be said, there can be no such thing as a libel. (Richard Bradley, attorney general of New York, prosecuting John Peter Zenger, New York City, August 4, 1735, from *A Brief Narrative of the Case and Tryal of John Peter Zenger of the New-York Weekly Journal*.)

29. I freely acknowledge that there are such things as libels, yet I must insist at the same time that what my client is charged with is not a libel; and I observed just now, that Mr. Attorney in defining libel, made use of the words "scandalous," "seditious," and "tend to disquiet the people"; but (whether with design or not I will not say) he omitted the word "false." (Andrew Hamilton, defense attorney, Ibid.)

[Hamilton argued that the published articles regarding colonial governor William Cosby were true and therefore not libelous. The jury found Zenger not guilty. Ever since, American courts have recognized truth as a defense against libel.]

A DIFFERENT VIEW OF EDUCATION

30. We know that you highly esteem the kind of learning taught in those colleges, and that the maintenance of our young men while with you would be very expensive to you. We are convinced, therefore, that you mean to do us good by your proposal, and we thank you heartily.

But you, who are wise, must know that different nations have different conceptions of things, and you will therefore not take it amiss if our ideas of this kind of education happen not to be the same with yours.

We have had some experience of it. Several of our young people were formerly brought up at the colleges of the northern provinces; they were instructed in all your sciences; but when they came back to us they were bad runners, ignorant of every means of living in the woods, unable to bear either cold or hunger, knew neither how to build a cabin, take a deer, nor kill an enemy, spoke our language imperfectly; were therefore neither fit for hunters, warriors, nor counselors—they were therefore totally good for nothing.

We are, however, not the less obliged by your kind offer; though we decline accepting it; and to show our grateful sense of it, if the gentlemen of Virginia will send us a dozen of their sons we will take great care of their education, instruct them in all we know, and make men of them. (Conassatego, Lancaster, Pennsylvania, 1744, quoted in *Poor Richard's Almanac*, by Benjamin Franklin.)

[At the Lancaster meeting, Virginia commissioners had invited the Six Nations of the Iroquois to send some of their sons to William and Mary College for formal education. Though Franklin did not name the speaker, he was later identified as Conassatego.]

LEARNING THE ALPHABET

31.

In *Adam's* fall
We sinned all. [Pictures Adam, Eve, and the Serpent.]

(*New England Primer*, 1749 edition.)

32.

Thy life to mend
This *Book* attend. [Pictures the Holy Bible.]

(Ibid.)

33.

The *Cat* doth play
And after slay. [Pictures cat and mouse.]

(Ibid.)

34.

The *Dog* doth bite
The thief at night. [Pictures dog catching thief.]

(Ibid.)

[The school textbook continues the alphabet through Z, with many biblical references.]

ALBANY PLAN

35. It is proposed that humble application be made for an act of Parliament of Great Britain, by virtue of which the general government may be formed in America. . . .

That the said general government be administered by a President-General, to be appointed and supported by the crown; and a Grand Council, to be chosen by the representatives of the people of the several Colonies in their respective assemblies. (Albany Plan of Union, 1754.)

NO TAXES FOR AN UNJUST WAR

36. [B]eing painfully apprehensive that the large sum granted by the late Act of Assembly for the King's use is principally intended for purposes inconsistent with our peaceable testimony, we therefore think that as we cannot be concerned in wars and fightins, so neither ought we to contribute thereto by paying the tax directed by the said Act, though suffering be the consequence of our refusal, which we hope to bear with patience. And we take this [position] though some part of the money to be raised by the said Act is said to be for such benevolent purposes as supporting our friendship with our Indian neighbors and relieving the distress of our fellow subjects who have suffered in the present calamities, for whom our hearts are pained; and we affectionately and with bowels of tenderness sympathize with them therein. And we could most cheerfully contribute to those purposes if they were not so mixed that we cannot in the manner proposed show our hearty concurrence therewith without at the same time assuming to, or allowing ourselves in, practices which we apprehend contrary to the testimony which the Lord hath given us to bear for his name and Truth's sake. (An Epistle of Tender Love and Friendship to Friends [Quakers] in Pennsylvania, Philadelphia, December 16, 1755, cited in *The Universe Bends toward Justice: A Reader on Christian Nonviolence in the U.S.*, edited by Angie O'Gorman.)

[This was a declaration of conscience signed by a number of Quakers in Philadelphia. They feared that the new taxes being levied would be used to carry on a war against the Indians.]

POOR RICHARD SAYS

37. A word to the wise is enough.

38. [T]he taxes are indeed very heavy . . . but we have many others, and much more grievous to some of us. We are taxed twice as much by our IDLENESS, three times as much by our PRIDE, and four times as much by our FOLLY; and from these taxes the commissioners cannot ease or deliver us by allowing an abatement.

39. God helps them that help themselves.

40. The used key is always bright.

41. Dost thou love life? Then do not squander time, for that's the stuff life is made of.

42. Lost time is never found again.

43. Sloth makes all things difficult, but industry all things easy.

44. Laziness travels so slowly that poverty soon overtakes him.

45.

Early to bed and early to rise
Makes a man healthy, wealthy, and wise.

46. He that lives on hope will die fasting.

47. There are no gains without pains.

48. Diligence is the mother of good luck.

49.

Then plow deep while sluggards sleep,
And you shall have corn to sell and to keep.

50. One today is worth two tomorrows.

51. For want of a nail the shoe was lost, for want of a shoe the horse was lost, and for want of a horse the rider was lost; being overtaken and slain by the enemy; all for want of a little care about a horseshoe nail!

52. The borrower is a slave to the lender and the debtor to the creditor. (Benjamin Franklin, *Poor Richard's Almanac*, July 7, 1757.)

FOLK SONG

53.

Father and I went down to camp,
Along with Captain Gooding;
And there we saw the men and boys,
As thick as hasty pudding.

Yankee doddle, keep it up,
Yankee doodle dandy;

Mind the music and the step,
And with the girls be handy.

There was Captain Washington
Upon a slapping stallion,
A-giving orders to his men,
I guess there was a million.

(Folk song, ca. 1763.)

[The sources disagree on the authorship of "Yankee Doodle." *Bartlett's* labels the piece anonymous. Other sources credit a British army surgeon, Dr. Richard Shuckburgh, as the author. All sources agree that the British sang the song to poke fun at the continentals but that the Americans embraced it as their own.]

FROM A BLACK POETESS

54.

Some view our sable race with scornful eye,
"Their colour is a diabolic dye."
Remember, Christians, Negroes black as Cain,
May be refined, and join the angelic train.

(Phillis Wheatley, *On Being Brought from Africa to America*, 1768.)

ADVERTISEMENT

55. Run away from the subscriber in Albemarle [Virginia], a Mulatto slave called Sandy, about 35 years of age. . . . He is a shoemaker by trade, in which he uses his left hand principally, can do coarse carpenter's work. . . . He took with him a white horse . . . of which it is expected he will endeavor to dispose; he also carried his shoemaker's tools, and will probably endeavor to get employment that way. Whoever conveys the said slave to me in Albemarle, shall have 40s reward. (Thomas Jefferson, advertisement, *Virginia Gazette*, 1769, cited by Lynn A. Curtis in *Quiet Riots*, compiled by Fred R. Harris and Roger W. Wilkins.)

ADVERTISEMENT

---

56. TO BE SOLD,

On Thursday the third Day of August next,
  A CARGO OF
  NINETY-FOUR
  PRIME, HEALTHY
  N E G R O E S
  consisting of
Thirty-nine MEN, Fifteen BOYS,
  Twenty-four WOMEN, and
  Sixteen GIRLS.
  Just arrived
  in the Brigantine Dembia,
    Francis Bare, Master, from SIERRA-LEON,
    by DAVID & LEON

(Handbill, Charlestown, July 24, 1769.)

Washington and Lafayette inspect the troops at Valley Forge, 1777.

4

The American Revolution

It was the first colonial war in the history of the world. Officially, it began in 1775 at Lexington, Massachusetts, but its origins began much earlier—in the mid-1760s with what colonists regarded as unfair taxes. The first deaths of the war came in 1770, with the so-called Boston Massacre. Whenever the war began, it ended with British recognition of the infant United States of America and set an example for Europeans, Asians, Latin Americans, and Africans in the centuries to come.

POLITICAL SLOGAN

57. Taxation without representation is tyranny! (Slogan, early 1770s.)

MASSACRE—OR SELF-DEFENSE?

On March 5, 1770, five Bostonians were killed and six wounded when British troops fired on what they thought was a threatening mob. The incident would become known in American history as the

"Boston Massacre." Months later, a murder trial was held. The following are excerpts from the concluding arguments of both sides.

58. If an assault was made to endanger their lives, the law is clear they [the British soldiers] had a right to kill in their own defense. If it was not so severe as to endanger their lives, yet if they were assaulted at all, struck and abused by blows of any sort, by snowballs, oyster shells, cinders, the law reduces the offense of killing down to manslaughter, in consideration of those passions of our nature which cannot be eradicated. (John Adams, defense attorney, address to the jury, Boston, December 7, 1770, cited in *The Case for Courage*, by William M. Kunstler.)

59. [The evening of the violence] a number of soldiers had come out of their barracks, armed with clubs, bayonets, cutlasses and instruments of diverse kinds, and in the most outrageous manner were ravaging the streets, assaulting everyone they met . . . and even vented their inhumanity on a little boy of 12 years of age. . . .

They [Bostonian civilians] had been fully sensible of the evil disposition and abusive behavior of many of the soldiers towards them, and the most peaceable among them had found it necessary to arm themselves with heavy walking sticks as weapons of defense when they went abroad. (Robert Treat Paine, chief prosecutor, representing the Crown, address to the jury, Ibid.)

[Six British soldiers were acquitted. Two were convicted of manslaughter and were branded on the hand as punishment. In an earlier trial, Captain Thomas Preston—commanding officer of the British soldiers on trial—had also been defended by Adams and was acquitted.]

THE SOUND OF SILENCE

60. If the people are at present hushed into silence, is it not a sort of sullen silence, which is far from indicating that the glorious spirit of liberty is vanquished and left without hope but in miracles? (Samuel Adams, 1771, cited in *Voices of the American Revolution*, by the Peoples Bicentennial Commission.)

LAND OF ASYLUM

61. Preserve America therefore an asylum for the distressed of all nations, and a land of liberty for yourselves. Let the oppression that forced them . . . to leave their native soil, teach you wisdom; let it teach you to value the envied blessings you enjoy, purchased by the perilous toil and stern virtue of your ancestors. Therefore leave these blessings which they left you, unimpaired to your posterity. If you suffer the iron rod of oppression to reach and scourge you here, remember you have no America to flee to for asylum. Here you must be free men, or the most abject and mortified slaves. There is no alternative; therefore, stand firm, acquit yourselves like free men, who value liberty and life alike. (Anonymous broadside, 1773, cited in *Voices of the American Revolution*, by the Peoples Bicentennial Commission.)

JAUNDICED VIEW

62. The business of the Congress is tedious beyond expression. . . . Every man in it is a great man, an orator, a critic, a statesman; and therefore every man upon every question must show his oratory, his criticism, and his political abilities. (John Adams, delegate to the First Continental Congress, Letter to Abigail Adams, October 9, 1774.)

LIBERTY OR DEATH

63. They tell us, sir, that we are weak; unable to cope with so formidable an adversary. But when shall we be stronger? Will it be the next week, or the next year? Will it be when we are totally disarmed, and when a British guard shall be stationed in every house? . . .

Shall we acquire the means of effectual resistance by lying supinely on our backs, and hugging the delusive phantom of hope, until our enemies shall have bound us hand and foot? . . .

Three millions of people, armed in the holy cause of liberty, and in such a country as that which we possess, are invincible by any force which our enemy can send against us. . . .

The battle, sir, is not to the strong alone; it is to the vigilant, the active, the brave. Besides, sir, we have no election. If we were base enough to desire it, it is now too late to retire from the contest. There is no retreat but in submission and slavery. Our chains are forged! Their clanking may be heard on the plains of Boston! The war is inevitable—and let it come! I repeat, sir, let it come! (Patrick Henry, Virginia House of Burgesses, March 23, 1775.)

64. Gentlemen may cry peace, peace—but there is no peace. The war is actually begun! The next gale that sweeps from the North will bring to our ears the clash of resounding arms! Our brethren are already in the field! Why stand we here idle? What is it that gentlemen wish? What would they have? Is life so dear, or peace so sweet, as to be purchased at the price of chains and slavery? Forbid it, Almighty God! I know not what course others may take; but as for me, give me liberty, or give me death! (Ibid.)

THE BRITISH MOVE

65. About ten o'clock last night [April 18], the troops in Boston were discovered to be in motion in a very secret manner, and it was found they were embarking in boats. . . . at the lower end of the common. Expresses [messengers] set off immediately to alarm the country. . . .

[After landing, the British troops] proceeded with great silence to Lexington, six miles below Concord. A company of militia, numbering about 80 men, had mustered. . . . Just before sunrise the King's troops came in sight, when the militia began to disperse. The troop[s] then set out upon the road, hallooing and huzzaing. . . . [T]he commanding officer cried out in words to this effect, "Disperse, you damned rebels! Damn you, disperse!" Upon which the troops again huzzaed, and at the same time one or two officers discharged their pistols, which were instantaneously followed by the firing of four or five of the soldiers, and then there seemed to be a general discharge from the whole. . . . [T]hey fired upon the militia as they were dispersing agreeably to their command. . . . [T]hey did not even return the fire. Eight of our men were killed, and nine wounded. The troops then laughed, and damned the Yankees, and said they could not bear the smell of gunpowder. (News article, *Pennsylvania Journal* (May 24, 1775), citing events of April 18–19, 1775, from *The Diary of the American Revolution*, edited by Frank Moore.)

LEXINGTON: THE OFFICIAL STORY

66. It will appear that on the night preceding the 19th of April instant, a body of the king's troops, under the command of colonel Smith, were secretly landed at Cambridge, with an apparent design to take or destroy the military and other stores, provided for the defence of this colony, and deposited at Concord.

Some inhabitants of the colony, on the night aforesaid, whilst traveling peaceably on the road, between Boston and Concord, were seized and greatly abused by armed men, who appeared to be officers of general Gage's army. The town of Lexington, by these means, was alarmed, and a company of the inhabitants mustered on the occasion. The regular troops on their way to Concord, marched into the said town of Lexington, and the said company, on their approach, began to disperse. Notwithstanding this, the regulars rushed on with great violence and first began hostilities, by firing on said Lexington company, whereby they killed eight and wounded several others. The regulars continued their fire, until those of said company, who were neither killed nor wounded, had made their escape.

Colonel Smith, with the detachment then marched to Concord, where a number of provincial were again fired on by the troops, two of them killed and several wounded, before the provincial fired on them. [This] produced an engagement that lasted through the day, in which many of the provincial and more of the regular troops were killed and wounded.

To give a particular account of the ravages of the troops, as they retreated from Concord to Charlestown, would be very difficult, if not impracticable. Let it suffice to say, that a great number of the houses on the road were plundered and rendered unfit for use, several were burnt. Women in child-bed were driven by the soldiery naked into the streets. Old men peaceably in their houses were shot dead, and such scenes exhibited as would disgrace the annals of the most uncivilized nation. (Joseph Warren, Massachusetts Provincial Congress, Watertown, Massachusetts, April 26, 1775, from *Principles and Acts of the Revolution*, edited by H. Niles.)

BATTLE ON BREED'S HILL

67. Intelligence had been received that it was the intention of [British] General Gage to post a part of his troops . . . on a promontory just at the entrance of the peninsula at Charlestown, called Bunker's hill. . . . Accordingly orders were given to Colonel Prescott . . . with one thousand men, to march silently in the evening of 16th of June, and throw up some intrenchments on the height of Bunker's hill. By some mistake they took possession of Breed's hill, which, being about one-fourth of a mile nearer Boston, was less capable of being defended. . . .

About four o'clock in the morning the British were astonished to behold the works which had been thrown up in a single night. . . . They immediately commenced a tremendous cannonade from their shipping, their floating batteries, and from all their fortifications. . . .

At about one o'clock, 17th of June, the royal forces were observed to cross the river from Boston, and land on the shore at Charlestown. . . . Their force consisted of about three thousand men, well provided with field-artillery. They formed in two lines, their officers haranguing them probably in such language as this: "Those cowardly rebels must and shall be put to flight. See the dastardly Yankees with rusty guns and scarcely a bayonet among them. March on, my lads, march on! . . ."

Hear the voice of Putnam, of Prescott and Warren: "See, my brave soldiers, that phalanx approaching. . . . These are the cruel enemies to your freedom; they have come to enslave you. Remember their barbarous murders of our friends at Lexington. Fight manfully, and they shall be vanquished. Reserve your fire till their near approach; then with a sure aim cut them down, and the victory shall be ours."

The regulars deliberately advance to the attack. . . . The Americans reserve their fire till the enemy are within eight or ten rods, then . . . by a general discharge of musketry and field-artillery, several officers and men are seen to fall.

"They are thinned. See the ground covered with the stain. See those wounded officers borne off the field."

[T]he regulars retreat in disorder, and many of them flee even to their boats. The officers, greatly agitated, pursue their men, and threaten them with their swords. With great difficulty they are rallied, and commanded to advance again to the attack. The provincials are prepared, and when sufficiently near, a deadly fire from their ranks puts the enemy a second time to flight, leaving such numbers of dead and wounded that several of their officers exclaim, "It is downright butchery to lead the men on afresh against the lines." At this critical moment Major-General Clinton . . . entered the field . . . for the purpose of forcing the regulars to renew the attack. . . .

[I]t was now discovered that their [the provincials'] powder was nearly expended, and another supply could not be procured. The enemy now . . . rake the inside of our breastworks in its whole course, which at length obliges the provincials to retire. . . . The firing from the British ships, and other armed vessels and batteries, is now pushed to the utmost extremity. [T]he regulars are impelled forward by their officers. . . . Our brave men continue their resistance, and actually confront the enemy with the butt-end of their muskets. . . . The British light infantry attempted . . . to cut off the retreat of our troops. In this they displayed the greatest bravery, but their opposers poured forth their reserved and formidable fire in such a manner as to produce astonishing execution, and to arrest their progress, till the whole of the Americans could effect a retreat. . . .

Certain it is, that on the first and second onset, the veterans were fairly repulsed, and whatever advantage was ultimately obtained, was at the expense of some of their most valuable officers and the flower of the British grenadiers and light infantry. These two corps, at the moment of their first onset, lost three-fourths of their number. . . . [O]f the enemy, 19 commissioned officers were killed and 70 wounded; and their total loss, according to General Gage, was 1,054. Of the provincials, the killed and dead of their wounds, are 139. . . . Other wounded, 200. . . .

The provincials have much reason to triumph on the successful issue of this first general conflict with veteran troops; it must tend greatly to increase their confidence in their own powers, and give them a serious impression that we are favored with the smiles of Heaven. (James Thacher, from *Military Journal of the American Revolutionary War, 1775 to 1783*, June 17, 1775.)

SAVING AMMUNITION

68. Men, you are all marksmen. Don't one of you fire until you see the whites of their eyes. (Israel Putnam, at the Battle of "Bunker Hill" [Breed's Hill], June 17, 1775.)

[The sources differ on the author of this quotation. *Bartlett's* credits William Prescott.]

THREE ROADS TO "INDEPENDANCY"

69. There are three different ways by which an independancy may hereafter be effected; and that one of those three, will, one day or other, be the fate of America, viz. By the legal voice of the people in Congress; by a military power; or by a mob. . . . Should an independancy be brought about by the first of those means, we have every opportunity and every encouragement before us, to form the noblest, purest constitution on the face of the earth. We have it in our power to begin the world over again. (Thomas Paine, Appendix to *Common Sense*, 1776.)

70. The birthday of a new world is at hand, and a race of men, perhaps as numerous as all Europe contains, are to receive their portion of freedom from the events of a few months. (Ibid.)

71. Let the names of Whig and Tory be extinct; and let none other be heard among us, than those of a good citizen; an open and resolute friend; and a virtuous supporter of the RIGHTS of MANKIND, and of the FREE AND INDEPEN-DANT STATES OF AMERICA. (Ibid.)

RESOLUTION INTRODUCED

72. RESOLVED: That these United Colonies are, and of right ought to be, free and independent States, that they are absolved from all allegiance to the British Crown, and that all political connection between them and the State of Great Britain is, and ought to be totally dissolved. (Richard Henry Lee, Second Continental Congress, Philadelphia, June 7, 1776.)

73. That it is expedient forthwith to take the most effectual measures for forming foreign Alliances. (Ibid.)

74. That a plan of confederation be prepared and transmitted to the respective Colonies for their consideration and approbation. (Ibid.)

WRITING THE DECLARATION

75. You inquire why so young a man as Jefferson was placed at the head of the Committee for preparing a Declaration of Independence. . . .

Mr. Jefferson came into Congress in June, 1775, and brought with him a reputation for literature, science, and a happy talent of composition. Writings of his were handed about, remarkable for the peculiar felicity of expression. Though a silent member in Congress, he was so prompt, frank, explicit and decisive upon committees and in conversation, not even Samuel Adams was more so, that he soon seized upon my heart, and upon this occasion I gave him my vote, and did all in my power to procure the votes of others. I think he had one more vote than any other, and that placed him at the head of the committee. I had the next highest number, and that placed me the second. The committee met, discussed the subject, and then appointed Mr. Jefferson and me to make the draught. I suppose because we were the first two on the list.

The sub-committee met. Jefferson proposed to me to make the draught. I said, "I will not." . . .

"Why will you not? . . . What are your reasons?" . . .

"Reason first—You are a Virginian, and a Virginian ought to appear at the head of this business. Reason second—I am obnoxious, suspected, and unpopular. You are very much otherwise. Reason third—You can write ten times better than I can."

"Well," said Jefferson, "if you have drawn it up, we will have a meeting."

A meeting we accordingly had. . . . I was delighted with its high tone and flights of oratory with which it abounded, especially that concerning Negro slavery, which, (though I knew his Southern brethren would never suffer to pass in Congress), I certainly never would oppose. There were other expressions which I would not have inserted, if I had drawn it up, particularly that which called the King tyrant. I thought this too personal; for I never believed George to be a tyrant in disposition and in nature; I always believed him to be deceived by his courtiers on both sides of the Atlantic. . . . I thought it would not become me to strike it out. I counseled to report it, and do not now remember that I made or suggested a single alteration. . . .

Congress cut out about a quarter of it, as I expected they would; but they obliterated some of the best of it. (John Adams, recalling events of June–July 1776, letter to Timothy Pickering, August 6, 1822, from *The Works of John Adams*, edited by Charles Francis Adams.)

AFTER VOTING INDEPENDENCE

76. We must all hang together, or most assuredly we shall all hang separately. (Benjamin Franklin, following the adoption of the Declaration of Independence, Philadelphia, July 4, 1776.)

DECLARATION OF INDEPENDENCE

77. We hold these truths to be self-evident, that all men are created equal, that they are endowed by their Creator with certain inalienable Rights, that among these are Life, Liberty and the pursuit of Happiness. That to secure these rights, Governments are instituted among Men, deriving their just powers from the consent of the governed. That whenever any Form of Government becomes destructive of these ends, it is the Right of the People to alter or to abolish it, and to institute new Government, laying its foundation on such principles and organizing its powers in such form, as to them shall seem most likely to effect their Safety and Happiness. (Thomas Jefferson, Declaration of Independence, Philadelphia, July 4, 1776.)

78. And for the support of this Declaration, with a firm reliance on the Protection of Divine Providence, we mutually pledge to each other our Lives, our Fortunes and our sacred Honor. (Ibid.)

ON SUNSHINE PATRIOTS

79. These are the times that try men's souls. The summer soldier and the sunshine patriot will, in this crisis, shrink from the service of their country; but he that stands it now, deserves the love and thanks of man and woman. Tyranny, like hell, is not easily conquered; yet we have this consolation with us, that the harder the conflict, the more glorious the triumph. (Thomas Paine, *The Crisis*, December 23, 1776.)

VICTORY AT SARATOGA

80. The voice of fame, ere this reaches you, will tell how greatly fortunate we have been in this department. Burgoyne and his whole army have laid down their arms, and surrendered themselves to me and my Yankees. Thanks to the Giver of all victory for this triumphant success. . . .

Major-General Phillips, who wrote me that saucy note last year from St. John's, is now my prisoner. . . .

If Old England is not by this lesson taught humility, then she is an obstinate old slut, bent upon her ruin. (Horatio Gates, letter to his wife, October 17, 1777, from the Gates Papers of the New York Historical Society, cited in *The Diary of the American Revolution*, edited by Frank Moore.)

A NEW GOVERNMENT

81. Articles of Confederation and perpetual Union between the states. . . . The stile of this confederacy shall be "The United States of America." (Articles of Confederation, November 15, 1777.)

82. Each state retains its sovereignty, freedom and independence, and every Power, Jurisdiction and right, which is not by this confederation expressly delegated to the United States, in Congress assembled. (Ibid.)

83. The said states hereby severally enter into a firm league of friendship with each other, for their common defence, the security of their Liberties, and their mutual and general welfare, binding themselves to assist each other, against all force offered to, or attacks made upon them, or any of them, on account of religion, sovereignty, trade, or any other preference whatever. (Ibid.)

84. [T]he free inhabitants of each of these states, paupers, vagabonds and fugitives from Justice excepted, shall be entitled to all privileges and immunities of free citizens in the several states. (Ibid.)

NEGOTIATING AN ALLIANCE

85. We must move, but with caution. There must be no terms of which we will later repent. As for our court, be assured that we are resolved to take no advantage of the situation. Whatever we do must be founded upon the basis of mutual interest, as to make it last as long as human institutions will endure.

When we enter into a treaty with you, we will be affirming your independency. Necessarily this will bring about war with England. We cannot do this without consulting Spain, without whose concurrence nothing can be done. (Comte de

Vergennes, French foreign minister, conversation with Benjamin Franklin and other American commissioners, Versailles, France, December 10, 1777, cited in *Triumph in Paris: The Exploits of Benjamin Franklin*, by David Schoenbrun.)

[Spain refused to join the proposed alliance. Nevertheless, France and the United States signed two treaties—one of commerce and one of alliance—on February 6, 1778.]

OUTRUNNING THEIR LEADERS

86. [The government of King George says] that this Revolution has been the work of a faction, a junto of ambitious men against the sense of the people of America. On the contrary, nothing has been done without the approbation of the people, who have indeed outrun their leaders, so that no capital measure has been adopted until they called loudly for it. (George Mason, 1778, cited in *Voices of the American Revolution*, by the Peoples Bicentennial Commission.)

SEEKING A REWARD

87. In a former letter, you mentioned that the gentlemen of the state of New York were satisfied with my conduct when commanding in the state, and wished to give me some mark of their approbation of my conduct. I have thought of proposing to the state to purchase a tract of forfeited or unlocated lands [seized from Loyalists] on the frontiers of the state, and making a settlement whenever the times will admit. (Benedict Arnold, letter to General Philip Schuyler, November 30, 1778, cited in *Secret History of the American Revolution*, by Carl Van Doren.)

TREASON

88. About the month of June 1779 [more likely May], General [Benedict] Arnold sent for me and, after some general conversation, opened his political

sentiments respecting the war carrying on between Great Britain and America, declaring his abhorrence of a separation of the latter from the former as that would be ruinous to both. That General Arnold then communicated to me, under a solemn obligation of secrecy, his intention of opening his services to the commander-in-chief of the British forces in any way that would most effectually restore the former government and destroy the then usurped authority of Congress, either by immediately joining the British army or co-operating on some concealed plan with Sir Henry Clinton. (Joseph Stansbury, recalling events of spring 1779, West Point, New York, cited in *Secret History of the American Revolution*, by Carl Van Doren.)

[Statement made in London on March 4, 1784. This was in support of Benedict Arnold's claim for compensation from the Crown for his services.]

SEEKING A POSITION

89. I have not had the pleasure of receiving a line from you since you arrived at camp [Washington's headquarters at Morristown, New Jersey], and know not who is to have the command at the North river [the Hudson, headquartered at West Point]. (Benedict Arnold, letter to General Philip Schuyler, May 25, 1779, cited in *Secret History of the American Revolution*, by Carl Van Doren.)

[Schuyler raised the issue with Washington, who would appoint Arnold to the post.]

AN EXCHANGE BETWEEN CAPTAINS

90. Has your ship struck its colors? (Captain Richard Pearson, HMS *Serapis*.)

91. I have not yet begun to fight! (Captain John Paul Jones, USS *Bon Homme Richard*, off the coast of Yorkshire, England, September 23, 1779.)

[The *Serapis* surrendered. The *Bon Homme Richard* was so badly damaged that the American sailors had to abandon it and take over the British vessel. Their own ship sank two days after the battle.]

TREACHERY AT WEST POINT

92. I . . . desired Colonel [Alexander] Hamilton to go forward, and inform General [Benedict] Arnold that I would breakfast with him. Soon after he arrived at Arnold's quarters, a letter was delivered to Arnold which threw him into the greatest confusion. He told Colonel Hamilton that something required his immediate attendance at the garrison, which was on the opposite side of the [Hudson] river to his quarters; and immediately ordered a horse, to take him to the river, and the barge, which he kept to cross to be ready. . . .

When I got to his quarters, [I] did not find him there. . . . The impropriety of his conduct when he knew I was to be there, struck me very forcefully, and my mind misgave me; but I had not the least idea of the real cause. When I returned to Arnold's quarters about two hours later, and told Colonel Hamilton that I had not seen him, he gave me a packet which had just arrived for me from Col. Jemmison, which immediately brought the matter to light. [It reported the seizure of John Andre with papers apparently in Arnold's handwriting. Arnold escaped to a British ship on the Hudson.] (General George Washington, West Point, New York, ca. September 24, 1780, from *Occasional Productions: Political, Diplomatic, and Miscellaneous*, by Richard Rush.)

SWAN SONG

93. "The World Turned Upside Down." (Song played by British band following British surrender to American and French forces, Yorktown, Virginia, October 19, 1781.)

AMERICAN PARADOX

94. It [society in America] is not composed, as in Europe, of great lords who possess every thing, and of a herd of people who have nothing. Here are no aristocratical families, no courts, no kings, no bishops . . . ; no great manufacturers employing thousands, no great refinements of luxury. The rich and the poor are not so far removed from each other as they are in Europe. Some few towns excepted, we are all tillers of the earth . . . scattered over an immense territory, communicating with each other by means of good roads and navigable rivers, united by the silken bands of mild government, all respecting the laws, without dreading their power, because they are equitable. We are all animated with the spirit of an industry which is unfettered and unrestrained, because each person works for himself. . . . We are the most perfect society now existing in the world. Here man is free as he ought to be. (J. Hector St. John Crevecoeur, Letter III, *Letters from an American Farmer*, 1782.)

95. [A] sound resembling a deep rough voice, uttered, as I thought, a few inarticulate monosyllables. Alarmed and surprized, I precipitately looked all round, when I perceived at about six rods distance something resembling a cage suspended to the limbs of a tree; all the branches of which appeared covered with large birds of prey, fluttering about, and anxiously endeavoring to perch on the cage. Actuated by an involuntary motion of my hands, more than by any design of my mind, I fired at them; they all flew to a short distance, with a most hideous noise; when, horrid to think and painful to repeat, I perceived a negro, suspended in the cage, and left there to expire!

I shudder when I recollect that the birds had already picked out his eyes, his cheek bones were bare; his arms had been attacked in several places, and his body seemed covered with a multitude of wounds. From the edges of the hollow sockets and from the lacerations with which he was disfigured, the blood slowly dropped, and tinged the ground beneath. No sooner were the birds flown, than swarms of insects covered the whole body of this unfortunate wretch, eager to feed on his mangled flesh and to drink his blood.

I found myself suddenly arrested by the power of affright and terror; my nerves were convulsed; I trembled, I stood motionless, involuntarily contemplating the fate of this negro, in all its dismal latitude. The living spectre, though deprived of his eyes, could still distinctly hear, and in his uncouth dialect begged me to give him some water to allay his thirst. Humanity herself would have recoiled back with horror; she would have balanced whether to lessen such reliefless distress, or mercifully with one blow to end this dreadful scene of agonizing torture! Had I had a ball in my gun, I certainly should have despatched him; but finding myself unable to perform so kind an office, I sought, though trembling, to relieve him as well as I could. A shell ready fixed to a pole, which had been used by some negroes, presented itself to me; filled it with water, and with trembling hands I guided it to the quivering lips of the wretched sufferer. Urged by the irresistible power of thirst, he endeavored to meet it as he instinctively guessed its approach by the noise I made in passing through the bars of the cage. "Tanke you white man, tanke you, pute some poyson and give me." How long have you been hanging there? I asked him. "Two days, and me no die; the birds, the birds; aaah me!"

[Later] I heard that the reason for this slave being thus punished, was on account of his having killed the overseer of the plantation. They told me that the laws of self-preservation rendered such executions necessary. (Letter IX, Ibid.)

[J. Hector St. John was the pseudonym of Michel Crevecoeur. He wrote 12 "letters," or essays, between 1770 and 1781. All were published in a single volume in 1782.]

5

The New Nation

At the time, the new nation was a magnificent experiment in self-government. There was no king. A system of checks and balances was to prevent tyranny and to protect a Bill of Rights. Only a George Washington could have provided the leadership to carry it out. Slaves, Indians, and women were still left out, however.

A GENERAL SAYS FAREWELL

96. With a heart full of love and gratitude, I now take leave of you. I most devoutly wish that your latter days may be as prosperous and happy as your former ones have been glorious and honorable.

I cannot come to each of you to take my leave, but shall be obliged to you, if each of you will come and take me by the hand. (General George Washington, farewell to his officers, Francis' Tavern, New York City, December 4, 1783, cited in *Military Journal of the American Revolution*, by James Thacher.)

[Thacher describes what happened next: "General Knox, being nearest, turned to him. Incapable of utterance, Washington, in tears, grasped his hand, embraced and kissed him. In the same affectionate manner he took leave of each succeeding officer. In every eye was the tear of dignified sensibility; and not a word was articulated to interrupt the eloquent silence and tenderness of the scene."]

Benjamin Franklin was the only man to sign the four basic documents of American government: the Albany Plan of Union, the Declaration of Independence, the Articles of Confederation, and the Constitution. The portrait is by Joseph Duplessis.

THE CONVENTION: HISTORIAN'S VIEW

97. A survey of the economic interests of the members of the [Constitutional] Convention presents certain conclusions:

A majority of the members were lawyers by profession.

Most of the members came from regions in which personalty [personal property] was largely concentrated.

Not one member represented in his immediate personal economic interests the small farming or mechanic classes.

The overwhelming majority of members, at least five-sixths, were immediately, directly, and personally interested in the outcome of their labors at Philadelphia, and were to a greater or less extent economic beneficiaries from the adoption of the Constitution.

1. Public security interests were extensively represented in the Convention. Of the 55 members who attended no less than 40 appear on the records of the Treasury Department for sums varying from a few dollars up to more than 100,000 dollars. . . .

2. Personalty invested in lands for speculation was represented by at least 14 members. . . .

3. Personalty in the form of money loaned at interest was represented by at least 24 members. . . .

4. Personalty in mercantile, manufacturing, and shipping lines was represented by at least 11 members. . . .

5. Personalty in slaves was represented by at least 15 members. . . .

It cannot be said, therefore, that the members of the Convention were "disinterested." On the contrary, we are forced to accept the profoundly significant conclusion that they knew through their personal experiences in economic affairs the precise results which the new government that they were setting up was designed to attain. . . . [A]s practical men they were able to build the new government upon the only foundations which could be stable: fundamental economic interests. (Charles A. Beard, events of 1787, from *An Economic Interpretation of the Constitution of the United States*, by Charles A. Beard.)

IDEALS FOR THE NEW TERRITORY

98. Religion, morality, and knowledge, being necessary to good government and the happiness of mankind, schools and the means of education shall forever be encouraged. The utmost good faith shall always be observed towards the Indians; their lands and property shall never be taken from them without their consent; and, in their property, rights, and liberty, they shall never be invaded or disturbed unless in just and lawful wars authorized by Congress; but laws founded in justice and humanity, shall from time to time be made for preventing wrongs being done to them, and for preserving peace and friendship with them. (Northwest Ordinance, July 13, 1787.)

99. There shall be neither slavery nor involuntary servitude in the said territory, otherwise than in the punishment of crimes. (Ibid.)

NEW IDEAS, NEW IDEALS

100. We the People of the United States, in order to form a more perfect Union, establish Justice, insure domestic Tranquility, provide for the common defence, promote the general Welfare, and secure the blessings of Liberty for ourselves and our Posterity, do ordain and establish this Constitution for the United States of America. (Preamble, U.S. Constitution, September 17, 1787.)

101. Treason against the United States shall consist only in levying War against them, or in adhering to their Enemies, giving them Aid and Comfort. No Person shall be convicted of Treason unless on the Testimony of two Witnesses to the same overt Act, or of Confession in open Court.

The Congress shall have Power to declare the Punishment of Treason, but no Attainder of Treason shall work Corruption of Blood, or Forfeiture except during the Life of the Person attainted. (Article III, Section 3, Ibid.)

A NEW GOVERNMENT

102. A republic—if you can keep it. (Benjamin Franklin, Philadelphia, September 18, 1787.)

[Following the Constitutional Convention, he was asked the question: "Is it to be a monarchy or a republic?"]

FAVORING THE CONSTITUTION

103. I propose in a series of papers to discuss the following interesting particulars—

The unity of the UNION to your political prosperity—

The insufficiency of the present Confederation to preserve that UNION—

The necessity of a government at least equally energetic with the one proposed to the attainment of this object—

The conformity of the proposed constitution to the true principles of republican government—

Its analogy to your own state constitution—and lastly,

The additional security, which its adoption will afford to the preservation of that species of government, to liberty and to property.

In the progress of this discussion I shall endeavor to give a satisfactory answer to all the objections which shall have made their appearance that may seem to have any claim to your attention. ("Publius" [Alexander Hamilton], *The Independent Journal*, October 27, 1787, cited in *The Federalist*, edited by Jacob E. Cooke.)

[As "Publius," Alexander Hamilton, James Madison, and John Jay wrote a series of 84 essays supporting the new Constitution.]

OPPOSING THE CONSTITUTION

104. Have they said, we the States? Have they made a proposal of a compact between States? If they had, this would be a confederated government. The question turns, Sir, on . . . the expression, *We, the People*, instead of the States of America. . . .

[T]he principles of this system are extremely pernicious, impolitic, and dangerous. . . . It is not a democracy, wherein the people retain all their rights securely. . . .

Here is a revolution as radical as that which separated us from Great Britain. It is as radical, if in this transition our rights and privileges are endangered, and the sovereignty of the States be relinquished: And cannot we plainly see, that this is actually the case?

The rights of conscience, trial by jury, liberty of the press, all our immunities and franchises, all pretensions to human rights and privileges, are rendered insecure, if not lost, by this change so loudly talked of by some, and inconsiderately by others. Is this same relinquishment of rights worthy of freemen? (Patrick Henry, speech, Virginia Convention to ratify the new Constitution, June 5, 1788, cited in *The Complete Anti-Federalist*, edited by Herbert J. Storing.)

ON THE VICE PRESIDENCY

105. My country has, in its wisdom, contrived for me the most insignificant office that ever the invention of man contrived or his imagination conceived.

(Vice President John Adams, letter to Abigail Adams, December 19, 1789, cited in *Presidential Wit*, edited by Bill Adler.)

FREEDOM, NOT TOLERATION

---

106. The Citizens of the United States of America have a right to applaud themselves for having given to mankind examples of an enlarged and liberal policy, a policy worthy of imitation. All possess alike liberty of conscience and immunities of citizenship. It is now no more that toleration is spoken of, as if it was by the indulgence of one class of people, that another enjoyed the exercise of their inherent natural rights. For happily the Government of the United States, which gives to bigotry no sanction, to persecution no assistance requires only that they who live under its protection should demean themselves as good citizens, in giving it on all occasions their effectual support. . . .

May the Children of the Stock of Abraham, who dwell in this land, continue to merit and enjoy the good will of the other Inhabitants; while every one shall sit in safety under his own vine and figtree, and there shall be none to make him afraid. (President George Washington, letter to the Hebrew Congregation in Newport, Rhode Island, 1790.)

A BILL OF RIGHTS

---

107. Congress shall make no law respecting an establishment of religion, or prohibiting the free exercise thereof; or abridging the freedom of speech, or of the press, or the right of the people peaceably to assemble, and to petition the government for a redress of grievances. (Bill of Rights, effective November 3, 1791.)

108. Right of the people to keep and bear arms. . . . Right of the people against unreasonable searches and seizures. . . . Nor shall any person be subject for the same offence to be twice put in jeopardy. . . . Nor compelled in any criminal case to be a witness against himself. . . . Due process of law. . . . Right to a speedy trial by impartial jury. . . . To have the Assistance of Counsel for his defence. . . . No excessive bail. . . . No cruel and unusual punishment. (Ibid.)

109. The powers not delegated to the United States by the Constitution, nor prohibited by it to the States, are reserved to the States respectively, or to the people. (Ibid.)

A CITY PLANNER CONSIDERS COLOR

110. The color of the skin is in no ways connected with strength of the mind or intellectual powers. (Benjamin Banneker, *Banneker's Almanac*, 1796.)

FAREWELL ADDRESS

111. I should now apprise you of the resolution I have formed to decline being considered among the number of those out of which a choice is to be made [for President]. (George Washington, September 17, 1796.)

112. Observe good faith and justice toward all nations. Cultivate peace and harmony with all. . . . In the execution of such a plan nothing is more essential than that permanent, inveterate antipathies against particular nations and passionate attachments for others should be excluded, and that in place of them just and amicable feelings toward all should be cultivated. The nation which indulges toward another an habitual hatred or an habitual fondness is in some degree a slave. It is a slave to its animosity or its affection, either of which is sufficient to lead it astray from its duty and its interest. (Ibid.)

113. Europe has a sea of primary interests which to us have none or a very remote relation. Hence she must be engaged in frequent controversies, the causes of which are essentially foreign to our concerns. Hence, therefore, it must be unwise to us to implicate ourselves by artificial ties in the ordinary combinations and collisions of her friendships or enmities. . . . It is our true policy to steer clear of permanent alliances with any portion of the foreign world. (Ibid.)

TOAST

114. Millions for defense, but not one cent for tribute! (Robert G. Harper, congressman from South Carolina, toasting John Marshall, Philadelphia, June 18, 1798.)

[Marshall had been part of an American diplomatic mission to France in 1797. There, three French agents proposed a U.S. loan to France plus a bribe for Foreign Minister Talleyrand. Charles Pinckney, one of the American commissioners, is supposed to have shouted, "No! No! Not a sixpence!" For years, the "millions for defense" quote was attributed to a more popular rendering of what Pinckney had said. Historians now agree that Harper said the words at a dinner honoring Marshall. The incident with the three French agents—who were called X, Y, and Z in the official correspondence—has gone down in history as "the XYZ Affair."]

BACKING DEPORTATIONS

115. It shall be lawful for the President of the United States at any time during continuance of this act, to order all such aliens as he shall judge dangerous to the peace and safety of the United States, or shall have reasonable grounds to suspect are concerned in any treasonable or secret machinations against the government thereof, to deport out of the territory of the United States. (Alien Act, June 25, 1798.)

SECURING THE BORDERS

116. Whenever there shall be a declared war between the United States and any foreign nation or government, or any invasion or predatory incursion shall be perpetrated, attempted, or threatened against the territory of the United States, by any foreign nation or government . . . all natives, citizens, or subjects of the hostile nation or government, being males of the age of 14 years and upwards, who shall be within the United States, and not actually naturalized, be liable to be apprehended, restrained, secured and removed, as alien enemies. (Enemy Aliens Act, July 6, 1798.)

PROTECTING AGAINST CRITICISM

117. If any person shall write, print, utter, or publish, or shall procure to be written, printed, uttered, or published, or shall knowingly and willingly assist or aid in writing, printing, uttering, or publishing any false, scandalous and malicious writing or utterings against the government of the United States . . . , with intent to defame the same government . . . , or to excite against them . . . , the hatred of the good people of the United States, or to stir up sedition . . . or to excite any unlawful combinations therein, for opposing or resisting any law . . . , or any act of the President . . . , or to resist, oppose or defeat any such law or act, or to aid, encourage or abet any hostile design of any foreign nation against the United States, their people or government, then such persons being thereby convicted . . . shall be punished by a fine not exceeding $2,000, and by imprisonment not exceeding two years. (Sedition Act, July 14, 1798.)

JAUNDICED VIEW OF THE COURTS

118. The Federalists have retired into the judiciary as a stronghold—and from that battery all the works of republicanism are to be beaten down and erased. (Thomas Jefferson, Letter, 1801.)

OF RULE AND REASON

119. All, too, will bear in mind this sacred principle, that though the will of the majority is in all cases to prevail, that to be rightful must be reasonable; that

the minority possess their equal rights, which equal law must protect, and to violate would be oppression. (Thomas Jefferson, First Inaugural Address, March 4, 1801.)

120. It is proper you should understand what I deem the essential principles of our Government. . . . Equal and exact justice to all men, of whatever state or persuasion, religious or political; peace, commerce, and honest friendship with all nations, entangling alliances with none. (Ibid.)

UNCONSTITUTIONAL

---

121. The authority . . . given to the supreme court, by the act establishing the judicial courts of the United States, to issue writs of mandamus to public officers, appears not to be warranted by the constitution. . . .

Certainly all those who have framed written constitutions contemplate them as forming the fundamental and paramount law of the nation, and consequently the theory of every such government must be that an act of the legislature repugnant to the Constitution is void. (Chief Justice John Marshall, Opinion, *Marbury v. Madison*, February 24, 1803.)

6

Westward Expansion

America's march to the Pacific began in 1803 with the purchase of the Louisiana Territory from France by President Jefferson. It would end in California following the Mexican War.

But ideas would also be expanding. There were new stirrings among women, among African slaves, among white workingmen, and among Native Americans. It was a new cry for freedom: social and political rights for women, basic human rights for slaves, organization rights for workers, and freedom to be allowed to live in ancient hunting grounds without molestation.

SEEKING THE NORTHWEST PASSAGE

122. Your mission has been communicated to the ministers here from France, Spain & Great Britain, and through them to their governments, & such assurances given them as to its objects, as we trust will satisfy them. . . .

The object of your mission is to explore the Missouri river, & such principal stream of it, as by its course and communication with the waters of the Pacific ocean, whether the Columbia, Oregon [sic], Colorado or any other river may offer the most direct & practicable water communication across this continent for the purposes of commerce.

Beginning at the mouth of the Missouri, you will take careful observations of

Lewis and Clark, exploring the Louisiana Territory, meet with friendly Indians. Their exploration will take them all the way to the Pacific. Engraving by Patrick Gass, 1810.

latitude & longitude, at all remarkable points on the river, & especially at the mouths of rivers, at rapids, at islands, & other places & objects distinguished by such natural marks & characters of a durable kind, as that they may with certainty be reorganized hereafter. . . .

The interesting points of the portage between the heads of the Missouri, & of the water offering the best communication with the Pacific ocean, should also be fixed by observation, & the course of that water to the ocean, in the same manner as that of the Missouri.

Your observations are to be taken with great pains & accuracy, to be entered distinctly & intelligibly for others as well as yourself to comprehend all the elements necessary, with the aid of the usual tables, to fix the latitude and longitude of the places at which they were taken, and are to be rendered to the War-office, for the purpose of having the calculations made concurrently by proper persons within the U.S. Several copies of these as well as of your other notes should be made at leisure times, & put into the care of the most trust-worthy of your attendants, to guard, by multiplying them, against the accidental losses to which they will be exposed. (President Thomas Jefferson, instructions to Captain Meriwether Lewis, Washington, D.C., June 20, 1803, cited in *Letters of the Lewis and Clark Expedition*, edited by Donald Jackson.)

TWO DISTINCT CHOICES

123. The Electors shall meet in their respective states and vote by ballot for President and Vice President . . . and they shall make distinct lists of all persons voted for as President, and of all persons voted for as Vice President, and of the number of votes for each. (12th Amendment, Ratified June 15, 1804.)

[Up to this point, the person who received the highest number of votes became president, and the person receiving the second highest number of votes became vice president.]

A DUEL AT WEEHAWKEN

124. Colonel [Aaron] Burr arrived first on the ground, as had been previously agreed. When General [Alexander] Hamilton arrived, the parties exchanged sal-

utations, and the seconds proceeded to make their arrangements. They measured the distance, ten full paces, and cast lots for the choice of position, as also to determine by whom the word should be given, both of which tell to the second of General Hamilton. They then proceeded to load the pistols in each other's presence, after which the parties took their stations. The gentleman who was to give the word then explained to the parties the rules which were to govern them in firing. . . .

He then asked if they were prepared; being answered in the affirmative, he gave the word *present*, as had been agreed on, and both parties presented and fired in succession. (Matthew L. Davis, describing events at Weehawken, New Jersey, July 11, 1804, from *Memoirs of Aaron Burr*, by Matthew L. Davis.)

[The eyewitnesses do not agree on precisely what happened during the duel. Either Hamilton fired first, or he did not. *If* he fired first, he either did or did not fire at Burr. Both sides agree on the outcome: Vice President Burr shot and killed former treasury secretary Hamilton.]

RESPONSE TO A MISSIONARY

---

125. Brother! . . . Your forefathers crossed the great waters, and landed on this island. Their numbers were small. They found friends and not enemies. They told us they had fled from their own country for fear of wicked men, and come here to enjoy their religion. They asked for a small seat. We took pity on them, granted their request, and they sat down amongst us. We gave them corn and meat. They gave us poison in return. The white people had now found our country. Tidings were carried back, and more came amongst us. Yet we did not fear them. We took them to be friends. They called us brothers. We believed them, and gave them a larger seat. At length their numbers have greatly increased. They wanted more land. They wanted our country. (Red Jacket, statement to missionary, 1805, cited in *Indian Biography*, by B. B. Thatcher.)

126. Brother! You have got our country, but are not satisfied. You want to force your religion upon us. . . . Brother! We understand that your religion is written in a book. If it was intended for us as well as for you, why has not the Great Spirit given it to us? (Ibid.)

EMBARKATION

127. Having acquired information & provisions of the Mandans on the evening of the 7th of April, 1805 we embarked with our baggage on board 2 large perogues [keelboats] and six small canoes at Fort Mandan [in central North Dakota] on a Voyage of Discovery to the Pacific Ocean. The party consisted of the following persons my friend and Colleague Capt. Wm. Clark, Interpreters George Drewyer and Tuasanat Charbono, Sergts. John Ordway Nathanial Pryor and Patric Gass, privates John Sheilds &c. a Shoshone Woman [Sacagawea] and her child wife and Infant of Toust. Charbono and York a black man servant of Capt. Clark making a total with myself of 33 persons. A Man of the Mandan nation also set out with us under promis to accompany us to the Rocky Mountains with a view to reestablishing peace between the Minnetares & Ahwahaways and the Shoshones and others at the head of the Missouri, but becoming very early tired of his mission he abandoned us on the 8th and returned to his village. (Captain Meriwether Lewis, letter to President Jefferson, events of April 7, 1805, cited in *The Letters of the Lewis and Clark Expedition*, edited by Donald Jackson.)

[The letter to Jefferson was dated September 21, 1806. It was sent from St. Louis, where the party had ended the expedition. The group had reached the Pacific Ocean on November 7, 1805.]

CONSPIRACY UNCOVERED

128. Some time in the latter part of September [1806], I received intimations that designs were in agitation in the western country, unlawful and unfriendly to the peace of the Union; and that the prime mover in these was Aaron Burr, heretofore distinguished by the favor of his country. . . .

It was not until the latter part of October, that the objects of the conspiracy began to be perceived, but still so blended and involved in mystery that nothing distinct could be singled out for pursuit. In this state of uncertainty as to the crime contemplated, the acts done, and the legal course to be pursued, I thought it best to send to the scene . . . a person, in whose integrity, understanding, and discretion, entire confidence could be reposed, with instructions to investigate the plots going on. [He was] to enter into conference (for which he had sufficient credentials) with the governors and all other officers, civil and military, and with their aid to do on the spot whatever should be necessary to discover the designs of the conspirators, arrest their means, bring their persons to punishment, and to call out the force of the country to suppress any unlawful enterprise. . . .

Besides despatching the confidential agent . . . others were at the same time sent to the governors of the Orleans and Mississippi territories, and to the commanders of the land and naval forces there, to be on their guard against surprise. . . .

By a letter received from [General James Wilkinson] on the 25th of November, but dated October 21st, we learn that a confidential agent of Aaron Burr had been deputed to him, with communications partly written in cipher and partly oral, explaining his designs. . . .

It appeared that he [Burr] contemplated two distinct objects. . . . One of these was the severance of the Union of these States by the Allegheny mountains; the other an attack on Mexico. A third object was . . . the settlement of a pretended purchase of a tract of country on the Washita, claimed by a Baron Basstrop. This was to serve as the pretext for all his preparations, an allurement for such followers as really wished to acquire settlements in that country. . . .

He [Burr] found at once that the attachment of the western country to the present Union was not to be shaken; that its dissolution could not be effected with the consent of its inhabitants, and that his resources were inadequate, as yet, to effect it by force. He took his course then at once, determined to seize on New Orleans, plunder the bank there, possess himself of the military and naval stores, and proceed on his expedition to Mexico, and to this object all his means and preparations were now directed. . . .

Orders were despatched [by me] to every intersecting point on the Ohio and Mississippi, from Pittsburg to New Orleans, for the employment of such force either of the regulars or of the militia, and . . . the civil authorities, as might enable them to seize on all the boats and stores provided for the enterprise, to arrest the persons concerned, and to suppress effectually the further progress of the enterprise. (President Thomas Jefferson, report to Congress on the Burr Conspiracy, January 22, 1807, cited in *Thomas Jefferson: Writings*, notes and text selection by Merrill D. Peterson.)

A CHARGE TO THE JURY

---

129. The present indictment charges the prisoner [Aaron Burr] with levying war against the United States, and alleges an overt act of levying war. The overt act must be proved . . . by two witnesses. It is not proved by a single witness. . . .

The arguments on both sides have been . . . deliberately considered. . . . No testimony relative to the conduct of declarations of the prisoner elsewhere and subsequent to the transaction on Blennerhassett's island can be admitted, because such testimony, being in its nature merely corroborative and incompetent to prove the overt act itself, is irrelevant until there be proof of the overt act by two witnesses. . . . The jury have now heard the opinion of the court on the law of the case. They will apply that law to the facts, and will find a verdict. . . . as their consciences may direct. (Chief Justice John Marshall, presiding at the treason trial of Aaron Burr, Richmond, Virginia, September 1, 1807, cited in *Aaron Burr: The Conspiracy and Years of Exile, 1805–1836*, by Milton Lomask.)

[The only crime specifically defined in the Constitution is treason, including the kind of evidence required for conviction. In charging the jury, Justice Marshall stuck strictly to that definition. The jurors came back with the verdict, "Aaron Burr is not proved to be guilty under this indictment by any evidence submitted to us. We therefore find him not guilty."]

A SATIRICAL HISTORY

130. In the ever-memorable year of our Lord, 1609, on a Saturday morning, the five-and-twentieth day of March, old style, did that "worthy and irrecoverable discoverer (as he has justly been called), Master Henry Hudson," set sail from Holland in a stout vessel called the *Half-Moon*, being employed by the Dutch East India Company, to seek a northwest passage to China.

Henry (or, as the Dutch historians call him, Hendrick) Hudson was a seafaring man of renown, who had learned to smoke tobacco under Sir Walter Raleigh, and is said to have been the first to introduce it into Holland, which gained him much popularity in that country, and caused him to find great favor in the eyes of their High Mightinesses, and Lords States-General, and also of the honorable West India Company. He was a short, square, brawny old gentleman, with a double chin, a mastiff mouth, and a broad copper nose, which was supposed in those days to have acquired its fiery hue from the constant neighborhood of his tobacco-pipe. . . .

He wore . . . a commodore's cocked hat on one side of his head. He was remarkable for always jerking up his breeches when he gave out his orders, and his voice sounded not unlike the prattling of a tin trumpet—owing to the number of hard northwesters which he had swallowed in the course of his seafaring.

Such was Hendrick Hudson, of whom we have heard so much, and know so little. (Washington Irving, from *Knickerbocker's History of New York*, 1809.)

131. From all that I can learn, few incidents worthy of remark happened on the voyage. Suffice it to say, the voyage was prosperous and tranquil; the crew, being a patient people, much given to slumber and vacuity and but little troubled with the disease of thinking—a malady of the mind, which is the sure breeder of discontent. Hudson had laid in abundance of gin and sourkrout, and every man was allowed to sleep quietly at his post unless the wind blew. True it is, some slight disaffection was shown on two or three occasions. . . .

[B]eing under the especial guidance of Providence, the ship was safely conducted to the coast of America; where, after sundry unimportant touchings and standings off and on, she at length, on the fourth day of September, entered that majestic bay which at this day expands its ample bosom before the city of New York, and which had never before been visited by any European.

When the great navigator was first blessed with a view of this enchanting island, he was observed, for the first and only time in his life, to exhibit strong symptoms of astonishment and admiration. He is said to have turned to Master Juet, and uttered these remarkable words, while he pointed towards the paradise of the new world—"See! There!"—and thereupon, as was always his way when he was uncommonly pleased, he did puff out such clouds of dense tobacco smoke, that in one minute the vessel was out of sight of land, and Master Juet was fain to wait until the winds had dispersed this impenetrable fog. (Ibid.)

132. Of the transactions of our adventurers with the savages, and how the latter smoked copper pipes, and ate dried currants; how they brought great store of tobacco and oysters; how they shot one of the ship's crew, and how he was buried, I shall say nothing; being that I consider them unimportant to my history. After tarrying a few days seafaring, our voyagers weighed anchor, to explore a mighty river which emptied into the bay. . . .

Being satisfied that there was little likelihood of getting to China . . . he forthwith re-crossed the sea to Holland, where he was received with great welcome by the honorable East India Company, who were very much rejoiced to see him come back safe—with their ship. At a large and respectable meeting of the merchants and burgomasters of Amsterdam, it was determined, that, as a munificent reward for the important discovery he had made, the great river . . . should be called after his name! And it continues to be called Hudson River unto this very day. (Ibid.)

APPEALING FOR ALLIES

133. Brothers—the white people are like poisonous serpents: when chilled, they are feeble and harmless, but invigorate them with warmth, and they sting their benefactors to death. (Tecumseh, address to the Osage tribe, 1811, from *Memoirs of a Captivity among the Indians of North America*, by John D. Hunter.)

134. Brothers—who are the white people that we should fear them? . . . They are only men; our fathers have killed many of them; we are not squaws, and we will stain the earth red with their blood.

Brothers—we must be united; we must smoke the same pipe; we must fight each other's battles; and more than all, we must love the Great Spirit; he is for us; he will destroy our enemies, and make his red children happy. (Ibid.)

FIGHTING WORDS

---

135. Don't give up the ship! (James Lawrence, commander of the American frigate *Chesapeake*, 30 miles from Boston, June 1, 1813.)

[During a fierce battle with the British frigate *Shannon*, Lawrence had been mortally wounded. The *Chesapeake* was captured.]

VICTORY MESSAGE

---

136. We have met the enemy, and they are ours! 2 ships, 2 brigs, 1 schooner, and 1 sloop. (Oliver H. Perry, commander of the brig *Niagara*, message to William Henry Harrison following the Battle of Lake Erie, September 10, 1813.)

ON NATURAL ARISTOCRACY

---

137. I agree with you that there is a natural aristocracy among men. The grounds of this are virtue and talents. Formerly, bodily powers gave place among the aristoi. But since the invention of gunpowder has armed the weak as well as the strong with missile death, bodily strength, like beauty, good humor, politeness and other accomplishments, has become but an auxiliary ground for distinction. (Thomas Jefferson, letter to John Adams, October 28, 1813.)

A FUTURE ANTHEM

138.

O! thus be it ever, when freemen shall stand
  Between their loved homes and the war's desolation!
Blest with victory and peace, may the Heav'n-rescued land
  Praise the Power that hath made and preserved us a nation.
Then conquer we must, when our cause it is just,
And this be our motto,—'In God is our trust,'
And the star-spangled banner in triumph shall wave
O'er the land of the free, and the home of the brave.

(Francis Scott Key, "The Star-Spangled Banner," 1814.)

[During the War of 1812, Key wrote this after witnessing the British bombardment of Fort McHenry, Maryland. As long as the flag flew over the fort, Key knew that the battle continued without surrender. This is the poem's final stanza, which became especially meaningful—and popular—during World War II.]

WASHINGTON PUT TO THE TORCH

139. [T]he troops advanced forthwith into the town [Washington], and having first put to the sword all who were found in the house from which the shots were fired and reduced it to ashes [The British troops had been fired on when approaching under a flag of truce.]. . . .

In this general devastation were included the Senate-house, the President's palace, an extensive dock-yard and arsenal, barracks for 2–3,000 men, several large store-houses filled with naval and military stores, some hundred of cannon of different descriptions, and nearly 20,000 stand of small arms. There were also two or three public rope-works which shared the same fate, a fine frigate pierced for 60 guns, and just ready to be launched, several gun-brigs and armed schooners, with a variety of gun-boats and small craft.

The powder magazines were of course set on fire, and exploded with a tremendous crash, throwing down many houses in their vicinity, partly by pieces of the walls striking them, and partly by the concussion of the air; whilst quantities of shot, shell, and hand-grenades, which could not otherwise be rendered useless, were thrown into the river. . . .

[U]nfortunately, it did not stop there; a noble library, several offices, and all the national archives were likewise committed to the flames, which, though no doubt the property of government, might better have been spared. (George Glieg, a British officer recalling the burning of Washington, August 24–25, 1814, from *The Campaigns of the British Army at Washington and New Orleans*, by George Robert Glieg.)

DEFINING THE REVOLUTION

---

140. What do we mean by the Revolution? The war? That was no part of the Revolution: it was only an effect and consequence of it. The Revolution was in the minds of the people, and this was effected, from 1760 to 1775, in the course of 15 years, before a drop of blood was shed at Lexington. (John Adams, 1815, cited in *Voices of the American Revolution*, by the Peoples Bicentennial Commission.)

AWAKENING

---

141. "Surely," thought Rip, "I have not slept here all night." He recalled the occurrences before he fell asleep. The strange man with a keg of liquor. . . .

The flagon—"Oh! that flagon!"—thought Rip—"What excuse shall I make to Dame Van Winkle?"

He looked round for his gun, but in place of the clean well-oiled fowling piece, he found an old firelock lying by him, the barrel incrusted with rust, the lock falling off, and the stock worm-eaten. . . .

Wolf, too, had disappeared, but he might have strayed away after a squirrel or partridge. He whistled after him and shouted his name, but all in vain; the echoes repeated his whistle and shout, but no dog was to be seen. . . .

As he approached the village, he met a number of people, but none whom he knew. . . .

He had now entered the skirts of the village. A troop of strange children ran at his heels, hooting after him, and pointing at his grey beard. The dogs, too, not one of which he recognized . . . barked at him as he passed. The very village was altered: it was larger and more populous. . . .

He now hurried forth, and hastened to his old resort, the village inn—but it too was gone. . . .

Instead of the great tree that used to shelter the quiet little Dutch inn of yore, there now was reared a tall naked pole, with something on the top that looked like a red nightcap, and from it was fluttering a flag, on which was a singular assemblage of stars and stripes—all this was strange and incomprehensible. He recognized on the sign, however, the ruby face of King George, under which he had smoked so many a peaceful pipe; but even this was singularly meta-morphosed. The red coat was changed for one of blue and buff, a sword was held in the hand instead of a scepter, the head was decorated with a cocked hat, and underneath was painted in large characters, GENERAL WASHINGTON. . . .

"Alas, gentlemen," cried Rip, somewhat dismayed, "I am a poor, quiet man, a native of the place, and a loyal subject of the king, God bless him!"

Here a general shout burst from the bystanders—"A Tory! a Tory! a spy! a refugee! hustle him! away with him!" (Washington Irving, from his short story "Rip Van Winkle," 1819.)

[This is a legend of the "Kaatskill" Mountains area of New York. Washington Irving used Rip Van Winkle's 20 years of sleep to illustrate how rapidly changes had come to the infant United States.]

ON TAXATION

142. The power to tax involves the power to destroy. (Chief Justice John Marshall, opinion, *McCulloch v. Maryland*, U.S. Supreme Court, 1819.)

HOME, SWEET HOME

143.

> 'Mid pleasures and palaces though we may roam,
> Be it ever so humble, there's no place like home.

(John Howard Paine, song from his play *Clari, the Maid of Milan*, 1823.)

MONROE DOCTRINE

144. The American continents, by the free and independent condition which they have assumed and maintained, are henceforth not to be considered as subjects for future colonization by any European powers. (James Monroe, address to Congress, August 7, 1823.)

145. Our policy in regard to Europe, which was adopted at an early stage of the wars which have so long agitated that quarter of the globe, nevertheless remains the same, which is, not to interfere in the internal concerns of any of its powers, to consider the government de facto as the legitimate government for us, to cultivate friendly relations with it, and to preserve those relations by a frank, firm, and manly policy, meeting in all instances the just claims of every power, submitting to injuries from none. But in regard to those [American] continents circumstances are eminently and conspicuously different. It is impossible that the allied powers should extend their political system to any portion of either [American] continent without endangering our peace and happiness; nor can anyone believe that our southern brethren, if left to themselves, would adopt it of their own accord. It is equally impossible, therefore, that we should behold such interposition in any form with indifference. (Ibid.)

PURSUED IN THE WILDERNESS

146. Led by the scout, Hawk-eye, the canoe moves speedily along the lake. The party had been pursued by Hurons, but they are no longer in sight. The canoe is beached, and Hawk-eye and Heyward climb to the top of a bluff to look over the lake.

[A]fter considering the expanse of water beneath him, [Hawk-eye] pointed out to [Heyward] a small black object, hovering under a head-land, at the distance of several miles.

"Do you see it?" demanded the scout. "Now, what would you account that spot, were you left alone to white experience to find your way through this wilderness?"

"But for its distance and its magnitude, I should suppose it a bird. Can it be a living object?"

" 'Tis a canoe of good birchen bark, and paddled by fierce and crafty Mingoes! Though Providence has lent to those who inhabit the woods eyes that would be needless to men in the settlements, where there are inventions to assist the sight, yet no human organs can see all the dangers which at this moment circumvent us. These varlets pretend to be bent chiefly on their sun-down meal, but the moment it is dark, they will be on our trail, as true as hounds on the scent. We must throw them off, or our pursuit of le Renard Subtil may be given up. These lakes are useful at times, especially when the game takes the water," continued the scout, gazing about him with a countenance of concern, "but they give no cover, except it be to the fishes. God knows what the country would be, if the settlements should ever spread far from the two rivers. Both hunting and war would lose their beauty!"

"Let us not delay a moment. . . ."

"I little like that smoke, which you may see worming up along the rock above the canoe," interrupted the abstracted scout. "My life on it, other eyes than ours see it, and know its meaning. Well, words will not mend the matter, and it is time that we were going." (James Fenimore Cooper, from his novel *The Last of the Mohicans*, 1826.)

[This historical novel was set during the French and Indian War. Readers of the time were thrilled by this action adventure, which featured such characters as a white man who knew the wilderness and Indians who were heroes as well as villains.]

ON THE ABUSES OF POWER

147. There is nothing more corrupting, nothing more destructive of the noblest and finest feelings of our nature, than the exercise of unlimited power. The man who in the beginning of such a career, might shudder at the idea of taking away the life of a fellow being, might soon have his conscience so scarred by the repetition of crime, that the agonies of his murdered victims might become music to his soul, and the drippings of his scaffold afford blood enough to swim in. History is full of such examples. (William Henry Harrison, U.S. minister to Colombia, letter to Simón Bolívar, September 27, 1829, cited in *The Bully Pulpit*, edited by Elizabeth Frost.)

[Harrison apparently sympathized with a group of revolutionaries in Colombia who wanted to overthrow Bolívar. President Jackson subsequently recalled Harrison from the diplomatic post.]

A WARNING ON LAND SALES

148. If any citizen or citizens of this [Cherokee] nation should treat and dispose of any lands belonging to this nation without special permission from the national authorities, he or they shall suffer death. . . .

Any person or persons who shall violate the provisions of this act, and shall refuse, by resistance, to appear at the place designated for trial, or abscond, are hereby declared to be outlaws; and any person or persons of this nation, may kill him or them so offending, in any manner most convenient, within the limits of this nation, and shall not be accountable for the same. (National Council of the Cherokee Nation, *Cherokee Phoenix*, October 29, 1829.)

[The Cherokee Council made a written law out of a long-standing tradition.]

TO A PROUD SHIP

149.

Ay, tear her tattered ensign down!
    Long has it waved on high,
And many an eye has danced to see
    That banner in the sky;
Beneath it rung the battle shout,
    And burst the cannon's roar;
The meteor of the ocean air
    Shall sweep the clouds no more! . . .
O better that her shattered hulk
    Should sink beneath the wave,
Her thunders shook the mighty deep,
    And there should be her grave;
Nail to the mast her holy flag,
    Set every thread-bare sail,
And give her to the god of storms—
    The lightning and the gale!

(Oliver Wendell Holmes Sr., from his poem "Old Ironsides," 1830.)

[Holmes wrote this poem after he heard that the U.S. Navy was planning to scrap the USS *Constitution*, also known as "Old Ironsides." Publication of the poem aroused such a furor that the navy relented.]

WHOSE GOVERNMENT IS IT?

150. This leads us to inquire into the origin of this Government and the source of its power. Whose agent is it? Is it the creature of the State Legislatures, or the creature of the people? . . . It is, sir, the people's Constitution, the people's Government; made for the people; made by the people; and answerable to the people. . . .

[H]ow is it that a State Legislature acquires any power to interfere? Who or what gives them the right to say to the people, "We who are your agents and servants for one purpose, will undertake to decide that your other agents and servants, appointed by you for another purpose, have transcended the authority you gave them?" The reply would be, I think, not impertinent: "Who made you a judge over another's servants?" (Daniel Webster, speech, U.S. Senate, January 26, 1830.)

151. Liberty and Union, now and forever, one and inseparable! (Ibid.)

A JUSTICE IS OVERRULED

152. [Chief Justice] John Marshall has made his decision, now let him enforce it! (President Andrew Jackson, comment attributed to Jackson following Marshall's decision on the rights of the Cherokee Nation to their land in Georgia, 1831, cited in *Encyclopedia of American History*, edited by Richard B. Morris and Jeffrey B. Morris.)

EDITORIAL ON MODERATION

153. I am aware that many object to the severity of my language; but is there not cause for severity? I will be as harsh as truth, and as uncompromising as justice. On this subject [slavery], I do not wish to think, or speak, or write, with

moderation. No! No! Tell a man whose house is on fire, to give a moderate alarm; tell him to moderately rescue his wife from the hands of the ravisher; tell the mother to gradually extricate her babe from the fire into which it has fallen; —but urge me not to use moderation in a cause like the present. I am in earnest— I will not equivocate—I will not excuse—I will not retreat a single inch—and I will be heard. (William Lloyd Garrison, *The Liberator*, January 1, 1831.)

SLAVE LEADER SPEAKS

The leader of the slave rebellion—a preacher—began his confession by telling of visions and signs that he had seen since he was a child. He had concluded that he was destined for some great purpose. He would conclude that God had directed him to lead a slave uprising. It began on August 21, 1831.

154. It was quickly agreed we should commence at home on that night; and until we had armed and equipped ourselves, and gained sufficient force, neither age nor sex was to be spared—which was invariably adhered to. We remained at the feast until about two in the night, when we went to the house. . . .

I took my station in the rear, and, as it was my object to carry terror and devastation wherever we went, I placed 15 or 20 of the best armed and most to be relied on in front, who generally approached the houses as fast as their horses could run. This was for two purposes—to prevent their escape, and strike terror to the inhabitants; on this account I never got to the houses, after leaving Mrs. Whitehead's, until the murders were committed, except in one case, I sometimes got in sight in time to see the work of death completed; viewed the mangled bodies as they lay, in silent satisfaction, and immediately started in quest of other victims. Having murdered Mrs. Waller and ten children, we started for Mr. Wm. Williams,—having killed him and two little boys that were there; while engaged in this, Mrs. Williams fled and got some distance from the house, but she was pursued, overtaken, and compelled to get up behind one of the company, who brought her back, and, after showing her the mangled body of her lifeless hus- band, she was told to get down and lay by his side, where she was shot dead. (Nat Turner, statement in prison, Southampton County, Virginia, ca. October 1831, from *The Confessions of Nat Turner*, edited by Thomas R. Gray.)

[More than 50 whites were killed during the rebellion. The 60 slaves taking part in the rebellion dispersed in different directions. Turner hid in a cave for more than six weeks. He was captured and executed.]

CAN A STATE NULLIFY A LAW?

155. The ordinance [by South Carolina nullifying a tariff act] is founded, not on the indefeasible right of resisting acts which are plainly unconstitutional and too oppressive to be endured, but on the strange position that any one State may not only declare an act of Congress void, but prohibit its execution. . . .

I consider . . . the power to annul a law of the United States, assumed by one State, incompatible with the existence of the Union, contradicted expressly by the letter of the Constitution, unauthorized by its spirit, inconsistent with every principle on which it was joined, and destructive of the great object for which it was formed. . . .

Because the Union was formed by a compact, it is said [by South Carolina that] the parties to that compact may, when they feel themselves aggrieved, depart from it; but it is precisely because it is a compact that they can not. A compact is an agreement or binding obligation. . . .

The governor of that State has recommended to the legislature the raising of an army to carry the secession into effect, and that he may be empowered to give clearances to vessels in the name of the State. No act of violent opposition to the laws has yet been committed, but such a state of things is hourly apprehended. And it is the intent of this instrument to proclaim, not only that the duty imposed on me by the Constitution "to take care that the laws be faithfully executed" shall be performed to the extent of the powers already vested in me by law, or of such others as the wisdom of Congress shall devise and intrust to me for that purpose, but to warn the citizens of South Carolina who have been deluded into an opposition to the laws of the danger they will incur by obedience to the illegal and disorganizing ordinance of the convention. . . . Disunion by armed force is treason. . . . (President Andrew Jackson, proclamation to the people of South Carolina, December 10, 1832.)

[The tariff law was amended by Congress, and the Nullification Ordinance was rescinded by South Carolina.]

HISTORIAN'S VIEW

156. The Jacksonians believed that there was a deep-rooted conflict in society between the "producing" and "nonproducing" classes—the farmers and laborers, on the one hand, and the business community on the other. The business community was considered to hold high cards in the conflict through its network of banks and corporations, its control of education and the press, above all, its power over the state: it was therefore able to strip the working classes of the fruits of their labor. "Those who produce all wealth," said Amos Kendall [writing in 1834], "are themselves left poor. They see principalities extending and palaces built around them, without being aware that the entire expense is a tax upon themselves."

If they wished to preserve their liberty, the producing classes would have to unite against the movement "to make the rich richer and the potent more powerful." . . .

The specific problem was to control the power of the capitalistic groups, mainly Eastern, for the benefit of the noncapitalist groups, farmers and laboring men, East, West and South. The basic Jacksonian ideas came naturally enough from the East, which best understood the nature of business power and reacted most sharply against it. The legend that Jacksonian democracy was the explosion of the frontier, lifting into the government some violent men filled with rustic prejudices against big business, does not explain the facts, which were somewhat more complex. Jacksonian democracy was rather a second American phase of that enduring struggle between the business community and the rest of society which is the guarantee of freedom in a liberal capitalist state. (Arthur M. Schlesinger Jr., historian, reviewing Jacksonian democracy, ca. 1834, from *The Age of Jackson*.)

IMMIGRATION PLOT SEEN

157. We have to resist the *momentous* evil that threatens us from *Foreign Conspiracy*. There is no doubt we are in serious danger, and it is madness not to see it, not to guard against it. We are under attack by foreign powers. The despots of Europe—those governments who keep the people in obedience at the point of the bayonet—have combined to attack us at every vulnerable point.

They are led by self-preservation to attempt our destruction—they must destroy democracy. To them it is a case of life and death—they must succeed or perish. If they do not overthrow American liberty, American liberty will overthrow their despotism. . . .

Americans, you are marked for their prey, not by foreign bayonets, but *by weapons surer of effecting the conquest of liberty* than all the guns and bombs of Europe. Wake up to the reality of your danger! . . .

Your enemies, pretending to be friends, are at this moment rushing to your ruin through the open doors of *naturalization*. Stop them, or you are lost. The first battle is here at the gates. (Samuel F. B. Morse, *Imminent Dangers to the Free Institutions of the United States through Foreign Immigration and the Present State of the Naturalization Law*, 1835.)

158. Do you doubt the cry of danger? Well, so be it. Go ahead and believe the foreigner instead of your own countrymen. Open wide your doors. Yes, throw down your walls. Invite your enemies in!

Enlarge your poorhouses and your prisons; do not spare your money. Complain not of crime in your streets, nor the burden of your taxes. You will be repaid in praises of your generosity.

So what that European despots have forced you to care for their sick, and blind, and naked, and the keepers of their criminals. So what that they have forced you to spend your lives toiling and providing for their outcast poor, and have caused you to be outraged by the violence in their cities, instead of allowing you to rejoice in the prosperity, and happiness, and peaceful neighborhood of your own well-provided, well-instructed children. (Ibid.)

APPEAL FOR HELP

During the 1830s, the Mexican province of Texas, with many American settlers, fights for independence.

159. I am besieged by a thousand or more of the Mexicans, under Santa Anna. I have sustained a continual bombardment and cannonade for 24 hours, and have not lost a man. The enemy have demanded a surrender . . . , otherwise the garrison is to be put to the sword, if the fort is taken. I have answered the summons with a cannonshot, and our flag still waves proudly from the walls. *I shall never surrender or retreat*; then I call on you, in the name of Liberty, of Patriotism, and of every thing dear to the American character, to come to our aid with all despatch. . . .

I am determined to sustain myself as long as possible, and die like a soldier, who never forgets what is due to his own honour and that of his country. *Victory or Death!* (Lieutenant Colonel William B. Travis, the Alamo, San Antonio, Texas, February 24, 1836, from *Texas and the Texans*, by Henry Stuart Foote.)

[Several days later, 32 volunteers made their way through Mexican lines to join the Alamo defenders. The siege lasted from February 23 to March 6, when the Texas force of 187 men was wiped out. Some historians claim that a woman and child survived. This desperate siege would inspire the battle cry "Remember the Alamo!"]

CONCORD HYMN

160.

By the rude bridge that arched the flood,
Their flag to April's breeze unfurled,
Here once the embattled farmers stood,
And fired the shot heard round the world.

(Ralph Waldo Emerson, *Hymn: Sung on the Completion of the Concord Monument,* Concord, Massachusetts, April 19, 1836.)

[The monument commemorated one of the first battles of the Revolutionary War.]

INFECTED

161. I have never called a white man a dog, but today I do pronounce them to be a set of black-hearted dogs. . . . I do not fear death, my friends. You know it. But to die with my face rotten [from the smallpox], that even the wolves will shrink with horror at seeing me. . . .

Listen well to what I have to say, as it will be the last time you will hear me. Think of your wives, children, brothers, sisters, with their faces all rotten, caused by those dogs the whites. Think of all that my friends, and rise all together and not leave one of them alive. (The Four Bears, 1837, cited in *Red & White: Indian Views of the White Man,* by Annette Rosenstiel.)

SOUTHERN VIEWPOINT

162. I fearlessly assert, that the existing relation between the two races in the South, against which . . . blind fanatics are waging war, forms the most solid and durable foundation on which to rear free and stable political institutions. . . .

There is, and always has been, in an advanced stage of wealth and civilization, a conflict between labor and capital. The condition of society in the South exempts us from the disorders and dangers resulting from this conflict, and which explains why it is that the political condition of the slaveholding states has been so much more stable and quiet than that of the North. (Senator John C. Calhoun of South Carolina, speech, U.S. Senate, February 6, 1837.)

[Following Calhoun's death in 1850, a paper was published in which he advocated two presidents serving concurrently. One would be from the North and one from the South, and each would have the veto power.]

AGAINST ANNEXATION

---

163. I do believe slavery to be a sin before God, and that is the reason and the only unsurmountable reason why we should not annex Texas to this Union. (Representative John Quincy Adams, speech, House of Representatives, February 1838.)

GOING, GOING, GONE

---

164. In the first place we were required to wash thoroughly. . . . We were then furnished with a new suit each, cheap, but clean. The men had hat, coat, suit, pants and shoes; the women frocks of calico, and handkerchief to bind about their heads. We were now conducted into a large room in the front part of the building to which the yard was attached, in order to be properly trained, before the admission of customers. . . .

[Auction owner Theoophilus] Freeman . . . exhorted us to appear smart and lively. . . .

Next day many customers called to examine Freeman's "new lot." [Freeman] was very loquacious, dwelling at much length upon our several good points and qualities. He would make us hold up our heads, walk briskly back and forth, while customers would feel of our hands and arms and bodies, turn us about, ask us what we could do, make us open our mouths and show our teeth, precisely as a jockey examines a horse which he is about to barter for or purchase. Sometimes a man or woman was taken back to the small house in the yard, stripped, and inspected more minutely. Scars upon a slave's back were considered evidence of a rebellious or unruly spirit, and hurt his sale. . . .

[After her son is purchased by a man from Baton Rouge, the mother begs the buyer to purchase her, as well. But the purchaser says he cannot afford her, too.]

The planter from Baton Rouge, with his new purchase, was ready to depart.

"Don't cry, mama. I will be a good boy. Don't cry," said Randall, looking back, as they passed out of the door.

What has become of the lad, God knows. It was a mournful scene indeed. (Solomon Northrup, describing a slave auction, New Orleans, 1841, from *Twelve Years a Slave*.)

INTEGRITY AND IDENTITY

165. Who so would be a man, must be a nonconformist. He who would gather immortal palms must not be hindered by the name of goodness. . . . Nothing is at last sacred but the integrity of your own mind. (Ralph Waldo Emerson, from his essay "Self-Reliance," 1841.)

WORKMEN'S SOCIETY OR CONSPIRACY?

The Journeymen Bootmakers Society of Boston is charged with being a criminal conspiracy. The members are found guilty in the lower courts, and the case goes to the state's supreme court.

166. The . . . count set forth, that the defendants . . . on the day and at the place named, being workmen, and journeymen, in the art and occupation of bootmakers, unlawfully, perniciously, and deceitfully designing and intending to . . . form, and unite themselves into an unlawful club, society, and combination; and make unlawful bylaws, rules, and orders among themselves, and thereby govern themselves and other workmen in their said art, and unlawfully and unjustly to extort great sums of money by means thereof, did unlawfully assemble and meet together, and being so assembled, did unjustly and corruptly conspire, combine, confederate, and agree together that no one of them should thereafter, and that none of them would, work for any master or person whatsoever in the said art, mystery, and occupation, who should employ any workman or journeyman, [or] other person . . . who was not a member of said club, society, or combination, . . . to the great damage and oppression etc. [of the employers]. . . .

The manifest intent of the association is, to induce all those engaged in the same occupation to become members of it. Such a purpose is not unlawful. It would give them a power which might be exerted for useful and honorable purposes, or for dangerous and pernicious ones. If the latter were the real and actual object, and susceptible of proof, it should have been specially charged. Such an association might be used to afford each other assistance in times of poverty, sickness, and distress; or to raise their intellectual, moral, and social condition; or to make improvement in their art; or for other proper purposes. Or the association might be designed for purposes of oppression and injustice. But in order to charge all those who become members of an association with the guilt of a criminal conspiracy, it must be averred and proved. . . .

The law is not to be hoodwinked by colorable pretenses. It looks at truth and reality through whatever disguise it may assume. But to make such an association, ostensibly innocent, the subject of prosecution as a criminal conspiracy, the secret agreement which makes it so, is to be averred and proved as the gist of the offense. . . . In this case, no such secret agreement, varying the objects of the association from those avowed, is set forth in this count of the indictment. . . .

[W]e cannot perceive that it is criminal for men to agree together to exercise their own acknowledged rights in such a manner as best to subserve their own interests. . . .

Suppose a class of workmen, impressed with the manifold evils of intemperance, should agree with each other not to work in a shop in which ardent spirit was furnished, or not to work in a shop with any one who used it. . . . [A]s the object would be lawful, and the means not unlawful, such an agreement could not be propounded a criminal conspiracy. . . .

[L]ooking solely at the indictment, disregarding the qualifying epithets, recitals, and immaterial allegations, and confining ourselves to facts so averred as to be capable of being traversed and put in issue, we cannot perceive that it charges a criminal conspiracy punishable by law. (Chief Justice Lemuel Shaw, Massachusetts Supreme Court, opinion, *Commonwealth v. Hunt*, March 1842.)

[This is the first legal victory for organized labor in America.]

A QUESTION OF LATITUDE

167. Fifty-four forty or fight! (Senator William Allen, speech calling for the northern boundary line of the Oregon Territory to be set at 54 degrees 40 minutes latitude, U.S. Senate, Washington, D.C., 1844.)

[The boundary dispute was settled with Great Britain in 1846. The northern boundary was set at the 49th parallel.]

A LETTER HOME

A runaway slave responds to a letter from his former master.

168. I am happy to inform you that you are not mistaken in the man whom you sold as property, and received pay for as such. But I thank God that I am not property now, but am regarded as a man like yourself, and although I live far north, I am enjoying a comfortable living by my own industry. If you should ever chance to be traveling this way, and will call on me, I will use you better than you did me while you held me as a slave. Think not that I have any malice against you, for the cruel treatment which you inflicted on me while I was in your power. As it was the custom of your country, to treat your fellow men as you did me and my little family, I can freely forgive you. . . .

To be compelled to stand by and see you whip and lash my wife without mercy, when I could afford her no protection, not even my offering myself to suffer the lash in her place, was more than I felt it to be the duty of a slave husband to endure, while the way was open to Canada. My infant child was also frequently flogged by Mrs. Gatewood, for crying, until his skin was bruised literally purple. This kind of treatment was what drove me from home and family, to seek a better home for them. But I am willing to forget the past. I should be pleased to hear from you again . . . and should also be very happy to correspond with you often, if it should be agreeable to yourself. (Henry Bibb, letter to W. H. Gatewood, his former master, who lived in Kentucky, March 23, 1844, from *Narrative of the Life and Adventures of Henry Bibb, An American Slave.*)

TELEGRAPH MESSAGE

169. What hath God wrought! (Samuel F. B. Morse, first telegraph message from Washington, D.C., to Baltimore, May 24, 1844.)

A BLACK BIRD

170.

> "Tell this soul with sorrow laden if, within the distant Aidenn,
> It shall clasp a sainted maiden whom the angels name Lenore—
> Clasp a rare and radiant maiden whom the angels name Lenore."
> Quoth the Raven "Nevermore."

(Edgar Allan Poe, from his poem "The Raven," 1845.)

NEW POLITICAL SLOGAN

171. Manifest Destiny. (John L. O'Sullivan, from article in *Democratic Review*, July 1845.)

[This apparently was the first time that the phrase appeared in public print.]

BORDER INCIDENT

172. About six o'clock P.M. General R. Jones, the Adjutant-General of the army, called and handed to me despatches received from General [Zachary] Taylor . . . giving information that a part of the Mexican army had crossed the Del Norte and attacked and killed and captured two companies of dragoons of General Taylor's army consisting of 63 officers and men. The despatch also stated that he had on that day [April 26] made a requisition on the Governors of Texas and Louisiana for four regiments each, to be sent . . . at the earliest practicable period. Before I had finished reading the despatches, the Secretary of War [William L. Marcy] called. I immediately summoned the Cabinet to meet . . . this evening. (President James K. Polk, diary entry, May 9, 1846, from *Polk: The Diary of a President*, edited by Allan Nevins.)

173. [A]fter repeated menaces, Mexico has passed the boundary of the United States, invaded our territory, and shed American blood upon the American soil. . . . [War] exists by the act of Mexico herself. (President James K. Polk, war message to Congress, May 11, 1846, Ibid.)

[On May 13, Polk signed Congress' war declaration. An army of 50,000 was authorized, and $10 million was appropriated.]

WHAT IF . . .

174. [If I had defeated Polk for the presidency in 1844] there would have been no annexation of Texas, no war with Mexico, no National debt . . . no imputation against us, by the united voice of all the nations of the earth, of a spirit of aggression and inordinate Territorial aggrandizement. (Henry Clay, once and future senator from Kentucky, letter to Epes Sargent, an early Clay biographer, February 15, 1847, cited in *Henry Clay: Statesman for the Union*, by Robert V. Remini.)

IN DEFENSE OF SLAVERY

175. So far as slavery is concerned, we of the south must throw ourselves on the constitution & defend our rights under [it] to the last, & when arguments will no longer suffice, we will appeal to the sword, if necessary to do so. I will be the last to yield one inch. (General Zachary Taylor, letter to Jefferson Davis, July 27, 1847, cited in *The Bully Pulpit*, edited by Elizabeth Frost.)

TRIUMPH IN MEXICO

176. Another victory, glorious in its results and which has thrown additional luster upon the American arms, has been achieved today by the army under General [Winfield] Scott. The proud capital of Mexico has fallen into the power of a mere handful of men compared with the immense odds arrayed against them, and Santa Anna, instead of shedding his blood as he had promised, is wandering with the remnant of his army no one knows whither. . . .
[The battle for Mexico City is described in detail.]

General Scott, with his staff, rode in and took quarters in the national palace, on the top of which the Stars and Stripes was already flying. An immense crowd of blanketed *leperos*, the scum of the capital, were congregated in the plaza as the commander-in-chief entered it. They pressed upon our soldiers and eyed them as though they were beings of another world. (George Wilkins Kendall, newspaper dispatch, reporting events of September 14, 1847, *New Orleans Picayune*, published October 14, 1847.)

[Using riders and boats—the fastest means of transmission available to him—Kendall was able to get his story into print a month after the event.]

EDUCATION AS EQUALIZER

177. A cardinal object which the government of Massachusetts . . . should propose to themselves is the physical well-being of all the people—the sufficiency, comfort, competence, of every individual in regard to food, raiment, and shelter. And these necessities and conveniences of life should be obtained by each individual for himself, or by each family for themselves, rather than accepted from the hand of charity or extorted by poor-laws. . . .

According to the European theory, men are divided into classes,—some to toil and earn, others to seize and enjoy. According to the Massachusetts theory, all are to have an equal chance for earning, and equal security in the enjoyment of what they earn. . . .

To what extent can competence displace pauperism? . . .

Education . . . beyond all other devices of human origin, is a great equalizer of the conditions of men—the balance wheel of social machinery. (Horace Mann, report of the Massachusetts Board of Education, 1848, from *The Life and Work of Horace Mann*.)

ON OFFICE SEEKERS

---

178. In the midst of the annoyances of the herd of lazy, worthless people who come to Washington for office instead of going to work and by some honest calling making a livelihood, I am sometimes amused at their applications. A case of this kind occurred on Saturday last. One of these office-seekers placed his papers of recommendation in the hands of Judge Mason to present to me. No particular office was specified in the papers, and the Judge reported to me that he enquired of him what office he wanted, to which he answered that he thought he would be a good hand at making treaties, and that as he understood there were some to be made soon he would like to be a minister abroad. This is about as reasonable as many other applications which are made to me. (President James K. Polk, diary entry, April 10, 1848, from *Polk: The Diary of a President, 1845–1849*, edited by Allan Nevins.)

A NEW DECLARATION

---

179. We hold these truths to be self-evident, that all men and women are created equal; that they are endowed by their Creator with certain inalienable rights; that among these are life, liberty, and the pursuit of happiness. . . .

The history of mankind is a history of repeated injuries and usurpations on the part of man toward woman, having in direct object the establishment of an absolute tyranny over her. . . .

He has compelled her to submit to laws, in the formation of which she had no voice.

He has withheld from her rights which are given to the most ignorant and degraded men—both natives and foreigners.

Having deprived her of this first right of a citizen, the elective franchise, thereby leaving her without representation in the halls of legislation, he has oppressed her on all sides.

He has made her, if married, in the eye of the law, civilly dead. . . .

Resolved, That all laws which prevent woman from occupying such a station in society as her conscience shall dictate, or which place her in a position inferior to that of many, are contrary to the great precept of nature, and therefore of no force or authority.

Resolved, That woman is man's equal—was intended to be so by the Creator, and the highest good of the race demands that she should be recognized as such. . . .

Resolved, That it is the duty of the women of this country to secure to themselves their sacred right to the elective franchise. (Seneca Falls Declaration, Seneca Falls, New York, July 19, 1848, from *The History of Woman Suffrage*, edited by E. C. Stanton, S. B. Anthony, and M. J. Gage.)

A FEAR OF DISUNION

---

180. The result of leaving the slavery question an open one [in the organization of territorial governments in Oregon, California, and New Mexico], to be agitated by ambitious political aspirants and gamblers and their friends, will be to produce an organization of parties upon geographical lines, which must prove dangerous to the harmony if not the existence of the Union itself. (President James K. Polk, diary excerpt, July 28, 1848, from *Polk: The Diary of a President*, edited by Allan Nevins.)

THE INDIVIDUAL AND THE STATE

---

181. I heartily accept the motto, "That government is best which governs least." (Henry David Thoreau, *Civil Disobedience*, 1849.)

182. A common and natural result of an undue respect for law is, that you may see a file of soldiers, colonel, captain, corporal, privates, powder-monkeys, and all, marching in admirable order over hill and dale to the wars, against their wills, ay, against their common sense and consciences. . . . It is a damnable business in which they are concerned. . . . Now, what are they? Men at all? or small

mobile forts and magazines, at the service of some unscrupulous man in power? . . .

The mass of men serve the state thus, not as men mainly, but as machines, with their bodies. They are the standing army, and the militia, jailers, constables, posse comitatus, &c. In most cases there is no free exercise whatever of the judgment or of the moral sense; but they put themselves on a level with wood and earth and stones; and wooden men can perhaps be manufactured that will serve the purpose as well. (Ibid.)

183. Most legislators, politicians, lawyers, ministers, and office-holders serve the state chiefly with their heads; and, as they rarely make any moral distinctions, they are as likely to serve the Devil, without *intending* it, as God. A very few, as heroes, patriots, martyrs, reformers in the great sense, and *men*, serve the state with their consciences also, and so necessarily resist it for the most part; and they are commonly treated as enemies by it. (Ibid.)

184. All voting is a sort of gaming, like checkers or backgammon, with a slight moral tinge to it, a playing with right and wrong, with moral questions. (Ibid.)

185. Is a democracy, such as we know it, the last improvement possible in government? Is it not possible to take a step further towards recognizing and organizing the rights of man? There will never be a really free and enlightened State, until the State comes to recognize the individual as a higher and independent power, from which all its own power and authority are derived, and treats him accordingly. I please myself with imagining a State at last which can afford to be just to all men, and to treat the individual with respect as a neighbor. (Ibid.)

WHAT DOES WOMAN WANT?

186. The question is often asked, "What does woman want, more than she enjoys? What is she seeking to obtain? Of what rights is she deprived? What privileges are withheld from her?" I answer, she asks nothing as favor, but as right, she wants to be acknowledged a moral, responsible being. She is seeking not to be governed by laws, in the making of which she has no voice. She is deprived of almost every right in civil society, and is a cypher in the nation, except in the right of presenting petition. In religious society her disabilities . . . have greatly retarded her progress. Her exclusion from the pulpit or ministry— her duties marked out for her by her equal brother man, subject to creeds, rules,

and disciplines made for her by him—this is unworthy of her true dignity. In marriage, there is assumed superiority, on the part of the husband, and admitted inferiority, with a promise of obedience, on the part of the wife. This subject calls loudly for examination in order that the wrong may be redressed. Customs suited to darker ages in Eastern countries, are not binding upon enlightened society. The solemn covenant of marriage may be entered into without these lordly assumptions, and humiliating concessions and promises. (Lucretia Mott, from *Discourse on Woman*, 1849.)

7

House Divided

The annexation of new territories led to great sectional disputes between North and South. Antislavery and pro-slavery forces literally killed each other to make a new territory slave or free. Violence broke out even on the floor of Congress itself. There was a series of congressional compromises on how to divide up the country.

A TOKEN OF SHAME

187. Stretching forth the official staff in his left hand, he laid his right upon the shoulder of a young woman, whom he thus drew forward, until, on the threshold of the prison door, she repelled him, by an action marked with natural dignity and force of character, and stepped into the open air, as if by her own free-will. She bore in her arms a child, a baby of some three months old, who winked and turned aside its little face from the too vivid light of day; because its existence, heretofore, had brought it acquainted only with the gray twilight of a dungeon, or other darksome apartment of the prison.

When the young woman—the mother of this child—stood fully revealed before the crowd, it seemed to be her first impulse to clasp the infant closely to her bosom; not so much by an impulse of motherly affection, as that she might thereby conceal a certain token, which was wrought or fastened into her dress. In a moment, however, wisely judging that one token of her shame would but poorly serve to hide another, she took the baby on her arm, and, with a burning

Rep. Preston Brooks of South Carolina canes Sen. Charles Sumner of Massachusetts on the floor of the U.S. Senate, May 22, 1856.

blush, and yet a haughty smile, and a glance that would not be abashed, looked around at her townspeople and neighbors.

On the breast of her gown, in fine red cloth, surrounded with an elaborate embroidery and fantastic flourishes of gold thread, appeared the letter A. (Nathaniel Hawthorne, from his novel *The Scarlet Letter*.)

[The novel gave mid-19th-century Americans an insight into sin, guilt, and punishment in 17th-century Boston. The scarlet "A" was a label for adultery.]

COMPROMISE: HISTORIAN'S VIEW

Following the Mexican War, the annexation of new territory in the West aroused bitter debate between North and South. Should the new territories be slave or free? The decision would have profound implications for congressional control and future national policy. Senator Henry Clay drafted a group of bills that would become known as the Compromise of 1850. Finally approved in September

1850, the legislation included free status for the state of California, "popular sovereignty" for the new territories of Utah and New Mexico, abolition of the slave trade in the District of Columbia, and a strengthened Fugitive Slave Law.]

188. The Compromise of 1850 postponed secession and civil war by ten years, and many historians have argued that had secession and war occurred in 1850, the South would undoubtedly have won its independence. By giving the North ten years to develop further its enormous industrial potential and find Abraham Lincoln to lead the nation, the Compromise of 1850 did, in a very real sense, prevent the permanent separation of the Union—thanks to Henry Clay.

The country quieted after its near brush with disaster. The Nashville Convention reconvened on schedule, but because the compromise had proved acceptable to both sides, the delegates took no further action and adjourned. Only the Fugitive Slave Act, the one bill that infuriated many northerners, met their [the Nashville delegates'] total approbation. Still peace had been achieved, and for that most Americans expressed their gratitude and delight. (Robert V. Remini, historian, analyzing events following passage of the Compromise bills, September 1850, from *Henry Clay: Statesman for the Union.*)

[In June 1850, while the Clay proposals were being debated, southern officials had convened in Nashville to discuss possible options to preserve slavery and what they regarded as southern rights. The Nashville Convention reconvened in November 1850, but by that time the various bills in the Compromise package had become law.]

WARNING TO SLAVE CATCHERS

189. Now, this bill [the Fugitive Slave Act] strips us of all manner of protection, by the writ of habeas corpus, by jury trial, or by any other process known to the laws of civilized nations, that are thrown as safeguards round personal liberty. But while it does this, it throws us back upon the natural and inalienable right of self-defence—self-protection. It solemnly refers to each of us, individually, the question, whether we will submit to being enslaved by the hyenas which this law creates and encourages, or whether we will protect ourselves, even if, in so doing, we have to peril our lives, and *more than peril the useless and devilish carcasses of Negro-catchers*. It gives us the alternative of dying freemen, or living slaves. Let the men who would execute this bill beware. Let them know that the business of catching slaves, or kidnapping freemen is an open warfare upon the rights and liberties of the black men of the North. Let them know that to enlist in that warfare is present, certain, inevitable death and damnation. Let us teach them, that none should engage in this business, but those who are ready to be offered upon the polluted altar of accursed slavery. (Samuel R. Ward, editorial, *The Impartial Citizen*, reprinted in *The Liberator*, October 11, 1850.)

A GATHERING STORM?

190. Addressing the crowds, he [Jefferson Davis] asked again and again, "What are we to do?" "That's it, that's the question," his listeners responded. Of course, Davis had an answer for them. Every Southern state should follow Mississippi's lead, call a convention, and send delegates to a general Southern convention. Then that body could proclaim the guarantees that Southerners demanded to protect their rights. "A body thus chosen would carry with it a moral force," he said, "which the fierce abolitionists dare not oppose." If Northerners ignored that convention's mandates, then the South would have to leave the Union. (Description of speaking tour by Senator Jefferson Davis, Mississippi, events of October–November 1850, from *Jefferson Davis: The Man and His Hour*, by William C. Davis.)

HARVARD MEDICAL: FOR MEN ONLY?

Three years earlier—in 1847—Dr. Harriot K. Hunt had tried to obtain permission to attend lectures at the Harvard Medical School. She had been turned down. Now she was trying again.

191. [T]he idea that delicacy, propriety, and necessity require for woman one of her own sex, properly educated, to consult with in many cases, has gained a stronger foothold. . . .

The want and need of female physicians must be seen, I should think, by every philanthropic and delicate mind. . . .

I now . . . would respectfully ask you to investigate this subject further, and . . . open your institution (as in other States) to prepare woman for one of the noblest callings in life, or through refusal again, cause further agitation on this great subject. (Dr. Harriot K. Hunt, letter to Medical Faculty of Harvard, Boston, November 12, 1850, from *Glances and Glimpses*, by Harriot K. Hunt, cited in *The Female Experience: An American Documentary*, by Gerda Lerner.)

192. [Response from Harvard:]

It was voted by the Medical Faculty of Harvard University. . . . That Miss Hunt be admitted to the lectures on the usual terms, provided that her admission be not deemed inconsistent with the statutes.

On communicating this vote to the President and Fellows, the answer was returned that no objection was perceived arising from the statutes of the Medical School to admitting female students to the lectures, but that no opinion was expressed by that answer as to the claims of such students to a medical degree.

You can therefore obtain tickets. (Oliver Wendell Holmes, dean of the faculty, response to Dr. Hunt, December 5, 1850, Ibid.)

193. [Response from Harvard medical students in the form of a petition:]

[W]e deem it proper both to testify our disapprobation of such measure, and to take such action thereon as may be necessary to preserve the dignity of the school, and our own self-respect.

[N]o woman of true delicacy would be willing in the presence of men to listen to the discussion of the subjects that necessarily come under the consideration of the student of medicine.

Resolved, That we object to having the company of any female forced upon us, who is disposed to unsex herself, and to sacrifice her modesty, by appearing with men in the medical lecture room.

Resolved, That we are not opposed to allowing woman her rights, but do protest against her appearing in places where her presence is calculated to destroy our respect for the modesty and delicacy of her sex. (Petition published in the *Boston Evening Transcript*, ca. late December 1850, Ibid.)

OFFSPRING OF HELL

194. The very accompaniments of the slave system stamp it as an offspring of hell itself. To insure good behavior, the slaveholder relies on his whip; to induce proper humility, he relies on the whip; to bind down the spirit of the slave, to imbrute and destroy his manhood, he relies on the whip, the chain, the gag, the thumb-screw, the pillory, the Bowie knife, the pistol, and the blood-hound. (Frederick Douglass, speech, Rochester, New York, December 1, 1850.)

THE WHITE WHALE

195. [A]fter repeated, intrepid assaults, the White Whale had escaped alive; it cannot be much matter of surprise that some whalemen should go still further in their superstitions, declaring Moby-Dick not only ubiquitous, but immortal for immortality is but ubiquity in time; that though groves of spears should be planted in his flanks, he would still swim away unharmed; or if indeed he should ever be made to spout thick blood, such a sight would be but a ghastly deception; for again in unsanguined billows hundreds of leagues away, his unsullied jet would once more be seen.

But even stripped of these supernatural surmisings, there was enough in the earthly make and incontestable character of the monster to strike the imagination with unwonted power. For, it was not so much his uncommon bulk that so much distinguished him from other sperm whales, but . . . a peculiar snow-white wrinkled forehead, and a high, pyramidical white hump. These were his prominent features, the tokens whereby, even in the limitless, uncharted seas, he revealed his identity, at a long distance, to those who knew him. (Herman Melville, from his novel *Moby-Dick*, 1851.)

[This novel deals with Captain Ahab's quest to track down Moby-Dick. Critics have described the novel as a literal as well as metaphysical quest. The symbolism of Moby-Dick has enjoyed many interpretations over the years.]

RUNAWAY SLAVE

196. An hour before sunset, she entered the village of T—, by the Ohio river, weary and foot-sore, but still strong in heart. Her first glance was at the river, which lay, like Jordan, between her and the Canaan of liberty on the other side.

It was now early spring, and the river was swollen and turbulent, great cakes of floating ice were swinging heavily to and fro in the turbid waters. . . .

It was about three-quarters of an hour after Eliza had laid her child to sleep in the village tavern that the party came riding into the same place. Eliza was standing by the window, looking out in another direction, when Sam's quick eye caught a glimpse of her. Haley and Andy were two yards behind. At this crisis, Sam contrived to have his hat blown off, and uttered a loud and characteristic ejaculation, which startled her at once; she drew suddenly back; the whole train swept by the window, round to the front door.

A thousand lives seemed to be concentrated in that one moment in Eliza. Her room opened by a side door to the river. She caught her child, and sprang down the steps towards it. The trader caught a full glimpse of her, just as she was disappearing down the bank; and throwing himself from his horse, and calling loudly on Sam and Andy, he was after her like a hound after a deer. In that dizzy moment her feet to her scarce seemed to touch the ground, and a moment brought her to the water's edge. Right on behind they came; and, nerved with strength such as God gives only to the desperate, with one wild cry and flying leap, she vaulted sheer over the turbid current by the shore, on to the raft of ice beyond. It was a desperate leap—impossible to anything but madness and despair; and Haley, Sam, and Andy, instinctively cried out, and lifted up their hands, as she did it.

The huge green fragment of ice on which she alighted pitched and creaked as her weight came on it, but she stayed there not a moment. With wild cries and desperate energy she leaped to another and still another cake;—stumbling—leaping—slipping—springing upwards again! Her shoes are gone—her stockings cut from her feet—while blood marked every step, but she saw nothing, felt nothing, till dimly, as in a dream, she saw the Ohio side, and a man helping her up the bank. (Harriet Beecher Stowe, from her novel *Uncle Tom's Cabin*, 1852.)

[The novel was an immediate sensation. It has been reported that when Lincoln met the author in the White House, he said to her, "So this is the little lady who made this great big war!" Two of the main characters in the book have had their names added to the American vocabulary. Uncle Tom, who was too fond of his original white master, is perceived as a sellout. Simon Legree is the embodiment of a demanding taskmaster, a slave driver.]

ON REVOLUTIONS

197. Let us remember that revolutions do not always establish freedom. Our own free institutions were not the offspring of our Revolution. They existed before. (President Millard Fillmore, annual message to Congress, Washington, D.C., December 5, 1852.)

SIZING UP AN ORATOR

198. It was a warmish day in early October, and Mr. Lincoln was in his shirt sleeves when he stepped on the platform. I observed that, although awkward, he was not in the least embarrassed. He began in a slow and hesitating manner, but without any mistakes of language, dates, or facts. It was evident that he had mastered his subject, that he knew what he was going to say, and that he knew he was right. He had a thin, high-pitched, falsetto voice of much carrying power, and could be heard a long distance in spite of the bustle and tumult of the crowd. He had the accent and pronunciation peculiar to his native State, Kentucky. . . . Progressing with his theme, his words began to come faster and his face to light up with the rays of genius and his body to move in unison with his thoughts. His gestures were made with his body and head rather than with his arms. They were the natural expression of the man, and so perfectly adapted to what he was saying that anything different would have been quite inconceivable. Sometimes his manner was very impassioned and he seemed transfigured with his subject. Perspiration would stream down his face, and each particular hair would stand on end. . . . In such transfigured moments as these he was the type of the Hebrew prophet. (Horace White, recalling a Springfield, Illinois, speech, October 1854, cited in *Lincoln and Herndon*, by Joseph Fort Newton.)

EMPATHY

199.

> I am the hounded slave, I wince at the bite of the dog, Hell and despair
>   are upon me, crack and again crack the marksmen,
> I clutch the rails of the fence, my gore drips, thinn'd with the ooze of my
>   skin,
> I fall on the weeds and stones,
> The riders spur their unwilling horses, haul close,
> Taunt my dizzy ears and beat me violently over the head with whip-
>   stocks.
>
> Agonies are one of my changes of garments,
> I do not ask the wounded person how he feels, I myself become the
>   wounded person,
> My hurts turn livid upon me as I lean on a cane and observe.

(Walt Whitman, from *Song of Myself*, 1855.)

LEARNING PROCESS

200.

There was a child went forth every day,
And the first object he looked upon and received with wonder or pity or
   love or dread, that object he became.

(Walt Whitman, from *Leaves of Grass*, 1855.)

KANSAS BLEEDS

When Congress voted territorial status to Kansas and Nebraska, it provided that residents would vote on whether the new states would be slave or free. This led to violence between pro-slavery and free-soil groups. Following an attack on Lawrence, Kansas, by pro-slavery men, John Brown led a small group of antislavery men into the area of Potawatomie Creek. One of those in the band describes what happened.

201. After my team was fed and the party had taken supper, John Brown told me for the first time what he proposed to do. He said he wanted me to pilot the company up to the forks of the creek, some five or six miles above, into the neighborhood where I lived, and show them where all the pro-slavery men resided; that he proposed to sweep the creek as he came down of all the pro-slavery men living on it. I positively refused to do it. He insisted upon it, but when he found that I would not go, he decided to postpone the expedition until the following night. I then wanted to take my team and go home, but he would not let me do so, and said I should remain with them. . . .

The old man Doyle and two sons were called out and marched some distance from the house . . . in the road, where a halt was made. Old John Brown drew his revolver and shot the old man Doyle in the forehead, and Brown's two youngest sons immediately fell upon the younger Doyles with their short two-edged swords. . . .

[Brown] hoped to find George Wilson, Probate Judge of Anderson County . . . and intended, if he did, to kill him too. Wilson had been notifying Free-Soil men to leave the territory. I had received such a notice from him myself. (James Townsley, recalling events of May 24–25, 1856, Potawatomie Creek, Kansas, from *The Kansas Conflict*, by Charles Robinson.)

[Five pro-slavery settlers—men and boys—were killed in Brown's foray. By the time the small-scale civil war in Kansas was over, more than 200 would be killed. Townsley was the only member of the group to be arrested, but he was never tried. His written statement was made on December 6, 1879.]

A SENATOR IS BEATEN

202. There is high excitement in Washington. You will have heard, through telegraphic reports, that Col. Brooks, of your State, punished Mr. Sumner, of Massachusetts last Thursday [May 22], for a libel on South Carolina and a slander against Judge Butler.

[Preston S. Brooks was a U.S. representative from South Carolina. Andrew P. Butler, his uncle, was a U.S. senator from the same state. Charles Sumner was a U.S. senator from Massachusetts.]

Sumner, on Monday and Tuesday [May 19 and 20], delivered a coarse and malignant Abolition speech, in which he assailed South Carolina and Judge Butler with great bitterness. [It would later be known as the "Crime against Kansas" speech, attacking the violence in that area over the slavery issue.] The speech was so coarse and insulting, that even his own faction condemned it, and the Southern men freely said he should be chastised. . . .

Col. Brooks waited about an hour after the adjournment, until all the ladies had left [the Senate chamber], Mr. Sumner having remained in his seat. . . .

Mr. Brooks went up to Mr. Sumner, and facing him, said: "Mr. Sumner, I have read your speech with great care, and all the impartiality in my power, and I have come to tell you that you have libelled my State, and slandered my relative, who is old and absent, and I deem it my duty to punish you, which I shall now proceed to do." Col. Brooks thereupon struck Mr. Sumner, who was rising, across the face with a gutta percha cane. He continued repeating the blows until Mr. Sumner fell upon the floor, crying out for help. Col. Brooks then desisted voluntarily, saying "I did not wish to hurt him much, but only punish him."

Sumner was well and elegantly whipped, and he richly deserved it. . . .

The whole South sustains Brooks, and a large part of the North also. All feel that it is time for freedom of speech and freedom of the cudgel to go together. (News report, *Charleston* [South Carolina] *Mercury*, May 28, 1856.)

[Attempts were made in the House and Senate either to expel or to censure Brooks. Both attempts failed. Brooks resigned in July but was overwhelmingly reelected. Sumner was so badly beaten that he became an invalid and did not return to the Senate until late in 1859.]

PROPERTY RIGHTS

203. If the Constitution recognizes the right of property of the master in a slave, and makes no distinction between that description of property and other property owned by a citizen, no tribunal, acting under the authority of the United States, whether it be legislative, executive, or judicial, has a right to draw such a distinction, or deny to it the benefit of the provisions and guarantees which have been provided for the protection of private property against the encroachments of the Government. . . . The right of property in a slave is distinctly and expressly affirmed in the Constitution. . . . And no word can be found in the Constitution which gives Congress a greater power over slave property, or which entitles property of that kind to less protection than property of any other description. (Chief Justice Roger B. Taney, opinion, [*Dred*] *Scott v. Sandford*, U.S. Supreme Court, 1857.)

AN EXPERIMENT WITH CAMELS

204. Left San Antonio at 1 P.M., and encamped at the beautiful spring of the San Lucas, having made 16 miles, the camels carrying, each, including pack saddles, nearly 576 pounds. This being the first day, and the animals not having performed any service for a long time, they seemed tired on our arrival at camp; but I hope, as we proceed, and they harden in flesh, to find them carrying their burdens more easily. Unfortunately, the only men in America who understand them, and who are thoroughly acquainted with the mode of packing and journeying with them, are some Turks, who came over with them, and who left at San Antonio, refusing to go so long a journey, and alleging that they had been badly treated by the government, not having received the pay due them since January. It seems the appropriation having been exhausted, no one is authorized to pay them, although they left their own country under special contract with officers of the government and have performed their duties very faithfully. (Edward Fitzgerald Beale, report to Secretary of War John B. Floyd, events of June 25, 1857, from *Concerning the Wagon Road from Fort Defiance to the Colorado River*, April 26, 1858, 35th Congress, 1st Session House of Representatives Ex. Doc. No. 124.)

[Following the Mexican War, Congress had sought alternative transportation for the newly acquired areas, which lacked railroad lines. In 1855 Congress appropriated $30,000 to buy camels, and the War Department conducted some exploratory trips with camels. Eventually, the exploration ended, and the camels were sold—mainly to circuses or zoos.]

ANSWERING HIS BRAVES

205. Taoyateduta [Little Crow] is not a coward, and he is not a fool! When did he run away from his enemies? When did he leave his braves behind him on the warpath and turn back to his tepee? When he ran from your enemies, he walked behind on your trail with his face to the Ojibways and he covered your backs as a she-bear covers her cubs. (Little Crow, addressing braves who accused him of turning his back on his own people, ca. 1858, from *Minnesota History*, Volume 38, September 1962.)

206. Braves! . . . You are like dogs in the Hot Moon when they snap at their own shadows. . . . See! The white men are like the locusts when they fly so thick that the whole sky is a snowstorm. . . . Kill one, two, ten, and ten times ten will come to kill you. . . .
You cannot see the face of your chief; your eyes are full of smoke; your ears are full of roaring waters. Braves! . . . You will die like the rabbits when the hungry wolves hunt them in the Hard Moon. Taoyateduta is not a coward: he will die with you. (Ibid.)

[Little Crow would later take part in the Sioux uprising of 1862.]

FOLK SONG

207.

Oh, don't you remember Sweet Betsey from Pike,
Who crossed the big mountains with her lover, Ike;

With two yoke of cattle, a large yellow dog,
A tall Shanghai rooster, and one spotted hog. . . .
They stopped at Salt Lake to inquire the way,
When Brigham declared that Sweet Betsey should stay;
But Betsey got frightened and ran like a deer,
While Brigham stood pawing the ground like a steer. . . .
This Pike County couple got married of course;
And Ike became jealous—obtained a divorce;
Sweet Betsey, well satisfied, said with a shout,
"Good-by, you big lummux, I'm glad you backed out!"

(Anonymous, folk song, ca. 1858.)

A HOUSE DIVIDED

208. A house divided against itself cannot stand. I believe this government cannot endure permanently half slave and half free. I do not expect the Union to be dissolved; I do not expect the house to fall; but I do expect it will cease to be divided. It will become all one thing or all the other. Either the opponents of slavery will arrest the further spread of it, and place it where the public mind shall rest in the belief that it is in the course of ultimate extinction, or its advocates will push it forward till it shall become alike lawful in all the States, old as well as new, North as well as South. (Abraham Lincoln, Republican State Convention, June 16, 1858.)

THE EQUALITY ISSUE

209. I am not in favor of . . . the social and political equality of the white and black races. . . . I am not in favor of negro citizenship. . . . I did not at any time say I was in favor of negro suffrage. (Abraham Lincoln, debates with Stephen Douglas for U.S. Senate seat in Illinois, August 21–October 15, 1858, cited in *Lincoln the President, Springfield to Gettysburg*, by James G. Randall.)

210. Physical difference [would] forever forbid the two races living together on terms of social and political equality. (Ibid.)

211. [I do not favor] a tendency to dehumanize the negro, to take away from him the right of ever striving to be a man. (Ibid.)

POPULAR SOVEREIGNTY

In answer to the following question by Lincoln: "Can the people of a United States Territory, in any lawful way, against the wish of any citizen of the United States, exclude slavery from its limits prior to the formation of a State constitution?"

212. A majority of the people thereof have the lawful means to introduce or exclude it as they please, for the reason that slavery cannot exist a day or an hour anywhere unless it is supported by local police regulations. These police regulations can only be established by the local legislature and if the majority of the people of the territory are opposed to slavery they will elect representatives to that body who will by unfriendly legislation, effectually prevent the introduction of it into their midst. If, on the contrary, they are for slavery, their legislature will favor its admission and extension. (Stephen Douglas, debate with Lincoln, Freeport, Illinois, August 27, 1858, cited in *The Lincoln Reader*, edited by Paul M. Angle.)

ANSWER TO A PRAYER

Harriet Tubman leads a party of fugitive slaves on board a steamboat. They are heading north, toward Canada and freedom. There is a hitch. For some reason the ticket clerk does not give her boarding tickets, telling her to wait.

213. I drew in my breath, and I sent it out to the Lord, and I said, O Lord! you know who I am, and what I am, and what I want; and that was all I could say; and again I drew in my breath and I sent it out to the Lord, but that was all I could say; and then again the third time and just then I felt a touch on my shoulder, and looked round, and the clerk said, "Here's your tickets." (Harriet Tubman, interviews between 1859 and 1865, cited in *Slave Testimony*, edited by John W. Blassingame.)

214. They say the Negro has no rights a white man is bound to respect; but it seems to me they send men to Congress, and pay them eight dollars a day, for nothing else but to talk about the Negro. (Ibid.)

215. I've been studying and studying upon it [the John Brown raid], and it's clear to me, it wasn't John Brown that died on that gallows. When I think how he give up his life for our people, and how he never flinched, but was so brave to the end; it's clear to me it wasn't mortal man, it was God in him. When I think of all the groans and tears and prayers I've heard on the plantations, and remember that God is a prayer-hearing God, I feel that his time is drawing near. God's time is always near. He gave me my strength, and he set the North star in the heavens [to guide fugitive slaves north to freedom]; he meant I should be free. (Ibid.)

A CONDEMNED MAN SPEAKS

216. I deny everything but what I have all along admitted: of a design on my part to free slaves. I intended certainly to have made a clean thing of that matter, as I did last winter, when I went into Missouri and there took slaves without the snapping of a gun on either side, moving them through the country, and finally leaving them in Canada. I designed to have done the same thing again on a larger scale. . . .

I never had any design against the life of any person, nor any disposition to commit treason or excite slaves to rebel or make any general insurrection. I never encouraged any man to do so, but always discouraged any idea of that kind. (John Brown, address to the court after he was sentenced to death, Charlestown, Virginia, November 2, 1859.)

SONG OF THE TIMES

217.

Gone are the days when my heart was young and gay,
Gone are my friends from the cotton fields away,
Gone from this earth to a better land I know.

I hear those gentle voices calling, "Old Black Joe."
I'm coming,
I'm coming,
Though my head is bending low,
I hear those gentle voices calling, "Old Black Joe."

(Stephen Foster, from his song "Old Black Joe," 1860.)

DISUNION OPPOSED

218. To the Union of the States this nation owes its unprecedented increase in population, its surprising development of material resources, its rapid augmentation of wealth, its happiness at home and its honor abroad; and we hold in abhorrence all schemes for Disunion, come from whatever source they may. (Republican Party platform, Chicago, May 16, 1860.)

ALL THE SOUTH WANTS

219. All for which the slave states have ever contended, is to be let alone and permitted to manage their domestic institutions in their own way. (President James Buchanan, annual message to Congress, December 3, 1860.)

FIRST SECESSION

220. We, the people of the State of South Carolina, in Convention assembled, declare and ordain . . . that the ordinance adopted by us in Convention, of the 23d day of May, in the year of our Lord 1788, whereby the Constitution of the United States of America was ratified, and also all Acts . . . of this State ratifying the amendments of the said Constitution, are hereby repealed, and that the union now subsisting between South Carolina and other States under the name of the United States of America is hereby dissolved. (Ordinance, state legislature, Charleston, South Carolina, December 20, 1860.)

"HOPE"

221.

> "Hope" is the thing with feathers—
> That perches in the soul—
> And sings the tune without the words—
> And never stops—at all—
>
> And sweetest—in the Gale—is heard
> And sore must be the storm—
> That could abash the little Bird
> That kept so many warm—
>
> I've heard it in the chillest land—
> And on the strangest Sea—
> Yet, never, in Extremity,
> It asked a crumb—of Me.

(Emily Dickinson, ca. 1861.)

A MIDNIGHT RIDE

222.

> So through the night rode Paul Revere;
> And so through the night went his cry of alarm
> To every Middlesex village and farm—
> A cry of defiance and not of fear,
> A voice in the darkness, a knock at the door,
> And a word that shall echo forevermore!
> For, borne on the night-wind of the Past,
> Through all our history, to the last,

In the hour of darkness and peril and need,
The people will waken and listen to hear
The hurrying hoof-beats of that steed,
And the midnight message of Paul Revere.

(Henry Wadsworth Longfellow, *Paul Revere's Ride*, 1861.)

[This poem about a time of peril during the American Revolution foreshadowed a new crisis facing America.]

AS SECESSION LOOMS

223. I'm a plane man. I don't know nothin' about no ded languages and am a little shaky on livin' ones. There4, expect no flowry talk from me. What I shall say will be to the pint, right strate out.

I'm not a politician, and my other habits air good. I've no enemys to reward, nor friends to sponge. But I'm a Union man. I luv the Union—it is a big thing—and it makes my hart bleed to see a lot of ornery peple a-movin' heaven—no, not heaven, but the other place—and earth, to bust it up. Too much good blud was spilt in courtin' and marryin' that hily respectable female, the Goddess of Liberty, to git a divorce from her now. My own State of Injianny is celebrated for unhitchin' marrid peple with neatness and despatch, but you can't git a divorce from the Goddess up there. Not by no means. The old gal has behaved herself too well to cast her off now. (Artemus Ward, "Oration," ca. January 1861, from *Mark Twain's Library of Humor*, edited by Samuel Langhorne Clemens, William Dean Howells, and Charles Hopkins Clark.)

224. The house, dooryard, barn and woodshed was now all full, and when another crowd cum, I told 'em not to go away for want of room, as the hog-pen was still empty. One patrit from a small town in Michygan went up on top the house, got into the chimney, and slid down into the parler, where Old Abe was endeverin to keep the hungry pack of offis-seekers from chawin' him up and without benefit of clergy. The minit he reached the fire-place he jumpt up, brusht the soot out of his eyes, and yelled: "Don't make eny pintment at the Spunkville postoffiss till you've read my papers. All the respectful men in our town is signers to that there dockyment."

"Good God!" cride Old Abe, "they cum upon me from the skize—down the chimneys, and from the bowels of the erth!" He hadn't more'n got them words out of his delikit mouth before two fat offiss-seekers from Wisconsin, in endeverin to crawl atween his legs for the purpuss of applyin' for the toll-gateship at Milwawky, upset the President eleck, & he would hev gone sprawlin' into the fire-place if I hadn't caught him in these arms. ("Interview with President Lincoln," ibid.)

[The "Oration" was first delivered in 1859 but was updated two years later. Ward explained, "I have revised the orashhun, and added sum things which makes it appropposser to the times than it otherwise would be. I have also corrected the grammars and punktooated it." The fictitious "Interview" delighted Lincoln.]

A PLEA FOR RECONCILIATION

225. Apprehension seems to exist among the people of the Southern States that by the accession of a Republican administration their property and their peace and personal security are to be endangered. There has never been any reasonable cause for such apprehension. Indeed, the most ample evidence to the contrary has all the while existed and been open to their inspection. It is found in nearly all the published speeches of him who now addresses you. I do but quote from one of those speeches when I declare that "I have no purpose, directly or indirectly, to interfere with the institution of slavery in the States where it exists. I believe I have no lawful right to do so, and I have no inclination to do so." (Abraham Lincoln, First Inaugural Address, March 4, 1861.)

226. If the United States be not a government proper, but an association of States in the nature of contract merely, can it as a contract be peaceably unmade by less than all the parties who made it? (Ibid.)

227. In your hands, my dissatisfied fellow-countrymen, and not in mine, is the momentous issue of civil war. . . . You have no oath registered in heaven to destroy the government, while I shall have the most solemn one to preserve, protect, and defend it. (Ibid.)

Union forces had to be brought in from Gettysburg to quell the New York draft riots of July 1863. Men who could afford it could pay to have someone substitute for them in the draft. Above, rioting on Second Avenue in Manhattan.

8

Civil War

The bloodiest conflict in the history of the United States, the Civil War was also the first modern war, not merely in terms of deadly weaponry but in terms of cutting off enemy resources. Since the Confederate army relied on the support of its civilian population, the Union forces could deprive it of food, munitions, and other supplies by burning crops, killing livestock, destroying warehouses, and tearing up railroad lines. Southern bitterness against the Union armies would last for generations.

WAR SONG

228.

> Den I wish I was in Dixie—
> Hooray, hooray!
> In Dixie land I'll take my stan'
> To lib an' die in Dixie
> Away, away,
> Away down south in Dixie.

(Daniel Emmett, "Dixie.")

[This most famous Confederate war song was actually composed in 1859.]

WAR SONG

229.

John Brown's body lies a-mold'ring in the grave,
John Brown's body lies a-mold'ring in the grave,
John Brown's body lies a-mold'ring in the grave,
  His soul is marching on. . . .
They'll hang Jeff Davis on a sour apple tree,
They'll hang Jeff Davis on a sour apple tree,
They'll hang Jeff Davis on a sour apple tree,
  As they go marching on. . . .

(Thomas B. Bishop, "John Brown's Body," 1861)

THE FIRST DEFEAT

230. Having defended Fort Sumter for 34 hours, until the quarters were entirely burned, the main gates destroyed by fire, the gorge walls seriously injured, the magazine surrounded by flames, and its door closed from the effects of heat, four barrels and three cartridges of powder only being available, and no provisions remaining but pork, I accepted terms of evacuation offered by General Beauregard, being the same offered by him on the 11th instant, prior to the commencement of hostilities, and marched out of the fort Sunday afternoon, the 14th instant, with colors flying and drums beating, bringing away company and private property, and saluting my flag with 50 guns. (Major Robert Anderson, report on Fort Sumter evacuation, April 18, 1861, from *The War of the Rebellion: A Compilation of the Official Records of Union and Confederate Armies.*)

A CONFLICT OF CONSCIENCE

231. The whole South is in a state of revolution, into which Virginia, after a long struggle, has been drawn. . . .

With all my devotion to the Union and the feeling of loyalty and duty of an American citizen, I have not been able to make up my mind to raise my hand against my relatives, my children, my home. I have therefore resigned my commission in the Army, and save in defense of my native State, with the sincere hope that my poor services may never be needed, I hope I may never be called on to draw my sword. (Robert E. Lee, letter to his sister, Arlington, Virginia, April 20, 1861, from *Recollections and Letters of General Robert E. Lee.*)

LETTER FROM A SOLDIER

232. The indications are very strong that we shall move in a few days perhaps tomorrow. Lest I should not be able to write again, I feel impelled to write a few lines that may fall under your eye when I shall be no more. . . .

I have no misgivings about, or lack of confidence in, the cause in which I am engaged, and my courage does not halt or falter. I know how strongly American Civilization now leans on the triumph of the Government, and how great a debt we owe to those who went before us through the blood and sufferings of the Revolution. And I am willing—perfectly willing—to lay down all my joys in this life, to help maintain this Government, and to pay that debt. . . .

Sarah my love for you is deathless. . . .

The memories of the blissful moments I have spent with you come creeping over me, and I feel most gratified to God and to you that I have enjoyed them so long. And hard it is for me to give them up and burn to ashes the hopes of future years, when, God willing, we might still have lived and loved together, and seen our sons grown up to honorable manhood around us. I have, I know, but few and small claims upon Divine Providence, but something whispers to me—perhaps it is the wafted prayer of my little Edgar—that I shall return to my loved ones unharmed; if I do not my dear Sarah, never forget how much I love you, and when my last breath escapes me on the battlefield, it will whisper your name. Forget my many faults, and the many pains I have caused you. . . . How gladly would I wash out with my tears every little spot upon your happiness, and struggle with all the misfortunes of this world to shield you and your children from harm. But I cannot. I must watch you from the Spirit-land and hover near you, while you buffet the storm, with your precious little freight, and wait with sad patience till we meet to part no more.

But, O Sarah! If the dead can come back to this earth and flit unseen around those they loved, I shall always be near you; in the gladdest days and darkest nights, advised to your happiest scenes and gloomiest hours, always, always, and if there be a soft breeze upon your cheek, it shall be my breath; as the cool air fans your throbbing temple, it shall be my spirit passing by. Sarah do not mourn me dead; think I am gone and wait for thee, for we shall meet again. (Major Sullivan Ballou, letter to his wife, Camp Clark, Washington, D.C., July 14, 1861, cited in *Letters of a Nation*, edited by Andrew Carroll.)

[A week later, Sullivan Ballou was killed at the battle of Bull Run.]

WINNING A NICKNAME

---

233. There stands Jackson like a stone wall! (General Barnard E. Bee, at the Battle of Bull Run, Virginia, ca. July 19, 1861.)

[How General Thomas Jackson got his nickname.]

FROM PRIDE TO PANIC

---

234. Some senators and many congressmen have already gone to join McDowell's army or to follow in his wake in the hope of seeing the Lord deliver the Philistines into his hands. . . . Every carriage, rig, wagon, and hack has been engaged by people going out to see the fight. The price is enhanced by mysterious communications respecting the horrible slaughter in the skirmishes at Bull Run. The French cooks and hotelkeepers, by some process of reasoning, have arrived at the conclusion that they must treble the prices of their wines and of the hampers of provisions which the Washington people are ordering to comfort themselves at their bloody Derby. . . .

The spectators were all excited, and a lady with an opera glass who was near me was quite beside herself when an unusually heavy discharge roused the current of her blood—"That is splendid. Oh, my! Is not that first-rate? I guess we will be in Richmond this time tomorrow." These, mingled with coarser exclamations, burst from the politicians who had come out to see the triumph of the Union armies. (William H. Russell, Bull Run, Virginia, July 20, 1861, from *My Diary North and South*.)

235. Loud cheers suddenly burst from the spectators as a man dressed in the uniform of an officer . . . galloped along the front, waving his cap and shouting at the top of voice. . . . "We've whipped them on all points," he cried. . . . "They are retreating as fast as they can, and we are after them." . . . The congressmen shook hands with each other. (Ibid.)

236. My attention was attracted by loud shouts . . . and I perceived several wagons coming from the direction of the battlefield. . . . Drivers and men cried out with the most vehement gestures: "Turn back! Turn back! We are whipped." (Ibid.)

237. In an instant the mass of vehicles and retreating soldiers, teamsters, and civilians, as if agonized by an electric shock, quivered throughout the tortuous line. With dreadful shouts and cursings the drivers lashed their maddened horses and, leaping from the carts, left them to their fate and ran on foot. Artillery men and foot soldiers and Negroes, mounted on gun horses with the chain traces and loose trappings trailing in the dust, spurred and flogged their steeds down the road or by the side paths. The firing continued and seemed to approach the hill, as it were, with a fresh convulsion.

Once more the dreaded cry: "The cavalry! Cavalry are coming!" rang through the crowd, and looking back to Centerville, I perceived coming down the hill, between me and the sky, a number of mounted men who might at a hasty glance be taken for horsemen in the act of sabering the fugitives. In reality they were soldiers and civilians, with, I regret to say, some officers among them, who were whipping and striking their horses with sticks or whatever else they could lay hands on. I called out to the men who were frantic with terror beside me, "They are not cavalry at all; they are your own men"—but they did not heed me. (Ibid.)

INTERNATIONAL INCIDENT

238. As the *Trent* approached she hoisted English colors; whereupon our ensign was hoisted and a shot was fired across her bow. As she maintained her speed and showed no disposition to heave to, a shell was fired across her bow which brought her to. Captain [Charles] Wilkes [of the Union ship *San Jacinto*] hailed that he intended to send a boat on board. . . .

Boarding the vessel, I was escorted by one of her officers to the upper or promenade deck and was introduced to Captain Moir. . . . I immediately asked if I might see his passenger-list, saying that I had information that a Messrs. [James] Mason and [John] Slidell were on board [The two were Confederate commissioners on their way to London and Paris, respectively.]. . . . .

I informed Captain Moir that I had been sent by my commander to arrest Mr. Mason and Mr. Slidell and their secretaries, and send them prisoners on board the United States war vessel nearby. As may readily be understood, when it was known why I had boarded the *Trent*, there was an outburst of rage and indignation from the passengers, who numbered nearly one hundred, many of them Southerners. The captain and the four gentlemen bore themselves with great composure, but the irresponsible lookers-on sang out, "Throw the d—— fellow overboard!" I called on Captain Moir to preserve order, but, for the benefit of the excited passengers, I reminded them that our every move was closely observed from the *San Jacinto*. . . .

I sent the boat [back] to Captain Wilkes to say that these gentlemen were all on board, and had objected to being sent to the *San Jacinto*, and that I must use force to accomplish my orders. . . .

When all was ready and the boats were in waiting, I notified both Mr. Mason and Mr. Slidell that the time had come to send them to the *San Jacinto*. They came quietly down to the main-deck, and they repeated that they would not go unless force was used—whereupon two officers, previously instructed, escorted each commissioner to the side, and assisted them into the comfortable cutter sent especially for them. (Donald M. Fairfax, international waters off Cuba, November 8, 1861, from *Battles and Leaders of the Civil War*.)

239. I gave my real reasons weeks afterward to Secretary [of the Treasury Salmon P.] Chase, . . . [who] asked me to explain why I had not literally obeyed Captain Wilkes's instructions [to claim the *Trent* as a prize for violation of neutrality]. I told him that it was because I was impressed with England's sympathy for the South, and felt that she would be glad to have so grand a ground to declare war against the United States. Mr. Chase . . . exclaimed, "You have certainly relieved the Government from great embarrassment, to say the least." (Ibid.)

[An international crisis—and the danger of war with Britain—was averted when Mason and Slidell were freed and allowed to proceed to Europe.]

SPIRITUAL

240.

Go down, Moses,
Way down in Egypt land,
Tell old Pharaoh
Let my people go.

(Anonymous, spiritual, ca. 1862.)

WHERE IS OUR MONEY?

241. The snow is on the ground, and we have been waiting a long time to get our money. We are poor; white Father has plenty. His fires are warm, his tepees keep out the cold. We have nothing to eat. . . .

We may die because you will not pay us; we may die, but if we do we will leave our bones on the ground where our great Father may see where his Dakota children died. . . .

We have sold our hunting grounds and the graves of our fathers. We have sold our own graves. We have no place to bury our dead, and you will not pay us the money for our lands. (Red Iron, council meeting with white officials, 1862, from My Life and Experiences among Our Hostile Indians, by Oliver O. Howard.)

WAR SONG

242.

Mine eyes have seen the glory of the coming of the Lord;
He is trampling out the vintage where the grapes of wrath are stored;
He hath loosed the fateful lightning of His terrible swift sword;
His truth is marching on.

(Julia Ward Howe, "Battle Hymn of the Republic," Atlantic Monthly, February 1862.)

CONFEDERATE INAUGURAL

243a. Whatever of hope some may have entertained that a returning sense of justice would remove the danger with which our rights were threatened, and render it possible to preserve the Union of the Constitution, must have been dispelled by the malignity and barbarity of the Northern States in the prosecution of the existing war. The confidence of the most hopeful among us must have been destroyed by the disregard they have recently exhibited for all the time-honored bulwarks of civil and religious liberty.

Bastilles filled with prisoners, arrested without civil process or indictment duly found; the writ of habeas corpus suspended by executive mandate; a state legislature confronted by the imprisonment of members whose avowed principles suggested to the federal Executive that there might be another added to the list of seceded states; elections held under threats of military power; civil officers, peaceful citizens, and gentlewomen incarcerated for opinion's sake—[all of these] proclaimed the incapacity of our late associates to administer a government as free, liberal, and humane as that established for our common use. (President Jefferson Davis, Inaugural Address, Richmond, Virginia, February 22, 1862.)

[Up until this date, Davis had been serving as provisional president.]

243b. I deeply feel the weight of the responsibilities I now . . . am about to assume. . . . With humble gratitude and adoration, acknowledging the Providence which has so visibly protected the Confederacy during its brief but eventful career, to Thee, O God! I trustingly commit myself, and prayerfully invoke Thy blessing on my country and its cause. (Ibid.)

PRIORITIES

244. My paramount object in this struggle is to save the Union, and is not either to save or destroy Slavery. If I could save the Union without freeing any slave, I would do it; and if I could save it by freeing all the slaves, I would do it; and if I could do it by freeing some and leaving others alone, I would also do that. What I do about slavery and the colored race, I do because I believe it helps to save this Union; and what I forbear, I forbear because I do not believe it would help to save the Union. (Abraham Lincoln, letter to Horace Greeley, Washington, D.C., August 22, 1862, cited in *The Rebellion Record*, edited by Frank Moore.)

COMMENT

245. It is well war is so terrible, or we should get too fond of it. (Robert E. Lee, comment to General W. N. Pendleton, Fredericksburg, Virginia, December 13, 1862, quoted in *Recollections and Letters of General Robert E. Lee*.)

THE OLD LADY AND THE GENERAL

246.

Forty flags with their silver stars,
Forty flags with their crimson bars,
Flapped in the morning wind; the sun
Of noon looked down, and saw not one.
Up rose old Barbara Frietchie then,
Bowed with her fourscore years and ten;
Bravest of all in Frederick town,
She took up the flag the men hauled down. . . .
Up the street came the rebel tread,
Stonewall Jackson riding ahead.
Under his slouched hat left and right
He glanced: the old flag met his sight.
"Halt!"—the dust-brown ranks stood fast.
"Fire!"—out blazed the rifle-blast. . . .
Quick, as it fell, from the broken staff
Dame Barbara snatched the silken scarf. . . .
"Shoot, if you must, this old gray head,
But spare your country's flag," she said.
A shade of sadness, a blush of shame,
Over the face of the leader came. . . .
"Who touches a hair of yon gray head
Dies like a dog! March on!" he said.

(John Greenleaf Whittier, from his poem "Barbara Frietchie," 1863.)

WAR SONG

247.

> The Union forever,
> Hurray! boys, Hurrah!
> Down with the traitor, up with the star;
> While we rally round the flag boys, rally once again,
> Shouting the battle cry of freedom.

(George F. Root, "The Battle Cry of Freedom.")

A PROCLAMATION

248. Whereas on the 22d day of September, A.D. 1862, a proclamation was issued by the President of the United States, containing, among other things, the following, to wit:

That on the 1st day of January, A.D. 1863, all persons held as slaves within any State or designated part of a State the people thereof shall then be in rebellion against the United States shall be then, henceforward, and forever free. (Abraham Lincoln, Emancipation Proclamation, January 1, 1863.)

FORTUNES OF WAR

249. Let us pass over the river, and rest under the shade of the trees. (Thomas (Stonewall) Jackson, last words, Chandler's Station, on the Richmond, Fredericksburg, and Potomac railroad, May 10, 1863.)

[Jackson was accidentally shot by his own Confederate troops during the Battle of Chancellorsville. He died of his wounds. Lee would later comment that with the death of Jackson he had lost his right arm.]

THE CHARGE

250. Pickett said, "General, shall I advance?"

The effort to speak the order failed, and I could only indicate it by an affirmative bow. He accepted the duty, and with seeming confidence of success, leaped on his horse, and rode gaily to his command. (James Longstreet, Cemetery Ridge, Gettysburg, Pennsylvania, July 3, 1863, *From Manassas to Appomattox*.)

251. General Armistead, of the second line, spread his steps to supply the places of fallen comrades. His colors cut down, with a volley against the bristling line of bayonets, he put his cap on his sword to guide the storm. The enemy's massing, enveloping numbers held the struggle until the noble Armistead fell beside the wheels of the enemy's battery. (Ibid.)

THE ENEMY APPROACHES

252. Every eye could see his legions, an overwhelming resistless tide of an ocean of armed men sweeping upon us. Regiment after regiment and brigade after brigade moved from the woods and rapidly take their places in the lines forming the assault. . . .

More than half a mile their front extends; more than a thousand yards the dull gray masses deploy, man touching man, rank pressing rank, and line supporting line. The red flags wave, then horsemen gallop up and down; the arms of 18,000 men, barrel and bayonet, gleam in the sun, a sloping forest of flashing steel. . . . They move as with one soul, in perfect order, without impediment of ditch, or wall or stream, over ridge and slope, through orchard and meadow, and cornfield, magnificent, grim, irresistible. (Frank A. Haskell, Gettysburg, Pennsylvania, July 3, 1860, from *The Battle of Gettysburg*.)

253. General Gibbon . . . said to the men, "Do not hurry, men, and fire too fast, let them come up close before you fire, and then aim low and steadily." . . .

All our available guns are now active, and from the fire of shells, as the range grows shorter and shorter, they change to shrapnel, and from shrapnel to canister; but in spite of shells, and shrapnel and canister, without wavering or halt, the hardy lines of the enemy continue to move on. The Rebel guns make no reply to ours, and no charging shout rings out today, as is the Rebel wont; but the courage of these silent men amid our shots seems not to need the stimulus of other noise. . . .

And so across that broad open ground they have come, nearer and nearer, nearly half the way, with our guns bellowing in their faces, until now a hundred yards, no more, divide our ready left from their advancing right. The eager men there are impatient to begin. Let them. First, Harrow's breastworks flame; then Hall's; then Webb's. As if our bullets were the fire coals that touched off their muskets the enemy in front halts, and his countless level barrels blaze back upon us. (Ibid.)

254. Great heaven! Were my senses mad? The larger portion of Webb's brigade—my God it was true—there by the group of trees and the angles of the wall, was breaking from the cover of their works, and, without orders or reason, with no hand lifted to check them, was falling back, a fear-stricken flock of confusion! The fate of Gettysburg hung upon a spider's single thread! . . .

My sword, that had always hung idle by my side . . . I drew, bright and gleaming, the symbol of command. . . . All rules and proprieties were forgotten, all considerations of person, and danger and safety despised; for, as I met the tide of these rabbits, the damned red flags of the rebellion began to thicken and flaunt along the wall they had just deserted, and one was already waving over one of the guns of the dead Cushing. I ordered these men to halt, and "face about," and "fire," and they heard my voice and gathered my meaning, and obeyed my commands. (Ibid.)

DRAFT RIOTS IN NEW YORK

255. Gangs of men and boys, composed of railroad employees, workers in machine shops, and a vast crowd of those who lived by preying upon others, thieves, pimps, professional ruffians, the scum of the city, jailbirds, or those who were running with swift feet to enter the prison doors, began to gather on the corners and streets and alleys where they lived. . . .

A body of these, five or six hundred strong, gathered about one of the enrolling offices in the upper part of the city, where the draft was quietly proceeding, and opened the assault upon it by a shower of clubs, bricks, and paving stones torn from the streets, following it up by a furious rush into the office. Lists, records, books, the drafting wheel, every article of furniture or work in the room, was rent in pieces and strewn about the floor or flung into the streets, while the law officers, the newspaper reporters—who are expected to be everywhere—and the few peaceable spectators, were compelled to make a hasty retreat through an opportune rear exit, accelerated by the curses and blows of the assailants. (Anna Dickinson, New York City, July 13, 1863, from *What Answer?*)

256. Late in the afternoon a crowd which could have numbered not less than ten thousand, the majority of whom were ragged, frowzy, drunken women, gathered about the Orphan Asylum for Colored Children—a large and beautiful building and one of the most admirable and noble charities of the city. When it became evident from the menacing cries and groans of the multitude that danger, if not destruction, was meditated to the harmless and inoffensive inmates, a flag of truce appeared. . . .

Whatever human feeling had ever, if ever, filled these souls was utterly drowned and washed away in the tide of rapine and blood in which they had been steeping themselves. The few officers who stood guard over the doors . . . were beaten down and flung one side, helpless and stunned, whilst the vast crowd rushed in. All the articles upon which they could seize—beds, bedding, carpets, furniture, the very garments of the fleeing inmates, some of these torn from their persons as they sped by—were carried into the streets and hurried off by the women and children. . . .

The little ones, many of them assailed and beaten—all, orphans and caretakers, exposed to every indignity and every danger—driven off to the street, the building was fired. . . .

In less than two hours the walls crashed in, a mass of smoking blackened ruins, whilst the children wandered through the streets, a prey to beings who were wild beasts in everything save the superior ingenuity of man to agonize and torture his victims. (Ibid.)

A MEMORY OF CRUELTY

257. [T]he most shocking thing that I have seen [as a slave] was on the plantation of Mr. Farrarby. . . .

I went up to his house one morning from my work for drinking water, and heard a woman screaming awfully in the door-yard. On going up to the fence and looking over I saw a woman stretched out, face downwards, on the ground her hands and feet being fastened to stakes. Mr. Farrarby was standing over and striking her with a leather trace belonging to his carriage-harness. As he struck her the flesh of her back and legs was raised in welts and ridges by the force of the blows. Sometimes when the poor thing cried too loud from pain Farrarby would kick her in the mouth.

After he had exhausted himself whipping her he sent to his house for sealing wax and a lighted candle and, melting the wax, dropped it upon the woman's lacerated back. He then got a riding whip and, standing over the woman, picked on the hardened wax by switching at it. Mr. Farrarby's grown daughters were looking at all this from a window of the house through the blinds.

This punishment was so terrible that I was induced to ask what offence the woman had committed and was told by her fellow servants that her only crime was in burning the edges of the waffles that she had cooked for breakfast. (Solomon Bradley, interview, American Freedman's Inquiry Commission, Hilton Head, South Carolina, August 27, 1863, cited in *Slave Testimony*, edited by John W. Blassingame.)

[At the time of the interview, Bradley was not only free but a soldier in the 21st U.S. Colored Troops.]

HOSPITAL FOR "CONTRABANDS"

---

258. North of Washington, in an open, muddy mire, are gathered all the colored people who have been made free by the progress of our Army. Sickness is inevitable, and to meet it these rude hospitals, only rough wooden barracks, are in use—a place where there is so much to be done. . . . We average here one birth per day, and have no baby clothes except as we wrap them up in an old piece of muslin, that even being scarce. Now the Army is advancing it is not uncommon to see from 40 to 50 arrivals in one day. . . . They have nothing that any one in the North would call clothing. . . . This hospital is the reservoir for all cripples, diseased, aged, wounded, infirm, from whatsoever cause; all accidents happening to colored people in employs around Washington are brought here. It is not uncommon for a colored driver to be pounded nearly to death by some of the white soldiers. (Cornelia Hancock, letter to her sister, Contraband Hospital, Washington, D.C., November 15, 1863, from *South after Gettysburg: Letters of Cornelia Hancock . . . 1863–1865*, edited by Henrietta Jaquette.)

259. One [freed slave] had his master's name branded on his forehead, and with him he brought all the instruments of torture that he wore at different times during 39 years of very hard slavery. . . . He wore an iron collar with 3 prongs standing up so he could not lay down his head; then a contrivance to render one leg entirely still and a chain clanking behind him with a bar weighing 50 lbs. This he wore and worked all the time hard. At night they hung a little bell upon the prongs above his head so that if he hid in any bushes it would tinkle and tell his whereabouts. The baton that was used to whip them he also had. It is so constructed that a little child could whip them till the blood streamed down their backs. (Ibid.)

A CEMETERY IS DEDICATED

260. Four score and seven years ago our fathers brought forth on this continent, a new nation, conceived in Liberty, and dedicated to the proposition that all men are created equal.

Now we are engaged in a great civil war, testing whether that nation or any nation so conceived and so dedicated, can long endure. (Abraham Lincoln, Gettysburg Address, November 19, 1863.)

261. We are met on a great battlefield of that war. We have come to dedicate a portion of that field, as a final resting place for those who here gave their lives that that nation might live. It is altogether fitting and proper that we should do this. But, in a larger sense, we can not dedicate—we can not consecrate—we can not hallow—this ground. The brave men, living and dead, who struggled here, have consecrated it, far above our poor power to add or detract. (Ibid.)

262. The world will little note, nor long remember what we say here, but it can never forget what they did here. It is for us the living, rather, to be dedicated here to the unfinished work which they who fought here have thus far so nobly advanced. It is rather for us to be here dedicated to the great task remaining before us—that from these honored dead we take increased devotion to that cause for which they gave the last full measure of devotion—that we here highly resolve that these dead shall not have died in vain—that this nation, under God, shall have a new birth of freedom—and that government of the people, by the people, for the people, shall not perish from the earth. (Ibid.)

BATTLE CRY

263. The Federal, or "Yankee," yell, compared with that of the Confederate, lacked in vocal breadth, pitch, and resonance. This was unquestionably attributable to the fact that the soldiery of the North was drawn and recruited entirely from large cities and towns, from factory districts, and from the more densely settled portions of the country.

Their surroundings, their circumstances of life and employment, had the effect of molding the character and temperament of the people, and at the same time of restraining their vocal development. People living and working in close proximity to one another have no absolute need for loud or strained vocal efforts. (J. Harve Dew, 9th Virginia Cavalry, Brandy Station, Virginia, fall 1863, from *Century Illustrated Magazine*, April 1892.)

264. To afford some idea of the difference between these "yells," I will relate an incident which occurred in battle. . . .

[We] found ourselves facing a [Union] battery of artillery with a regiment of cavalry drawn up on each side. . . . They came upon us in a body two or three times outnumbering us. Then was heard their peculiar characteristic [Yankee] yell—"Hoo-ray! Hoo-ray! Hoo-ray!" etc. . . . (The sound was as though the first syllable, if heard at all, was "hoo," uttered with an exceedingly short, low, and indistinct tone, and the second was "ray," yelled in a long and high tone slightly deflecting at its termination.) . . .

Our command was alone in the field, and it seemed impossible for us to withstand the coming shock; but our commander, as brave an officer as ever drew a saber, frequently repeated, as the charging column approached us, his precautionary orders, to "Keep steady, boys! Keep steady!" and so we remained till the Federals were within a hundred yards of us. Then, waving his sword in air, he gave the final order, loud enough to be heard the field over: "Now is your time, boys! Give them the saber! Charge them, men! Charge!"

In an instant every voice with one accord vigorously shouted that "Rebel yell," which was so often heard on the field of battle, "Woh-who-ey! Woh-who-ey!" etc. . . .

A moment or two later the Federal column wavered and broke. (Ibid.)

WAR SONG

265.

> Hurrah! Hurrah! we bring the jubilee!
> Hurrah! Hurrah! the flag that makes you free!
> So we sing the chorus from Atlanta to the sea,
> While we were marching through Georgia.

(Henry Clay Work, "Marching through Georgia.")

A NEW V.P. NOMINEE

266. Treason must be made odious, and traitors must be punished and impoverished. Their great plantations must be seized and divided into small farms, and sold to honest, industrious men. . . .

[T]he instigators [of the rebellion], the conscious intelligent traitors . . . ought to be hung. (Andrew Johnson, speech on his vice presidential nomination, June 9, 1864, cited in *The Papers of Andrew Johnson*, edited by LeRoy P. Graf, Ralph Haskins, and Paul H. Bergeron.)

NAVAL ASSAULT

267. Damn the torpedoes! Full speed ahead! (David G. Farragut, on board the *Hartford*, Mobile Bay, Alabama, August 5, 1864.)

[The Union fleet, despite heavy losses, forced its way into Mobile Bay. Within weeks, the city would be completely blockaded.]

FROM ATLANTA TO SAVANNAH

268. Behind us lay Atlanta smoldering and in ruins, the black smoke rising high in air and hanging like a pall over the ruined city. . . . Then we turned our horses' heads to the east; Atlanta was soon lost behind the screen of trees, and became a thing of the past. (William T. Sherman, on his march from Atlanta to the sea, November 16–December 10, 1864, from *Memoirs of General William T. Sherman*.)

269. The whole horizon was lurid with the bonfires of rail ties, and groups of men all night were carrying the heated rails to the nearest trees and bending them around the trunks. (Ibid.)

270. The Negroes were simply frantic with joy. Whenever they heard my name, they clustered about my horse, shouted and prayed in their peculiar style, which had a natural eloquence that would have moved a stone. . . .

I . . . explained to him [a freed slave] that we wanted the slaves to remain where they were and that to load us down with useless mouths, which would eat up the food needed for our fighting men . . . [and] that if they followed us in swarms of old and young, feeble and helpless, it would simply load us down and cripple us in our great task. (Ibid.)

271. No doubt, many acts of pillage, robbery, and violence were committed by these parties of foragers [for food], usually called bummers; for I have since heard of jewelry taken from women and the plunder of articles that never reached the commissary; but these acts were exceptional and incidental. I never heard of any cases of murder or rape, and no army could have carried along sufficient food and forage for a march of three hundred miles, so that foraging in some shape was necessary. (Ibid.)

[After a 10-day siege, Savannah would fall to Union forces on December 20, 1864.]

WAR SONG

272.

> Just before the battle the General hears a row,
> He says, "The Yanks are coming, I hear their rifles now,"
> He turns around in wonder, and what do you think he sees?
> The Georgia militia eating goober peas!
>   Peas! Peas! Peas! Peas! eating goober peas!
>   Goodness, how delicious, eating goober peas!

(A. Pender, "Goober Peas.")

[When provisions ran low, Confederate soldiers had to settle for "goober peas"—peanuts.]

WAR SONG

273.

> When Johnny comes marching home again, hurrah, hurrah!
> We'll give him a hearty welcome then, hurrah, hurrah!
> The men will cheer, the boys will shout,

The ladies they will all turn out,
And we'll all feel gay when Johnny comes marching home.

(Patrick Gilmore, "When Johnny Comes Marching Home.")

BURNING OF COLUMBIA

---

274. On the . . . 17th the city was evacuated by our soldiers and surrendered by the mayor. Oh God . . . the humiliation, the agony of knowing we were to be under the Yankees; that our beloved flag was to be pulled down and the USA flag, wave over the city, that flag, that carried loathing to every Southern heart. . . .

As the evening shades drew darker the sky was illumined with crimson, it was a fearfully windy night, and as we watched the sky, we heard the awful cry of fire. Oh God can I ever forget that night, but after a while we heard only Main Street was so burned, we gathered together in a room at the top of the house, and as we gazed we saw new fires burst forth in every direction; the flames were seen, leaping and dancing assisted by the winds in the work of destruction, and the air was filled with torpedoes, shells, hand grenades and all the . . . instruments of evil doers; the exultant shout of the infuriated soldiers met the ears, and from every heart went up to God a prayer that he would lull the wind, stay the flames, and put mercy in the hearts of our foes. . . . We at home did not think the fire would reach us, but it did so rapidly, and [we] were urged to put a change of clothing in a bag and leave our house. . . . [A]s I left all my comforts, all the accumulated treasures of a life time, the letters of loved absent ones, pictures of our precious relations, tokens and souvenirs of childhood, a feeling of fearful desolation came upon me. [B]y this time the streets were crowded with the "vandal foe," and as we reached the street, were greeted by curses too fearful to be entered in my book. (Eleanor Cohen Seixas, recalling events of February 17, 1865, Columbia, South Carolina, diary entry, February 28, 1865, from *Private Pages: Diaries of American Women, 1830s–1970s*, edited by Penelope Franklin.)

[Transcript of the diary was from the American Jewish Archives, Cincinnati, Ohio.]

MALICE TOWARD NONE

---

275. On the occasion corresponding to this four years ago [Lincoln's First Inaugural Address] all thoughts were anxiously directed to an impending civil war. All dreaded it, all sought to avert it. While the inaugural address was being delivered from this place, devoted altogether to saving the Union without war, insurgent agents were in the city seeking to destroy it without war—seeking to dissolve the Union and divide effects by negotiation. Both parties deprecated war, but one of them would make war rather than let the nation survive, and the other would accept war rather than let it perish, and the war came. (Abraham Lincoln, Second Inaugural Address.)

276. One eighth of the whole population was colored slaves, not distributed generally over the Union, but localized in the southern part of it. These slaves constituted a peculiar and powerful interest. All knew that this interest was somehow the cause of the war. To strengthen, perpetuate, and extend this interest was the object for which the insurgents would rend the Union even by war, while the Government claimed no right to do more than to restrict the territorial enlargement of it. (Ibid.)

277. Both [sides] read the same Bible and pray to the same God, and each invokes His aid against the other. It may seem strange that any men should dare to ask a just God's assistance in wringing their bread from the sweat of other men's faces, but let us judge not, that we be not judged. . . .

Fondly do we hope, fervently do we pray, that this mighty scourge of war may speedily pass away. Yet, if God will that it continue until all the wealth piled by the bondsman's 250 years of unrequited toil shall be sunk, and until every drop of blood drawn with the lash shall be paid by another drawn with the sword, as was said 3,000 years ago, so still it must be said, "The judgments of the Lord are true and righteous altogether." (Ibid.)

278. With malice toward none, with charity for all, with firmness in the right as God gives us to see the right, let us strive on to finish the work we are in, to bind up the nation's wounds, to care for him who shall have borne the battle and for his widow and his orphan, to do all which may achieve and cherish a just and lasting peace among ourselves and with all nations. (Ibid.)

RECOUNTING A DREAM

279. It seems strange how much there is in the Bible about dreams. . . . If we believe the Bible, we must accept the fact that in the old days God and His angels came to men in their sleep and made themselves known in dreams. Nowadays dreams are regarded as very foolish, and are seldom told, except by old women and by young men and maidens in love. . . .

I can't say that I do [believe in dreams], but I had one the other night which has haunted me ever since. . . .

About ten days ago, I retired very late. I had been up waiting for important dispatches from the front. I could not have been long in bed when I fell into a slumber, for I was weary. I soon began to dream. There seemed to be a death-like stillness about me. Then I heard subdued sobs, as if a number of people were weeping. I thought I left my bed and wandered downstairs. There the silence was broken by the same pitiful sobbing, but the mourners were invisible. I went from room to room; no living person was in sight, but the same mourning sounds of distress met me as I passed along. It was light in all the rooms; every object was familiar to me; but where were all the people who were grieving as if their hearts would break? I was puzzled and alarmed. What could be the meaning of this? Determined to find the cause of a state of things so mysterious and so shocking, I kept on until I arrived at the East Room, which I entered. There I met with a sickening surprise. Before me was a catafalque, on which rested a corpse wrapped in funeral vestments. Around it were stationed soldiers who were acting as guards; and there was a throng of people, some gazing mournfully upon the corpse, whose face was covered, others weeping pitifully. "Who is dead in the White House?" I demanded of one of the soldiers. "The President," was his answer, "he was killed by an assassin!" Then came a loud burst of grief from the crowd, which awoke me from my dream. I slept no more that night. (Abraham Lincoln, the White House, April 1865, from *Recollections of Abraham Lincoln, 1847–1865*, by Ward Hill Lamon.)

SURRENDER TERMS

280. General Lee was sitting at the side of the room; he rose and went to meet General Grant to take that paper and read it over. When he came to the part in which only public property was to be surrendered, and the officers were to retain their side arms and personal baggage, General Lee said: "That will have a very happy effect."

Lee then said to General Grant: "General, our cavalrymen furnish their own horses; they are not Government horses, some of them may be, but of course you will find them out—any property that is public property, you will ascertain that, but it is nearly all private property, and these men will want to plough ground and plant corn."

General Grant answered that as the terms were written, only the officers were permitted to take their private property, but almost immediately he added that he supposed that most of the men in the ranks were small farmers, that the United

States did not want their horses. He would give orders to allow every man who claimed to own a horse or mule to take the animal home.

General Lee . . . again said that this would have an excellent effect. . . .

General Grant said to [General] Sheridan: "Order your commissary to send to the Confederate Commissary 25,000 rations for our men [being held as prisoners] and his men." . . .

I took the letter over to General Lee, and he read it and said: "Don't say 'I have the honor to acknowledge the receipt of your letter of such a date'; he is here; just say, 'I accept these terms.' " (Charles Marshall, Appomattox Court House, Virginia, April 9, 1865, from *An Aide-de-Camp of Lee, Being the Papers of Colonel Charles Marshall*, edited by Frederick Maurice.)

MESSAGE TO HIS TROOPS

281. I need not tell the survivors of so many hard-fought battles, who have remained steadfast to the last, that I have consented to this result [the surrender] from no distrust of them; but, feeling that valor and devotion could accomplish nothing that could compensate for the loss that would have attended the continuation of the contest, I have determined to avoid the useless sacrifice of those whose past services have endeared them to their countrymen. (General Robert E. Lee, message to the Army of Northern Virginia. April 10, 1865.)

INCIDENT IN FORD'S THEATER

282. Like a clap of thunder out of a clear sky spread the announcement that President Lincoln was shot while sitting in a box at Ford's Theater. The city is wild with excitement. A gentleman who was present thus describes the event:

At about 10-½ o'clock, in the midst of one of the acts, a pistol shot was heard, and at the same instant a man leaped upon the stage from the same box occupied by the President, brandished a long knife, and shouted, *"Sic semper tyrannis!"* [thus always to tyrants!], then rushed to the rear of the scenes and out of the back door of the theater. So sudden was the whole thing that most persons in the theater supposed it a part of the play, and it was some minutes before the fearful tragedy was comprehended.

The man was pursued, however, by someone connected with the theater, to the outer door and seen to mount a horse and ride rapidly away. (Dispatch to the *New York Times* from Washington, D.C., April 14, 1865.)

EULOGY

283.

> O Captain! my Captain! our fearful trip is done,
> The ship has weathered every rack, the prize we sought is won,
> The port is near, the bells I hear, the people all exulting,
> While follow eyes the steady keel, the vessel grim and daring,
> But O heart! heart! heart!
>   O the bleeding drops of red,
>   Where on the deck my Captain lies,
>   Fallen cold and dead.

(Walt Whitman, "O Captain! My Captain!" April 1865.)

[On the assassination of Lincoln.]

RESPONSE TO TRAGEDY

---

284. I suppose all the children who were born about the time of the Civil War have recollections quite unlike those of the children who are living now. Although I was but four and a half years old when Lincoln died, I distinctly remember the day when I found on our two white gateposts American flags companioned with black. I tumbled down on the marsh gravel walk in my eager rush into the house to inquire what they were "there for." To my amazement I found my father in tears, something that I had never seen before, having assumed, as all children do, that grown-up people never cried. The two flags, my father's tears, and his impressive statements that the greatest man in the world had died, constituted my initiation, my baptism, as it were, into the thrilling and solemn interests of a world lying quite outside the two white gateposts. (Jane Addams, recollections of April 1865, from *Twenty Years at Hull-House.*)

285. The war touched children in many ways: I remember an engraved roster of names, headed by the words "Adams' Guard," and the whole surmounted by the insignia of the American eagle clutching many flags, which always hung in the family living room. As children we used to read this list of names again and again. We could reach it only by dint of putting the family Bible on a chair and piling the dictionary on top of it; using the Bible to stand on was always accompanied by a little thrill of superstitious awe, although we carefully put dictionary above that our profane feet might touch it alone. (Ibid.)

9

Reconstruction

Shortly before his assassination, Lincoln had talked of "binding up the nation's wounds." That was not to be. The Radical Republicans in Congress wanted to punish the South and grant all civil rights to the newly freed slaves, including the right to vote. President Andrew Johnson wanted to bring the southern states back into the Union as quickly as possible and spoke openly of a "white man's government." The antagonism would eventually lead to the impeachment of Johnson.

Meanwhile, the nation was being bound together from east to west by the building of the Transcontinental Railroad.

BLACK CODES

286. It shall not be lawful for any freedman, free negro, or mulatto to intermarry with any white person; nor for any white person to intermarry with any freedman, free negro, or mulatto. Any person who shall so intermarry, shall be deemed guilty of felony, and on conviction thereof shall be confined in the State penitentiary for life. (Mississippi law, 1865.)

287. All contracts for labor made with freedmen, free negroes, and mulattoes for a longer period than one month shall be in writing, and if the laborer shall quit the service of the employer before the expiration of his term of service, without good cause, he shall forfeit his wages for that year up to the time of quitting. (Ibid.)

At Promontory Point, Utah, the final link of the Transcontinental Railroad is joined, May 10, 1869.

288. Every civil officer shall, and every person may, arrest and carry back to his or her legal employer any freedman, free negro, or mulatto who shall have quit the service of his or her employer before the expiration of his or her term of service without good cause. Said officer and person shall be entitled to receive for arresting and carrying back every deserting employee the sum of $5.00 and ten cents per mile from the place of arrest to the place of delivery, and the same shall be paid by the employer, and held deducted from the wages of the deserting employee. (Ibid.)

TOWARD RECONCILIATION

289. General, there is no such thing as reconstruction. These States have not gone out of the Union, therefore reconstruction is unnecessary. . . . [I desire] to have the seceded States return back to their former condition as quickly as possible. (President Andrew Johnson, statement to General John A. Logan, *Washington Morning Chronicle*, July 1, 1865, cited in *The Papers of Andrew Johnson*, edited by LeRoy P. Graf, Ralph Haskins, and Paul H. Bergeron.)

ON RACE AND POLITICS

290. This is a country for white men, and by God, as long as I am President, it shall be a government for white men. (President Andrew Johnson, ca. summer 1865, cited in *The Reconstruction Presidents*, by Brooks D. Simpson.)

A PLEA FOR ONE CONDEMNED

291. Inasmuch as your petitioner [Mary Surratt] was a private citizen and not subject to military jurisdiction, and that all crimes committed . . . are under the Constitution and laws of the United States, to be tried only before its criminal tribunals, with the right of public trial by jury, she prays your Honor to grant unto her the United States' most gracious writ of *habeas corpus*. (Plea before Justice Andrew Wylie of the Supreme Court of the District of Columbia on behalf of Mary Surratt, Washington, D.C., 2 A.M., July 7, 1865, cited in *The Case for Courage*, by William M. Kunstler.)

[Mrs. Surratt, who owned the boardinghouse in which the Lincoln assassination had been planned, had been sentenced to death by a Military Commission. The writ was granted, but President Andrew Johnson ordered that the writ be suspended and the sentence of death carried out. That morning, Mrs. Surratt and three others condemned in the conspiracy were executed. Most historians believe that Mrs. Surratt was probably innocent.]

BUILDING THE
TRANSCONTINENTAL

292. [The Chinese railroad workers are] quiet, peaceable, industrious, economical—ready and apt to learn all the different kinds of work. (Leland Stanford, president, Central Pacific Railroad, ca. 1865, cited in *Strangers from a Different Shore: A History of Asian Americans*, by Ronald Takaki.)

293. They [Chinese laborers] prove nearly equal to white men in the amount of labor they perform, and are much more reliable. No danger of strikes among them. We are training them to all kinds of labor: blasting, driving horses, handling rock as well as pick and shovel. . . .

We can't get enough white labor to build this railroad, and build it we must, so we're forced to hire them. (Charles Crocker, superintendent, Central Pacific Railroad, ibid.)

[Eventually, 90 percent of the railroad workers were Chinese. Ironically, in the famous photograph showing Stanford driving the golden spike at the railroad's completion, not a single Chinese face can be found.]

A FRIENDLY WARNING

---

294. They [the Republicans] control 20 states, and both branches of Congress. Four-fifths of the soldiers sympathize with them. Can you afford to quarrel with these two millions of voters? . . . For God sake move gradually and carefully. . . . Better stick close to old friends who carried you into the White House than to exchange them for Copperheads & rebels who will garrote you after using you. (Joseph Medill, *Chicago Tribune* editor, message to President Andrew Johnson, September 15, 1865, from *The Papers of Andrew Johnson*, edited by LeRoy P. Graf, Ralph Haskins, and Paul H. Bergeron.)

FOR GRADUAL
RECONSTRUCTION

---

295. [It is better] to let them reconstruct themselves than to force them to it; for if they go wrong, the power is in our hands, and we can check them in any stage, and oblige them to correct their errors; we must be patient with them. . . .

[If I was in Tennessee] I should try to introduce Negro suffrage gradually. . . . [Otherwise it] would breed a war of races. (President Andrew Johnson, interview with George L. Stearns, October 3, 1865, from *The Papers of Andrew Johnson*, edited by LeRoy P. Graf, Ralph Haskins, and Paul H. Bergeron.)

NEWSPAPER AD

296. Information Wanted of Caroline Dodson, who was sold from Nashville, Nov. 1st, 1862, by James Lumsden to Warwick (a trader then in human beings), who carried her to Atlanta, Georgia, and she was last heard of in the sale pen of Robert Clarke, (human trader in that place), from which she was sold. Any information of her whereabouts will be thankfully received and rewarded by her mother. Lucinda Lowery, Nashville. (Advertisement, *Nashville Colored Tennessean*, Late 1865, cited in *Been in the Storm So Long: The Aftermath of Slavery*, by Leon P. Litwack.)

SLAVERY OUTLAWED

297. Neither slavery nor involuntary servitude, except as a punishment for crime . . . shall exist within the United States or any place subject to their jurisdiction. (13th Amendment, ratified Dec. 6, 1865.)

CULTURES IN CONTRAST

298. God made us not as you; we were born like the animals, in the dry grass, not on beds like you. This is why we do as the animals, go about of a night and rob and steal. If I had such things as you have, I would not do as I do, for then I would not need to do so. (Cochise, council meeting with General Gordon Granger, 1866, *Kansas State Historical Collections*, 1913–1914.)

299. When I was young I walked all over this country east and west, and saw no other people than the Apaches. After many summers I walked again and found another race of people had come to take it. (Ibid.)

THE IRON ROAD

300. Hear ye, Dakotas! When the Great Father at Washington sent us his chief soldier to ask for a path through our hunting grounds, a way for his iron road to the mountains and the western sea, we were told that they wished merely to pass through our country, not to tarry among us, but to seek for gold in the far west. Our old chiefs thought to show their friendship and good will, when they allowed this dangerous snake in our midst.

Yet before the ashes of the council fire are cold, the Great Father is building his forts among us. You have heard the sound of the white soldier's axe upon the Little Piney. His presence here is an insult and a threat. It is an insult to the spirits of our ancestors. Are we then to give up their sacred graves to be plowed for corn? Dakotas, I am for war! (Red Cloud, council meeting, Fort Laramie, Wyoming, 1866, cited in *Indian Heroes and Great Chieftains*, by Charles A. Eastman.)

ONE MEETING, TWO VIEWS

A delegation of blacks, led by Frederick Douglass, met with President Andrew Johnson at the White House. According to Douglass, the president delivered a "speech" to the group but then refused to answer any of their questions or comments. After the meeting, Douglass wrote a memo to the president summarizing Johnson's major points and responding to them. Johnson's reaction to the meeting appears in the quotation immediately following that of Douglass.

301. 1. The first point to which we feel especially bound to take exception is your [President Johnson's] attempt to found a policy opposed to our enfranchisement, upon the alleged ground of an existing hostility on the part of the former slaves toward the poor white people of the South. We admit the existence of this hostility, and hold that it is entirely reciprocated. . . .

There was no earthly reason why the blacks should not hate and dread the poor whites when in a state of slavery, for it was from this class that their masters received their slave catchers, slave drivers, and overseers. They were the men called in upon all occasions by the masters whenever any fiendish outrage was to be committed upon the slave. Now, sir, you cannot but perceive, that the cause of this hatred removed, the effect must be removed also. . . .

2. Besides, even if it were true, as you allege . . . that this enmity between the two races is even more intense in a state of freedom than in a state of slavery, in the name of heaven, we reverently ask how can you, in view of your desire to promote the welfare of the black man, deprive him of all means of defence, and clothe him whom you regard as his enemy in the panoply of political power? Can it be that you recommend a policy which would arm the strong and down the defenseless? Can you, by any possibility of reasoning, regard this as just, fair, or wise? Experience proves that those are most abused who can be abused with the greatest impunity. Men are whipped oftenest who are whipped easiest. Peace between races is not to be secured by degrading one race and exalting another, by giving power to one race and withholding it from another, but by maintaining a state of equal justice between all classes. . . .

3. On the colonization theory you were pleased to broach . . . much could be said. It is impossible to suppose, in view of the usefulness of the black man in time of peace as a laborer in the South, and in time of war as a soldier in the North, and the growing respect for his rights . . . and his increasing adaptation to a high state of civilization in his native land, that there can ever come a time when he can be removed from this country without a terrible shock to its prosperity and peace. Besides, the worst enemy of the nation could not cast upon its fair name a greater infamy than to admit that Negroes could be tolerated among them in a state of the most degrading slavery and oppression, and must be cast away, driven into exile, for no other cause than having been freed from their chains. (Frederick Douglass, Washington, D.C., memo to President Johnson summarizing a meeting with black leaders, February 7, 1866, from *Life and Times of Frederick Douglass*, by Frederick Douglass.)

302. Those damned sons of bitches thought they had me in a trap! I know that damned Douglass; he's just like any other nigger, and he would sooner cut a white man's throat than not. (President Andrew Johnson, remark after meeting the black delegation, February 7, 1866, cited in *The Reconstruction Presidents*, by Brooks D. Simpson.)

NEW ORLEANS RACE RIOT

In July 1866, freedmen assembled in New Orleans to press for changes in Louisiana's state constitution. They had been disfranchised and were seeking black voting rights. During their meeting, white mobs, including police, attacked those both outside and inside the meeting hall. A white spectator inside the hall told a congressional committee what had happened.

303. I looked through the windows, and saw the people on the fences with their revolvers, waiting to shoot anybody who would show themselves, and I saw the police shoot many colored people who attempted to escape. . . . I saw one policeman, while a Negro was kneeling before him and begging for mercy, shoot into his side. I saw another discharge his revolver into a Negro lying flat on the floor. All this time I was anxiously hoping the military [federal troops] would arrive and quell the riot, and allow those in the hall to get away, either as prisoners taken to jail or otherwise. . . .

I suggested that we barricade the hall, and hold it until the military should come. It was the only chance we had. I succeeded in getting the chairs placed against the doors. The doors, however, opened into the lobby, and the fastenings outside were very soon torn off. We had no protection except the chairs, and they constituted very little, as it was easy to fire through between them.

The police made another attack, and entered the hall. . . . [T]hose inside took the chairs and drove them out, and this they did two distinct times. On the third attack they entered again, headed by an officer who seemed to be a sergeant, from his uniform. He came to the door with a white handkerchief. I supposed they had become human again, and that this meant that they were willing to give us protection. . . .

I spoke to this policeman and asked him if they meant to give us protection against the mob, who would kill us. He said "Yes, we'll protect you." . . .

I pulled the chairs down and drove the colored people from the door, so that their presence should not provoke the police to any further acts of violence. . . . As the police entered the hall, one . . . advanced, calling out, "Yes, you G— d—— sons of bitches, we'll protect you." . . . [E]ven the man who had tendered me his hand rushed forward with the others, discharging their pistols indiscriminately. One of the police, pointing his pistol toward me, said, "So you will surrender, you G— d—— son of a bitch," and discharging his revolver towards my head, said, "Take that and go to hell, will you?" I was standing close to him, and had the presence of mind to throw up his hand, and the ball passed through my hat. . . .

[Later:] I jumped, and I suppose those persons below, not understanding what it meant, or thinking I was one of themselves, became panic-stricken. They went out and carried me along with them without knowing who I was. As I got on to the street, I saw a line of police standing like soldiers across Dryadess Street, towards Canal Street. Parties would leave their positions, go to the sides of the building and fire their revolvers into the hall. . . .

Their hat-bands, on which they wore the letters "police" and the [identification] number, were turned wrong side out. . . .

I then left and went down Canal and St. Charles Streets to General Baird's headquarters. I informed him that I had just left the hall and of the position of affairs there, and asked him, for God's sake, to send the military. (J. D. O'Connell, recalling events of July 30, 1866, at Mechanics Institute, New Orleans, testimony before a congressional committee, from H.R. Document No. 16, 39th Congress, Second Session.)

[Thirty-eight men were killed and 146 wounded in the riot.]

TEACHING FORMER SLAVES

304. Our school begun—*in spite of threatenings from the whites,* and *the conse-quent fear of the blacks*—with 27 pupils, four only of whom could read, even the simplest words. At the end of six weeks, we have enrolled 85 names, with *but 15 unable to read.* In seven years teaching at the North, I have not seen a parallel to their appetite for learning, and their active progress. Whether this zeal will abate with time, is yet a question. I have a little fear that it may. Meanwhile it is well to "work while the day lasts." Their spirit *now* may be estimated somewhat, when I tell you that three walk a distance of four miles, each morning, to return after the five hours session. Several come three miles, and quite a number from two and two-and-a-half miles.

The night school—taught by Miss Root—numbers about 40, mostly men, earnest, determined, ambitious. One of them walks six miles and returns after the close of school, which is often as late as ten o'clock. One woman walks three miles, as do a number of the men.

On Sabbath mornings, at half-past nine, we open our Sabbath school, which is attended by about 50 men, women and children, who give willing, earnest attention to our instruction. . . . [W]e take a text or passage of Scripture, enlarge upon and apply it as well as we are able, answering their questions, correcting erroneous opinions, extending their thoughts. (Mary S. Battey, Andersonville, Georgia, letter, December 1866, from the Everett Family Papers, Newberry Library, Chicago, cited in *The Female Experience: An American Documentary,* by Gerda Lerner.)

THE LIMITS OF MARTIAL LAW

In 1864, Lambdin Milligan, a civilian, was put on trial in Indiana for plotting to aid the Confederacy. He was convicted by military court-martial and sentenced to death. He appealed on the grounds that his civil rights had been violated. In 1866 the Supreme Court made its ruling.

305. It is claimed that martial law covers with its broad mantle the proceed-ings of this military commission. The proposition is this: that in a time of war the commander of an armed force (if in his opinion the exigencies of the country demand it, and of which he is to judge) has the power, within the lines of his military district, to suspend all civil rights and their remedies, and subject citizens as well as soldiers to the rule of his will; and in the exercise of his lawful authority cannot be restrained, except by his superior officer or the President of the United States.

If this position is sound to the extent claimed, then when war exists, foreign or domestic, and the country is subdivided into military departments for mere convenience, the commander of one of them can, if he chooses, within his limits, on the plea of necessity, with the approval of the Executive, substitute military force for and to the exclusion of the laws, and punish all persons, as he thinks right and proper, without fixed or certain rules.

The statement of this proposition shows its importance; for, if true, republican government is a failure, and there is an end of liberty regulated by law. (Justice David Davis, opinion, *Ex Parte Milligan*, December 17, 1866.)

306. Martial law cannot arise from a threatened invasion. The necessity must be actual and present; the invasion real, such as effectually closes the courts and deposes the civil administration.

It is difficult to see how the safety of the country required martial law in Indiana. If any of her citizens were plotting treason, the power of arrest could secure them, until the government was prepared for their trial, when the courts were open and ready to try them. It was as easy to protect witnesses before a civil as a military tribunal; and as there could be no wish to convict except on sufficient legal evidence, surely an ordained and established court was better able to judge of this than a military tribunal composed of gentlemen not trained to the profession of the law. (Ibid.)

[The court voted unanimously to free Milligan.]

HORATIO ALGER STORY

Dick is a bootblack who lives on the street. One morning, he shines the boots of Mr. Greyson. Though Dick charges a dime for a shine, Greyson has only a quarter and asks Dick to bring the change to his office. The following day, Dick does so.

307. "You're an honest boy," said Mr. Greyson. "Who taught you to be honest?"

"Nobody," said Dick. "But it's mean to cheat and steal. I've always knowed that."

"Then you've got ahead of some of our business men. Do you read the Bible?"

"No," said Dick. "I've heard it's a good book, but I don't know much about it."

"You ought to go to some Sunday School. Would you be willing?"

"Yes," said Dick, promptly. "I want to grow up 'spectable. But I don't know where to go."

"Then I'll tell you. The church I attend is at the corner of Fifth Avenue and 21st Street. . . . I have a class in the Sunday School there. If you'll come next Sunday, I'll take you into my class, and do what I can to help you." (Horatio Alger Jr., from the novel *Ragged Dick*, 1867.)

[This was the first of about 120 novels on the theme of the poor-but-honest boy—usually a bootblack or a newsboy—who makes good.]

VETOING MILITARY RULE

308. The bill places all the people of the ten States therein named [former Confederate states] under the absolute domination of military rulers; and the preamble undertakes to give the reason upon which the measure is based. . . . It declares that there exists in those States no legal governments and no adequate protection for life or property, and asserts the necessity of enforcing peace and good order within their limits. Is this true as matter of fact?

It is not denied that the States in question have each of them an actual government, with all the powers—executive, judicial, and legislative—which properly belong to a free state. . . .

I submit to Congress whether this measure is not in its whole character, scope, and object without precedent and without authority, in palpable conflict with the plainest provisions of the Constitution, and utterly destructive to those great principles of liberty and humanity for which our ancestors . . . have shed so much blood and expended so much treasure. . . .

It is plain that the authority given to the military officer amounts to absolute despotism. . . .

Have we the power to establish and carry into execution a measure like this? I answer, certainly not, if we derive our authority from the Constitution and if we are bound by the limitations which it imposes. . . .

[Item by item, it is shown how the proposed measure would violate specific rights guaranteed in the Constitution.]

The United States are bound to guarantee to each State a republican form of government. Can it be pretended that this obligation is not palpably broken if we carry out a measure like this, which wipes away every vestige of republican government in ten States and puts the life, property, liberty, and honor of all the people in each of them under the domination of a single person clothed with unlimited authority? (President Andrew Johnson, veto message on the First Reconstruction Act, March 2, 1867.)

[Johnson's veto was overridden by Congress.]

EMANCIPATION FOR MEN ONLY?

309. There is a great stir about colored men getting their rights, but not a word about colored women; and if colored men get their rights, and not colored women theirs, you see, the colored men will be masters over the women and it will be as bad as before. So I am for keeping the thing going while things are stirring, because if we wait till it is still, it will take a great while to get it going again. (Sojourner Truth, Equal Rights Convention, New York City, May 9, 1867.)

PRINCIPLES—ON PAPER

310. This is an institution of Chivalry, Humanity, Mercy, and Patriotism; embodying in its genius and its principles all that is chivalric in conduct, noble in sentiment, generous in manhood, and patriotic in purpose; its peculiar objects being:

First: To protect the weak, the innocent, and the defenseless, from the indignities, wrongs, and outrages of the lawless, the violent, and the brutal; to relieve the injured and oppressed; to succor the suffering and unfortunate; and especially the widows and orphans of Confederate soldiers.

Second: To protect and defend the Constitution of the United States, and all laws passed in conformity thereto; and to protect the States and the people thereof from all invasion from any source whatever.

Third: To aid and assist in the execution of all constitutional laws, and to protect the people from unlawful seizure, and from trial except by their peers in conformity to the laws of the land. (Ku Klux Klan, "Character and Objects of the Order," Nashville, Tennessee, ca. summer 1867, from *Documentary History of Reconstruction*, by Walter L. Fleming.)

[The Klan—and similar organizations—quickly spread throughout the South. These groups launched a campaign of violence, terror, and murder against freedmen, carpetbaggers, and scalawags. In 1869 the Klan's first grand wizard—Nathan Bedford Forrest—tried to disband it because of its reputation for violence. That would not come about until 1877, when President Rutherford B. Hayes withdrew the last federal troops from the former Confederate states. The Ku Klux Klan was reconstituted in Atlanta in 1915.]

THE DEFEATED SOUTH

311. Look to the South, and you who went with me through that land can best say if they too have not been fearfully punished. Mourning in every household, desolation written in broad characters across the whole face of their country, cities in ashes and fields laid waste, their commerce gone, their system of labor annihilated and destroyed. Ruin, poverty and distress everywhere, and now pestilence adding . . . to their stack of misery; her proud men begging for pardon and appealing for permission to raise food for their children; her five millions of slaves free and their value lost to their former masters forever. (General William T. Sherman, address to former members of his command, *Augusta* [Georgia] *Weekly Constitutionalist*, November 2, 1867.)

TO OLD MASTERS, NEW "FRIENDS"

312. Now, to keep a man in the hardest bondage, to crush his body by excessive labor and his soul by absolute ignorance, to whip him, to undertake a gigantic war in order to better deprive him of his liberty and shorten his chains, and after that . . . to tell us that you are our TRIED friends, is more than a lie, it is a cruel insult and nothing short of it. . . . What friendship is that, but the deceiving and false friendship of impostors and hypocrites? ("Accepting the Past, but Opposing the Future," *New Orleans Tribune* editorial, December 21, 1867, cited in *Black Voices from Reconstruction*, by John David Smith.)

[The *Tribune* was the first daily black newspaper published in the United States.]

A THIRST FOR LEARNING

313. The great cry throughout the State has been, send us teachers, send us men, send us women, who will teach us how to read and write, and we will pay them for it. The people are hungry and thirsty after knowledge. They seem inspired with spirit from on high that tells them knowledge is the only source by which they will rise from the low and degraded state in which they have been kept. (Jonathan J. Wright, delegate, *Proceedings of the South Carolina Constitutional Convention*, 1868, cited in *Black Voices from Reconstruction*, by John David Smith.)

SHOWDOWN

314. Didn't I tell you so? What good did our moderation do you? If you don't kill the beast, it will kill you. (Congressman Thaddeus Stevens, ca. February 21, 1868, responding to President Johnson's appointment of a successor to Secretary of War Edwin M. Stanton, cited in *Andrew Johnson: A Biography*, by Hans L. Trefousse.)

[By his action, President Johnson had violated the Tenure of Office Act, which would lead to his impeachment. This was a final showdown between the Radical Republicans in Congress, who wanted to punish the southern states and bring civil rights to former slaves, and a president who wanted to do the opposite.]

A PRESIDENT IS CHARGED

315. In obedience to the order of the House of Representatives and all the people of the United States we do impeach Andrew Johnson, President of the United States, of high crimes and misdemeanors in office. (Representative Thaddeus Stevens of Pennsylvania on the floor of the U.S. Senate,

Washington, D.C., February 25, 1868, cited in *Impeachable Offenses: A Documentary History from 1787 to the Present*, by Emily Field Van Tassel and Paul Finkelman.)

[Johnson had been impeached in the House. He was charged with violating the Tenure of Office Act and the Army Appropriations Act. The major charges were that Johnson had removed Secretary of War Edwin M. Stanton without Senate approval and had insulted and threatened members of Congress.]

316. Johnson's problems with Congress were a result of his views on race, Reconstruction, and the meaning of the Civil War. These problems were complicated by his personality, his lack of sophistication, his generally crude behavior, and the circumstances of his ascension to the White House. (Emily Field Van Tassel and Paul Finkelman, law professors, commenting on events of 1868, ibid.)

[The Senate trial ended on May 16, 1868. The Senate failed to convict Johnson by a single vote shy of a two-thirds majority. Van Tassel and Finkelman, however, point out that as many as four senators were ready to vote for acquittal if necessary to prevent Johnson's removal from office.]

RIGHTS, VOTES, AND DEBTS

317. All persons born or naturalized in the United States, and subject to the jurisdiction thereof, are citizens of the United States and of the State wherein they reside. No State shall make or enforce any law which shall abridge the privileges or immunities of citizens of the United States, nor shall any State deprive any person or life, liberty, or property, without due process of law; nor deny to any person within its jurisdiction the equal protection of the laws. (14th Amendment, July 20, 1868.)

318. Representatives shall be apportioned among the several States according to their respective numbers, counting the whole number of persons in each State, excluding Indians not taxed. But when the right to vote at any election . . . is denied to any of the male inhabitants of such State, being 21 years of age, and citizens of the United States, or in any way abridged, except for participation in rebellion, or other crime, the basis of representation therein shall be reduced in the [same] proportion. (Ibid.)

319. No person shall be a Senator or Representative in Congress, or elector of President and Vice President, or hold any office, civil or military under the

United States, or under any State, who, having previously taken an oath as a member of Congress, or as an officer of the United States, or as a member of any State legislature, or as an executive or judicial officer of any State, to support the Constitution of the United States, shall have engaged in insurrection or rebellion against the same, or given aid or comfort to the enemies thereof. But Congress may by a vote of two-thirds of each House, remove such disability. (Ibid.)

320. Neither the United States nor any State shall assume or pay any debt or obligation incurred in aid of insurrection or rebellion against the United States, or any claim for the loss or emancipation of any slave; but all such debts, obligations and claims shall be held illegal and void. (Ibid.)

VALLEY OF THE SHADOW

321. The pleasantest room in the house was set apart for Beth, and in it was gathered everything that she most loved—flowers, pictures, her piano, the little work-table, and the beloved pussies. Father's best books found their way there, mother's easy chair, Jo's desk, Amy's loveliest sketches, and every day Meg brought her babies on a loving pilgrimage to make sunshine for Aunty Beth. . . .

So the spring days came and went, the sky grew clearer, the earth greener, the flowers were up fair and early, and the birds came back in time to say good-bye to Beth, who, like a tired but trustful child, clung to the hands that had led her all her life, as father and mother guided her tenderly through the valley of the shadow, and gave her up to God. . . .

As Beth had hoped, the "tide went out easily"; and in the dark hour before the dawn, on the bosom where she had drawn her first breath, she quietly drew her last, with no farewell but one loving look and a little sigh.

With tears, and prayers, and tender hands, mother and sisters made her ready for the long sleep that pain would never mar again—seeing with grateful eyes the beautiful serenity that soon replaced the pathetic patience that had wrung their hearts so long, and feeling with reverent joy, that to their darling death was a benignant angel—not a phantom full of dread.

When morning came, for the first time in many months, the fire was out, Jo's place was empty, and the room was very still. But a bird sang blithely on a budding bough, close by, the snowdrops blossomed freshly at the window, and the spring sunshine streamed in like a benediction over the placid face upon the pillow— a face so full of painless peace, that those who loved it best smiled through their tears, and thanked God that Beth was well at last. (Louisa May Alcott, from her novel *Little Women*, 1868–1869.)

[This novel dealt with women—especially young women—trying to cope during the Civil War, when the men were away fighting. It was also among the first American novels written for a juvenile audience.]

VOTES FOR FORMER SLAVES

322. The right of citizens of the United States to vote shall not be denied or abridged by the United States or by any State on account of race, color, or previous condition of servitude. (15th Amendment, March 30, 1870.)

DISCOVERY

323. An Englishman who was wrecked on a strange shore and wandering along the coast came to a gallows with a victim hanging on it, and fell down on his knees and thanked God that he at last beheld a sign of civilization. (Representative James A. Garfield, speech, House of Representatives, June 15, 1870, cited in *Presidential Wit*, edited by Bill Adler.)

A CONVICTED PRISONER SPEAKS

The judge has just directed a verdict of guilty. The prisoner, a woman, had violated election laws the previous November by voting in Rochester, New York.

324. [I]n your ordered verdict of guilty, you have trampled underfoot every vital principle of our government. My natural rights, my civil rights, my political rights, are all alike ignored. Robbed of the fundamental privilege of citizenship, I am degraded from the status of a citizen to that of a subject; and not only myself individually, but all of my sex, are, by your honor's verdict, doomed to political subjection under this so-called Republican government. . . .

I shall never pay a dollar of your unjust penalty. (Susan B. Anthony, Canandaigua, New York, June 18, 1873, from *The History of Woman Suffrage*, edited by Elizabeth Cady Stanton, Susan B. Anthony, and Matilda Joslyn Gage.)

LAISSEZ-FAIRE

325. [T]he let-alone policy seems now to be the true course [for Reconstruction]. (Rutherford B. Hayes, once and future governor of Ohio, letter to Guy M. Bryan, July 27, 1875, from *The Diary and Letters of Rutherford B. Hayes*, by Charles R. Williams.)

ELECTION IN DISPUTE

326. No man worthy of the office of President should be willing to hold it if "counted in" or placed there by fraud. Either party can afford to be disappointed in the result, but the country cannot afford to have the result tainted by the suspicion of illegal or false returns. (President Ulysses S. Grant, ca. December 1876, on the Hayes-Tilden deadlock in the 1876 presidential election, cited in *The Reconstruction Presidents*, by Brooks D. Simpson.)

[Two different sets of electoral results came in from several southern states. Congress set up an electoral commission to investigate. All the disputed electoral votes were awarded to Rutherford B. Hayes. He won the presidency, beating Samuel J. Tilden by a single electoral vote. Many historians believe that there was some kind of political deal made by which Hayes would end Reconstruction if elected. Whether that is true or not, the last federal troops did leave the South on April 24, 1877.]

DEATHBED STATEMENT

327. Soldiers were sent out in the winter, who destroyed our villages. Then "Long Hair" [General George Custer] came in the same way. They say we mas-

sacred him, but he would have done the same to us had we not defended ourselves and fought to the last. Our first impulse was to escape with our squaws and papooses, but we were so hemmed in that we had to fight. (Crazy Horse, on his deathbed, Fort Robinson, Nebraska, 1877, from *Twenty Years among Our Savage Indians*, by J. Leo Humfreville.)

In the late 19th and early 20th centuries, it was common for young boys to work in the coal mines. This photo was taken by Lewis Hine at a mine in South Pittston, Pennsylvania.

10

Industrialism

The age of expanding American industry was also the age of a shrinking western frontier. American Indians were being pushed off their lands. Labor unions were battling strikebreakers and striving for recognition. Adventurers were turning greedy eyes toward Spanish possessions in both the Atlantic and the Pacific. Observers of the American scene were writing about industrialism from a wide variety of viewpoints.

A CHIEF SURRENDERS

328. I am tired of fighting. Our chiefs are killed. . . . The old men are all dead. It is the young men who say yes or no. He who led on the young men is dead. It is cold and we have no blankets. The little children are freezing to death. My people, some of them, have run away to the hills, and have no blankets, no food, no one knows where they are—perhaps freezing to death. I want to have time to look for my children and see how many of them I can find. Maybe I shall find them among the dead. Hear me, my chiefs! I am tired, my heart is sick and sad. From where the sun now stands I will fight no more forever. (Chief Joseph, statement of surrender to General Nelson Miles, Bear Paw Mountains, Montana, October 1877, from Secretary of War Report 1877.)

[The Nez Perce chief was trying to avoid confinement to a reservation by fleeing to Canada. He was 30 miles from the border when he was forced to surrender.]

THE LEAVING

329. It was lonesome, the leaving. Husband dead, friends buried or held prisoners. I felt that I was leaving all that I had but I did not cry. You know how you feel when you lose kindred and friends through sickness—death. You do not care if you die. With us it was worse. Strong men, well women and little children killed and buried. They had not done wrong to be so killed. We had asked to be left in our own homes, the homes of our ancestors. Our going with heavy hearts, broken spirits. But we would be free. . . . All lost, we walked silently on into the wintry night. (Wetatonmi, recollections of October 1877, following the surrender of Chief Joseph, cited in *Hear Me My Chiefs!*, by Lucullus V. McWhorter.)

GETTING ORGANIZED

330. The recent alarming development and aggression of aggregated wealth, which, unless checked, will invariably lead to the pauperization and hopeless degradation of the toiling masses, render it imperative . . . that a check should be placed on its power and upon unjust accumulation, and a system adopted which will secure to the laborer the fruits of his toil; and as this much-desired object can only be accomplished by the thorough unification of labor. (Preamble to the constitution of the Knights of Labor, January 1, 1878, from *Thirty Years of Labor*, by T. V. Powderly.)

[The Knights of Labor began in 1869 with clothing workers in Philadelphia. By the time of its constitution, it had a membership of several hundred thousand. Anyone gainfully employed could join, except bankers, lawyers, stockbrokers, saloon keepers, professional gamblers, and other groups that it frowned upon. The more structured trade unions, such as the American Federation of Labor, would eclipse the Knights of Labor.]

ECONOMIC TWINGES AND SHOCKS

331. These industrial depressions, which cause as much waste and suffering as famines or wars, are like the twinges and shocks which precede paralysis. Everywhere is it evident that the tendency to inequality, which is the necessary result of material progress where land is monopolized, cannot go much further without carrying our civilization into that downward path which is so easy to enter and so hard to abandon. (Henry George, *Progress and Poverty*, 1879.)

332. Everywhere the increasing intensity of the struggle to live, the increasing necessity for straining every nerve to prevent being thrown down and trodden under foot in the scramble for wealth, is draining the forces which gain and maintain improvements. In every civilized country pauperism, crime, insanity, and suicides are increasing. In every civilized country the diseases are increasing which come from overstrained nerves, from insufficient nourishment, from squalid lodgings, from unwholesome and monotonous occupations, from premature labor of children, from the tasks and crimes which poverty imposes upon women. . . .

It is not an advancing civilization that such figures show, it is a civilization which in its undercurrents has already begun to recede. . . . As sure as the running tide must soon run full ebb, as sure as the declining sun must bring darkness, so sure is it, that though knowledge yet increases and invention marches on, and new states are being settled, and cities still expand, yet civilization has begun to wane when, in proportion to population, we must build more and more prisons, more and more almshouses, more and more insane asylums. It is not from top to bottom that societies die; it is from bottom to top. (Ibid.)

333. What has destroyed every previous civilization has been the tendency to the unequal distribution of wealth and power. This same tendency, operating with increasing force, is observable in our civilization today. . . . Wages and interest tend constantly to fall, rent to rise, the rich to become very much richer, the poor to become more helpless and hopeless, and the middle class to be swept away. (Ibid.)

UNCLE REMUS STORY

334. [B]imeby here come Brer Rabbit pacin' down de road—lippity-clippity, clippity-lippity—dez ez sassy ez a jay-bird. Brer Fox, he lay low. Brer Rabbit come prancin' 'long twel he spy de Tar-Baby, en den he fotch up on his behine legs like he wuz 'stonished. De Tar-Baby, she sot dar, she did, en Brer Fox, he lay low.

"Mawnin'!" sez Brer Rabbit, sezee—nice wedder dis mawnnin'," sezee.

Tar-Baby ain't sayin' nuthin', en Brer Fox, he lay low. . . .

"Youer stuck up, dat's wat you is," says Brer Rabbit, sezee. . . .

"I'm gwineter larn you how ter talk ter'specttubble fokes ef hit's de las ack," says Brer Rabbit, sezee. . . .

Brer Rabbit draw back wid his fis, he did, en blip he tuck 'er side er de head. . . . His fis stuck, en he can't pull loose. Brer Fox, he lay low.

"Tu'n me loose, fo' I kick de natal stuffin' outen you," sez Brer Rabbit, sezee, but de Tar-Baby, she ain't sayin' nuthin'. . . .

"Howdy, Brer Rabbit," sez Brer Fox, sezee, and den he rolled on de ground, en laft en laft. . . . "I speck you'll take dinner with me dis time, Brer Rabbit." (Joel Chandler Harris, "The Tar-Baby," 1880, from the *Atlanta Constitution*.)

WHAT IS JUSTICE?

335. Liberty means the security given to each man that, if he employs his energies to sustain the struggle on behalf of himself and those he cares for, he shall dispose of the product exclusively as he chooses. It is impossible to know whence any definition or criterion of justice can be . . . if it is not . . . that each shall enjoy the fruit of his own labor and self-denial, and of injustice that the idle and the industrious, the self-indulgent and the self-denying, shall share equally in the product. Aside from the *a priori* speculations of philosophers who have tried to make equality an essential element of justice, the human race has recognized, from the earliest times, the above conception of justice as the true one, and has founded upon it the right of property. . . .

[I]t is the utmost folly to denounce capital. To do so is to undermine civilization, for capital is the first requisite of every social gain, educational, ecclesiastical, political, aesthetic, or other. (William Graham Sumner, professor of sociology, 1880, from *Essays of William Graham Sumner*, edited by Albert C. Keller and Maurice R. Davie.)

A CENTURY OF DISHONOR

---

336. So long as there remains on our frontier one square mile of land occupied by a weak and helpless owner, there will be a strong and unscrupulous frontiersman ready to seize it, and a weak and unscrupulous politician, who can be hired for a vote or for money, to back him. The only thing that can stay this is a mighty outspoken sentiment and purpose of the great body of the people. . . .

What an opportunity for Congress . . . to redeem the name of the United States from the stain of a century of dishonor! (Helen Hunt Jackson, from her tract *A Century of Dishonor*, 1881.)

THINK TANK

---

337. Our club [the Economic and Sociological Club, formed several years before the American Federation of Labor] was in reality a group of trade unionists who naturally drifted together because of common belief and banded together for the purpose of extending and defending the principles of trade unionism. . . .

It was this little group that refused to subordinate the trade union to any "ism" or political "reform." We knew that the trade union was the fundamental agency through which we could achieve economic power, which would in turn give us social and political power. We refused to be entangled by Socialist partyism, not only because we realized that partisan political methods are essentially different from those of industry, but because legislation could affect the lives of men at work in a very few points—and those not vitally important for progressively improving conditions. . . .

We believed we ought to concentrate on the development of economic power and that political discussion would dissipate energy. Labor organizations had been the victims of so much political trickery that we felt the only way to keep this new organization free from taint was to exclude all political partisan action. (Samuel Gompers, labor leader, recalling events of the early 1880s, from *Seventy Years of Life and Labor*.)

FOLK SONG FOR AN OUTLAW

338.

Jesse James was a man that killed a-many a man;
He robbed the Danville train,
But that dirty little coward that shot Mister Howard,
Has laid poor Jesse in his grave.

Poor Jesse had a wife to mourn for his life,
Three children, they were brave.
But that dirty little coward that shot Mister Howard,
Has laid poor Jesse in his grave.

It was Robert Ford, that dirty little coward,
I wonder how does he feel.
For he ate of Jesse's bread, and he slept in Jesse's bed,
Then laid poor Jesse in his grave.

Jesse was a man, a friend to the poor,
He never would see a man suffer pain;
And with his brother Frank he robbed the Chicago bank,
And stopped the Glendale train.

(Folk song, ca. 1882.)

[Jesse James robbed banks and held up trains, but he had the reputation of being a Robin Hood. In 1882, at the age of 35, he was shot in the back by Bob Ford for a $10,000 reward.]

WORDS OF CONTEMPT

339. I hate all the white people. You are thieves and liars! You have taken away our land and made us outcasts. (Sitting Bull, speech before a white audience, 1883, cited in *Bury My Heart at Wounded Knee*, by Dee Brown.)

A QUESTION OF MORALITY

340. Well, one thing was dead sure, and that was, that Tom Sawyer was in earnest and was actually going to help steal that nigger out of slavery. That was the thing that was too many for me. Here was a boy that was respectable, and well brung up; and had a character to lose; and folks at home that had characters; and he was bright and not leather-headed; and knowing and not ignorant; and not mean, but kind; and yet here he was, without any more pride, or rightness, or feeling, than to stoop to this business, and make himself a shame, and his family a shame, before everybody. I *couldn't* understand it, no way at all. It was outrageous, and I knowed I ought to just up and tell him so, and so be his true friend, and let him quit the thing right where he was, and save himself. And I *did* start to tell him, but he shut me up, and says:

"Don't you reckon I know what I'm about? Don't I generly know what I'm about?" (Mark Twain, from his novel *The Adventures of Huckleberry Finn*, 1884.)

[The novel takes place around 1834 along the Mississippi. The narrator is Huck Finn. He is having second thoughts about involving his friend in a scheme to help a runaway slave escape to freedom.]

CAMPAIGN SLOGAN BACKFIRES

341. The [Democratic] party . . . antecedents have been rum, Romanism, and rebellion. (Rev. Samuel D. Burchard, speaking in support of the candidacy of Republican James G. Blaine, New York City, October 29, 1884.)

[Blaine failed to disavow the statement. It cost him the state of New York—and the election.]

THE NEW COLOSSUS

342.

Give me your tired, your poor,
Your huddled masses yearning to breathe free,

The wretched refuse of your teeming shore,
Bring these, the homeless, tempest-tossed to me:
I lift my lamp beside the golden door.

(Emma Lazarus, poem inscribed at the base of the Statue of Liberty, 1886.)

ARBITRATE LABOR DISPUTES?

343. The consciousness that arbitration can be forced upon them would induce both employer and employee to get together and to try to adjust their own differences, and thus nearly always results in a settlement. (John Peter Altgeld, Chicago attorney, "Protection of Non-Combatants: or, Arbitration of Strikes," article in the *Chicago Mail*, April 26, 1886, cited in *The Case for Courage*, by William M. Kunstler.)

[The article was in response to a statement by President Grover Cleveland that arbitration of labor disputes was "unworkable and undemocratic."]

VISION OF THE GHOST DANCE

344. When the sun died [was eclipsed] I went up to Heaven and saw God and all the people who had died a long time ago. God told me to come back and tell my people they must be good and love one another, and not fight or steal, or lie. He gave me this dance to give my people. (Wovoka, 1888, cited in Bureau of Indian Affairs, *Famous Indians, a Collection of Short Biographies*.)

[The Ghost Dance was supposed to result in many miracles, including the restoration of Indian lands, the return of the buffalo, and invincibility from the white man's bullets.]

HOW MUCH IS THAT YACHT?

345. Any man who has to ask about the annual upkeep of a yacht can't afford one. (Attributed to J. P. Morgan, banker and financier, undated, cited in *Familiar Quotations*, edited by John Bartlett and Emily Morison Beck.)

HUMAN RIGHTS DECLARATION

346. The earth is the common heritage of the people; every person born into the world is entitled equally with all others to a place to live . . . and earn a living, and any system of government that does not maintain and protect this inalienable right is wrong and should be changed or abolished. (People's Party platform, Kansas, 1890, cited in *Populism: The Humane Preference in America, 1890–1900*, by Gene Clanton.)

ANTI-TRUST ACT

347. Every contract, combination in the form of trust or otherwise, or conspiracy, in restraint of trade or commerce among the several States, or with foreign nations, is hereby declared to be illegal. (Sherman Anti-Trust Act, July 2, 1890.)

WOUNDED KNEE

348. Fully three miles from the scene of the massacre we found the body of a woman completely covered with a blanket of snow, and from this point on we found them scattered along as they had been relentlessly hunted down and slaughtered while fleeing for their lives. (Charles A. Eastman, describing events at Wounded Knee, South Dakota, December 1890, *From the Deep Woods to Civilization.*)

349. When we reached the spot where the Indian camp had stood among the fragments of burned tents and other belongings we saw the frozen bodies lying close together or piled one on another. I counted eighty bodies of men who had been in council and who were almost as helpless as the women and babes when the deadly fire began, for nearly all their guns had been taken from them. A reckless and desperate young Indian had fired the first shot when the search for weapons was well under way, and immediately the troops opened fire from all sides, killing not only unarmed men, women, and children, but their own comrades who stood opposite them, for the camp was entirely surrounded. (Ibid.)

ON THE GHOST DANCE

350. If our messiah does come we shall not force you into our belief. We will never burn innocent women at the stake or pull men to pieces with horses because they refuse to join in our ghost dances. (Masse Hadjo, "An Indian on the Messiah Craze," letter to the editor, *Chicago Tribune*, December 5, 1890.)

EYEWITNESS TESTIMONY

351. The men were separated, . . . from the women, and they were surrounded by the soldiers. Then came next the village of the Indians that was entirely surrounded by the soldiers also. When the firing began, . . . the people who were standing immediately around the young [Indian] man who fired the first shot were killed right together, and then they [the soldiers] turned their guns, Hotchkiss guns, etc., upon the women who were in the lodge, standing there under a flag of truce, and of course as soon as they were fired upon they fled. . . .

Right near the flag of truce a mother was shot down with her infant, the child not knowing that his mother was dead was still nursing. . . . The women as they were fleeing with their babes were killed together, shot right through, and the women who were very heavy with child were also killed. . . .

After most all of them [the Indians] had been killed a cry was made that all those who were not killed or wounded should come forth and they would be safe. Little boys who were not wounded came out of their places of refuge, and as soon as they came in sight a number of soldiers surrounded them and butchered them there. (American Horse, statement to the commissioner of Indian Affairs on the 1890 massacre at Wounded Knee, South Dakota, Washington, D.C., February 11, 1891, *14th Annual Report*, Bureau of American Ethnology, Part 2, 1896.)

VIOLENCE AT HOMESTEAD

On July 1, 1892, the Amalgamated Association of Iron and Steel Workers called a strike against the Carnegie Steel Company in Homestead, Pennsylvania. The company hired 300 Pinkerton detectives to guard nonstrikers and protect company property. The Pinkertons were brought to Homestead by barges, and a gun battle ensued on July 6. Most of the firing was done by the strikers. Abandoned by the tugboat that had brought them there, the trapped Pinkertons surrendered. One of them later testified before a congressional committee, describing what had happened.

352. [T]he steam tug had pulled out, taking all those who had charge of us. I concluded I would look out for my life, and if anything was said about my leaving and not staying there I would say I did not intend to work for them any more. . . .

[S]urrender was effected, and I started up the embankment with the men who went out, and we were glad to get away and did not expect trouble; but I looked up the hill and there were our men being struck as they went up, and it looked rather disheartening. . . .

[I]n front of the miners' cottages there were crowds of miners, women, etc., and as we all went by they commenced to strike at us again, and a man picked up a stone and hit me upon the ear. . . .

I got on further toward the depot and there were tremendous crowds on both sides and the men were just hauling and striking our men, and you would see them stumble as they passed by. I tried to get away from the crowd. . . . I put my hat on and walked out of the line of Pinkerton men, but some one noticed me, and I started to run and about 100 got after me. I ran down a street and ran through a yard. I ran about half a mile I suppose, but was rather weak and had had nothing to eat or drink and my legs gave out, could not run any further, and some man got hold of me by the back of my coat, and about 20 to 30 men came up and kicked me and pounded me with stones. I had no control of myself then. I thought I was about going and commenced to scream, and there were 2 or 3 strikers with rifles rushed up then and kept off the crowd and rushed me forward to a theater, and I was put in the theater and found about 150 of the Pinkerton men there, and that was the last violence offered me. (Former Pinkerton detective, recalling events of July 6, 1892, testimony before a congressional committee investigating the use of private armies by corporations, from Senate Report No. 1280, 53rd Congress, Second Session.)

[Seven Pinkertons were killed at Homestead. On July 12, the state militia was called out. Strikebreakers replaced union workers. By November 20, 1892, the strike was over.]

INFLUENCE OF THE FRONTIER

353. In a recent bulletin of the Superintendent of the Census for 1890 appear these significant words: "Up to and including 1880 the country had a frontier of settlement, but at present the unsettled area has been so broken into by isolated bodies of settlement that there can hardly be said to be a frontier line. In the discussion of its extent, its westward movement, etc., it can not, therefore, any longer have a place in the census reports." This brief official statement marks the closing of a great historic movement. Up to our own day American history has been in a large degree the history of the colonization of the Great West. The existence of an area of free land, its continuous recession, and the advance of American settlement westward, explain American development. (Frederick Jackson Turner, *The Significance of the Frontier in American History*, 1893.)

354. What the Mediterranean Sea was to the Greeks, breaking the bond of custom, offering new experiences, calling on new institutions and activities, that, and more, the ever retreating frontier has been to the United States directly, and to the nations of Europe more remotely. And now, four centuries from the discovery of America, at the end of a hundred years of life under the Constitution, the frontier has gone, and with its going has closed the first period of American history. (Ibid.)

IN TRIBUTE

355.

> O beautiful for spacious skies,
>   For amber waves of grain,
> For purple mountain majesties
>   Above the fruited plain!
>   America! America!

God shed His grace on thee
And crown thy good with brotherhood
From sea to shining sea!

(Katherine Lee Bates, from her poem "America the Beautiful," 1893.)

LOOKING AT A PANIC

356. The panic of 1893, like all periods of business depression, was a dismal time of radiating destruction. But it had its bright side, inside; it was good for the bears and for my education. The shorts rejoiced in the ruin; they made money, and they were happy. As a reporter on the side lines in the Stock Exchange I could see and hear and feel the wild joy of the bears on a day of tumbling prices, and it was a never-ending surprise to me, because everything I had read, heard, or imagined had pictured the dark depression, despair, and an anguish of the losers. And of course there were sufferers, some of them on the floor, others in the banks and brokerage houses, most of all, however, far from the market, out in the country—the public. Among the brokers generally, whether "on the floor" or in their offices, an active market, whether prices are rising or falling, means that business is good; and that's what one felt—the joy of a panic.

It's like a war, a revolution, a strike—like any crisis in human affairs when men have to walk up and face the consequences of their ignorance, folly, or wickedness—the panic of '93 was a period of bad times chiefly for the innocent. (Lincoln Steffens, remembering the Panic of 1893, *Autobiography*.)

A PLAN TO CURB LYNCHING

357. The recent terrible holocaust at Paris [Texas] is but an illustration to what extent the mob spirit will go when the laws are inadequate to check it. While the victim of that affair was guilty of an atrocious, barbarous crime, appalling to contemplate, for which he was certain of full punishment under the Constitution and laws of our State, our civilization stands aghast, a helpless witness to the most revolting execution of the age, in which large numbers of citizens openly, in broad day, publicly became murderers by methods revolting to humanity. . . .

To aid in suppressing mob violence in this State, I respectfully suggest a law embodying the following features:

1. That when any person, being a prisoner, or in a jail or other place of confinement . . . shall be taken from such place or authority in violation of law and put to death, the county within which such person was so held or confined, and from which he may have been so taken, shall be liable to pay a specified large sum to the surviving husband, wife, children, or parents of said person who shall so suffer death.

2. Make the county also liable for damages when any person not being a prisoner or under legal duress, is mobbed by two or more persons. . . .

3. Make such person or corporation also liable for damages who takes part in, or aids by acts, encourages by words or gestures, or who keeps watch, or in any way abets in the mobbing of a person.

4. Give the surviving relatives an action in the district court of any county where the murder was committed. . . .

5. Render the sheriff ineligible to hold his office, and provide for his removal when a prisoner is taken. . . .

6. Provide for a change of venue, either before or after indictment, in all cases of mob violence. (Governor James Hogg, message to the Texas legislature, February 6, 1893, from *Addresses and State Papers of James Stephen Hogg*, edited by Robert C. Cotner.)

[The lynching referred to by Hogg was of a "colored man" who had killed a three-year-old white child. Many hundreds of Texans had taken part in the torture and burning of the lynch victim. Two years after Hogg left office, the Texas legislature passed an anti-lynching law.]

HAYMARKET PARDONS

358. No man has the right to allow his ambition to stand in the way of the performance of a simple act of justice. (Governor John Peter Altgeld of Illinois, message pardoning the last three Haymarket defendants, Springfield, Illinois, June 26, 1893.)

[On May 4, 1886, a mass demonstration had been held in Haymarket Square, Chicago, by the eight-hour-day advocates. During the demonstration, police tried to disperse the crowd. A bomb was hurled, and several police were killed. Some of the demonstrators were arrested, tried, and executed for murder. Three were given long jail sentences, and these were the three pardoned by Altgeld. The act virtually ended his political career.]

REFLECTIONS

359. The holy passion of Friendship is of so sweet and steady and loyal and enduring a nature that it will last through a whole lifetime, if not asked to lend money. (Mark Twain, *Pudd'nhead Wilson's Calendar*, 1893–1894.)

360. When I reflect upon the number of disagreeable people I know have gone to a better world, I am moved to lead a different life. (Ibid.)

361. Nothing so needs reforming as other people's habits. (Ibid.)

362. If you pick up a starving dog and make him prosperous, he will not bite you. That is the principal difference between a dog and a man. (Ibid.)

VIEWS OF A COMPANY TOWN

363. [Pullman is a town] where all that is ugly and discordant and demoralizing is eliminated, and all that inspires to self-respect is generously provided. (Pullman Company official, early 1890s, cited in *The Great Struggle: Labor in America*, by Irving Werstein.)

364. You liked it or you lumped it. We had no choice, and we took what was dished out because in those days, jobs were hard to come by. (Pullman Company employee, recollection of early 1890s, ibid.)
[Pullman was a company town located just outside Chicago. The Pullman Palace Car Company owned everything in the town. Pullman workers lived there, paying rent and buying food from company-owned stores. Whatever an employee owed for rent, food and so on was deducted from his paycheck. The problem came when wages were cut while prices remained the same. In one instance, an employee received a paycheck for two cents. In the spring of 1894, the Pullman workers went out on strike.]

SETTLING UP ON THE FARM

365. Mrs. Vigell came up this morning, washed floor of little room, pantry & dining room, cleaned out cellar and white-washed walls—she is coming again in morning to wash safe & stain & scrub tables, clean up back room & help move stove. Also wash screen doors & refrigerator if there is time. When we settled last I forgot to count in the floor. I let her have 27 lbs. = .54 cts. and I owe her only for this day's work = .75 cts. I therefore owe her tonight .21 cts. She brought me 10 duck eggs also & I gave her a big satchel full of clothes, good, bad & indifferent. (Sarah Christie Stevens, diary excerpt, Minnesota, June 6, 1894, from James C. Christie and Family Papers, Minnesota Historical Society, St. Paul, cited in *The Female Experience: An American Documentary*, by Gerda Lerner.)

[Farmhands—especially domestic help—were often paid the equivalent of cash in produce or goods. Barter was common.]

PROTEST TELEGRAM

---

366. You have ordered Federal troops to go into service in the State of Illinois. Surely the facts have not been correctly presented to you in this case or you would have not taken this step, for it is entirely unnecessary, and, it seems to me, unjustifiable. . . . The local authorities have been able to handle the situation. . . . The Federal government has been applied to by men who had political and selfish motives for wanting to ignore the State government. (Governor John Peter Altgeld, telegram to President Grover, Cleveland, Springfield, Illinois, July 1894, cited in *The Great Struggle: Labor in America*, by Irving Werstein.)

[The troops had been called in during a strike against the Pullman Palace Car Company. The official reason for the troop movement was to protect U.S. mail delivery. By early August, the strike was broken.]

PANIC

---

367. They were bursting from their coats and their equipments as from entanglements. They charged down upon him like terrified buffaloes.

Behind them blue smoke curled and clouded above the treetops, and through the thickets he could sometimes see a distant pink glare. The voices of the cannon were clamoring in interminable chorus. . . .

The fight was lost. The dragons were coming with invincible strides. The army, helpless in the matted thickets and blinded by the overhanging night, was going to be swallowed. War, the red animal, war, the blood-swollen god, would have bloated fill. (Stephen Crane, from *The Red Badge of Courage*, a novel of the Civil War, 1895.)

CAST DOWN YOUR BUCKET

---

368. A ship lost at sea for many days suddenly sighted a friendly vessel. From the mast of the unfortunate vessel was seen a signal: "Water, water; we die of thirst!" The friendly vessel signalled: "Cast down your bucket where you are!"

The captain of the distressed vessel, at last heeding the call, cast down his bucket, and it came up full of fresh sparkling water from the mouth of the Amazon river.

To those of my race who depend on bettering their condition in a foreign land, or who underestimate the importance of cultivating friendly relations with the Southern white man, who is their next-door neighbor, I would say: "Cast down your bucket where you are." . . .

Cast it down in agriculture, mechanics, in commerce, in domestic service, in the professions.

Our greatest danger is that, in the great leap from slavery to freedom, we may overlook the fact that the masses of us are to live by our hands; and to keep in mind that we shall prosper in proportion as we learn to dignify and glorify common labor, and put brains and skill into the common occupations of life. (Booker T. Washington, speech, Atlanta, Georgia, September 1895.)

369. No race can prosper till it learns that there is as much dignity in tilling a field as in writing a poem. It is at the bottom of life we must begin, and not at the top. Nor should we permit our grievances to overshadow our opportunities. (Ibid.)

370. To those of the white race who look to the incoming of those of foreign birth and strange tongue and habits for the prosperity of the South, were I permitted I would repeat what I say to my own race, "Cast down your bucket where you are. . . .

Cast down your bucket among those people who have—without strikes and labor wars—tilled your fields, cleared your forests, built your railroads and cities, and brought forth treasures from the bowels of the earth, and helped show this magnificent progress of the South." (Ibid.)

371. In all things that are purely social we [blacks and whites] can be as separate as the fingers, yet one as the hand in all things essential to mutual progress. (Ibid.)

SEPARATE CAN BE EQUAL

372. The object of the [14th] Amendment was to enforce the full equality of the two races before the law. But this could not have meant complete social equality, as distinguished from political equality.

Laws permitting, and even requiring, the separation of blacks and whites do not necessarily mean the inferiority of either race to the other. Such laws have been recognized as part of the police power of the state. The most common instance of this is the establishment of separate schools for white and colored children, which has been upheld even by courts of States where the political rights of the colored race have been longest and most earnestly enforced. (*Plessy v. Ferguson*, U.S. Supreme Court, 1896.)

CROSS OF GOLD

373. There are two ideas of government. There are those who believe that, if you will only legislate to make the well-to-do prosperous, their prosperity will leak through on those below. The Democratic idea, however, has been that if you legislate to make the masses prosperous, their prosperity will find its way up through every class which rests upon them. (William Jennings Bryan, speech, Democratic National Convention, Chicago, July 8, 1896.)

374. It is the issue of 1776 over again. Our ancestors, when but three millions in number, had the courage to declare their political independence of every other nation; shall we, their descendants, when we have grown to 70 millions, declare that we are less independent than our forefathers? No, my friends, that will never be the verdict of our people. Therefore, we care not upon what lines the battle is fought. If they say bimetallism is good, but that we cannot have it until other nations help us, we reply that, instead of having a gold standard because England

has, we will restore bimetallism, and then let England have bimetallism because the United States has it. If they dare to come out in the open field and defend the gold standard as a good thing, we will fight them to the uttermost. Having behind us the producing masses of this nation and the world, supported by the commercial interests, the laboring interests, and the toilers everywhere, we will answer their demand for a gold standard by saying to them: You shall not press down upon the brow of labor this crown of thorns, you shall not crucify mankind upon a cross of gold. (Ibid.)

CONTROVERSIAL CABLES

In 1897 newspaper publisher William Randolph Hearst sent the team of war correspondent Richard Harding Davis and illustrator Frederic Remington to cover a reported rebellion on the island of Cuba, then owned by Spain. That much is agreed on by all historians. What is *not* agreed on is the authenticity of the following exchange of cables.

375. Everything is quiet. There is no trouble here. There will be no war. I wish to return. (Frederic Remington, cable to William Randolph Hearst from Cuba, 1897.)

376. Please remain. You furnish the pictures and I'll furnish the war. (William Randolph Hearst, response to Frederic Remington, from New York, 1897.)

[The immediate source for the cables is *Citizen Hearst*, by W. A. Swanberg. He cites as his own source *On the Great Highway*, by James Creelman, published in 1901. Some scholars now question Creelman's reliability, pointing out that neither Remington nor Davis ever confirmed it and that Hearst flatly denied it. The quotes appear in this book as a piece of Americana.]

EDITORIAL RESPONSE

Eight-year-old Virginia O'Hanlon writes a letter to the *New York Sun*. Some of her friends have told her that there is no Santa Claus, and Virginia wants to know the truth. Is there a Santa Claus? The answer appears in an editorial.

377. Yes, Virginia, there is a Santa Claus. He exists as certainly as love and generosity and devotion exist, and you know that they abound and give to your life its highest beauty and joy. Alas! how dreary would be the world if there were no Santa Claus! . . . There would be no child-like faith, no poetry, no romance to make tolerable this existence. . . .

You might get your papa to hire men to watch in all the chimneys on Christmas eve to catch Santa Claus, but even if you did not see Santa Claus coming down, what would that prove? Nobody sees Santa Claus, but that is no sign that there is no Santa Claus. The most real things in the world are those that neither children nor men can see. . . .

Nobody can conceive or imagine all the wonders there are unseen and unseeable in the world. . . . Only faith, fancy, poetry, love, romance, can push aside that curtain and view and picture the supernal beauty and glory beyond. Is it all real? Ah, Virginia, in all this world there is nothing else real and abiding.

No Santa Claus? Thank God he lives, and he lives forever. A thousand years from now, Virginia, nay, ten times ten thousand years from now, he will continue to make glad the heart of childhood. (Francis P. Church, editorial, *New York Sun*, September 27, 1897.)

ITCHING FOR WAR

378. I would regard war with Spain from two viewpoints: First, the advisability on the ground both of humanity and self-interest of interfering on behalf of the Cubans, and of taking one more step forward the complete freeing of America from European domination; second, the benefit done to the people by giving them something to think of which isn't material gain, and especially the benefit done our military forces by trying both the Army and Navy in actual practise. I should be very sorry not to see us make the experiment of trying to land, and therefore to feed and clothe, an expeditionary force, if only for the sake of learning from our blunders. I should hope that the force would have some fighting to do. It would be a great lesson, and we would profit much by it. (Theodore Roosevelt, assistant secretary of the navy, private correspondence, November 18, 1897, cited in *Theodore Roosevelt: A Biography*, by Henry F. Pringle.)

CALL FOR INTERVENTION

379. The forcible intervention of the United States as a neutral to stop the war [between Cuba and Spain], according to the large dictates of humanity and following many historical precedents where neighboring states have interfered to check the hopeless sacrifices of life by internecine conflicts beyond their borders, is justifiable on rational grounds. It involves, however, hostile constraint upon both the parties to the contest, as well to enforce a truce as to guide the eventual settlement.

The grounds for such intervention may be briefly summarized as follows:

First. In the cause of humanity and to put an end to the barbarities, bloodshed, starvation, and horrible miseries now existing there. . . .

Second. We owe it to our citizens in Cuba to afford to them . . . protection and indemnity for life and property. . . .

Third. The right to intervene may be justified by the very serious injury to the commerce, trade, and business of our people and by the wanton destruction of property and devastation of the island.

Fourth. . . . The present condition of affairs in Cuba is a constant menace to our peace and entails upon this Government enormous expense. With such a conflict waged for years in an island so near us and with which our people have such trade and business relations; when the lives and liberty of our citizens are in constant danger and their property destroyed and themselves ruined; where our trading vessels are liable to seizure and are seized at our very door by warships of a foreign nation; . . . [these things] are a constant menace to our peace and compel us to keep on a semi war footing with a nation with which we are at peace.

These elements of danger and disorder . . . have been strikingly illustrated by a tragic event which has deeply and justly moved the American people. . . . the destruction of the battleship *Maine* in the harbor of Havana during the night of the 15th of February. . . .

I ask the Congress to authorize and empower the President to take measures to secure a full and final termination of hostilities between the Government of Spain and the people of Cuba, and to secure in the island the establishment of a stable government, capable of maintaining order. (William McKinley, message to Congress, April 11, 1898.)

ASSESSING A WAR

380. It has been a splendid little war, begun with the highest motives, carried on with magnificent intelligence and spirit, favored by that fortune which loves the brave. (John Hay, U.S. ambassador to England, letter to Colonel Theodore Roosevelt, Summer 1898, cited in *The Splendid Little War*, by Frank Freidel.)

PORTENT IN A PAINTING

381.

Bowed by the weight of centuries he leans
Upon his hoe and gazes on the ground,
The emptiness of ages in his face,
And on his back the burden of the world.
A thing that grieves not and that never hopes,
Stolid and stunned, a brother to the ox?
Who loosened and let down this brutal jaw?
Whose was the hand that slanted back this brow?
Whose breath blew out the light within this brain? . . .
There is no shape more terrible than this—
More tongued with censure of the world's blind greed—
More filled with signs and portents for the soul—
More fraught with menace to the universe. . . .
O masters, lords and rulers in all lands,
How will the Future reckon with this Man?
How answer his brute question in that hour
When whirlwinds of rebellion shake the world?

(Edwin Markham, from his poem "The Man with the Hoe," 1899.)

[Markham wrote the poem after viewing Millet's painting.]

THE ROLE OF CHARACTER

382. [T]here is much less need for genius or oratory or special brilliancy in the administration of our government than there is need of such homely virtues and qualities as common sense, honesty, and courage. (Governor Theodore Roosevelt, Inaugural Address as governor, Albany, New York, January 2, 1899, cited in *The Inaugural Addresses of 20th-Century American Presidents*, edited by Halford Ryan.)

A FAMOUS ESSAY

383. In all this Cuban business there is one man stands out on the horizon of my memory. . . . When war broke out between Spain and the United States, it was very necessary to communicate quickly with the leader of the Insurgents. Garcia was somewhere in the mountain fastnesses of Cuba. . . . The President must secure his cooperation, and quickly. What to do?

Someone said to the President, "There is a fellow by the name of Rowan will find Garcia for you, if anybody can." . . .

How the fellow . . . took the letter, sealed it up in an oilskin pouch, strapped it over his heart . . . , landed by night on the coast of Cuba from an open boat, disappeared into the jungle, and in three weeks came out on the other side of the island, having traversed a hostile country on foot, and delivered his letter to Garcia—are things I have no special desire now to tell in detail. The point I wish to make is this: McKinley gave Rowan a letter to be delivered to Garcia; Rowan took the letter and did not ask, "Where is he at?" By the Eternal, there is a man whose form should be cast in deathless, bronze and the statue placed in every college of the land. It is not book-learning young men need, nor instruction about this and that, but a stiffening of the vertebrae which will cause them to be loyal to a trust, to act promptly, concentrate their energies, do the thing— "Carry a message to Garcia." . . .

You, reader, put this matter to a test: . . . Summon any one [of your clerks] and make this request: "Please look in the encyclopedia and make a brief memorandum for me concerning the life of Correggio."

Will the Clerk quietly say, "Yes, sir," and go the task?

On your life he will not. He will look at you out of a fishy eye and ask one or
more of the following questions:

Who was he?

Which encyclopedia?

Where is the encyclopedia?

Was I hired for that?

Don't you mean Bismarck?

What's the matter with Charlie doing it?

Is he dead?

Is there any hurry? . . .

What do you want to know for? . . .

And this incapacity for independent action, this moral stupidity, this infirmity
of the will, this unwillingness to cheerfully catch hold and lift—these are things
that put pure Socialism so far into the future. If men will not act for themselves,
what will they do when the benefit of their effort is for all? . . .

We have recently been hearing much maudlin sympathy expressed for the
"downtrodden denizens of the sweat-shop" and the "homeless wanderer searching
for the honest employment," and with it all often go many hard words for the
men in power.

Nothing is said about the employer who grows old before his time in a vain
attempt to get frowsy ne'er-do-wells to do intelligent work. . . .

My heart goes out to the man who does his work when the "boss" is away, as
well as when he is at home. And the man who, when given a letter for Garcia,
quietly takes the missive, without asking any idiotic questions, and with no lurk-
ing intention of chucking it into the nearest sewer. . . .

Civilization is one long, anxious search for just such individuals. . . . The world
cries out for such; he is needed, and needed badly—the man who can carry A
MESSAGE TO GARCIA. (Elbert Hubbard, "A Message to Garcia," article in
the *Philistine*, March 1899.)

[This was the most famous essay of its time, not just in the United States but around the
world in many languages. Hubbard embellished the history. Lieutenant Andrew Rowan
was assigned to the Military Information Bureau, better known today as military intelligence. The army sent Rowan on a mission to Cuba to meet with General Calixto Garcia,
the Cuban rebel leader. The mission was to get information on the disposition of Spanish
military forces on the island. It was the message *from* Garcia that was crucial.]

DUTY OF THE VERY RICH

384. To set an example of modest, unostentatious living, shunning display or
extravagance; to provide moderately for the legitimate wants of those dependent

upon him; and, after doing so, to consider all surplus revenues which come to him simply as trust funds, which he is called upon to administer, and strictly bound as a matter of duty to administer in the manner which, in his judgment, is best calculated to produce the most beneficial results for the community—the man of wealth thus becoming the mere trustee and agent for his poorer brethren, bringing to their service his superior wisdom, experience, and ability to administer, doing for them better than they would or could do for themselves. (Andrew Carnegie, from *The Gospel of Wealth*, 1900.)

Editorial cartoon from 1906 shows President Theodore Roosevelt at La Boca, the Pacific entrance to the Panama Canal, then under construction.

11

America as a World Power

With the conclusion of the Spanish-American War, the United States became a global power. President Theodore Roosevelt began building a strong navy and took the necessary military steps to support Panamanian independence from Colombia. This ensured America's stake in a Panama Canal. When World War I erupted, both sides in the conflict sought American aid. When Imperial Germany decided on a policy of unrestricted submarine warfare—and promised Mexico the territory that it had lost in the Mexican War—America tilted in favor of the Allies. American military power helped decide the outcome of the war.

HYPOCRISY IN THE HOUSE?

385. [Turning to the Democratic side of the congressional aisle:]
   It is amazing to a Populist to hear members upon this side of the House declare that "this is a white man's government," and justify a property and educational qualification to exclude the black man from the right of suffrage and at the same time denounce the Republican party for trying to govern the brown man without his consent [This is a reference to American rule over the Philippines.]. . . .
   [Turning to the Republican side of the aisle:]
   As a Populist, I am much more amazed to observe members upon the other side of this House dramatize indignation because a black man is occasionally deprived of life without due process of law [lynched], and in the same breath laud

the Administration for shooting salvation and submission into the brown man because he wants to be free. . . .

Nations should have the same right among nations that men have among men. The right to life, liberty, and the pursuit of happiness is as dear to the black and brown man as to the white; as precious to the poor as to the rich; as just to the ignorant as to the educated; as sacred to the weak as to the strong, and as applicable to nations as to individuals, and the nation which subverts such right by force is not better governed than the man who takes the law in his own hands. (Representative William Neville, speech, House of Representative, Washington, D.C., February 6, 1900, *Congressional Record*, 56th Congress, First Session, cited in *Populism: The Humane Preference in America, 1890–1900*, by Gene Clanton.)

PHILOSOPHY

386. Speak softly and carry a big stick; you will go far. (President Theodore Roosevelt, speech, Minnesota State Fair, September 2, 1901.)

HISTORIC OCCASION

387. Dear Mr. President: I shall be very glad to accept your invitation for dinner this evening at 7:30. (Booker T. Washington, note to President Theodore Roosevelt, Washington, D.C., October 16, 1901, cited in *Theodore Roosevelt: A Biography*, by Henry F. Pringle.)

ON CORPORATE POWER

388. [When I became president] [t]he total absence of governmental control had led to a portentous growth of corporations. In no other country was such power held by the men who had gained these fortunes. The Government [was] practically impotent. Of all forms of tyranny the least attractive and the most vulgar is the tyranny of mere wealth, the tyranny of a plutocracy. (Theodore Roosevelt, recalling events of 1901, from his memoirs, cited in *Theodore Roosevelt: A Biography*, by Henry F. Pringle.)

ON THE PHILIPPINE INSURRECTION

389. Th' counthry [the Philippines] may be divided into two parts, pollytically—where th' insurrection continues an' where it will soon be. Th' brave but I fear not altogether cheery army conthrols th' insurrected parts be martiyal law, but th' civil authorities are supreme in their own house. Th' diff'rence between civil law an' martiyal law in th' Ph'lippeens is what kind iv coat th' judge wears. Th' raysult is much th' same. Th' two branches wurruks in perfect harmony. We bag thim in th' city an' they round them up in th' counthry. ("Mr. Dooley" [Finley Peter Dunne] satirically quoting an "expert" on American policy in the Philippines, 1902.)

390. It is not always necessary to kill a Filipino American right away. Me desire is to idjacate thim slowly in the ways an' customs iv th' counthry. We ar-re givin' hundherds iv these pore benighted haythen th' well-known, ol'-fshioned American wather cure. Iv course, ye know how 'tis done. A Filipino, we'll say, niver heerd iv th' histhry iv this counthry. He is met be wan iv our sturdy boys . . . who asts him to cheer f'r Abraham Lincoln. He rayfuses. He is thin placed upon th' grass an' given a dhrink, a baynit bein' fixed in his mouth so he cannot reject th' hospitality. Undher th' inflooence iv th' hose that cheers but does not inebriate, he soon warms or perhaps I might say swells up to a ralization iv th' granjoor iv his adoptive counthry. One gallon makes him give three groans f'r th' constitchoochion. At four gallons, he will ask to be wrapped in th' flag. . . .

Among th' mos' useful Spanish customs is reconcenthration. Our reconcenthration camps is among th' mos' thickly popylataed in the wurrld. (Ibid.)

PROBLEM OF THE CENTURY

391. The problem of the 20th century is the problem of the color line. (W.E.B. Du Bois, *The Souls of Black Folk*, 1903.)

392. One ever feels his twoness—an American, a Negro; two souls, two thoughts, two unreconciled strivings; two warring ideals in one dark body, whose dogged strength alone keeps it from being torn asunder. (Ibid.)

393. We are absolutely certain that the way for a people to gain their reasonable rights is not by voluntarily throwing them away and insisting that they do not want them. The way for a people to gain respect is not by continually belittling and ridiculing themselves. On the contrary, Negroes must insist continually, in season and out of season, that voting is necessary to modern manhood, that color discrimination is barbarism, and that black boys need education as well as white boys. (Ibid.)

12 SECONDS OF HISTORY

394. Wilbur having used his turn in the unsuccessful attempt on the 14th [of December], the right to the first trial now belonged to me. After running the motor a few minutes to heat it up, I released the wire that held the machine to the track, and the machine started forward into the wind. Wilbur ran at the side of the machine, holding the wing to balance it on the track. Unlike the start on the 14th, made in a calm, the machine, facing a 27-mile wind, started very slowly. Wilbur was able to stay with it till it lifted from the track after a forty-foot run. . . .

The course of the flight up and down was exceedingly erratic, partly due to the irregularity of the air and partly to lack of experience in handling this machine. The control of the front rudder was difficult on account of its being balanced too near the center. This gave it a tendency to turn itself when started, so that it turned too far on one side and then too far on the other. As a result, the machine would rise suddenly to about ten feet, and then as suddenly dart for the ground. . . .

[T]he speed of the machine . . . was over 45 feet per second, and the length of the flight was equivalent to a flight of 540 feet made in calm air.

This flight lasted only 12 seconds, but it was the first in the history of the world in which a machine carrying a man had raised itself by its own power into the air in full flight, had sailed forward without reduction of speed, and had finally landed at a point as high as that from which it started. (Orville Wright, Kitty Hawk, North Carolina, events of December 17, 1903, quoted in *The Wright Brothers*, by Fred C. Kelly.)

BUSINESS AND POLITICS

395. I have sometimes heard men say politics must have nothing to do with business, and I have often wished that business had nothing to do with politics. (Woodrow Wilson, president of Princeton University, speech, American Institute of Bank Clerks, New York, May 13, 1904, cited in *Presidential Wit*, edited by Bill Adler.)

TAMMANY POLITICS

396. There's only one way to hold a district; you must study human nature and act accordin'. You can' study human nature in books. Books is a hindrance more than anything else. If you have been to college, so much the worse for you. You'll have to unlearn all you learned before you can get right down to human nature, and unlearnin' takes a lot of time. . . . To learn real human nature you have to go among the people, see them and be seen. I know every man, woman, and child in the 15th District, except them that's been born this summer—and I know some of them, too. I know what they like and what they don't like, what they are strong at and what they are weak in, and I reach them by approachin' at the right side. (George Washington Plunkitt, quoted in *Plunkitt of Tammany Hall*, by William L. Riordon, 1905.)

397. Everybody is talkin' these days about Tammany men growin' rich on graft, but nobody thinks of drawin' the distinction between honest graft and dishonest graft. There's all the difference in the world between the two. There's many of our men have grown rich in politics. I have myself. I've made a big fortune out of the game, and I'm gettin' richer every day, but I've not gone in for dishonest graft—blackmailin' gamblers, saloonkeepers, disorderly people, etc. . . .

There's an honest graft, and I'm an example of how it works. I might sum up the whole thing by sayin': "I seen my opportunities and I took 'em."

Just let me explain by examples. My party's in power in the city, and it's goin' to undertake a lot of public improvements. Well, I'm tipped off, say, that they're going to lay out a new park at a certain place.

I see my opportunity and I take it. I go to that place and I buy up all the land I can in the neighborhood. Then the board of this or that makes its plan public, and there is a rush to get my land, which nobody cared particular for before. (Ibid.)

A QUESTION OF DUTY

---

398. Esteemed Editor:

I hope that you will advise me in my present difficulty.

I am a "greenhorn," only five weeks in the country, and a jeweler by trade. I come from Russia, where I left a blind father and a stepmother. Before I left, my father asked me not to forget him. I promised that I would send him the first money I earned in America.

When I arrived in New York I walked around for two weeks looking for a job, and the bosses told me it was after the season. In the third week I was lucky, and found a job at which I earn eight dollars a week. I worked, I paid my landlady board, I bought a few things to wear, and I have a few dollars in my pocket.

Now I want you to advise me what to do. Shall I send my father a few dollars for Passover, or should I keep the little money for myself? In this place the work will end soon and I may be left without a job. The question is how to deal with the situation. I will do as you tell me.

EDITOR'S ANSWER:

The answer to this young man is that he should send his father the few dollars for Passover because, since he is young, he will find it easier to earn a living than would his blind father in Russia. (Letter to the editor, *Jewish Daily Forward*, and the editor's response, 1906, from *A Bintel Brief*, edited by Isaac Metzker.)

THE SPOILED-MEAT INDUSTRY

---

399. It was the custom . . . whenever meat was so spoiled that it could not be used for anything else, either to can it or else to chop it up into sausage. . . . [Those working on the inside] could now study the whole of the spoiled-meat industry . . . and read a new and grim meaning into that old Packingtown jest— that they use everything of the pig except the squeal. (Upton Sinclair, from his novel *The Jungle*, 1906.)

400. Jonas had told them how the meat that was taken out of pickle would often be found sour, and how they would rub it up with soda to take away the smell, and sell it to be eaten on free-lunch counters; also of all the miracles of chemistry which they performed, giving to any sort of meat, fresh or salted, whole or chopped, any color and any flavor and any odor they chose. (Ibid.)

401. In the pickling of hams they had an ingenious apparatus, by which they saved time and increased the capacity of the plant—a machine consisting of a hollow needle attached to a pump; by plunging this needle into the meat and working with his foot a man could fill a ham with pickle in a few seconds. And yet, in spite of this, there would be hams found spoiled, some of them with an odor so bad that a man could hardly bear to be in the room with them. To pump into these the packers had a second and much stronger pickle which destroyed the odor. . . . Also, after the hams had been smoked, there would be found some that had gone to the bad. Formerly these had been sold as "Number Three Grade," but later on some ingenious person had hit upon a new device, and now they would extract the bone, about which the bad part generally lay, and insert in the hole a white-hot iron. After this invention there was no longer Number One, Two, and Three Grade—there was only Number One Grade. (Ibid.)

[Years after his book was published, Sinclair commented that he had tried to reach the heart of America—but had apparently succeeded in reaching only its stomach.]

VISIONARY

---

402. The public must learn that the blind man is neither a genius nor a freak nor an idiot. He has a mind which can be educated, a hand which can be trained, ambitions which it is right for him to strive to realize, and it is the duty of the public to help him make the best of himself so that he can win light through work. (Helen Keller, 1907, cited in *Helen Keller: A Life*, by Dorothy Herrmann.)

A BIG STICK

---

403. Proceed to duty assigned. (President Theodore Roosevelt, message to U.S. fleet, Hampton Roads, Virginia, December 16, 1907.)

[Ostensibly on a goodwill tour, the American fleet was intended to show to the world—but especially to Japan—that the United States had a powerful navy that it was ready to use. The fleet cruised around the world, completing its voyage on February 22, 1909.]

GOD'S CRUCIBLE

---

404. America is God's crucible, the great melting pot where all the races of Europe are melting and reforming. (Israel Zangwill, from his play *The Melting Pot*, 1908.)

MAN AND DOG IN THE YUKON

It is the dead of winter. A man and his husky set out on foot for a camp in the Alaska wilderness. It is 75 degrees below zero. Along the trail, where a hidden spring lies beneath the snow, the man falls through into the icy water. His feet are soaked halfway to his knees. He starts a fire to dry off, but it is doused by snow from an over-hanging bough. He tries to start a second fire, but by now his hands are frozen. He strikes a match with his teeth, but it fails to ignite the wet twigs. Nothing works, and he realizes that he will surely freeze to death unless he can find some way to get warm.

405. The sight of the dog put a wild idea into his head. He remembered the tale of the man, caught in a blizzard, who killed a steer and crawled inside the carcass, and so was saved. He would kill the dog and bury his hands in the warm body until the numbness went out of them. Then he could build another fire. He spoke to the dog, calling it to him, but in his voice was a strange note of fear that frightened the animal, who had never known the man to speak in such a way before. Something was the matter, and its suspicious nature sensed danger—it knew not what danger, but somewhere, somehow, in its brain arose an apprehension of the man. It flattened its ears down at the sound of the man's voice. . . . [B]ut it would not come to the man.

He got on his hands and knees and crawled toward the dog. This unusual posture again excited suspicion, and the animal sidled mincingly away.

The man sat up in the snow for a moment and struggled for calmness. Then he pulled on his mittens, by means of his teeth, and got up on his feet. He glanced down at first in order to assure himself that he was really standing up, for the absence of sensation in his feet left him unrelated to the earth. His erect position in itself started to drive the webs of suspicion from the dog's mind; and when he spoke peremptorily, with the sound of whip lashes in his voice, the dog rendered its customary allegiance and came to him. As it came within reaching distance, the man lost his control. His arms flashed out to the dog, and he experienced genuine surprise when he discovered that his hands could not clutch, that there was neither bend nor feeling in his fingers. He had forgotten for the moment that they were frozen and that they were freezing more and more. All this happened quickly, and before the animal could get away, he encircled its body with his arms. He sat down in the snow, and in this fashion held the dog, while it snarled and whined and struggled.

But it was all he could do, hold its body encircled in his hands and sit there. He realized that he could not kill the dog. There was no way to do it, with his helpless hands he could neither draw nor hold his sheath knife nor throttle the animal. He released it, and it plunged wildly away, with tail between its legs, and still snarling. It halted forty feet away and surveyed him curiously, with ears sharply pricked forward. The man looked down at his hands in order to locate them, and found them hanging on the ends of his arms. It struck him as curious that one should have to use his eyes in order to find out where his hands were. . . .

Then the man drowsed off into what seemed to him the most comfortable and satisfying sleep he had ever known. The dog sat facing him and waiting. . . . But the man remained silent. Later the dog whined loudly. And still later it crept close to the man and caught the scent of death. This made the animal bristle and back away. A little longer it delayed, howling under the stars that leaped and danced and shone brightly in the cold sky. Then it turned and trotted up the trail in the direction of the camp it knew, where there were other food providers and fire providers. (Jack London, from his short story "To Build a Fire," 1908.)

RACIAL VIEWS

406. My chief purpose is not to effect a change in the electoral vote of the Southern States [for denying the vote to blacks]. That is a secondary consideration. (President William Howard Taft, Inaugural Address, Washington, D.C., March 4, 1909.)

407. The colored men must base their hope on the results of their own industry, self-restraint, thrift, and business success, as well as upon the aid and comfort and sympathy which they may receive from their white neighbors of the South. (Ibid.)

408. The negroes are now Americans. Their ancestors came here years ago against their will and this is their only country and their only flag. They have shown themselves anxious to live for it and to die for it. (Ibid.)

THE MEANING OF AMERICA

409. Our country—this great Republic—means nothing unless it means the triumph of a real democracy, the triumph of popular government, and, in the long run, of an economic system under which each man shall be guaranteed the opportunity to show the best that there is in him. That is why the history of America is now the central feature of the history of the world; for the world has set its face hopefully toward our democracy. (Theodore Roosevelt, *The New Nationalism*, 1910.)

410. I stand for the square deal. But when I say that . . . I mean not merely that I stand for fair play under the present rules of the game, but that I stand for having those rules changed so as to work for a more substantial equality of opportunity and of reward for equally good service . . . When I say I want a square deal for the poor man, I do not mean that I want a square deal for the man who remains poor because he has not got the energy to work for himself. (Ibid.)

LABOR SONG

411. [To the tune of "In the Sweet Bye and Bye":]

You will eat, bye and bye,
In that glorious land above the sky;
Work and pray, live on hay,
You'll get pie in the sky when you die.

(Joe Hill, from his song "The Preacher and the Slave," *The Little Red Song Book*, 1911.)

ABOUT THE CANAL

412. I am interested in the Panama Canal because I started it. If I had followed conventional, conservative methods, I should have submitted a dignified state paper to the Congress and the debate would have been going on yet, but I took the canal zone and let Congress debate, and while the debate goes on the canal does also. (Theodore Roosevelt, speech, University of California, March 23, 1911, cited in *Theodore Roosevelt: A Biography*, by Henry F. Pringle.)

THE TRIANGLE FIRE

413. I got in at half past eight, and we got out at four o'clock. When we left, we never went out of the front door. We always went one by one out the back. There was a man there searching, because the people were afraid we would take something, so that door was always locked.

We were just leaving that Saturday. I was fixing my hair at my [sewing] machine. The cutters were right there. They generally lit a cigarette when they got out. The man was right there. His match lit the scraps under the table. Suddenly, another cutter said, "C'mon, let's run!"

I said, "Ooh, my God, a fire." I ran and I left everything—pocketbook. I was running and the people were all at the door. I saw the people throwing themselves out the window. . . . The door was locked. . . . We were hollering and crying. "Open the door!" [Finally the door was unlocked and workers fled down to the street.] (Pauline Cuoio Pepe, Triangle Shirtwaist Factory, New York City, recalling events of March 25, 1911, quoted in *You Must Remember This*, by Jeff Kisselhoff.)

[Some 147 lives were lost, mostly women and girls. Triangle had the top three floors of a 10-story building, but fire ladders could reach no higher than the sixth floor. Factory owners were tried and acquitted, but new labor and fire laws were enacted.]

THE RIGHT TO KNOW

414. The concern of patriotic men is to put our government again on its right basis, by substituting the popular will for the rule of guardians, the processes of common counsel for those of private arrangement. In order to do this, a first necessity is to open the doors and let in the light on all affairs which the people have a right to know about.

In the first place, it is necessary to open up all the processes of our politics. They have been too secret, too complicated, too roundabout; they have consisted too much of private conferences and secret understandings, of the control of legislation by men who were not legislators, but who stood outside and dictated, controlling oftentimes by very questionable means, which they would not have dreamed of allowing to become public. The whole process must be altered. . . . The very fact that so much in politics is done in the dark, behind closed doors, promotes suspicion. Everybody knows that corruption thrives in secret places and avoids public places, and we believe it a fair presumption that secrecy means impropriety. . . .

"Let there be light!" (Governor Woodrow Wilson, presidential campaign speech, autumn 1912.)

TAXING INCOME

415. The Congress shall have power to lay and collect taxes on incomes, from whichever source derived, without apportionment among the several States and without regard to any census or enumeration. (16th Amendment, February 25, 1913.)

TIME TO CLEANSE

416. Our duty is to cleanse, to reconsider, to restore, to correct the evil without impairing the good, to purify and humanize every process of our common life without weakening or sentimentalizing it. There has been something crude and heartless and unfeeling in our haste to succeed and be great. Our thought has been "Let every man look out for himself, let every generation look out for itself," while we reared giant machinery which made it impossible that any but those who stood at the levers of control should have a chance to look out for themselves. (President Woodrow Wilson, First Inaugural Address, Washington, D.C., March 4, 1913.)

417. The Nation has been deeply stirred, stirred by a solemn passion, stirred by the knowledge of wrong, of ideals lost, of government too often debauched and made an instrument of evil. (Ibid.)

418. We shall deal with our economic system as it is and as it may be modified, not as it might be if we had a clean sheet of paper to write upon; and step by step we shall make it what it should be, in the spirit of those who question their own wisdom and seek counsel and knowledge, not shallow self-satisfaction or the excitement of excursions whither they can not tell. Justice, and only justice, shall always be our motto. (Ibid.)

POPULAR VOTE FOR SENATE

419. The Senate of the United States shall be composed of two senators from each State, elected by the people thereof. (17th Amendment, May 31, 1913.)

ANTI-SALOON LEAGUE: HISTORIAN'S VIEW

Founded in 1895, the Anti-Saloon League campaigned to prohibit the production and sale of alcoholic beverages in the United States. Its campaign for a constitutional amendment began in 1913. By 1919 the 18th Amendment—on Prohibition—would be ratified.

420. The decision of 1913 to seek what became the 18th Amendment signified that the Anti-Saloon League was in a position to operate on a national scale as a political arm of American evangelical Protestantism. The decision, moreover, was taken at a time of general reform, "progressivism," that proved, in retrospect, special in American history. Public sentiment favorable to prohibition appeared to be growing as part of a more general reform consensus among Protestant Americans. Most important for the league as a reform organization, almost all prohibitionists were accepting its leadership and nonpartisan methods. . . .

[W]ith a new administration entering the White House determined to achieve important social and economic reforms, and with so much of the nation's territory already under dry statutes, not only did conditions seem favorable for the national campaign, but a constitutional amendment was apparently the only practical method of exercising control over the large urban areas that resisted all dry reform efforts.

The campaign for national prohibition involved much more than electioneering and lobbying. The campaign reshaped the Anti-Saloon League in important ways. The league needed to enlarge the dry constituency, a task that required far larger organization and one supplied by adequate funds. The league needed to reach out to persons who did not attend services regularly in the Protestant churches. The league had, in short, to mount a tremendous educational and propaganda campaign to expand public support while maintaining its strength in the areas that had already chosen to outlaw the liquor traffic. (K. Austin Kerr, historian, events of 1913, from *Organized for Prohibition: A New History of the Anti-Saloon League.*)

CAN A LENDER BE NEUTRAL?

421. Morgan Company of New York have asked whether there would be any objection to their making a loan to the French Government. . . . I have conferred with Mr. [Robert] Lansing [counsel to the State Department on legal affairs] and he knows of no legal objection to financing this loan. [B]ut I have suggested to him the advisability of presenting to you an aspect of the case which is not legal but . . . whether it would be advisable for this Government to take the position that it will not approve of any loan to a belligerent nation. The reasons. . . . :

First: Money is the worst of all contrabands because it commands everything else. . . . I know of nothing that would do more to prevent war than an international agreement that neutral nations would not loan to belligerents. . . .

Second: . . . If we approved of a loan to France we could not, of course, object to a loan to Great Britain, Germany, Russia, Austria or to any other country, and if loans were made to these countries, our citizens would be divided into groups, each group loaning money to the country which it favors and this money could not be furnished without expressions of sympathy. These expressions of sympathy are disturbing enough when they do not rest upon pecuniary inter-ests—they would be still more disturbing if each group was pecuniarily interested in the success of the nation to whom its members had loaned money.

Third: The powerful financial interests which would be connected with these loans would be tempted to use their influence through the newspapers to support the interests of the Government to which they had loaned because the value of the security would be directly affected by the results of the war. We would thus find our newspapers violently arrayed on one side or the other, each paper sup-porting a financial group and pecuniary interest. . . .

As we cannot prevent American citizens going abroad at their own risk, so we cannot prevent dollars going abroad at the risk of the owners, but the influence of the Government is used to prevent American citizens from doing this. Would the Government not be justified in using its influence against the enlistments of the nation's dollars in a foreign war? (William Jennings Bryan, secretary of state, memo to President Woodrow Wilson, August 10, 1914, cited in Senate Inves-tigation of the Munitions Industry, 74th Congress, second session.)

[In 1915 Bryan would resign, to be replaced by Lansing.]

AMERICAN VALUES

422. I have tried to know what America is, what her people think, what they are, what they most cherish and hold dear. I hope that some of their finer passions are in my own heart—some of the great conceptions and desires which gave birth to this Government and which have made the voice of this people a voice of peace and hope and liberty among the peoples of the world, and that speak my own thoughts. I shall, at least in part, speak theirs also, however faintly and inadequately, upon this vital matter.

We are at peace with all the world. No one who speaks counsel based on fact or drawn from a just and candid interpretation of realities can say that there is reason to fear that from any quarter our independence or the integrity of our territory is threatened. Dread of the power of any other nation we are incapable of. We are not jealous of rivalry in the fields of commerce or of any other peaceful achievement. We mean to live our own lives as we want; but we mean also to let live. We are, indeed, a true friend to all the nations of the world, because we threaten none, covet the possessions of none, desire the overthrow of none. Our friendship can be accepted and is accepted without reservation, because it is offered in a spirit and for a purpose which no one need ever question or suspect. Therein lies our greatness. (President Woodrow Wilson, annual message to Con-gress, December 8, 1914.)

THE RIGHT TO FISH

423. God created this Indian country and it was like He spread out a big blanket. He put the Indians on it. They were created here in this country, truly and honestly, and that was the time this river started to run. Then God created fish in this river and put deer in these mountains and made laws through which has come the increase of fish and game. (Meninock, testimony at his trial for violating the salmon fishing code of the state of Washington, 1915, from *The Washington Historical Quarterly*, July 1928.)

424. I was not brought from a foreign country and did not come here. I was put here by the Creator. We had no cattle, no hogs, no grain, only berries and roots and game and fish. We never thought we would be troubled about these things, and I tell my people, and I believe, it is not wrong for us to get this food. (Ibid.)

WHITE HOUSE SCREENING

425. It is like writing history with lightning. And my only regret is that it is all so terribly true. (President Woodrow Wilson, attributed, following a screening of the movie *The Birth of a Nation*, February 18, 1915, cited in *D. W. Griffith: An American Life*, by Richard Schickel.)

[*The Birth of a Nation*, directed by D. W. Griffith, is one of the most controversial movies ever made. Based on the book *The Clansman*, by Thomas Dixon Jr., it told the story of the Civil War and Reconstruction. But it portrayed the Ku Klux Klan in a favorable light, protecting southern womanhood. Following protests by blacks and liberals, the White House denied the endorsement. Most film scholars believe that the quotation is accurate. Wilson and Dixon had been academic colleagues, and Dixon had asked the president if he could show the movie to him in the White House. It was, he had promised, an extraordinary new medium.]

ADVERTISEMENT

426. NOTICE!

Travellers intending to embark on the Atlantic voyage are reminded that a state of war exists between Germany and her allies and Great Britain and her allies; that the zone of war includes the waters adjacent to the British Isles; that, in accordance with formal notice given by the Imperial German Government, vessels flying the flag of Great Britain, or of any of her allies, are liable to destruction in those waters and that travellers sailing in the war zone on ships of Great Britain or her allies do so at their own risk. (Imperial German Embassy, Washington, D.C., April 22, 1915, advertisement placed in several New York newspapers, May 1, 1915.)

[On May 1 the British ship *Lusitania* sailed out of New York and headed for Liverpool, England. On May 7 the ship was hit by two German torpedoes off the Irish coast and sank in 18 minutes. Some 1,198 died, including 128 Americans.]

BEING RIGHT

427. There is such a thing as a man being too proud to fight. There is such a thing as a nation being so right that it does not need to convince others by force that it is right. (President Woodrow Wilson, speech, Philadelphia, May 10, 1915.)

ON BEING AN AMERICAN

428. There is no room in this country for hyphenated Americanism . . . [This] would . . . permit it to become a tangle of squabbling nationalities. (Theodore Roosevelt, speech, New York, October 12, 1915.)

LAST WORDS

429. Don't waste any time mourning—organize! (Joe Hill, message to Bill Haywood, head of the Industrial Workers of the World prior to Hill's execution for murder, Salt Lake City, Utah, November 18, 1915.)

PEACE EFFORTS

430. We'll have the boys out of the trenches by Christmas. (Henry Ford, *New York Tribune*, November 25, 1915.)

431. On a bright, bitterly cold Saturday afternoon early in December 1915 a great and joyful crowd stood on a Hoboken [New Jersey] pier cheering, singing and waving handkerchiefs as passengers pushed their way through the throng, past hustling stevedores and brass bands and up the gangplank to Henry Ford's festively decorated peace ship, eager to embark upon their crusade to end the World War. Former Secretary of State William Jennings Bryan waved his umbrella at the departing pacifists, and Thomas Edison and John Burroughs attended their good friend Henry Ford, who stood at the ship's rail throwing roses to his wife on the pier below. (Barbara S. Kraft, relating events of December 4, 1915, from *The Peace Ship: Henry Ford's Pacifist Adventure in the First World War*.)

[Ford chartered the ship *Oscar II* to transport a group of pacifists to Europe. The idea was to get neutral nations to mediate a peaceful solution to the war. The effort failed. Ford continued his activities for peace until February 1917. Two months later, President Wilson asked Congress for a declaration of war.]

ELECTION SLOGAN

432. He kept us out of war! (Democratic Party slogan on behalf of Woodrow Wilson, 1916.)

BELIEVING IN AMERICA

433. I believe in the United States of America as a government of the people, by the people, for the people; whose just powers are derived from the consent of the governed; a democracy in a republic; a sovereign nation of many sovereign states; a perfect union, one and inseparable; established upon those principles of freedom, equality, justice, and humanity for which American patriots sacrificed their lives and fortunes.

I therefore believe it is my duty to my country to love it; to support its Constitution; to obey its laws; to respect its flag; and to defend it against all enemies. (William Tyler Page, *The American's Creed*, 1917.)

[Prizewinning entry in a competition to express the basic American values. It was officially adopted by the House of Representatives in 1918.]

A FATEFUL TELEGRAM

434. WE PROPOSE TO BEGIN ON FEBRUARY 1 UNRESTRICTED SUBMARINE WARFARE. IN DOING THIS HOWEVER WE SHALL ENDEAVOR TO KEEP AMERICA NEUTRAL. . . . IF WE SHOULD NOT SUCCEED IN DOING SO WE PROPOSE MEXICO AN ALLIANCE. . . . YOUR EXCELLENCY SHOULD FOR THE PRESENT INFORM THE PRESIDENT [OF MEXICO] SECRETLY THAT WE EXPECT WAR WITH THE U.S.A. (Arthur Zimmerman, German foreign secretary, telegram to Johann von Bernstorff, German ambassador to the United States, intercepted and decoded by British Intelligence, January 17, 1917, cited in *The Zimmerman Telegram*, by Barbara Tuchman.)

435. WE MAKE WAR TOGETHER, MAKE PEACE TOGETHER, GENEROUS FINANCIAL SUPPORT, AND AN UNDERSTANDING ON OUR PART THAT MEXICO IS TO RECONQUER THE LOST TERRITORY IN TEXAS, NEW MEXICO, AND ARIZONA. (Section of telegram decoded later, cited in *Biographical Dictionary of World War I*, by Holger H. Herwig and Neil M. Heyman.)

[The proposal was to go to the German envoy in Mexico for transmission. The British made sure that Wilson received a copy.]

A CALL FOR WAR

436. It is a fearful thing to lead this great peaceful people into war, into the most terrible and disastrous of all wars, civilization itself seeming to be in the balance. But the right is more precious than peace, and we shall fight for the things which we have always called nearest our hearts—for democracy, for the right of those who submit to authority to have a voice in their own Governments, for the rights and liberties of small nations, for a universal dominion of right by such a concert of free peoples as shall bring peace and safety to all nations and make the world itself at last free. To such a task we can dedicate our lives and our fortunes, everything that we are and everything that we have, with the pride of those who know that the day has come when America is privileged to spend her blood and her might for the principles that gave her birth and happiness and the peace which she has treasured. God helping her, she can do no other. (President Woodrow Wilson, message to Congress calling for a declaration of war against Germany, April 2, 1917.)

PROPAGANDA

437. From the first we held that undocumented "atrocity stories" were bound to have bad reactions, for if the Germans could manage to refute one single charge, they would use it to discredit our entire indictment. . . . The chauvinists, however, managed to figure largely in the Liberty Loan drives, over which the Committee [on Public Information] had no control, and flooded the country with posters showing "bloody boots," trampled children, and mutilated women. . . .

The National Security League and the American Defense Society, officered by prominent citizens, were easily the most active and obnoxious. At all times their patriotism was a thing of screams, violence, and extremes, and their savage intolerances had the burn of acid.

From the first they leveled attacks against the foreign language groups, and were chiefly responsible for the development of a mob spirit in many sections. . . .

A principal demand of the chauvinists was for a prohibition against every other language but English. No effort or distinction was made, for along with their attacks on German they also clamored for a ban against Italian, French, Czech, Spanish, Russian, Danish, Norse, and Swedish, the languages of our allies and the neutrals. Several states yielded to this vicious pressure, an example being this proclamation by the governor of Iowa:

"First, English should and must be the only medium of instruction in public, private, denominational or other similar schools.

"Second, conversation in public places, on trains or over the telephone must be in the English Language.

"Third, all public addresses should be in the English language; and

"Fourth, let those who cannot speak or understand English conduct their religious worship in their homes." (George Creel, head of the Committee on Public Information, created April 14, 1917, purpose to increase public support for the war effort, recollecting events of 1917–1918, from *Rebel at Large.)*

[The National Security League had been founded in 1914 after the war had broken out in Europe. Stressing military preparedness on the part of the United States, it was led by former president Theodore Roosevelt and Senator Henry Cabot Lodge of Massachusetts.]

REMARKS AT A CEMETERY

438. What we have of blood and treasure are yours. In the presence of the illustrious dead, we pledge our hearts and our honor in carrying this war to a successful conclusion. Lafayette, we are here! (Colonel Charles E. Stanton, speech at Lafayette's tomb, Picpus Cemetery, Paris, July 4, 1917, cited in *Black Jack: The Life and Times of John J. Pershing,* by Frank E. Vandiver.)

[The remark is often attributed to General John J. Pershing.]

AN ATTACK ON DISSENTERS

439. DISTRICT JUDGE WOULD LIKE TO TAKE SHOT AT TRAITORS IN CONGRESS

Houston, Texas, October 1, 1917: Judge Walter T. Burns, of the United States district court, in charging a Federal grand jury at the beginning of the October term today, after calling by name Senators Stone of Missouri, Hardwick of Georgia, Vardaman of Mississippi, Gronna of North Dakota, Gore of Oklahoma, and

LaFollette of Wisconsin [the six senators who voted against a declaration of war against Germany], said:

"If I had a wish, I would wish that you men had jurisdiction to return bills of indictment against these men. They ought to be tried promptly and fairly, and I believe this court could administer the law fairly; but I have a conviction, as strong as life, that this country should stand them up against an adobe wall tomorrow and give them what they deserve. If any man deserves death, it is a traitor. I wish that I could pay for the ammunition. I would like to attend the execution, and if I were in the firing squad I would not want to be the marksman who had the blank shell." (Associated Press story, cited by Senator Robert LaFollette in Senate speech, October 6, 1917.)

DOUGHBOYS IN FRANCE

440. The most important thing is to keep the men healthy. A hundred different human frailties now assert themselves. Jealousies and pettiness and selfishness. And then out of it all stand a few strong figures who are true and patriotic and unselfish. This school should be good to teach us humility. We come here from fairly comfortable billets to a different arrangement all together. We are on the side of a high hill. Mud just tenacious and much more abundant and long staying predominates. We are in barracks much on the style of the officers' camps only without floors. No light but candle and lanterns. Cots, muddy floors and dampness. I am rather glad of it all myself, because it means a little taste of inconvenience and I was beginning to think it was war de luxe. (Major William J. Donovan, letter to his wife, Ruth, France, November 24, 1917, cited in *The Last Hero: William J. Donovan*, by Anthony Cave Brown.)

LETTER FROM A RECRUIT

441. Dere Mable,

Having nothin better to do I take up my pen to rite.

We have been here now three weeks. As far as I am concerned I am all ready to go. I told the Captin that I was ready any time. He said yes, but that wed have to wait for the slow ones cause all goin together. I says was I to go out to drill with the rest. He said yes more for the example than anything else. . . .

In the mean time I been doin guard duty. . . .

Guard duty is something like extemperaneus speakin. You got to know everything your goin to say before you start. Its very tecknickle.

For instance you walk a post but there aint no post. An you mount guard but you dont really mount nothin. An you turn out the guard but you dont really turn em out. They come out them selves. . . .

I dont kno my address. Just rite me care of the General.

I got the red muffler that your mother sent me. Give her my love just the same. Bill (Edward Streeter, from *Dere Mable*, a series of fictional letters from an army rookie to his girl, 1918.)

POET-WARRIOR

442.

My shoulders ache beneath my pack
(Lie easier, Cross, upon His back).
I march with feet that burn and smart
(Tread, Holy Feet, upon my heart).
Men shout at me who may not speak
(They scourged Thy back and smote Thy cheek).
I may not lift a hand to clear
(My eyes of salty drops that sear).
Then shall my fickle soul forget
(Thy agony of Bloody Sweat?)
My rifle hand is stiff and numb
(From Thy pierced palm red rivers come).
Lord, Thou must suffer more for me
(Than all the hosts of land and sea).
So let me render back again
(This millionth of Thy gift. Amen).

(Joyce Kilmer, "Prayer of a Soldier in France," 1918, From *Joyce Kilmer*, edited by Robert Cortes Holliday.)

[Kilmer, best known for "Trees," was killed in action in France.]

PROPOSAL FOR PEACE

443. What we demand in this war . . . is nothing peculiar to ourselves. It is that the world be made fit and safe to live in; and particularly that it be made safe for every peace-loving nation which, like our own, wishes to live its own life, determine its own institutions, be assured of justice and fair dealing by the other peoples of the world as against force and selfish aggression.

All the peoples of the world are in effect partners in this interest, and for our own part we see very clearly that unless justice be done to others it will not be done to us. The program of the world's peace, therefore, is our program, and that program, the only possible program, as we see it, is thus:

1. Open covenants of peace, openly arrived at. . . .

2. Absolute freedom of navigation upon the seas. . . .

3. The removal, so far as possible, of all economic barriers and the establishment of equality of trade conditions among all the nations. . . .

4. Adequate guarantees given and taken that national armaments will be reduced to the lowest point consistent with domestic safety.

5. A free, open-minded, and absolutely impartial adjustment of all colonial claims. . . .

6. The evacuation of all Russian territory. . . .

7. Belgium . . . must be evacuated. . . .

8. All French territory should be freed. . . .

9. A readjustment of the frontiers of Italy. . . .

10. The peoples of Austria-Hungary . . . should be accorded the freest opportunity of autonomous development. . . .

11. Rumania, Serbia, and Montenegro should be evacuated. . . .

12. The Turkish portions of the present Ottoman Empire should be assured a secure sovereignty, but the other nationalities which are now under Turkish rule should be assured an undoubted security of life and an absolutely unmolested opportunity of autonomous development. . . .

13. An independent Polish state should be erected. . . .

14. A general association of nations must be formed under specific covenants for the purpose of affording mutual guarantees of political independence and territorial integrity to great and small states alike. (President Woodrow Wilson, Fourteen Points message to Congress, January 8, 1918.)

ON CASUALTY LISTS

444. As soon as our troops began serving in the front line in quiet sectors, we were faced with the problem of handling casualty lists. The solution reached was to defer cabling the lists until some time after the engagement and then to send them in groups, to be given out by the War Department, so that the particular battle in which the casualty occurred could not be identified. If we had given the names to the press at home immediately, it would have been equivalent to telling the enemy the engagement in which they occurred. The French published no lists, but the information was sent to the local mayor, who in turn notified the family of the soldier, at the same time extending them his condolences. Contrasted with this quiet, sympathetic way of giving such news to relatives, the method of publishing column after column of killed and wounded in the papers which people would eagerly scan day after day seemed inconsiderate and cruel. (General John J. Pershing, from *My Experiences in the World War*, recollection of events of 1918.)

ETHNIC ARMY DIVISION
REJECTED

445. Cabled disapproval of suggestion by Mr. [Jan] Paderewski for organization of division of men with Polish antecedents. (General John J. Pershing, diary entry, March 10, 1918, from *My Experiences in the World War*.)

[Paderewski, a gifted pianist, would serve as president of a newly freed Poland in 1919.]

AN AMERICAN GENERAL
REPORTS

446. I have come to tell you that the American people would consider it a great honor for our troops to be engaged in the present battle. I ask you for this in their name and my own.

At this moment there are no other questions but of fighting. Infantry, artillery, aviation, all that we have are yours; use them as you wish. More will come, in numbers equal to requirements.

I have come especially to tell you that the American people will be proud to take part in the greatest battle of history. (General John J. Pershing to General Ferdinand Foch, Clermont-sur-Oise, France, ca. March 28, 1918, cited in *Black Jack: The Life and Times of John J. Pershing*, by Frank E. Vandiver.)

[During the war, however, Pershing insisted that American forces operate as a separate command, without being "amalgamated" into other armies.]

FIRST KILL

447. I knew it was a Hun the moment I saw it, for it had the familiar lines of their new Pfalz. . . .

The Hun was steadily approaching us, unconscious of his danger, for we were full in the sun.

With the first downward dart of Jimmy's [Captain James Hall's] machine I was by his side. We had at least a thousand feet advantage over the enemy and we were two to one numerically. . . .

The Boche hadn't a chance to outfly us. His only salvation would be in a dive toward his own lines. . . .

While Hall went in for his attack I would maintain my altitude and work toward a position on the other side of the Pfalz, hoping to cut off his retreat.

No sooner had I changed my line of flight than the German pilot saw me clear of my sun cover. Hall was already halfway to him when the Hun nosed up and climbed furiously for a higher level. I let him pass me and found myself on the other side just as Hall began firing. . . .

Surprised by discovering Hall just ahead of him, the Pfalz abandoned all ideas of an attack and instead banked around to the right and started for home—just as I had expected him to do. In a trice I was on his tail. Down, down we sped with throttles both fully open. . . . The Boche had no heart for evolutions or maneuvers. He was running like a scared rabbit. . . . I was gaining upon him every instant and had my sights trained dead upon his cockpit before I fired my first shot.

At 150 yards I pressed my fingers. The tracer bullets cut a streak of flying fire into the rear of the Pfalz tail. Raising the nose of my airplane slightly the fiery streak turned itself like the stream of water from a garden hose. Gradually it settled into the pilot's seat. . . . [T]he Pfalz circled a little to the south and the next minute crashed onto the ground just at the edge of the woods a mile inside their own lines. I had brought down my first enemy airplane and had not been subjected to a single shot! (Lieutenant Eddie Rickenbacker, recalling events of April 29, 1918, from *Fighting the Flying Circus*.)

[Jimmy Hall—full name James Norman Hall—would later become famous as coauthor of the *Bounty* trilogy.]

MARINES AT BELLEAU WOOD

448. Reconnaissance had been lulled by appearances, and the men walked almost nonchalantly out into the wheatfields. Poppies beckoned a few pickers, some officers smoked pipes on an afternoon stroll. One Medal of Honor noncom with veteran shrewdness yelled "Come on, you sons of bitches. Do you want to live forever?" Long lines of khaki filed out through the fields west of Belleau Wood, neat, good lines that rolled on almost like human scythes through the grain; then the machine guns hidden in the woodland opened in ranging bursts, settled into killing cadence, and the men went down in those neat lines and lay still in a reddening stain. Anger filled the survivors; they leaned into the race now, broke up into bunches, ran for the guns, for some cover of trees. Some men reached the wood line, smashed against an unseen tangle of wire and heavy German trenches, broke and recoiled to the edge of the road, and hung on for contact with [Major Berton W.] Sibley's men.

Out against the village through open fields, lines bent a little to hit the wood flush, Sibley's men also strolled into the slaughter of crossfire, of nests spurting bullets that mowed them down in windrows. Clutches of men, formation gone, raced for the village, for the woods, for those terrible killing guns. Sharp mortar fire broke the formations further, but finally hand-to-hand struggles pushed the enemy from Bouresches and back into the southern feather of the woods. Sibley's men held the town, refused to yield their thin strip of woods. By dark the attack ended with limited success. It had been the costliest day in Marine Corps history: 1,087 casualties.

And that merely began the battle. (Frank E. Vandiver, recounting events of June 6, 1918, Belleau Wood, France, from *Black Jack: The Life and Times of John J. Pershing*, vol. 2.)

[The Belleau Wood offensive began on June 6. By June 21, the wood was virtually in American hands. Total casualties of the offensive: 9,500.]

TURKEY SHOOT

449. The veteran of many a Fentress County turkey shoot . . . waited for heads to bob up. Keeping a .45 Colt automatic dangling from a finger of his right hand, [Corporal Alvin C.] York "teched off" Germans with his Enfield the way he had so often killed turkeys back home; only now the stakes were higher and, to York's delight, so were the targets. With machine gun fire clattering over his head . . . York sat calmly in the mud and scanned his front. When an enemy head popped up for a better look, York shot it.

After several minutes, however, the Germans managed to approximate York's position and decided to rush him with bayonets. Knowing York was firing from a five-round clip, a [German] lieutenant and five others jumped up and charged. . . . The Germans apparently reasoned that at least one should be able to reach him before he could reload, but York, now on his feet and shooting "offhand," used the pistol instead. As the Germans ran toward him, York once again drew on the instincts of a Tennessee hunter and shot the last man, then the fifth, and so on. Back home, York killed wild turkeys starting from the back so the others would not realize what was happening and scatter. Similarly, he realized that if he shot the lead man first, the others "would drop down and pump a volley into me and get me." York later remembered he "[g]ot the lieutenant right through the stomach and he dropped and screamed a lot. All the boches who were hit squealed just like pigs." His barrel hot and ammunition low, York turned back to the rifle and began to shout at the survivors to surrender. (David D. Lee, from *Sergeant York: An American Hero*, citing events of October 8, 1918, Argonne campaign.)

[In this engagement, York killed 20 German soldiers, captured 35 machine guns, and took 132 Germans prisoner. It won him the Congressional Medal of Honor.]

ON THE NATURE OF SURRENDER

450. Instead of requiring the German forces to retire at once, leaving material, arms and equipment behind, the Armistice terms permitted them to march back to their homeland with colors flying and bands playing, posing as the victims of political conditions.

If unconditional surrender had been demanded, the Germans would, without doubt, have been compelled to yield, and their troops would have returned to Germany without arms, virtually as paroled prisoners of war. The surrender of the German armies would have been an advantage to the Allies in the enforcement of peace terms and would have been a greater deterrent against possible future German aggression. (General John J. Pershing, recalling events at war's end, November 1918, from My Experiences in the World War.)

[Pershing's memoirs were published in 1931, when the Nazi party was reaching for power in Germany. The aggressive tone of the Nazis may have concerned Pershing, with their charge of Germany having been "stabbed in the back" by politicians in the First World War. The old general's remarks may have served as a warning for the future.]

MESSAGE TO HIS MEN

451. The enemy has capitulated. It is fitting that I address myself in thanks directly to the officers and soldiers of the American Expeditionary Forces who by their heroic efforts have made possible this glorious result. Our armies, hurriedly raised and hastily trained, met a veteran enemy, and by courage, discipline and skill always defeated him. Without complaint you have endured incessant toil, privation and danger. You have seen many of your comrades make the supreme sacrifice that freedom may live. . . . Your deeds will live forever on the most glorious pages of American history. (General John J. Pershing, General Order No. 203, France, November 12, 1918, cited in Black Jack: The Life and Times of John J. Pershing, by Frank E. Vandiver.)

AMERICA'S ROLE IN THE GREAT WAR

452. Arrays of figures and statistics may frighten the general reader; they certainly do not attract him. Yet, who can tell without a few figures the story of this part of the world's greatest military adventure—in which a nation engaged in war, across seas, 3,500 miles from its own shores, transported its soldiers by the millions, its material resources in millions of tons, and counted the cost in billions of dollars. Nothing on such a scale had been seen in war since Xerxes crossed the world of his time in the attempt to overwhelm Greece. No such difficulties had been encountered in war since Xenophon and the Ten Thousand reached the sea at Trebizond, or Alexander crossed the mountain passes into India. The only considerable war waged overseas in modern times was that in South Africa, for which the British transported by sea something like 300,000 men. At the time of the Armistice there were over 668,000 soldiers in the Services of Supply, including several combat divisions. There were then over 2,000,000 American soldiers in France. Napoleon took the Grand Army of about one-fourth that number to Russia in 1812. (Major General James G. Harbord, from *The American Army in France, 1917–1919*, recalling 1919.)

12

Boom and Bust

America, having become a world power, now turned its back on the rest of the world by refusing to participate in the League of Nations.

The decade of the 1920s was dubbed the Roaring Twenties. Women won the right to vote. Prohibition outlawed alcohol and ushered in an era of rumrunners, speakeasies, and bootleggers. Defiance of the law corrupted law enforcement, while gangsters fought wars over turf. There was a new way for people to get rich: the stock market. That bubble would burst in the fall of 1929.

PROHIBITION

453. After one year from the ratification of this article, the manufacture, sale, or transportation of intoxicating liquors within, the importation thereof into, or the exportation thereof from the United States and all territory subject to the jurisdiction thereof for beverage purposes is hereby prohibited. (18th Amendment, January 29, 1919.)

Editorial cartoon shows the strain on Uncle Sam for trying to carry out the "Noble Experiment" of Prohibition.

FREE SPEECH IN WARTIME

454. The most stringent protection of free speech would not protect a man in falsely shouting fire in a theater and causing a panic. It does not even protect a man from an injunction against uttering words that may have all the effect of force. The question in every case is whether the words used are used in such circumstances and are of such a nature as to create a clear and present danger that they will bring about the substantive evils that Congress has a right to protect. It is a question of proximity and degree. When a nation is at war many things that might be said in time of peace are such a hindrance to its effort that their utterance will not be endured so long as men fight and that no Court could regard them as protected by any constitutional right. (Justice Oliver Wendell Holmes Jr., opinion, *Schenck v. United States*, U.S. Supreme Court, March 3, 1919.)

STRIKEOUT

455. There is no right to strike against the public safety by anybody; anywhere, any time. (Governor Calvin Coolidge, of Massachusetts, telegram to Samuel Gompers of the American Federation of Labor, September 14, 1919.)

[This was at the conclusion of the Boston police strike. Coolidge had sent in the state militia to preserve order. The action made Coolidge a national figure overnight, and the following year he was picked as running mate for Warren G. Harding.]

PLEA FOR THE LEAGUE OF NATIONS

456. You will say, "Is the League an absolute guaranty against war?" No; I do not know any absolute guaranty against the errors of human judgment or the violence of human passion. . . .

If it is not an absolute insurance against war, do you want no insurance at all? Do you want nothing? Do you want not only no probability that war will not recur, but the probability that it will recur? (President Woodrow Wilson, speech, Pueblo, Colorado, September 25, 1919.)

RESERVATIONS TO A TREATY

457. The United States assumes no obligation to preserve the territorial integrity or political independence of any other country or to interfere in controversies between nations . . . or to employ the military or naval forces of the United States under any article of the [Versailles] treaty for any purpose, unless in any particular case the Congress, which, under the Constitution, has the sole power to declare war or authorize the employment of the military or naval forces of the United States, shall by act or joint resolution so provide. (Senator Henry Cabot Lodge, one of more than a dozen reservations to the Treaty of Versailles and the proposed League of Nations, November 19, 1919.)

[Even with the Lodge reservations to the treaty, it still failed to get a two-thirds majority of the Senate.]

FORBIDDEN

458. No blue material—no jokes lousing up the town—or the trolley or the railroad—no foul punch lines in songs—*or you will be cancelled!* (Sign posted backstage at vaudeville and legitimate theaters, 1920s, cited in *Joey Adams Encyclopedia of Humor.*)

WOMEN MAY VOTE

459. The right of citizens of the United States to vote shall not be denied or abridged by the United States or by any States on account of sex. (19th Amendment, August 26, 1920.)

CAMPAIGN SLOGAN

460. Return to Normalcy. (Republican campaign slogan on behalf of Warren G. Harding, fall 1920.)

WALL STREET BOMBING

461. An explosion, believed to have been caused by a time bomb, killed 30 persons and injured probably 300 others at Broad and Wall Streets [New York City] yesterday at noon.

The blast shattered windows for blocks around, threw the financial district into a panic, and strewed the streets in the immediate vicinity with the bodies of the dead and injured victims.

Twelve hours later investigating authorities were almost-certain the disaster was due to an infernal machine left on an uncovered one-horse-vehicle on Wall Street directly in front of the United States Assay Office next door to the Sub-Treasury, and directly across the street from the J. P. Morgan Building. . . .

Federal, State and City authorities were agreed that the devastating blast signalled the long threatened Red outrages.

Throughout the nation . . . public buildings and great storehouses of wealth, as well as conspicuous men in several cities, were placed under vigilant guard. (Newspaper account, *New York Times*, September 17, 1920.)

NATIONALITY VERSUS INTERNATIONALITY

462. The success of our popular government rests wholly upon the correct interpretation of the deliberate, intelligent, dependable popular will of America. In a deliberate questioning of a suggested change of national policy, where internationality was to supersede nationality, we turned to a referendum, to the American people. There was ample discussion, and there is a public mandate of manifest understanding. (President Warren G. Harding, Inaugural Address, Washington, D.C., March 4, 1921.)

OBITUARY

Mary White died when she struck her head on an overhanging branch during a horseback ride. In an editorial, her father, a Kansas newspaper editor, told of her young life and early death.

463. She used the car as a jitney bus. It was her social life. She never had a "party" in her nearly 17 years—wouldn't have one, but she never drove a block in the car in her life that she didn't fill it with pick-ups! Everybody rode with Mary White—white and black, old and young. She liked nothing better than to

fill the car full of long-legged high school boys and an occasional girl, and parade the town. . . .

[T]he last endeavor of her life was to try to get a rest room for colored girls in the high school. She found one girl reading in the toilet, because there was no better place for a colored girl to loaf, and it inflamed her sense of injustice and she became a nagging harpy to those who, she thought, could remedy the evil. . . .

She hungered and thirsted for righteousness. . . .

She joined the church without consulting her parents, not particularly for her soul's good. . . . But even as a little child, she felt the church was an agency for helping people to more of life's abundance, and she wanted to help. . . .

A rift in the clouds in a gray day threw a shaft of sunlight upon her coffin as her nervous, energetic little body sank to its last sleep. But the soul of her, the glowing, gorgeous, fervent soul of her, surely was flaming in eager joy upon some other dawn. (William Allen White, *Emporia* [Kansas] *Gazette*, May 17, 1921.)

[For decades after her death, the obituary was reprinted in newspapers and anthologies. The complete text may be found in *The Autobiography of William Allen White*.]

THE DECLARATION—
REWRITTEN

---

464. When things get so balled up that the people of a country have to cut loose from some other country and go it on their own hook, without asking no permission from nobody, excepting maybe God Almighty, then they ought to let everybody know why they done it so that everybody can see they are on the level, and not trying to put nothing over nobody.

All we got to say on this proposition is this: First, you and me is as good as anybody else, and maybe a damn sight better; second, nobody ain't got no right to take away none of our rights; third, every man has got a right to live, to come and go as he pleases, and to have a good time however he likes, so long as he don't interfere with nobody else. That any government that don't give a man these rights ain't worth a damn; also people ought to choose the kind of government they want themselves, and nobody else ought to have no say in the matter. That whenever any government don't do this, then the people have got a right to can it and put in one that will take care of their interests. . . .

And we swear on the Bible on this proposition, one and all, and agree to stick to it no matter what happens, whether we win or we lose, and whether we get away with it or get the worst of it, no matter whether we lose all our property by it or even get hung for it. (H. L. Mencken, columnist and social critic, "Essay in American," *Baltimore Evening Sun*, November 7, 1921.)

[Mencken decried the misuse of the American language. He rewrote and revised the Declaration of Independence over a period of several years. The complete text may be found in *The Impossible H. L. Mencken*, edited by Marion Elizabeth Rodgers.]

WORD PORTRAIT

465. His name was George F. Babbitt. He was 46 years old now, in April 1920, and he made nothing in particular, neither butter nor shoes nor poetry, but he was nimble in the calling of selling houses for more than people could afford to pay. (Sinclair Lewis, from his novel *Babbitt*, 1922.)

HUNGER AND POVERTY

466. Hungry men have no respect for law, authority or human life. (Marcus Garvey, *Philosophy and Opinions*, 1923.)

467. [Poverty is] a hellish state to be in. It is no virtue. It is a crime. (Ibid.)

ARGUING FOR NATIONAL DEFENSE

468. [T]hrough the years we, the people, and those who make our laws, have gone from bad to worse, learning little, doing less, still prejudiced, lulled into inaction by an unwarranted sense of security and by false ideas of economy, instead of using plain, practical common sense and making reasonable provision in time of peace for the maintenance of a moderate policy of national defense. . . .

A group of pacifists, who, by carrying placards and applying epithets, think they can end wars, proclaim in favor of our complete disarmament as a beginning to world peace, entirely ignoring the experience of the World War and the palpable fact that we should [then] be in a class by ourselves and probably become at once the object of aggression by wiser nations. It is one of the inconsistencies of this group to be among the first to demand protection at home and intervention abroad. (John J. Pershing, U.S. Army chief of staff, "A Discussion of National Defense," *Saturday Evening Post*, March 10, 1923.)

TAKING THE OATH

469. I was awakened by my father coming up the stairs calling my name. I noticed that his voice trembled. . . . He told me that President Harding had just passed away. . . .

[T]he oath of office . . . was administered by my father . . . a notary public . . . in the sitting room by the light of the kerosene lamp. (Calvin Coolidge, recalling events of August 2, 1923, Plymouth Notch, Vermont, from *The Autobiography of Calvin Coolidge*.)

CAMPAIGN SLOGAN

470. Keep Cool with Coolidge! (Republican campaign slogan on behalf of Calvin Coolidge, fall 1924.)

A TILT TOWARD INTERNATIONALISM?

471. If we are to judge by past experience, there is much to hope for in international relations from frequent conferences and consultations. We have before us the beneficial results of the Washington conference and the various consultations recently held upon European affairs, some of which were in response to our suggestions and in some of which we were active participants. Even the failures cannot not be accounted useful and an immeasurable advance over threatened or actual warfare. I am strongly in favor of continuation of this policy, whenever conditions are such that there is even a promise that practical and favorable results might be secured. . . .

Much may be hoped for from the earnest studies of those who advocate the outlawing of aggressive war. (President Calvin Coolidge, Inaugural Address, Washington, D.C., March 4, 1925.)

[The Washington Conference on the Limitation of Naval Armaments was held from 1921 to 1922.]

THE RIGHT TO TEACH

472. I feel that I have been convicted of violating an unjust statute. I will continue to oppose this law. Any other action would violate my ideal of academic freedom—that is, to teach the truth as guaranteed in our Constitution. (John T. Scopes, address to the court, following his conviction for teaching the theory of evolution, Dayton, Tennessee, July 21, 1925.)

HARASSMENT IN THE WORKPLACE

Richard Wright gets a job in an optical company. He is resented by two white workers, Pease and Reynolds, who feel he has taken a "white man's job." There are taunts and insults. Finally, the situation comes to a head.

473. "Richard, I want to ask you something," Pease began pleasantly. . . .
Reynolds came over and stood blocking the narrow passage. . . . He folded his arms and stared at me solemnly.

I looked from one to the other, sensing trouble. Pease looked up and spoke slowly, so there would be no possibility of my not understanding.

"Richard, Reynolds here tells me that you called me Pease," he said.

I stiffened. . . . I knew that this was the showdown.

He meant that I had failed to call him Mr. Pease. I looked at Reynolds; he was gripping a steel bar in his hand. I opened my mouth to speak, to protest, to assure Pease that I had never called him simply Pease, and that I had never had any intention of doing so, when Reynolds grabbed me by the collar, ramming my head against a wall.

"Now, be careful, nigger," snarled Reynolds, baring his teeth.

"I heard you call 'im. And if you say you didn't, you're calling me a liar, see?" He waved the steel bar threateningly.

If I had said, No, sir, Mr. Pease, I never called you Pease, I would by inference have been calling Reynolds a liar, and if I had said: Yes, sir, Mr. Pease, I called you Pease, I would have been pleading guilty to the worst insult that a Negro can offer to a southern white man. . . .

"I don't remember calling you Pease, Mr. Pease," I said cautiously. "And if I did, I sure didn't mean. . . ."

"You black sonofabitch! You called me Pease, then!" he spat, rising and slapping me till I bent sideways over a bench. . . .

I wilted. . . . I knew what they what they wanted. They wanted me to leave the job.

"I'll leave," I promised. "I'll leave right now!" (Richard Wright, Memphis, Tennessee, 1926, from *Black Boy*.)

ENTER ARCHY THE COCKROACH

---

474. We came into our room earlier than usual in the morning, and discovered a gigantic cockroach jumping about upon the keys. He did not see us, and we watched him. He would climb painfully upon the framework of the machine and cast himself with all his force upon a key, head downward, and his weight and the impact of the blow were just sufficient to operate the machine, one slow letter after another. He could not work the capital letters, and he had a great deal of difficulty operating the mechanism that shifts the paper so that a fresh line may be started.

We never saw a cockroach work so hard or perspire so freely in all our lives before. After about an hour of this frightfully difficult literary labor he fell to the floor exhausted, and we saw him creep feebly into a nest of the poems which are always there in profusion.

Congratulating ourself that we had left a sheet of paper in the machine the night before so that all this work had not been in vain, we made an examination, and this is what we found:

expression is the need of my soul
i was once a vers libre bard
but i died and my soul went into the body of a cockroach
it has given me a new outlook upon life
i see things from the under side now
thank you for the apple peelings in the wastepaper basket
but your paste is getting so stale i cant eat it
there is a cat here called mehitabel i wish you would have
removed she nearly ate me the other night why dont she
catch rats that is what she is supposed to be for. . . .
night after night i have written poetry for you
on your typewriter
and this big brute of a rat who used to be a poet
comes out of his hole when it is done
and reads it and sniffs at it
he is jealous of my poetry
he used to make fun of it when we were both human
he was a punk poet himself
and after he has read it he sneers
and then he eats it
i wish you would have mehitabel kill that rat
or get a cat that is onto her job
and i will write you a series of poems showing how things look
to a cockroach [. . . .]
dont you ever eat any sandwiches in your office
i havent had a crumb of bread for i dont know how long
or a piece of ham or anything but apple parings
and paste leave a piece of paper in your machine
every night you can call me archy

(Don Marquis, from *archy and mehitabel.*)

[Marquis was a humorist and newspaper columnist. His columns, which appeared in the *New York Sun*, were enormously popular in the 1920s. They were compiled into a book in 1927.]

AVIATOR HERO

475. The first indication of my approach to the European Coast was a small fishing boat. . . .

I have carried on short conversations with people on the ground by flying low with throttled engine, shouting a question, and receiving the answer by some signal. When I saw this fisherman I decided to try to get him to point towards land. I had no sooner made the decision than the futility of the effort became apparent. In all likelihood he could not speak English, and even if he could he would undoubtedly be far too astounded to answer. However . . . as the plane passed within a few feet of the boat I shouted, "Which way is Ireland?" Of course the attempt was useless. (Charles A. Lindbergh Jr., recalling events of May 21, 1927, from *We.*)

476. I flew low over the field once, then circled around into the wind and landed [at Le Bourget Field, outside Paris]. . . . The entire field ahead . . . was covered with thousands of people all running towards my ship. . . . I cut the switch to keep the propeller from killing some one. . . . [W]hen parts of the ship began to crack from the pressure of the multitude I decided to climb out of the cockpit in order to draw the crowd away. . . . [A]s soon as one foot appeared through the door I was dragged the rest of the way without assistance on my part. For nearly half an hour I was unable to touch the ground. . . .

The French military flyers very resourcefully took the situation in hand. . . . [A]t a given signal, they placed my helmet on an American correspondent and cried: "Here is Lindbergh." That helmet on an American was sufficient evidence. The correspondent immediately became the center of attraction, and while he was being taken protestingly . . . I managed to get inside one of the hangers. (Ibid.)

[Lindbergh had flown solo nonstop from New York to Paris—the first person to accomplish this. The flight had taken 33½ hours.]

ADDRESS TO THE COURT

477. If it had not been for these thing I might have live out my life talking at street corners to scorning men. I might have die, unmarked, unknown, a failure. Now we are not a failure. This is our career and our triumph. Never in our full life could we hope to do such work for tolerance, for justice, for man's understanding of man, as now we do by accident. Our words, our lives, our pains—nothing! The taking of our lives—lives of a good shoemaker and a poor fishpeddler—all! That last moment belongs to us—that agony is our triumph. (Bartolomeo Vanzetti, last address to the court, Boston, 1927, quoted in *The Poetry of Freedom*, edited by William Rose Benet and Norman Cousins.)

[Nicola Sacco and Bartolomeo Vanzetti were anarchists who were convicted in 1921 of killing two men during a robbery. They were sentenced to death. After six years of legal wrangling and official investigation, the sentence was carried out. Doubts remain over their guilt and the fairness of their trial. The presiding judge, Webster Thayer, commented later to a friend, "Did you see what I did to those anarchist bastards?" In 1977 Massachusetts governor Michael Dukakis signed a proclamation clearing Sacco and Vanzetti.]

THE HUMORIST'S VIEW

478. My ancestors did not come over on the *Mayflower*—they met the boat. (Will Rogers, wisecrack.)

479. They sent the Indians to Oklahoma. They had a treaty that said, "You shall have this land as long as grass grows and water flows." It was not only a good rhyme but looked like a good treaty, and it was till they struck oil. Then the government took us again. They said the treaty only refers to "water and grass; it don't say anything about oil." (Syndicated column, February 5, 1928.)

NOBLE EXPERIMENT

480. [Prohibition is] a great social and economic experiment, noble in motive, and far-reaching in purpose. (Herbert Hoover, secretary of commerce, acceptance speech as presidential nominee of the Republican Party, Republican National Convention, Kansas City, Missouri, June 15, 1928.)

WHY LEARN ARABIC IN AMERICA?

481. In my opinion, knowledge of Arabic would be a distinct asset to the Syrian-American generation and all efforts to spread its knowledge should be commended. That it is not now generally taught is, I must admit, the fault of the parents. I cannot shake off the conviction that most Syrian parents are woefully negligent in this respect. Some of them are even ashamed of their mother tongue and indifferent to their precious traditions.

In the same manner that we send our children to tutors for music, for instance, we can and should send them for Teaching Arabic. It should also be the general rule that only Arabic be spoken at home. The young generation may not appreciate all the benefits and advantages of knowing an extra language until later on in life, when it would be too late to atone for the past.

We surely could make a better contribution to our beloved adopted country if we were better equipped linguistically, and consequently rendered more able to appreciate our racial heritage and pass it along as our contribution to America. (Clara K. Bishara, Brooklyn, New York, letter to the Readers' Forum, *Syrian World*, August 1928.)

482. In Lansing the young Syrian people, ranging from the ages of 16 to 30, organized a club known as the "Young Phoenician Society" whose purpose is to create a better understanding among the young people.

Three months ago we decided to take 25 or 30 minutes from each club period which we held twice a month, and hold a class for the purpose of learning Arabic. The teacher chosen was a very well-educated young man, and an instructor in one of the best colleges in Michigan.

Everybody started out very enthusiastically for about four lessons, and after that nobody desired to advance any further. What was the trouble? It was that our parents didn't encourage us any further. They didn't have the patience to help their children, some wondered what good the Syrian language could do them in America, and others didn't approve of it at all, and we ceased learning. Therefore, I believe that the matter should be left to individuals to find means of teaching their children the Arabic language if they desire to, because it will be a tedious task to try to accomplish it universally. (Ruby Nakfoor, Lansing, Michigan, letter to Readers' Forum, *Syrian World*, September 1928.)

ECONOMIC PROGRAM

483. We were challenged [after the world war] with a peace-time choice between the American system of rugged individualism and a European philosophy of diametrically opposed doctrines—doctrines of paternalism and static socialism. The acceptance of these ideas would have meant the destruction of self-government through centralization of government. It would have meant the undermining of the individual initiative and enterprise through which our people have grown to unparalleled greatness. (Herbert Hoover, campaign speech, October 1928.)

A TRUE "UNTOUCHABLE"

484. I wasn't born to sell out; I wasn't built that way. The pay wasn't good; but I wasn't forced to go on the job. I was happy to go on the job. There weren't many of my kind in the [Prohibition Bureau of the Justice] department in that era, and I was proud of it. (Albert Wolff, recalling anti-gangster activities as an "untouchable" federal agent during Prohibition, ca. 1929, cited in *New York Times*, March 25, 1998.)

PHONE CALL

485. Groucho, the jig is up. (Unnamed stockbroker, phone call to Groucho Marx following the stock market crash, October 1929.)

CRASH!

486. Stock prices virtually collapsed yesterday, swept downward with gigantic losses in the most disastrous trading day in stock market history. Billions of dollars in open market values were wiped out as prices crumbled under the pressure of liquidation of securities which had to be sold at any price. . . .

Groups of men, with here and there a woman, stood about inverted glass bowls all over the city yesterday watching pools of ticker tape unwind and as the tenuous paper with its cryptic numerals grew longer at their feet their fortunes shrunk. Others sat stolidly on tilted chairs in the customers' rooms of brokerage houses and watched a motion picture of waning wealth as the day's quotations moved silently across a screen. (*New York Times* news article, October 30, 1929.)

JOKE OF THE DAY

487. I made a killing in the Stock Market today. I shot my broker. (Wisecrack, late 1929.)

13

Depression and New Deal

Banks closed, factories closed, millions were unemployed. The election of Franklin Roosevelt in 1932 signaled the beginning of the New Deal. Legislation was passed to get people back to work, feed the hungry, build public works, provide for union recognition, and protect bank deposits. The depression would last for nearly a decade—from the aftermath of the market crash to the outbreak of World War II.

SPEEDUP

488. I was working at the Briggs Highland Park plant when the stock market crash came in October 1929. In a matter of days they started to lay off men. After the first layoff of ten per cent, the rest worked so much faster that it was necessary to lay off another 20 per cent to reduce production by ten per cent. The slowest man was always in danger of being laid off. The greater the number of unemployed the greater the effort on the part of those working. As the Depression deepened, the men tended to work close to the limit of their capacities. It was this speed-up which became unbearable and finally caused the workers to organize. (John W. Anderson, Highland Park, Michigan, 1929–1930, from *Rank and File: Personal Histories by Working-Class Organizers*, edited by Alice Lynd and Staughton Lynd.)

Refugees from the Texas Dust Bowl at an overnight roadside camp near Calipatria, California, in the early 1930s. The photo was taken by Dorothea Lange for the Farm Security Administration.

MONEY AND POLITICS

489. Periodically the country is shocked by investigations revealing the expenditures of huge sums of money by candidates for Congress; these shocks have been intermittent since the close of the Civil War. A great deal of heat has been generated, escaping usually in talk, and Congress has skirted around the edges of the subject in several statutes. Generally speaking, "nothing has been done about it"; yet there are signs of change. Not long ago the Senate in the Vare case added a new qualification for membership in that body: a citizen presenting his election credentials to the Senate must show that he has not spent too much money in an irregular fashion in winning his seat. . . .

[T]here are Senators who hold that it cannot be solved until the use of private money in primaries and elections is forbidden entirely. But this involves heroic action. Especially does it throw upon the federal government the burden of providing machinery by which all aspirants and candidates may present their claims to constituents on an even plane at public expense. (Charles A. Beard, *The New Republic*, July 30, 1930.)

A VIEW OF LIFE

Referring to the poet's boast "I am the master of my fate, I am the captain of my soul."

490. A fine captain. Why, man isn't even a deckhand on a rudderless ship! . . . We are like a body of shipwrecked sailors clutching to a raft and desperately engaged in holding on. . . . The best that we can do is to be kindly and helpful toward our friends and fellow passengers who are clinging to the same speck of dirt while we are drifting side by side to our common doom. (Clarence Darrow, *The Story of My Life*, 1932.)

FINANCING RELIEF EFFORTS

491. The urgent question today is the prompt balancing of the budget. When that is accomplished I propose to support adequate measures for relief of distress and unemployment. In the meantime it is essential that there should be an understanding of the character of the draft bill [H.R.12353, the Emergency Relief and Construction bill]. . . . That draft bill supports some proposals we have already made in aid to unemployment through the use of the Reconstruction Finance Corporation to make loans for projects which have been in abeyance and which proposal makes no drain on the taxpayer.

But, in addition, it [the new draft bill] proposes to expend about $900 million for Federal public works.

I believe that the American people will grasp the economic fact that such action would require appropriations to be made to the Federal departments, thus creating a deficit in the budget that could only be met with more taxes and more Federal bond issues. This makes balancing of the budget hopeless. The country also understands that an unbalanced budget means the loss of confidence of our own people and of other nations in the credit and stability of the Government and that the consequences are national demoralization and the loss of 10 times as many jobs as would be created by this program even if it could be physically put into action. . . .

Detailed lists of these [proposed] projects have been broadcast to every part of the country during the past 24 hours, to the cities, towns, villages, and sections who would receive a portion of this pork barrel. It is apparently expected that the cupidity of these towns and sections will demand that their Congressmen and senators vote for this bill or threaten to penalize them if they fail to join in this squandering of money. (President Herbert Hoover, press conference, Washington, D.C., May 27, 1932.)

[On July 21, 1932, Congress passed the Relief and Construction Act. It gave the Reconstruction Finance Corporation the power to lend $1.5 billion to state and local agencies for public works that were "self-liquidating," plus $300 million for temporary loans to states that could not finance the relief of economic distress.]

CAMPAIGN PROMISE

492. I pledge you, I pledge myself, to a new deal for the American people. Let us all here assembled constitute ourselves prophets of a new order of competence and of courage. This is more than a political campaign: it is a call to arms. Give me your help, not to win votes alone, but to win in this crusade to restore America to its own people. (Franklin D. Roosevelt, acceptance speech, Democratic National Convention, July 2, 1932.)

THE BONUS ARMY

493. A challenge to the authority of the United States Government has been met, swiftly and firmly.

After months of patient indulgence, the Government met overt lawlessness as it always must be met if the cherished processes of self-government are to be preserved. We cannot tolerate the abuse of constitutional rights by those who would destroy all government, no matter who they may be. Government cannot be coerced by mob rule.

The Department of Justice is pressing its investigation into the violence which forced the call for Army detachments, and it is my sincere hope that those agitators who inspired yesterday's attack upon the Federal authority may be brought speedily to trial in the civil courts. . . .

Order and civil tranquility are the first requisites in the great task of economic reconstruction to which our whole people now are devoting themselves. . . . This national effort must not be retarded in even the slightest degree by organized lawlessness in the country. . . .

For your own information, while I am on the subject, the National Red Cross has undertaken to send all the women and children out of the District who want to go home, and they are actively in the field this afternoon gathering them up. This is not for publication, just for your own information. (President Herbert Hoover, press conference, Washington, D.C., July 29, 1932, from *Public Papers of the Presidents: Herbert Hoover.*)

[In May 1932 about 1,000 veterans of the World War had come to Washington to petition for the payment of a promised bonus. In the weeks that followed, an additional 10,000–15,000—including many nonveterans—had joined the original group. Along with their wives and children, they became known as the Bonus Army, and they took shelter in unoccupied government buildings and in shacks that they put together on the Anacostia Flats outside Washington. The House of Representatives passed a bill authorizing the bonus payments, but the Senate rejected it on June 17. The government paid for the travel expenses home of many of the veterans. A few thousand remained in Washington. Following a clash with police, the U.S. Army was called in. Under the personal direction of General Douglas MacArthur, the army drove out the remaining members of the Bonus Army, using cavalry and tanks. In all, four died in the confrontation—two members of the Bonus Army and two policemen.]

CHARGING A GRAND JURY

494. It appears that a considerable group of men, styling themselves as bonus marchers, have come to the District of Columbia from all parts of the country for the stated purpose of petitioning Congress for the passage of legislation providing for the immediate payment of the so-called bonus certificates. The number of these men has been variously estimated as from five to ten thousand.

It is reported that certain buildings in this city, belonging to the Government, were in the possession of members of this so-called bonus army, who had been requested to vacate but had declined to do so; . . . that yesterday agents of the

Treasury proceeding lawfully, went upon the premises to dispossess the bonus army, and a force of district police was present to afford protection and prevent disorder; that the bonus marchers were removed from the old building which the public contractor was waiting to demolish; that thereupon a mob of several thousand bonus marchers coming from other quarters, proceeded to this place for the purpose of resisting the officials and of regaining possession of the Government property. It appears that this mob, incited by some of their number, attacked the police, seriously injured a number of them, and engaged in riot and disorder. Their acts of resistance reached such a point that the police authorities were unable to maintain order and the Commissioners of the District were compelled to call upon the Federal authorities for troops to restore order and protect life and property.

It is obvious that the laws of the District were violated in many respects. You should undertake an immediate investigation of these events with a view to bringing to justice those responsible for this violence, as well as those inciting it as well as those who took part in acts of violence.

It is reported that the mob guilty of actual violence included few exservicemen, and was made up mainly of communists, and other disorderly elements. I hope you will find that is so and that few men who have worn the Nation's uniform engaged in this violent attack upon law and order. In the confusion not many arrests have been made, and it is said that many of the most violent disturbers and criminal elements in the unlawful gathering have already scattered and escaped from the city, but it may be possible yet to identify and apprehend them and bring them to justice. (Judge Oscar R. Luhring, charge to the grand jury, Supreme Court of the District of Columbia, July 29, 1932, from *Public Papers of the Presidents: Herbert Hoover.*)

A JOURNALIST'S ACCOUNT

495. The bonus army was retreating today—in all directions.

Its billets destroyed, its commissary wrecked, its wives and babies misplaced, its leaders lost in the confusion which followed its rout last night by troops of the Regular Army, the former soldiers tramped the streets of Washington and the roads of Maryland and Virginia, foraging for coffee and cigarettes. . . .

The latest casualty list showed about fifty or fifty-five wounded or gassed in the fighting. . . .

Few of the bonus marchers had any sleep last night. And many of them had been worn out by the scramble to get out of the way of cavalry sabers, bayonets, and tear-gas bombs. (Lee McCardell, news story, *Baltimore Evening Sun*, July 29, 1932.)

[This is from a remarkable newspaper account. The full text appears in *A Treasury of Great Reporting*, edited by Louis L. Snyder and Richard B. Morris.]

ADVICE TO A PRESIDENT

496. Soup is cheaper than tear gas bombs and bread better than bullets in maintaining law and order in these times of depression, unemployment, and hunger. (Congressman Fiorello La Guardia, telegram to President Hoover, ca. July 30, 1932, following the routing of the Bonus Army in Washington, cited in *A Treasury of Great Reporting*, edited by Louis L. Snyder and Richard B. Morris.)

FIGHTING THE DEPRESSION

497. Two courses were open. We might have done nothing. That would have been utter ruin. Instead, we met the situation with proposals to private business and the Congress of the most gigantic program of economic defense and counter-attack ever evolved in the history of the Republic. We put it into action.

Our measures have repelled these attacks of fear and panic. . . .

We have provided methods and assurances that there shall be none to suffer from hunger and cold. We have instituted measures to assist farmers and home owners. We have created vast agencies for employment. Above all, we have maintained the sanctity of the principles on which this Republic has grown great. . . .

Thus we have held that the Federal Government should in the presence of great national danger use its powers to give leadership to the initiative, the courage, and the fortitude of the people themselves; but it must insist upon individual, community, and State responsibility. That it should furnish leadership to assure the coordination and unity of all existing agencies, governmental and private, for economic and humanitarian action. That where it becomes necessary to meet emergencies beyond the power of these agencies by the creation of new Government instrumentalities, they should be of such character as not to supplant or weaken, but rather to supplement and strengthen, the initiative and enterprise of the people. That they must, directly or indirectly, serve all the people. Above all, that they should be set up in such form that once the emergency is passed they can and must be demobilized and withdrawn, leaving our governmental, economic, and social structure strong and whole. (President Herbert Hoover, reelection campaign speech, August 11, 1932.)

HANDLING THE HOMELESS

498. Dull mornings last winter the sheriff of Miami, Florida, used to fill a truck with homeless men and run them up to the county line. Where the sheriff of Fort Lauderdale used to meet them and load them into a second truck and run them up to <u>his</u> county line. Where the sheriff of Saint Lucie's would meet them and load them into a third truck and run them up to <u>his</u> county line. Where the sheriff of Brevard County would <u>not</u> meet them. And where they would trickle back down the roads to Miami. To repeat. (From "No One Has Starved," *Fortune*, September 1932.)

499. Next winter there will be no truck. . . . The sheriff of Miami, like the President of the U.S., will next winter think of transients and unemployed miners and jobless mill workers in completely different terms. The difference will be made by the Emergency Relief Act. . . . The passage of the Act . . . marks a turning in American political history. And the beginning of a new chapter in American unemployment relief. It constitutes an open and legible acknowledgment of governmental responsibility for the welfare of the victims of industrial unemployment. (Ibid.)

THE "WILD WEST"

500. Only to the white man was nature a "wilderness" and only to him was the land "infested" with "wild" animals and "savage" people. To us it was tame. Earth was bountiful and we were surrounded with the blessings of the Great Mystery. Not until the hairy man from the east came and with brutal frenzy heaped injustices upon us and the families that we loved was it "wild" for us. When the very animals of the forest began fleeing from his approach, then it was that for us the "Wild West" began. (Luther Standing Bear, *Land of the Spotted Eagle*, 1933.)

501. In the natural course of events, every Lakota boy became a hunter, scout, or warrior. . . . When I reached young manhood, the warpath for the Lakota was a thing of the past. The hunter had disappeared with the buffalo, the war scout had lost his calling, and the warrior had taken his shield to the mountain-top and given it back to the elements. The victory songs were sung only in the memory of the braves and even they soon went unsung under a cruel and senseless ban of our overseers. (Ibid.)

INSIGHT

The blind and deaf Helen Keller felt that those who had sight and hearing did not really appreciate those gifts. She wrote about what she would do if she had but three days to see.

502. The first day . . . I should call to me all my dear friends and look long into their faces, imprinting upon my mind the outward evidences of the beauty that is within them. . . .

I should like to look into the loyal, trusting eyes of my dogs, the little Scottie and the stalwart Great Dane. . . .

The next day I should arise with the dawn and see the thrilling miracle of which night is transformed into day. . . . This day I should devote to a hasty glimpse of the world, past and present. . . . I should go to the museums. . . .

[The] third day, I shall spend in the workaday world, amid the haunts of men going about the business of life. The city becomes my destination.

First, i stand at a busy corner, merely looking at people. . . . lives. I see smiles, and I am happy. I see serious determination, and I am proud. I see suffering, and I am compassionate. . . .

Only when darkness had again descended upon me should I realize how much I had left unseen. (Helen Keller, "Three Days to See," *Atlantic Monthly*, January 1933.)

"LAME DUCK" AMENDMENT

---

503. The terms of the President and Vice President shall end at noon on the 20th day of January, and the terms of Senators and Representatives at noon on the 3d day of January . . . and the terms of their successors shall begin. (20th Amendment, ratified January 23, 1933.)

NOTHING TO FEAR BUT FEAR

504. This great nation will endure as it has endured, will revive and will prosper.

So first of all let me assert my firm belief that the only thing we have to fear is fear itself—nameless, unreasoning, unjustified terror which paralyzes needed efforts to convert retreat into advance. (Franklin D. Roosevelt, First Inaugural Address, March 4, 1933.)

505. The money changers have fled from their high seats in the temple of our civilization. We may now restore that temple to the ancient truths.

The measure of the restoration lies in the extent to which we apply social values more noble than a mere monetary profit. (Ibid.)

506. I shall ask the Congress for the one remaining instrument to meet the crisis—broad executive power to wage war against the emergency as great as the power that would be given me if we were in fact invaded by a foreign foe. (Ibid.)

ARMISTICE DAY EDITORIAL

507. Fifteen years ago came the Armistice and we all thought it was to be a new world. It is: But a lot worse than it was before. . . .

Ten million men were killed and many more maimed . . .

And for what? Would it have been any worse if Germany had won? . . .

Is this old world as safe for democracy as it was before all these lives were lost?

There is no democracy east of the Rhine. Tyrants have risen where constitutional monarchs ruled twenty years ago. . . .

Look at Russia, ruled by the proletariat tyrant!

Behold Germany, governed by paranoiac sadists!

Italy has lost her liberty to fill her stomach and enthrone the rich!

Poland, the Balkans, and Central Europe—a super powder magazine—waiting for the match to blow civilization back to the dark ages! . . .

All wars are like that. The next one will be worse.

War is the devil's joke on humanity. So let's celebrate Armistice Day by laughing our heads off.

Then let us work and pray for peace when man can break the devil's chains and nations realize their nobler dreams! (William Allen White, editorial, *Emporia (Kansas) Gazette*, November 11, 1933.)

[The holiday now known as Veterans Day was originally called Armistice Day. It commemorated November 11, 1918, when an armistice was declared in World War I. When World War II broke out, White was one of the leading figures in an organization called the Committee to Defend America by Aiding the Allies.]

PROHIBITION ENDS

508. The 18th article of amendment to the Constitution of the United States is hereby repealed. (21st Amendment, December 5, 1933.)

THE NEW DEAL'S "ALPHABET SOUP"

509.

AAA: Agricultural Adjustment Administration
CCC: Civilian Conservation Corps
FCC: Federal Communications Commission
FDIC: Federal Deposit Insurance Corporation
FSA: Farm Security Administration
NLRB: National Labor Relations Board
NRA: National Recovery Administration
PWA: Public Works Administration
REA: Rural Electrification Administration
SEC: Securities and Exchange Commission
SSA: Social Security Administration
TVA: Tennessee Valley Authority
WPA: Works Progress Administration

(Some of the major federal agencies established 1933–1939.)

ALONE IN THE ANTARCTIC
WINTER

510. By May 17th, one month after the sun had sunk below the horizon, the noon twilight was dwindling to a mere chink in the darkness, lit by a cold reddish glow. . . . This was the polar night, the morbid countenance of the Ice Age. Nothing moved, nothing was visible. This was the soul of inertness. One could almost hear a distant creaking as if a great weight were settling. Out of the deepening darkness came the cold. (Admiral Richard E. Byrd, Antarctica, events of May 17, 1934, from *Alone*.)

511. The trapdoor [to the shelter built beneath the snow] was completely buried when I found it again. I pulled at the handle. . . . It did not give. It's a tight fit, anyway, I mumbled to myself. The drift has probably wedged the corners. Standing astride the hatch, I braced myself and heaved with all my strength. I might just as well have tried hoisting the Barrier.

Panic took me then, I must confess. Reason fled. I clawed at the three-foot square of timber like a madman. I beat on it with my fists, trying to shake the snow loose, and, when that did no good, I lay flat on my belly and pulled until my hands went weak from cold and weariness. Then I crooked my elbow, put my face down, and said over and over again, You damn fool, you damn fool. Here for weeks I had been defending myself against the danger of being penned inside the shack; instead, I was now locked out, and nothing could be worse. . . .

Just two feet below was sanctuary—warmth, food, tools, all the means of survival. All these things were an arm's length away, but I was powerless to reach them. (Ibid.)

[Byrd was conducting research for the U.S. Navy. He was working alone—about 100 miles from the main base at Little America. As he struggled to get the trapdoor opened in the midst of a fierce blizzard, he remembered a shovel that he had left behind in the snow a week before. Byrd found the shovel and used it to pry open the trapdoor—and save his life.]

FBI GETS ITS MAN

512. John Dillinger, ace bad man of the world, got his last night—two slugs through his heart and one through his head. He was tough and he was shrewd, but he wasn't as tough and shrewd as the Federals, who never close a case until the end. It took 27 of them to end Dillinger's career, and their strength came out of his weakness—a woman. . . .

As Dillinger emerged [from the Biograph movie theater], walking near him were two youngish women, one of them wearing a red dress. Hundreds were leaving the house at the time, and almost any number of women would naturally have been near him. But the one with the red dress hurried up the alley, and four Federals made a formation between her and Dillinger before the first shot was fired. It is my theory that she was with Dillinger and she was the tip-off party or in league with [Melvin] Purvis [of the FBI Chicago office]. (Jack Lait, news story, Chicago, International News Service, July 23, 1934.)

[During the 1930s, the FBI spotlighted "public enemies," equivalent to the "most wanted" of later years. These were often bank robbers or kidnappers. They included individuals, such as "Pretty Boy" Floyd, and small groups, such as the Ma Barker gang. When he was shot, Dillinger was officially listed as "Public Enemy No. 1."]

JOKE OF THE DAY

513. I'm so hungry that my stomach thinks my throat is cut. (Wisecrack, ca. 1935.)

"SHARE OUR WEALTH"

In February 1934, U.S. senator Huey Long of Louisiana inserted into the *Congressional Record* an appeal to all Americans to set up a "Share Our Wealth Society" in every community. Its slogan was "Every Man a King." Long pushed the idea into 1935, his eye on a White House run in 1936. Historian William Ivy Hair summarizes the plan.

514. Share Our Wealth was simple in outline. Personal and family fortunes above three or four million dollars would be confiscated. Annual income and inheritance taxes would be steeply raised—up to a flat 100 percent on anything above one million dollars. The national government would transfer this wealth

to the poor. Since wealth also consisted of goods, Huey proposed to redistribute in kind "so the poor devil who needs a house can get one from some rich bird who has too many houses"; stock in corporations might also be divided among the people. As to how such transfers could actually be accomplished, Huey confessed he had not worked out the details: "I am going to have to call in some great minds to help me." Being pressed for specifics annoyed him. Once, he shrugged off questions by saying that "as soon as I run the crooks out of government I'll get down to methods for putting the plan into effect."

Understandably, with close to half the nation's families in 1934 and 1935 earning less than the $1,250 considered minimal for a "maintenance level" of life, Huey's promised cornucopia of benefits from Share Our Wealth enjoyed widespread appeal.

"Every family" would make not less than $2,000 to $3,000 per year," he insisted. Moreover, the Long Plan (as he often called it) would shorten the work week to thirty hours or "maybe less," with a month's annual paid vacation or "maybe more." Each family able to work, he said, would have a guaranteed "family wealth" of "around $5,000—enough for a home, an automobile, a radio, and the ordinary conveniences" ($5,000 in 1934 dollars is the equivalent of almost $50,000 in 1990 dollars). (William Ivy Hair, events of 1935, from *The Kingfish and His Realm: The Life and Times of Huey P. Long.*)

[On September 8, 1935, Long was shot in Baton Rouge. He died two days later.]

ADVICE FOR GETTING ALONG

515. When dealing with people, remember you are not dealing with creatures of logic, but with creatures of emotion, creatures bristling with prejudices and motivated by pride and vanity. And if you want to stir up a resentment tomorrow that may rankle across the decades and endure until death, just indulge in a little stinging criticism—no matter how certain you are that it is justified. (Dale Carnegie, from *How to Win Friends and Influence People*, 1936.)

516. Remember that a man's name is to him the sweetest and most important sound in the English language. (Ibid.)

[The book proved to be one of the most successful self-improvement tomes in the history of American publishing.]

VAG

517. The young man waits at the edge of the concrete, with one hand grips a rubbed suitcase of phony leather, the other hand almost making a fist, thumb up

that moves in ever so slight an arc when a car slithers past, a truck roars, clatters, the wind of cars passing ruffles his hair, slaps grit in his face.

Head swims, hunger has twisted the belly tight,

he has skinned a heel through the torn sock, feet ache in the broken shoes, under the threadbare suit carefully brushed off with the hand, the torn drawers have a crummy feel, the feel of having slept in your clothes; in the nostrils lingers the staleness of discouraged carcasses crowded into a transient camp, the carbolic stench of the jail, on the taut cheeks the shamed flush from the boring eyes of cops and deputies, railroadbulls (they eat three squares a day, they are buttoned into well-made clothes, they have wives to sleep with, kids to play with after supper, they work for the big men who buy their way, they stick their chests out with the sureness of power behind their backs). Git the hell out, scram Know what's good for you, you'll make yourself scarce. Gittin tough, eh? Think you kin take it, eh?

The punch in the jaw, the slam on the head with the nightstick, the wrist grabbed and twisted behind the back, the big knee brought up sharp to the crotch,

the walk out of town with sore feet to stand and wait at the edge of the hissing speeding string of cars where the reek of ether and lead and gas melts into the silent grassy smell of the earth.

Eyes black with want seek out the eyes of the drivers, a hitch, a hundred miles down the road. (John Dos Passos, from the novel *The Big Money*, 1936.)

[This sketch of a vagrant on the road is from the third novel in a trilogy. All three were later published in a single volume called *U.S.A.* The trilogy offers a panoramic view of American life during World War I, the period of boom and bust, and the Great Depression.]

A NOVELIST LOOKS AT RECONSTRUCTION

518. The former slaves were now the lords of creation and, with the aid of the Yankees, the lowest and most ignorant ones were on top. The better class of them, scorning freedom, were suffering as severely as their white masters. . . .

In slave days . . . [t]hose consigned to the fields were the ones least willing or able to learn, the least energetic, the least honest and trustworthy, the most vicious and brutish. And now this class, the lowest in the black social order, was making life a misery for the South.

Aided by the unscrupulous adventurers who operated the Freedmen's Bureau and urged on by a fervor of Northern hatred almost religious in its fanaticism, the former field hands found themselves suddenly elevated to the seats of the mighty. There they conducted themselves as creatures of small intelligence might naturally be expected to do. Like monkeys or small children turned loose and among treasured objects whose value is beyond their comprehension, they ran wild—either from perverse pleasure in destruction or simply because of their ignorance. . . .

[T]hey were, as a class, childlike in mentality, easily led and from long habit accustomed to taking orders. Formerly their white masters had given the orders. Now they had a new set of masters, the Bureau and the Carpetbaggers, and their orders were: "You're just as good as any white man, so act that way. Just as soon as you can vote the Republican ticket, you are going to have the white man's property. It's as good as yours now. Take it, if you can get it!"

Dazzled by these tales, freedom became a never-ending picnic, barbecue every day of the week, a carnival of idleness and theft and insolence. (Margaret Mitchell, from her novel *Gone With the Wind*.)

[Two enormously popular novels about slavery have both reflected and shaped traditional regional attitudes about race in America. One was *Uncle Tom's Cabin*, by Harriet Beecher Stowe (*q.v.*), published nine years before the Civil War began. The Mitchell book was the other, published 60 years after the Reconstruction period ended. One was a northern view; the other, a southern view.]

RENDEZVOUS WITH DESTINY

519. There is a mysterious cycle in human events. To some generations much is given. Of other generations much is expected. This generation of Americans has a rendezvous with destiny. (President Franklin Roosevelt, acceptance speech, Democratic National Convention, Philadelphia, June 27, 1936.)

A PLEA FOR LABOR

520. There are those who fail to read both in the signs of the times and American history. They would try to refuse the worker any effective power to bargain collectively, to earn a decent livelihood and to acquire security. It is those short-sighted ones, not labor, who threaten this country with that class dissension which in other countries has led to dictatorship and the establishment of fear and hatred as the dominant emotions in human life. (President Franklin D. Roosevelt, "Fireside Chat" radio broadcast, September 6, 1936.)

ONE-THIRD OF A NATION

521. Here is the challenge to our democracy: In this nation I see tens of millions of its citizens—a substantial part of its whole population—who at this very moment are denied the greater part of what the very lowest standards of today call the necessities of life.

I see millions of families trying to live on incomes so meager that the pall of family disaster hangs over them day by day.

I see millions whose daily lives in city and on farm continue under conditions labeled indecent by a so-called polite society half a century ago.

I see millions denied education, recreation, and the opportunity to better their lot and the lot of their children.

I see millions lacking the means to buy the products of farm and factory and by their poverty denying work and productiveness to many other millions.

I see one-third of a nation ill-housed, ill-clad, ill-nourished. (President Franklin D. Roosevelt, Second Inaugural Address, January 20, 1937.)

KANSAS CITY MACHINE

522. We know that the [Thomas J.] Pendergast machine enjoys all the political patronage in Kansas City and Jackson Country, but that is only a small part

of the machine's perquisites. It controls State and city contracts. It sells construction materials which go into public buildings. It can, if it wishes, exercise a virtual monopoly of Kansas City's liquor business and its soft-drink business. The jackals of the machine enjoy the slot-machine, dice, roulette, and prostitution rackets—and a Parisian who recently visited Kansas City described it as the wickedest city he had ever seen. There is hardly a phase of Kansas City's life untouched by this monstrous outfit. . . .

In 1934, there was to be an election for the United States Senate. There was also to be an election for Collector of Jackson County. To this latter post a county judge (an administrative, not a judicial, post), Harry Truman, passionately aspired. It was a job paying a large sum of money, and Truman could use the money. The boss was sorry. He could not endorse Truman for the collectorship but he would put him in the United States Senate. He did. . . . In the senatorial primary, believe it or not, the county judge who wanted to be a collector polled 120,180 votes in Kansas City, and a brilliant and tremendously popular veteran . . . got 1,221 votes. (Ralph Coghlan, "Boss Pendergast," in *The Forum*, February 1937.)

REFORMING OR PACKING?

523. Last Thursday I described the American form of government as a three-horse team provided by the Constitution to the American people so that their field might be plowed. The three horses are, of course . . . the Congress, the executive, and the courts. Two of the horses are pulling in unison today; the third is not. . . .

In the last four years the sound rule of giving statutes the benefit of all reasonable doubt has been cast aside. The Court has been acting not as a judicial body, but as a policy-making body. . . . The majority of the Court has been assuming the power to pass on the wisdom of these acts of the Congress—and to approve or disapprove the public policy written into these laws. . . .

The Court . . . has improperly set itself up as a third House of the Congress—a super-legislature, as one of the Justices has called it—reading into the Constitution words and implications which are not there, and which were never intended to be there. . . . We must take action to save the Constitution from the Court and the Court from itself. (President Franklin D. Roosevelt, radio address, March 9, 1937.)

524. [My] conclusion . . . was to infuse new blood into all our courts. We must have men worthy and equipped to carry out impartial justice. But at the same time we must have judges who will bring to the courts a present-day sense of the Constitution—judges who will retain in the courts the judicial functions of a court and reject the legislative powers which the courts have today assumed.

In 45 out of 48 States of the Union, judges are chosen not for life but for a period of years. . . . In many States judges must retire at the age of 70. . . .

What is my proposal? It is simply this. Whenever a judge or Justice of any Federal court has reached the age of 70 and does not avail himself of the opportunity to retire on a pension, a new member shall be appointed by the President then in office, with the approval, as required by the Constitution, of the Senate. . . .

Those opposing this plan have sought to arouse prejudice and fear by crying that I am seeking to pack the Supreme Court and that a baneful precedent will be established. What do they mean by the words "packing the Court"? . . .

If by that phrase . . . it is charged that I wish to place on the bench spineless puppets who would disregard the law and would decide specific cases as I wished them to be decided, I make this answer: That no President . . . would appoint, and no Senate of honorable men fit for their office would confirm, that kind of appointees to the Supreme Court. . . .

I will appoint Justices who will not undertake to override the judgement of the Congress on legislative policy, that I will appoint Justices who will act as Justices and not as legislators. (Ibid.)

[The proposal died in the Senate Judiciary Committee.]

SCREENING

On Memorial Day 1937, strikers attempting to march by a struck Republic Steel mill were fired on by Chicago police. The incident was filmed by Paramount newsreel cameramen. The film was suppressed by Paramount but was shown in secret to members of the La Follette Civil Liberties Committee. A reporter told of the committee's reaction.

525. Those who saw it were shocked and amazed by scenes showing scores of uniformed policemen firing their revolvers into a dense crowd of men, women,

and children, and then pursuing and clubbing the survivors unmercifully as they made frantic efforts to escape.

The impression produced by these fearful scenes was heightened by the sound record which accompanies the picture, reproducing the roar of police fire and the screams of the victims. (News story, *St. Louis Post-Dispatch*, June 16, 1937.)

[Ten strikers died, and another 58 were injured. Sixteen policemen were also injured.]

HOW TO WIN

526. If Negroes secure their goals, immediate and remote, they must win them, and to win them they must fight, sacrifice, suffer, go to jail and, if need be, die for them. (A. Philip Randolph, speech, National Negro Congress, Philadelphia, October 1937.)

PROPAGANDA DEVICES

527. We can more easily recognize propaganda when we see it if we are familiar with the seven common propaganda devices. These are:
1. The Name Calling Device.
2. The Glittering Generalities Device.
3. The Transfer Device.
4. The Testimonial Device.
5. The Plain Folks Device.
6. The Card Stacking Device.
7. The Band Wagon Device.

Why are we fooled by these devices? Because they appeal to our emotions rather than to our reason. They make us believe and do something we would not believe or do if we thought about it calmly, dispassionately. (Institute for Propaganda Analysis, *Propaganda Analysis*, November 1937.)

WHO CAN DECLARE WAR?

528. Except in the event of an invasion of the United States or its Territorial possessions and attack upon its citizens residing therein, the authority of Congress to declare war shall not become effective until confirmed by a majority of all votes cast thereon in a Nation-wide referendum. Congress, when it deems a national crisis to exist, may by concurrent resolution refer the question of war or peace to the citizens of the States, the question to be voted on being, Shall the United States declare war on ————? (Joint Resolution proposed by Congressman Louis L. Ludlow of Indiana on February 5, 1937, shelved in the House of Representatives by a vote of 209–188, January 10, 1938.)

ROLE OF THE HIGH COURT

529. What . . . are the major constitutional issues on which the validity of the principal New Deal measures turned? They are three in number.

First, has Congress exercised some power not delegated to it? . . .

Second, has Congress, or have the states, exercised some power in a manner so arbitrary or unreasonable as to amount to a deprivation of liberty or property without due process of law?

Third, has Congress exercised some delegated power, such as the commerce power or the taxing power, for a purpose believed by the Court to be unconstitutional?

There are no sharp, clear lines here between the constitutional and the unconstitutional, no categories of black and white, and in settling these issues the Court has come to exercise a type of judgment and discretion which is essentially legislative in character. . . .

I have no patience with the pious verbal expressions and legal epigrams by which certain judges and lawyers seek to camouflage or to conceal the essentially legislative power which the Court exercises in the handling of these three groups of cases and many others. . . .

In interpreting due process of law it may read into the Constitution either a progressive social philosophy or a Mid-Victorian theory of "rugged individualism." In setting the limits to the commerce power it may swing the balance toward an aggressive federal centralization or toward an equally vigorous protection of state rights. In my judgment the legislative power which the Supreme Court now wields in the exercise of its power of judicial review of legislation is far greater than can be soundly adjusted to the principles of democratic government. Our constitutional system rests on the principle that the legislative power of the United States is vested in the Congress. It is not vested in the Supreme Court. (Robert E. Cushman, "The Role of the Supreme Court in a Democratic Nation," Edmund James Lecture, University of Illinois, March 9, 1938.)

NEWSPAPERS AND CHANGE

530. [I]n the last three years great improvement has been made by the metropolitan press as a whole. Trained reporters who know the implications of labor's struggle are now used by certain great newspapers to get at the exact truth, but reporters trained to handle labor struggles are few, and the struggles are many. And much room remains for improvement in the handling of labor news by the American press. (William Allen White, "How Free Is Our Press?" *The Nation*, June 18, 1938.)

531. [After reviewing technological changes of the early 20th century:] In the next ten years the press may change again—certainly in its material aspect. Rotary presses, linotypes, stereotyping machinery may join the crossbow, the neckyoke, and the portcullis upon the ashheap of forgotten gadgets. (Ibid.)

RADIO VERSUS NEWSPAPER

532. The [radio] advertiser is willing to pay the cost of assembling a great orchestra or of forming a troop of entertainers or supplying a dance band because he knows that millions will listen. All he asks is the privilege of interrupting the program at intervals to catch the ears of those millions of listeners. It is an old technique. The itinerant medicine man of former days carried about with him his banjo player and minstrel and clog dancer and magician to attract the crowd to his tent and to put them in a benevolent mood as a prologue to his own "high pitch" upon the wonders of his pills and potions.

Now the radio is hopelessly committed to this form of operation. . . .

Having gotten his crowd he [the radio advertiser] should be permitted within decent limits to advertise his product. But he should not be permitted to turn that crowd into a political, religious or economic meeting. He should not be permitted to employ the radio and the crowd to spread religious, social, economic or political propaganda. However bad the newspaper may have become it has not descended to this. It does not, as a rule, rent out its news or its editorial columns to advertisers. It does indeed succumb to the influence of commercial interests but it does not permit the editorial function to pass out of its hands. Its editorials and reports do not have to run the gauntlet of advertising agents, vice-presidents and presidents and managers of commercial corporations, as is the case in broadcasts. (John T. Flynn, "Radio: Medicine Show," *The American Scholar*, autumn 1938.)

WELLS + WELLES = PANIC

533. Ladies and gentlemen, I have a grave announcement to make. Incredible as it may seem, both the observations of science and the evidence of our eyes lead to the inescapable assumption that those strange beings who landed in the Jersey farmlands tonight are the vanguard of an invading army from the planet Mars. (From "The Invasion from Mars" radio drama, Columbia Broadcasting System, October 30, 1938, from *The Treasury of Science Fiction Classics*, edited by Harold W. Kuebler.)

[Barely a month after a major war scare in Europe, Orson Welles used radio news techniques to dramatize *The War of the Worlds*, by H. G. Wells. Welles had writer Howard Koch present the drama as a series of bulletins, interviews, and eyewitness accounts interrupting normal programming. The effect was so realistic that many thousands of listeners were thrown into panic.]

HIRING FRUIT PICKERS

534. The man said, "You men want to work?" . . .
"Sure we wanna work. Where's at's work?"
"Tulare County. Fruit's opening up. Need a lot of pickers."
Floyd spoke up. . . .

"What you payin'?" . . .

"Well, can't tell exactly, yet. 'Bout thirty cents [an hour], I guess. . . . But it's keyed to the price. Might be a little more, might be a little less." . . .

"You're a contractor, an' you got a license. You just show your license, an' then you give us an order to go to work, an' where, an' when an' how much we'll get, an' you sign that, an' we'll all go."

The contractor turned, scowling. "You telling me how to run my own business?"

Floyd said, " 'F we're workin' for you, it's our business too."

"Well, you ain't telling me what to do. I told you I need men."

Floyd said angrily, "You didn' say how many men, an' you didn' say what you'd pay. . . . You don't know, you got no right to hire men." . . .

Floyd turned to the crowd of men. . . .

"Twice't now I've fell for that. Maybe he needs a thousan' men. He'll get five thousan' there, an' he'll pay fifteen cents an hour. An' you poor bastards'll have to take it 'cause you'll be hungry." . . .

The contractor turned to the Chevrolet and called, "Joe!" . . .

His companion swung the car door. . . . On his brown shirt a deputy sheriff's star was pinned. . . .

"Ever see this guy before, Joe?" . . .

"What'd he do?" . . .

"He's talkin' red, agitating trouble." . . .

"Get in the car," he said, and he unhooked the strap that covered the butt of his automatic. (John Steinbeck, from his novel *The Grapes of Wrath*, 1939.)

MOVIE LINES

535. Frankly, my dear, I don't *give* a damn. (Clark Gable to Vivien Leigh, *Gone With the Wind* [Metro-Goldwyn-Mayer], 1939, screenplay by Sidney Howard, based on the novel by Margaret Mitchell.)

[Gable has told Leigh that he is leaving her, and she has just asked him what she will do. The line is the most famous in the history of moviemaking. The strict Hollywood code of the time frowned on curse words. Finally, the line was permitted, with the emphasis to be placed on the word *give*.]

THE AGE OF PROPAGANDA

536. [W]e are in what may be ironically called a new Golden Age of propaganda. The last Golden Age came with the discovery and spread of advertising technique, the revelations in the army intelligence tests of the low level of popular thinking, and the underscoring the [First] World War gave to the irrational character of all political thinking. The new Golden Age, using all that, has added to it the control—either by a state monopoly or by a class monopoly—of the channels and sources of opinion, and their systematic exploitation for state or class ends. As Harold Lasswell says, "A new skill group has come into existence in modern civilization . . . skill in propaganda has become one of the most effective roads to power in modern states." And that propaganda skill is at the service of those who are ruthless enough to use it and can pay for it. (Max Lerner, from *Ideas Are Weapons*, 1939.)

Fire sweeps the U.S.S. *Arizona* at Pearl Harbor, December 7, 1941. The sneak attack by Japan brought the United States into the war.

14

World War II

When the war began, the United States was staunchly isolationist, wanting no part in a European war, but the Roosevelt administration recognized the danger posed by Hitler and Japanese militarism. When France surrendered to Nazi Germany, the president moved to provide help to an England bracing itself for German invasion. When Japan attacked Pearl Harbor, isolationism died. The United States was in the war to final victory.

A LETTER TO THE PRESIDENT

537. In the course of the last four months it has been made probable through the work of Joliot, Fermi and Szilard in America, that it may become possible to set up a nuclear chain reaction in a large mass of uranium, by which vast amounts of power and large quantities of new radium-like elements would be generated. Now it appears this could be achieved in the immediate future. This phenomenon would also lead to the construction of bombs, and it is conceivable, though much less certain—that extremely powerful bombs of a new type may thus be constructed. A single bomb of this type, carried by boat and exploded in a port, might well destroy the whole port, together with some of the surrounding territory. (Albert Einstein, letter to President Roosevelt, August 2, 1939.)

AS WORLD WAR EMERGES

538. The United States Army . . . in September 1939 [when World War II broke out] ranked, with Reserves, 19th among the world's armed forces, after Portugal but ahead of Bulgaria. In percent of population under arms, it ranked 45th. The active Army numbered 174,000 men, less than two-thirds the peacetime strength authorized by Act of Congress in 1920. (Barbara W. Tuchman, recalling events of September 1, 1939, from *Stilwell and the American Experience in China, 1911–45.*)

ENTER WALTER MITTY

539. It was two blocks to the parking lot. At the drugstore on the corner she said, "Wait here for me. I forgot something. . . ." Walter Mitty lighted a cigarette. It began to rain, rain with sleet in it. He stood up against the wall of the drugstore, smoking.

. . . . He put his shoulders back and his heels together. "To hell with the handkerchief," said Walter Mitty scornfully. He took one last drag on his cigarette and snapped it away. Then, with that faint, fleeting smile playing about his lips, he faced the firing squad, erect and motionless, proud and disdainful, Walter Mitty the Undefeated, inscrutable to the last. (James Thurber, from his short story "The Secret Life of Walter Mitty," *The New Yorker*, ca. November 1939, reprinted in *The Thurber Carnival.*)

[The short story was made into a highly successful 1947 movie by Samuel Goldwyn. Thurber, however, hated the movie and exchanged open letters with Goldwyn in *Life* magazine.]

ANTIWAR SLOGAN

540. The Yanks are *not* coming! (Slogan of the American Communist Party during the Hitler–Stalin Non-Aggression Pact, Late 1939–June 22, 1941.)

PRELUDE TO A LYNCHING

541. "What is justice? Is it justice that we sweat ourselves sick and old every damned day of the year to make a handful of honest dollars, and then lose it all in one night to some miserable greaser because Judge Tyler, whatever God made him, says we have to fold out hands and wait for his eternal justice? Waiting for Tyler's kind of justice, we'd all be beggars in a year. . . .

"What led rustlers into this valley in the first place?" . . . I'll tell you what did it. Judge Tyler's kind of justice. . . . They don't wait for that kind of justice in Texas any more, do they? No, they don't. They know they can pick a rustler as quick as any fee-gouging lawyer that ever took his time in any courtroom. They go and get the man, and they string him up. . . .

"Maybe if we do one job with our own hands, the law will get a move on. Maybe. And maybe it never will. But one thing is sure. If we do this job ourselves, and now, it will be one that won't have to be done again. . . .

"But, by God," he begged, "if we stand here yapping and whining and wagging our tails. . . . we'll have every thieving Mex and Indian and runaway Reb in the whole territory eating on our own plates. I say, stretch the bastards." (Walter Van Tilburg Clark, from his novel *The Ox-Bow Incident*, 1940.)

[The novel tells the story of a lynching in Nevada in the 1890s. Clark later commented: "[I]t was a kind of American Nazism that I was talking about. I had the parallel in mind, all right, but what I was most afraid of was not the German Nazis, or even the Bund, but that ever-present element in any society which can always be led to act the same way, to use authoritarian methods to oppose authoritarian methods.

"What I wanted to say was, 'It can happen here. It has happened here, in minor but sufficiently indicative ways, a great many times.' " This quote is from Walter Prescott Webb's "Afterword" in the New American Library edition.]

THE HAND AND THE DAGGER

542. On this tenth day of June, 1940, the hand that held the dagger has struck it into the back of its neighbor. (President Franklin Roosevelt, speech following the Italian invasion of France, June 10, 1940.)

PROHIBITING SUBVERSION

543. It shall be unlawful for any person

(1) to knowingly or wilfully advocate, abet, advise, or teach the duty, necessity, desirability, or propriety of overthrowing or destroying any government in the United States by force or violence, or by the assassination of any officer of any such government;

(2) with the intent to cause the overthrow or destruction of any government in the United States, to print, publish, edit, issue, circulate, sell, distribute, or publicly display written or printed matter advocating, advising, or teaching the duty, necessity, desirability, or propriety of overthrowing . . . any government in the United States by force or violence;

(3) to organize or help to organize any society, group, or assembly of persons who teach, advocate, or encourage the overthrow of any government in the United States by force or violence; or to be or become a member of, or affiliate with, any such society, group or assembly of persons, knowing the purposes thereof. (Smith Act, June 28, 1940.)

ON OBSTACLES AND DELAY

544. We can delay and effectively stop for a temporary period of indefinite length the number of immigrants into the United States. We could do this by simply advising our consuls to put every obstacle in the way and to require additional evidence and to resort to various administrative advices which would postpone and postpone and postpone the granting of the visas. (Breckinridge Long, memo to State Department officials James Dunn and Adolf Berle Jr., summer 1940, cited in *The Politics of Rescue*, by Henry L. Feingold.)

CONFRONTING THE DANGER

545. More than half the world is ruled by men who despise the American idea and have sworn to destroy it. They know that while one great people remains independent and free because it is strong and is brave, they can never crush finally the people they have conquered. . . .

We must be ready to meet force with a stronger force. (General John J. Pershing, radio broadcast, August 4, 1940, cited in *Black Jack: The Life and Times of John J. Pershing*, by Frank E. Vandiver.)

CAMPAIGN PROMISE

546. I have said this before, but I shall say it again and again and again: Your boys are not going to be sent into any foreign wars. (President Franklin D. Roosevelt, campaign speech, Boston, October 30, 1940.)

THE FUTURE OF LABOR

547. I see an America where factory workers are not discarded after they reach their prime, where there is no endless chain of poverty from generation to generation, where impoverished farmers and farm hands do not become homeless wanderers, where monopoly does not make youth beggar for a job. (President Franklin Roosevelt, campaign speech, November 2, 1940.)

ARSENAL OF DEMOCRACY

548. The experience of the past two years has proven beyond doubt that no nation can appease the Nazis. No man can tame a tiger into a kitten by stroking it. There can be no appeasement with ruthlessness. There can be no reasoning with an incendiary bomb. We know now that a nation can have peace with the Nazis only at the price of total surrender. (President Franklin D. Roosevelt, radio address, December 29, 1940.)

549. We must be the great arsenal of democracy. (Ibid.)

MOVIE LINES

550. Rosebud. (Orson Welles, *Citizen Kane* [RKO Radio], 1941, screenplay by Herman J. Mankiewicz and Orson Welles.)

[The movie begins with Welles playing the dying Kane. He whispers the word, and the movie sets out to discover what it meant to Kane. Allegedly paralleling the life of publisher William Randolph Hearst, it is regarded by many film critics and historians as the greatest motion picture ever made.]

551. The stuff that dreams are made of. (Humphrey Bogart to Ward Bond, *The Maltese Falcon* [Warner Brothers], 1941, screenplay by John Huston, based on the novel by Dashiell Hammett.)

[It is the end of the movie. The culprits are being rounded up. Bond asks Bogart what that figure is in his hands. It is the figure of a black bird at the center of the story. This movie set the stage for the sophisticated detective drama. It was also the coming-out for director John Huston and a whole new look at Humphrey Bogart as a leading man.]

THE NEED FOR UNITY

552. I cannot bring a divided nation into war. I learned that from the First World War. I felt the same urgency then that your people feel now. But [President Woodrow] Wilson taught me a lesson. I am going to be sure, very sure, that if the United States publicly enters the war, it will enter united. (President Franklin D. Roosevelt, speaking to William Stephenson, British intelligence official, January 1941, quoted in *A Man Called Intrepid*, by William Stevenson.)

FOUR FREEDOMS

553. In the future days, which we seek to make secure, we look forward to a world founded upon four essential human freedoms.
The first is freedom of speech and expression—everywhere in the world.

The second is freedom for every person to worship God in his own way—everywhere in the world.

The third is freedom from want—which, translated into world terms, means economic understandings which secure to every nation a healthy peace time life for its inhabitants—everywhere in the world.

The fourth is freedom from fear—which, translated into world terms, means a world-wide reduction of armaments to such a point and in such a thorough fashion that no nation will be in a position to commit an act of physical aggression against any neighbor—anywhere in the world.

That is no vision of a distant millennium. It is a definite basis for a kind of world attainable in our own time and generation. (President Franklin Roosevelt, State of the Union, January 6, 1941.)

A BLANK CHECKBOOK

554. [President Roosevelt is] not asking for a blank check, he wants a blank checkbook with the power to write away our manpower, our laws and our liberties. (Robert E. Wood, commenting on the proposed Lend-Lease program to aid Britain, January 11, 1941.)

COMMENT ON LEND-LEASE

555. [The proposed Lend-Lease program is] the New Deal's triple-A foreign policy—it will plough under every fourth American boy. (Senator Burton K. Wheeler, radio broadcast, *American Forum of the Air*, January 12, 1941.)

THE PRESIDENT RESPONDS

556. [Wheeler's remark is] the most untruthful, the most unpatriotic thing that has ever been said. Quote me on that! That really is the rottenest thing that

has been said in public life in my generation. (President Franklin Roosevelt, press conference, January 14, 1941.)

AID FOR BRITAIN

557. The British people . . . need ships. From America, they will get ships. They need planes. From America they will get planes. . . . They need tanks and guns and ammunition and supplies of all kinds. From America they will get tanks and guns and ammunition and supplies of all kinds. . . .

Our country is going to be what our people have proclaimed it must be—the arsenal of democracy. (President Franklin Roosevelt, speech on the Lend-Lease Bill, March 15, 1941.)

A NATIONAL EMERGENCY

558. An unlimited national emergency confronts this country. . . .

Our patrols are helping now to insure delivery of the needed supplies to Britain. All additional measures necessary to deliver the goods will be taken. (President Franklin D. Roosevelt, radio broadcast, May 27, 1941.)

MEMO ON INTELLIGENCE NEEDS

559. Strategy, without information on which it can rely, is helpless. . . . Information is useless unless it is intelligently directed to the strategic purpose. . . .

The United States lacks an effective service for analyzing, comprehending, and appraising such information as we might obtain (or in some cases have obtained), relative to the intention of potential enemies and the limit of the economic and military resources of those enemies. (William J. Donovan, "Memorandum of Establishment of Service of Strategic Information," prepared for President Roosevelt, undated. ca. early June 1941, cited in *The Last Hero: William J. Donovan*, by Anthony Cave Brown.)

[On June 18, 1941, Roosevelt approved establishment of the new agency. Donovan was named to head the Office of Coordinator of Information. The name was changed during the war to Office of Strategic Services. After the war, it became the Central Intelligence Agency.]

PLAYING BOTH SIDES

560. If we see that Germany is winning the war we ought to help Russia, and if Russia is winning we ought to help Germany, and in that way let them kill as many as possible. (Senator Harry S Truman, attributed, ca. July 1941, cited in *Prime Time*, by Alexander Kendrick.)

LINDBERGH OPPOSES WAR

561. The three most important groups who have been pressing this country toward war are the British, the Jewish, and the Roosevelt administration. (Charles A. Lindbergh Jr., speech, Des Moines, Iowa, September 11, 1941.)

THE FIRST SHOT

562. Hitler has attacked shipping in areas close to the Americas in the North and South Atlantic.

Many American-owned merchant ships have been sunk on the high seas. One American destroyer [*Greer*] was attacked on September 4. Another destroyer [*Kearny*] was attacked and hit on October 7. Eleven brave and loyal men of our Navy were killed by the Nazis.

We have wished to avoid shooting. But the shooting has started. And history has recorded who fired the first shot. In the long run, however, all that will matter is who fired the last shot. (President Franklin D. Roosevelt, radio address, October 27, 1941.)

WAR WARNING

---

563. Negotiations with Japan appear to be terminated to all practical purposes, with only the barest possibilities that the Japanese Government might come back and offer to continue. Japanese future action unpredictable, but hostile action possible at any moment. If hostilities cannot, repeat, cannot, be avoided, the United States desires that Japan commit the first overt act. This policy should not, repeat not, be construed as restricting you to a course of action that might jeopardize your defense. (Henry L. Stimson, message to U.S. Pacific commanders, November 27, 1941.)

DUTY OF THE SENTINEL

---

564. The outpost commander is like a sentinel on duty in the face of the enemy. His fundamental duties are clear and precise. . . . It is not the duty of the outpost commander to speculate or rely on the possibilities of the enemy attacking at some other outpost instead of his own. It is his duty to meet him at his post at any time and to make the best possible fight that can be made against him with the weapons with which he has been supplied. (Henry L. Stimson, testimony before a congressional committee investigating Pearl Harbor, March 21, 1946, recalling events of December 7, 1941.)

CALL FOR WAR

---

565. Yesterday, December 7, 1941—a date which will live in infamy—the United States of America was suddenly and deliberately attacked by naval and air forces of the Empire of Japan.

The United States was at peace with that Nation and, at the solicitation of Japan, was still in conversation with its Government and its Emperor looking toward the maintenance of peace in the Pacific. (President Franklin D. Roosevelt, address to Congress seeking a declaration of war, December 8, 1941.)

566. Always will we remember the character of the onslaught against us.

No matter how long it may take us to overcome this premeditated invasion, the American people in their righteous might will win through to absolute victory.

I believe I interpret the will of the Congress and of the people when I assert that we will not only defend ourselves to the uttermost but will make very certain that this form of treachery shall never endanger us again.

With confidence in our armed forces—with the unbounded determination of our people—we will gain the inevitable triumph—so help us God. (Ibid.)

MOVIE LINES

567a. Play it, Sam. Play "As Time Goes By." (Ingrid Bergman to Dooley Wilson, *Casablanca* [Warner Brothers], 1942, screenplay by Julius J. Epstein, Philip G. Epstein, and Howard Koch.)

[The famous line "Play it again, Sam" does not exist. Humphrey Bogart, later in the movie, tells Wilson, "You played it for her, you can play it for me. . . . Play it!"]

567b. I am shocked, *shocked* to discover that gambling is going on. (Claude Rains to Humphrey Bogart, ibid.)

[Conrad Veidt has ordered Rains to find an excuse for shutting down Rick's café.]

568. Round up the usual suspects. (Claude Rains to his gendarmes, ibid.)

[Humphrey Bogart has just shot Conrad Veidt, the Nazi major. This movie was picked because it represented the spirit of self-sacrifice that manifested itself in America during the war. The last two quotes are often cited by pundits today to make fun of insincerity and hypocrisy wherever they may occur.]

HOW TO WIN

569. No fighter ever won by covering up—by merely fending off the other fellow's blows. The winner hits and keeps on hitting even though he has to take some stiff blows in order to be able to keep on hitting. (Ernest J. King, chief of naval operations, undated, quoted in *Master of Sea Power*, by Thomas B. Buell.)

RELIGION IN WARTIME

570. There are no atheists in the foxholes. (Chaplain William Cummings, field service, Bataan, the Philippines, 1942, cited in *I Saw the Fall of the Philippines,* by Carlos P. Romulo.)

I SHALL RETURN

571. The President of the United States ordered me to break through the Japanese lines and proceed from Corregidor to Australia for the purpose, as I understand it, of organizing the American offensive against Japan, a primary object of which is the relief of the Philippines. I came through and I shall return. (General Douglas MacArthur, on arrival in Australia, March 17, 1942.)

RELOCATION FOR JAPANESE AMERICANS

572. TO ALL PERSONS OF JAPANESE ANCESTRY LIVING IN THE FOLLOWING AREA: [Geographic boundaries in northern California are specified]

Pursuant to the provisions of Civilian Exclusion Order No. 27 all persons of Japanese ancestry both alien and non-alien, will be evacuated from the above area by 12 o'clock noon P.W.T. [Pacific War Time], Thursday, May 7, 1942. . . .

The Civil Control Station is equipped to assist the Japanese population affected by this evacuation in the following ways. . . .

Provide services with respect to the management, leasing, sale, storage or other disposition of most kinds of property, such as real estate, business and professional equipment, household goods, automobiles and livestock.

Provide temporary residence elsewhere. . . .

Transport persons and a limited amount of clothing and equipment to that new residence.

THE FOLLOWING INSTRUCTIONS MUST BE OBSERVED:

1. A responsible member of each family . . . and each individual living alone, will report to the Civil Control Station to receive further instructions. This must be done on . . . Friday, May 1 . . . or on Saturday, May 2, 1942.

2. Evacuees must carry with them on departure for the Assembly Center the following property:

(a) Bedding and linens (no mattress) for each member of the family;

(b) Toilet articles . . . ;

(c) Extra clothing . . . ;

(d) Sufficient knives, forks, spoons, plates, bowls and cups . . .

(e) Essential personal effects . . . ;

All items carried will be securely packaged, tied and plainly marked with the name of the owner and numbered. . . . The size and number of packages is limited to that which can be carried by the individual or family group.

3. No pets of any kind will be permitted.

4. No personal items and no household goods will be shipped to the Assembly Center.

5. The United States Government through its agencies will provide for the storage at the sole risk of the owner of the more substantial household items, such as iceboxes, washing machines, pianos, and other heavy furniture. Cooking utensils and other small items will be accepted for storage if crated, packed and plainly marked with the name and address of the owner. (J. L. DeWitt, lieutenant general, U.S. Army commanding, April 30, 1942.)

BUT NOT IN SHAME

573. With broken heart and head bowed in sadness but not in shame I report to your excellency that today I must arrange terms for the surrender of the fortified islands of Manila Bay. (General Jonathan Wainwright, last message from Corregidor, addressed to President Roosevelt, May 6, 1942.)

[At about this point in the message, transmission was interrupted. The rest of the text did not become known until after the war.]

574. There is a limit of human endurance and that limit has long since been passed. Without prospect of relief I feel it is my duty to my country and to my gallant troops to end this useless effusion of blood and human sacrifice. (Ibid.)

575. If you agree, Mr. President, please say to the nation that my troops and I have accomplished all that is humanly possible and that we have upheld the best traditions of the United States Army.

May God bless and preserve you and guide you and the nation in the effort to ultimate victory.

With profound regret and with continued pride in my gallant troops I go to meet the Japanese commander. Goodbye, Mr. President. (Ibid.)

CARTEL AGREEMENT

576. Standard Oil [of New Jersey] had agreed with the German I. G. Farben Company that in return for Farben giving Standard Oil a monopoly in the oil industry, Standard Oil would give the Farben Company complete control of patents in the chemical field, including rubber. Thus when certain American rubber manufacturers made overtures to Standard Oil Company for licenses to produce synthetic rubber, they were either refused or offered licenses on very unfavorable terms. . . . Needless to say, I. G. Farben's position was dictated by the German government. (Senator Harry S Truman, radio broadcast, "Rubber in America," Blue Network, National Broadcasting Company, June 15, 1942, cited in *Truman*, by David McCullough.)

[There are differing opinions on Truman's personal reaction to this cartel agreement. McCullough quotes from the Truman Committee's report that there was no "unpatriotic motive," only "big business playing the game according to the rules." But at the time the investigation was under way, Truman was quoted as saying, "It still sounds like treason to me."]

WARNING TO SABOTEURS

577. I . . . do hereby proclaim that all persons who are subjects, citizens or residents of any nation at war with the United States or who give obedience to or act under the direction of any such nation, and who during time of war enter or attempt to enter the United States or any territory or possession thereof, through coastal or boundary defenses, and are charged with committing or attempting or preparing to commit sabotage, espionage, hostile or warlike acts, or violations of the law of war, shall be subject to the law of war and to the jurisdiction of military tribunals. (President Franklin D. Roosevelt, proclamation, July 2, 1942, cited in *They Came to Kill*, by Eugene Rachlis.)

[The proclamation was made shortly after the arrest of eight would-be saboteurs who had landed by German submarines on Long Island and Florida beaches. After a secret military trial, six of the eight were executed. The other two were deported back to Germany after the war.]

WAR AIMS

578. As one of the sections of the oppressed darker races, and representing a part of the exploited millions of the workers of the world, we are deeply concerned that the totalitarian legions of Hitler, Hirohito, and Mussolini do not batter the last bastions of democracy. We know that our fate is tied with the fate of the democratic way of life. And so, out of the depth of our hearts, a cry goes up for the triumph of the United Nations. But we would not be honest with ourselves were we to stop with a call for a victory of arms alone. We know this is not enough. We fight that the democratic faiths, values, heritages and ideals may prevail.

Unless this war sounds the death knell to the old Anglo-American empire systems, the hapless story of which is one of exploitation for the profit and power of monopoly capitalist economy, it will have been fought in vain. Our aim then must not only be to defeat nazism, fascism, and militarism on the battlefield but to win the peace, for democracy, for freedom and the Brotherhood of Man without regard to his pigmentation, land of his birth or the God of his fathers. (A. Philip Randolph, speech, March on Washington movement, September 26, 1942, cited in *Let Freedom Ring*, edited by Peter B. Levy.)

LIBERATION FOR WHAT?

579. This is a war of liberation. . . . Are we yet agreed that . . . our common job of liberation includes giving to *all* peoples freedom to govern themselves as soon as they are able, and the economic freedom on which all lasting self-government inevitably rests?

It is these two aspects of freedom, I believe, which form the touchstone of our good faith in this war. I believe we must include them both in our idea of the freedom we are fighting for. Otherwise, I am certain we shall not win the peace, and I am not sure we can win the war. (Wendell L. Willkie, *One World*, 1943.)

PREVIEW OF AWAY WE GO

580. No gags, no legs, no chance. (Walter Winchell, newspaper column, *New York Daily Mirror*, early 1943.)

[Notice appeared prior to Broadway opening. When it opened on March 31, 1943, name had been changed to *Oklahoma!*]

GERMS OF A NEW WAR

581. Unless the peace that follows recognizes that the whole world is one neighborhood and does justice to the whole human race, the germs of another world war will remain as a constant threat to mankind. (President Franklin Roosevelt, speech, White House Correspondents Association, February 12, 1943.)

DETROIT RACE RIOT

In June 1943 a race riot erupted in Detroit. White mobs attacked blacks, while some police stood by—or participated.

582. One Negro who had been an employee of a bank in Detroit for the past 18 years was on his way to work on a Woodward Avenue street car when he was seized by one of the white mobs. In the presence of at least four policemen, he was beaten and stabbed in the side. He also heard several shots fired from the back of the mob. He managed to run to two of the policemen who proceeded to "protect" him from the mob. The two policemen, followed by two mounted policemen, proceeded down Woodward Avenue. While he was being escorted by those policemen, the man was struck in the face by at least eight of the mob, and at no time was any effort made to prevent him from being struck. After a short distance this man noticed a squad car parked on the other side of the street. In sheer desperation, he broke away from the two policemen who claimed to be protecting him and ran to the squad car, begging for protection. The officer in the squad car put him in the back seat and drove off, thereby saving his life. (Thurgood Marshall, head of the National Association for the Advancement of Colored People (NAACP) Legal Defense Fund, writing of events of June 20–21, 1943, from "The Gestapo in Detroit," in *The Crisis*, August 1943.)

[President Roosevelt called out federal troops to put down the rioting. Some 34 died, including 25 blacks and nine whites.]

PLANS FOR A G.I. BILL

583. We are, today, laying plans for the return to civilian life of our gallant men and women in the armed services. They must not be demobilized into an environment of inflation and unemployment, to a place on a bread line or on a corner selling apples. We must, this time, have plans ready. . . .

The least to which they are entitled, it seems to me, is: Mustering-out pay. . . . Unemployment insurance. . . . Further education or trade training. . . . Improved and liberalized provisions for hospitalization, rehabilitation, and medical care. . . . Sufficient pensions for disabled members of the armed forces. (President Franklin Roosevelt, speech, July 28, 1943.)

AIR RAID ON PLOESTI

584. It was more like an artist's conception of an air battle than anything I have ever experienced. We flew through sheets of flame, and airplanes were everywhere, some of them on fire and others exploding. It's indescribable to anyone who wasn't there. (Leon W. Johnson, relating the Army Air Force raid on the Ploesti oil fields of Romania, August 1, 1943, quoted in *The Brereton Diaries*, by Lewis H. Brereton.)

TIME TO CHOOSE

585. As I recall, [President Roosevelt] asked me after a great deal of beating about the bush just what I wanted to do [i.e., stay in Washington as chief of staff or go on to London to head the Allied invasion of Europe]. Evidently it was left up to me. . . . I just repeated again in as convincing language as I could that I wanted him to feel free to act in whatever way he felt was in the best interest of the country and to his satisfaction and not in any way to consider my feelings. I would cheerfully go whatever way he wanted me to go. . . . Then he evidently assumed that concluded the affair and that I would not command in Europe. Because he said, "Well I didn't feel I could sleep at ease if you were out of Washington." (General George C. Marshall, recalling events of December 1943 in Cairo, cited in *George C. Marshall: Organizer of Victory*, edited by Forrest C. Pogue.)

AMERICAN DILEMMA

586. The Negro problem in America would be of a different nature, and, would be simpler to handle scientifically, if the moral conflict raged only between valuations held by different persons and groups of persons. . . . The moral struggle goes on within people and not only between them. . . . We shall find that even a poor and uneducated white person in some isolated and backward rural region in the Deep South, who is violently prejudiced against the Negro and intent upon depriving him of civic rights and human independence, has also a whole compartment in his valuation sphere housing the entire American Creed of liberty, equality, justice, and fair opportunity for everybody. He is actually also a good Christian and honestly devoted to the ideals of human brotherhood and the Golden Rule.... At the other end, there are few liberals, even in New England, who have not a well-furnished compartment of race prejudice....

Even the American Negroes share in this community of valuations: they have eagerly imbued the American Creed and the revolutionary Christian teaching of common brotherhood; under study, they usually reveal also that they hold something of the majority prejudice against their own characteristics....

Although the Negro problem is a moral issue both to Negroes and to whites, we shall in this book have to give primary attention to what goes on in the minds of white Americans....

[P]ractically all the economic, social, and political power is held by whites....

It is thus the white majority group that naturally determines the Negro's "place." All our attempts to reach scientific explanations of why the Negroes are what they are and why they live as they do have regularly led to determinants on the white side of the race line. (Gunnar Myrdal, *An American Dilemma: The Negro Problem and Modern Democracy*, 1944.)

LETTER FROM A SON

587. F.D.R. motioned for me to sit down. He opened a desk drawer, picked out a letter, and read part of it.

"Dear Pop," it began, "I only hope one of us gets killed. Maybe then they will stop picking on the rest of the family."

I had seen and heard F.D.R. laugh at jokes and stories, but I had never seen a President weep. His eyes filled. He tried to swallow a lump that stuck in his throat. He put the letter back in the drawer. (Walter Winchell, from *Winchell Exclusive*, recalling events ca. 1944.)

LETTER TO YANK

588. What is the Negro soldier fighting for? On whose team are we playing? Myself and eight other soldiers were on our way from Camp Claiborne, La., to the hospital here at Fort Huachuca . . . We could not purchase a cup of coffee at any of the lunchrooms around there. As you know, Old Man Jim Crow rules. The only place where we could be served was at the lunchroom at the railroad station but, of course, we had to go into the kitchen. But that's not all; 11:30 A.M. about two dozen German prisoners of war, with two American guards, came to the station. They entered the lunchroom, sat at the tables, had their meals served, talked, smoked, in fact had quite a swell time. I stood on the outside looking on. . . . I could not help but ask myself these questions: Are these men sworn enemies of this country? Are they not taught to hate and destroy . . . all democratic governments? Are we not American soldiers, sworn to fight for and die if need be for this our country? Then why are they treated better than we are? . . . if we are to die for our country, then why does the Government allow such things to go on? (Corporal Rupert Trimmingham, letter to *Yank* magazine, 1944, cited in *The Best from* Yank.)

THE STATEMENT NEVER MADE

589. Our landings in the Cherbourg-Havre area have failed to gain a satis-factory foothold and I have withdrawn the troops. My decision to attack at this time and place was based upon the best information available. The troops, the air, and the Navy did all that bravery and devotion to duty could do. If any blame or fault attaches to the attempt it is mine alone. (Dwight D. Eisenhower, draft of a communiqué prepared for release if the D-Day landings on Normandy had failed, June 1944, cited in *My Three Years with Eisenhower*, by Harry C. Butcher.)

D-DAY

590. Coming in on the landing craft approaching Omaha beach, it was very peaceful. When we landed it was pandemonium; it was complete terror. You didn't know if you would be alive the next minute. You saw nothing. But you heard artillery shells, mortar shells, machine gun fire. There were bodies every-where.

Our mission was to get up on the bluffs overlooking Omaha beach and set up an anti-aircraft unit. That became impossible. We faced a hill of little stones. You couldn't drive a half-track up there. So we were called on to do other things.

An officer came running up to us, pointing out a German bunker which stood in the way of anyone trying to get up those bluffs. He wanted us to take out that bunker.

I went into the surf first to check for mines in the water. Then we drove the half-track into the water, aiming it the best way to give us a clear field of fire. We got a clear shot and we knocked it out. That was during my first five or ten minutes on the beach.

This action opened a route up the hill because that bunker had been blocking the way. They called that Exit E-1. That was one of the three exits that opened up. Once that happened, vehicular traffic moved up.

When we were going up the exit road to the bluffs, we passed the bunker. And there were the Germans we had shot. They were in an awful state. And you could say, "Look, thousands of our guys were hit, and I don't know how many died." Yet when I saw what we had done, I didn't feel too good. Because I had never really hurt anybody before. Those Germans were our enemies, and yet to see those guys bleeding from the mouth. . . . They just lay out there on the bunker. I don't know if they lived or not. (Hy Haas, U.S. Army, recalling events of June 6, 1944, Omaha Beach, Normandy, interview, August 29, 1996.)

WATCHDOG COMMITTEE REPORT

In February 1941 Senator Harry S Truman called for creation of a committee to investigate defense spending of $25 billion. The new committee was approved and allotted $15,000 for expenses. Officially the Special Committee to Investigate the National Defense Program, it became known as the Truman Committee, for its chairman. He later summarized three years of committee operations.

591. We saw the seamy side of the war effort. We had to investigate crooked contractors on camp construction, airplane engine manufacturers who made faulty ones, steel plate factories which cheated, and hundreds of other such sordid and unpatriotic ventures. We investigated procurement, labor hoarding, army and navy waste in food and other supplies. But when we were coming to our conclusions, we all decided that by and large the greatest production and war preparation job in history had been fine.

We looked into rubber. . . . We found cartel agreements by the great oil and aluminum companies which were helpful to the enemy, and we found labor leaders who were willing to sacrifice the country for their own aggrandizement.

Publicity is the best antidote for this sort of thing and the committee acted as a sounding board to the country. We made some 30 reports over a three-year period and . . . not one report contained minority views. (Senator Harry S Truman, recalling events from 1941–1944, from *The Autobiography of Harry S Truman*, edited by Robert H. Ferrell.)

ON THE EVE OF BATTLE

592. All real Americans love the sting of clash of battle. America loves a winner. America will not tolerate a loser. . . . America never will lose a war, for the very thought of losing is hateful to an American. (General George S. Patton Jr., address to his troops, France, July 1944, cited in *Memoirs of a Revolutionist*, by Dwight Macdonald.)

593. You've bitched about what you call "this chicken-shit drilling." That drilling was for a purpose: instant obedience to orders and to create alertness. If not, some son-of-a-bitch of a German will sneak up behind him and beat him to death with a sock full of shit. (Ibid.)

594. Thirty years from now, when you are sitting at the fire with your grandson on your knee and he asks you what you did in the Great World War II, you won't have to say: "I shoveled shit in Louisiana." (Ibid.)

LETTER TO A CANDIDATE

595a. This letter is being addressed to you solely on my own initiative. Admiral [Ernest J.] King having been consulted only after the letter was drafted, and I am persisting in the matter because the military hazards involved are so serious that I feel some action is necessary to protect the interests of our armed forces. (General George C. Marshall, letter to Governor Thomas E. Dewey, September 27, 1944.)

[General Marshall had learned that Governor Dewey, Republican candidate for president, had gotten word that the United States had broken the Japanese code. Dewey was preparing a speech to charge that—because of the broken code—President Roosevelt, his campaign rival, had known in advance about Pearl Harbor.]

595b. You will understand the utterly tragic consequences if the present political debates regarding Pearl Harbor disclose to the enemy, German or Jap, any suspicion of the vital sources of information we now possess. . . . I am presenting this matter to you . . . in the hope that you will see your way clear to avoid the tragic results with which we are now threatened in the present political campaign. (Ibid.)

[Dewey never mentioned the code issue during the campaign.]

UP FRONT

Cartoon depicts a weary group of American soldiers trudging through a driving rain as they guard captured German soldiers. Caption:

596. "Fresh, spirited American troops, flushed with victory, are bringing in thousands of hungry, ragged, battle-weary prisoners."—News item. (Bill Mauldin, from *Up Front*.)

FROM ADMIRAL TO ADMIRAL

597. The whole world wants to know where is Task Force 34. (Admiral Chester W. Nimitz, message to Admiral William F. Halsey Jr. during the Battle of Leyte Gulf, October 1944.)

[It happened during the battle to retake the Philippines. Halsey had left the San Bernardino strait unguarded to pursue a Japanese decoy force. Upon receiving the message, Halsey is said to have snapped to a subordinate, "Send him our latitude and longitude."]

CAUSTIC COMMENT

598. Nuts! (General Anthony McAuliffe, Bastogne, Belgium, in answer to a German demand for surrender of the town during the Battle of the Bulge, December 21, 1944.)

PRAYER FOR GOOD WEATHER

599. Almighty and most merciful Father, we humbly beseech Thee, of Thy great goodness, to restrain these immoderate rains with which we have had to contend. Grant us fair weather for battle. Graciously hearken to us as soldiers who call upon Thee that armed with Thy power, we may advance from victory to victory, and crush the oppression and wickedness of our enemies, and establish Thy justice among men and nations. Amen. (Chaplain James H. O'Neill, prayer written at the request of General George S. Patton Jr., Battle of the Bulge, Belgium, December 1944.)

THE PEACE TO COME

600. The structure of world peace cannot be the work of one man, or one party, or one nation. It cannot be an American peace, or a British peace, or a French, Russian or Chinese peace. It cannot be a peace of large nations. Or of small nations. It must be a peace which rests on the cooperative effort of the whole world. (President Franklin Roosevelt, address to Congress, March 1, 1945.)

ANTICIPATING VICTORY

601. In the joyousness of high spirits it is easy for us to forget the dead. Those who are gone would not want themselves to be a millstone of gloom around our necks.

But there are many of the living who have had burned into their brains forever the unnatural sight of cold dead men scattered over the hillsides and in the ditches along the high rows of hedge throughout the world.

Dead men by mass production—in one country after another—month after month and year after year. Dead men in winter and dead men in summer. . . .

Dead men in such monstrous infinity that you come almost to hate them.

These are things that you at home need not even try to understand. To you at home they are columns of figures, or he is a near one who went away and just didn't come back. You didn't see him lying so grotesque and pasty beside the gravel road in France.

We saw him, saw him by the multiple thousands. That's the difference. (Ernie Pyle, April 1945, from *Ernie's War*, edited by David Nichols.)

[This was part of a dispatch that war correspondent Pyle planned to publish upon the surrender of Nazi Germany. He was killed by a Japanese sniper on Ie Shima three weeks before the war ended in Europe.]

JAPANESE AMERICAN HERO

602. Of course, the arm had to come off. It wasn't an emotionally big deal for me. I knew it had to be done and had stopped thinking of it as belonging to me. (Lieutenant Daniel Inouye after his right arm was shattered by a German rifle grenade, Italy, recalling events of April 1945, cited in *Famous Asian Americans*, by Janet Nomura Morey and Wendy Dunn.)

[The arm of the future U.S. senator was amputated. The young lieutenant had been wounded during an attack on German positions. At the time it won him the Distinguished Service Cross. But 55 years later—in June 2000—he and a score of Japanese American soldiers would be awarded the Congressional Medal of Honor for their World War II valor.]

INDOCHINA'S FUTURE

603. There is . . . not the slightest possibility at the present time or in the foreseeable future that France will volunteer to place Indo-China under an international trusteeship, or will consent to any . . . international accountability which is not applied to the colonial possessions of other powers. If an effort were made to exert pressure on the French Government, such action would have to be taken by the United States alone for France could rely upon the support of other colonial powers, notably Great Britain and the Netherlands. . . .

The . . . United States should neither oppose the restoration of Indo-China to France . . . nor take any action toward French overseas possessions which it is not prepared to take or suggest with regard to the colonial possessions of our other Allies.

The . . . United States should continue to exert its influence with the French in the direction of having them effect a liberalization of their past policy of limited opportunities for native participation in government and administration, as well as a liberalization of restrictive French economic policies formerly pursued in Indo-China. (U.S. State Department, draft memorandum for President Truman, April 20, 1945, cited in *Vietnam: Anthology and Guide to a Television History,* edited by Steven Cohen.)

LETTER FROM A FLAG-RAISER

604. I am back again [overseas with his outfit instead of stateside promoting war bonds] . . . and I like it better this way. I have a reason for coming back. . . . I have not been over here twice for nothing. There were a few guys who went all through the battle of Iwo [Jima] with me. I've known them for a year, fought together, and were scared most of the time together. And they were back here while I was in the States, just for raising a flag, and getting all the publicity and glory. That I could not see. (Ira Hayes, letter to family, June 1945, Cited in *The Arizona Republic,* February 22, 1965.)

A THOUSAND SUNS

605. If the radiance of a thousand suns were to burst forth at once in the sky, that would be like the splendor of the Mighty One. . . . I am become death, the Scatterer of Worlds. (J. Robert Oppenheimer. This ancient verse is from the 2,000-year-old *Bhagavad Gita* of India. It flashed into Oppenheimer's mind at the first atomic explosion, Alamogordo, New Mexico, July 16, 1945.)

LEAST ABHORRENT CHOICE

606. The face of war is the face of death. . . . The decision to use the atomic bomb was a decision that brought death to over a hundred thousand Japanese.

No explanation can change that fact and I do not wish to gloss it over. But this deliberate, premeditated destruction was our least abhorrent choice. (Henry L. Stimson, article in *Harper's*, February 1947, recalling events of August 1945.)

HISTORIC SIGNING

607. BRANCH RICKEY: Suppose I'm a player . . . in the heat of an important ball game. Suppose I collide with you at second base. When I get up, I yell, "You dirty, black son of a bitch!" What do you do?

JACKIE ROBINSON: Mr. Rickey, do you want a ballplayer who's afraid to fight back?

BRANCH RICKEY: I want a ballplayer with guts enough *not* to fight back! You've got to do this job with base hits and stolen bases and fielding ground balls, Jackie. *Nothing else!* (Part of a three-hour conversation between the owner of the Brooklyn Dodgers and a ballplayer with the Kansas City Monarchs of the Negro American Baseball League, Brooklyn, New York, August 28, 1945, quotations from *Branch Rickey: American in Action*, by Arthur Mann.)

[Robinson played with the Montreal Royals—Brooklyn's farm team—until 1947. Then he began playing for the Dodgers, the first black player in the major leagues. During his 10 years with Brooklyn, the team won six National League pennants and a World Series championship. In 1962 Robinson was elected to the Baseball Hall of Fame—the first black so honored.]

ADVICE FOR PRESIDENTS

608. The buck stops here. (President Harry S Truman, sign on his Oval Office desk, the White House, 1945.)

609. If you can't stand the heat, get out of the kitchen. (Saying, undated.)

Television converted politicians into media stars. These members of the Committee to Investigate Organized Crime became folk heroes in 1950. Second from the right is Sen. Estes Kefauver of Tennessee, committee chairman. In 1956, he beat out for the Democratic Vice Presidential nomination a young senator from Massachusetts named John F. Kennedy.

15

Cold War

With the end of World War II—and the rise of an expansionist Soviet Union—the United States entered a period known as the Cold War. That meant fighting Communism at home and abroad. Isolationism was over. The United States created the Marshall Plan to rebuild Europe, provided help to defend Greece and Turkey from Russian domination, created the North Atlantic Treaty Organization, and sent troops to Korea and elsewhere.

It was also the era of television. One could not only watch a new president being inaugurated but see a gangster being grilled before a senatorial investigating committee and witness alleged Communist sympathizers confronting their accusers before klieg lights. Politics would never be the same.

Nor would race relations. One could not have fought Hitler's racial theories overseas and then justify them at home.

CARTOONS: POSTWAR

A soldier is being interviewed by two civilian reporters. An army public relations officer has his arm around the soldier's shoulder and speaks to the reporters.

610. He thinks the food over there was swell. He's glad to be home, but he misses the thrill and excitement of battle. You may quote him. (Bill Mauldin, 1945–1946, from *Back Home*.)

Soldier stands in front of a desk while a weeping executive addresses a nearby employee.

611. Sam, go tell poor old Jackson he'll have to put off his wife's operation and look for other work. Our hero has come back to take his old job. (Ibid.)

Two veterans are looking at a sign in front of an auto shop. The sign reads: "MEN WANTED: Applicants must be prepared to prove racial and religious background." One of the veterans comments.

612. I ain't got a chance, Joe—I had too many blood transfusions overseas. (Ibid.)

DISCLAIMER

613. This Autobiography, in spite of all the pains I have taken and the research I have put into it, is necessarily fiction. The fact that names, dates, and places seem to correspond with such things that may have occurred in real life does not guarantee the truth of these stories. So, in all candor, I wish to warn the reader not to confuse this story with reality. For God only knows the truth. I am hereby trying, in my finite way, to set down some facts which seem real and true to me. At best, this is only a tale that is told! (William Allen White, from *The Autobiography of William Allen White*, 1946.)

[The last half of the 20th century was filled with works of "nonfiction" with obvious recreations of incidents and conversations to which the respective authors could not possibly have been privy. There were so-called docudramas on television supposedly representing actual events. There was even a famous biography of Ronald Reagan, written by a prominent historian. He used the name of a fictional character as the biographer and included several fictional citations from fictional sources. White laid it all on the line. This, he said in effect, is how I remember it. Disclaimer or not, the book won the Pulitzer Prize for biography.]

CAMPAIGN SLOGANS

614. Had Enough? Vote Republican! (Republican campaign slogan on behalf of a Republican Congress, fall 1946.)

615. Vote Republican and You'll *Never* Have Enough! (Democratic campaign slogan on behalf of a Democratic Congress, fall 1946.)

THE ANGLE

As World War II ended, the horrors of the Holocaust became unmistakably clear. A civilized nation had turned to genocide. Novelist Hobson told the story of a magazine writer whose assignment is a series of articles on anti-Semitism in America. After much soul-searching, he hits on the best way to handle the subject.

616. "Every article you've done for us, Phil," Minify had said, "has a kind of human stuff in it. The right answers get in it somehow."

Sure. But he hadn't asked for them and pried for them. When he'd wanted to find out about a scared guy in a jalopy with his whole family behind him hoping for a living in California, he hadn't stood on Route 66 and signaled one of them to a stop so he could ask a lot of questions. He'd just bought himself some old clothes and a breaking-up car and taken Route 66 himself. He'd melted into the crowds moving from grove, ranch to ranch, picking till he dropped. He lived in their camps, ate what they ate, told nobody what he was. He'd found the answers in his own guts, not somebody else's. He'd *been* an Okie.

And the mine series. What had he done to get research for it? Go and tap some poor grimy guy on the shoulder and begin to talk? No, he'd damn well gone to Scranton, got himself a job, gone down into the dark, slept in a bunk in a shack. He hadn't dug into a man's secret being. He'd *been* a miner.

"Christ!"

He banged his fist on his thigh. His breath seemed to suck back into his lungs. The startled flesh of his leg still felt the impact of the blow.

"Oh, God, I've got it. It's the way. It's the only way. I'll *be* Jewish. I'll just say—nobody knows me—I can just say it. I can live it myself. Six weeks, eight weeks, nine months—however long it takes. Christ, I've got it." (Laura Z. Hobson, from her novel *Gentleman's Agreement*, 1947.)

[The novel apparently inspired journalist John Griffin to darken his skin and "become black" in the Deep South. The story is told in his book *Black like Me*.]

REPORT HITS LYNCHING

617. While available statistics show that, decade by decade, lynchings have decreased, this Committee has found that in the year 1947 lynching remains one of the most serious threats to the civil rights of Americans. It is still possible for a mob to abduct and murder a person in some sections of the country with almost certain assurance of escaping punishment for the crime. The decade from 1936 through 1946 saw at least 43 lynchings. No person received the death penalty, and the majority of the guilty persons were not even prosecuted.

The communities in which lynchings occur tend to condone the crime. Punishment of lynchers is not accepted as the responsibility of state or local governments in these communities. Frequently, state officials participate in the crime, actively or passively. Federal efforts to punish the crime are resisted. Condonation of lynching is indicated by the failure of some local law enforcement officials to make adequate efforts to break up a mob. It is further shown by failure in most cases to make any real effort to apprehend or try those guilty. If the federal government enters a case, local officials sometimes actively resist the federal investigation. Local citizens often combine to impede the effort to apprehend the criminals by convenient "loss of memory"; grand juries refuse to indict; trial juries acquit in the face of overwhelming proof of guilt.

The large number of attempted lynchings highlights, even more than those which have succeeded, the widespread readiness of many communities to resort to mob violence. Thus, for seven of the years from 1937 to 1946 for which statistics are reported, the conservative estimates of the Tuskegee Institute show 226 persons were rescued from threatened lynching. Over 200 of these were Negroes. . . .

Lynching is the ultimate threat by which his inferior status is driven home to the Negro. As a terrorist device, it reinforces all the other disabilities placed upon him. The threat of lynching always hangs over the head of the southern Negro; the knowledge that a misinterpreted word or action can lead to his death is a dreadful burden. . . .

Committee's Recommendations. . . .

The enactment by Congress of an anti-lynching law. (President's Committee on Civil Rights, *To Secure These Rights*, 1947.)

[Among other points dealt with in the report: establishment of a civil rights investigating unit in the FBI, establishment of a permanent Civil Rights Commission, and self-government for the District of Columbia, plus the issues of police brutality, involuntary servitude, poll taxes, voting in primaries as well as regular elections, and segregation laws.]

THE WAY THINGS ARE

618. Consider the case of Professor X, who is *any* Negro professor at [the black] Atlanta University. He works in close conjunction with several whites, but meeting him on the street after hours, they will not be likely to recognize or greet him. In a hotel, he must take the freight elevator, and under no circumstances can he eat in any but a quarantined restaurant or lunchroom. He is too proud to go to a Jim Crow theater; therefore he can scarcely ever see a first-run movie, or go to a concert. If he travels in a daycoach he is herded like an animal into a villainously decrepit wooden car. If he visits a friend in a suburb, he will find that water, electricity, and gas may literally stop where the segregated quarter begins. He cannot as a rule try on a hat or a pair of gloves in a white store. Not conceivably will a true southern white shake hands with him, and at a bus terminal or similar point he will, of course, have to use the "colored" toilet, and drink from a separate water fountain. He is expected to give the right of way to whites on the sidewalk, and he will almost never see the picture of a fellow Negro in a newspaper, unless of a criminal. His children must attend a segregated school; they could not possibly go to a white swimming pool, bowling alley, dance hall or other place of recreation. When they grow up, no state university in the entire South will receive them. (John Gunther, from *Inside U.S.A.*, 1947.)

LOYALTY ORDER

619. There shall be a loyalty investigation of every person entering the civilian employment of any department or agency of the Executive Branch of the Federal Government. . . .

An investigation shall be made of all applicants at all available pertinent sources of information and shall include reference to: F.B.I. files, Civil Service Commission files, military and naval intelligence files, files of any other appropriate government investigative or intelligence agency, House Committee on Un-American Activities files, local law-enforcement files at the place of residence and employment of the applicant, including municipal, county and state law-enforcement files, schools and colleges attended by applicant, former employers . . . , references . . . , and any other appropriate source.

Whenever derogatory information with respect to loyalty of an applicant is revealed, a full field investigation shall be conducted. (President Harry S Truman, executive order, March 22, 1947.)

620. Disloyalty may include one or more of the following:

Sabotage, espionage, or preparations thereof, knowingly associating with spies or saboteurs.

Treason or sedition. . . .

Advocacy of revolution or violence to alter the Constitution or Government of the United States. . . .

Intentional, unauthorized disclosure to any person, under circumstances which indicate disloyalty to the United States, of documents or information of a confidential or non-public character obtained by the person . . . as a result of his employment by the Government. . . .

Performing or attempting to perform his duties, or otherwise acting, so as to serve the interests of another government in preference to the interests of the United States.

Membership in, affiliation or sympathetic association with any foreign or domestic organization, association, movement group or combination of persons, designated by the Attorney General as totalitarian, Fascist, Communist, or subversive . . . or of advocating or adopting the commission of acts of force or violence to deny other persons their rights under the Constitution of the United States. (Ibid.)

A PLAN TO SAVE EUROPE

621. In considering the requirements for the rehabilitation of Europe the physical loss of life, the visible destruction of cities, factories, mines and railroads was correctly estimated, but it has become obvious during recent months that this visible destruction was probably less serious than the dislocation of the entire fabric of a European economy. . . .

It is logical that the United States should do whatever it is able to do to assist in the return of normal economic health in the world, without which there can be no political stability and no assured peace. . . .

Our policy is directed not against any country or doctrine but against hunger, poverty, desperation and chaos. Its purpose should be the revival of a working economy in the world so as to permit the emergence of political and social conditions in which free institutions can exist. . . .

With foresight, and a willingness on the part of our people to face up to the vast responsibility which history has clearly placed upon our country, the difficulties I have outlined can and will be overcome. (Secretary of State George C. Marshall, address at Harvard University, Cambridge, Massachusetts, June 5, 1947.)

[The program, later known as the Marshall Plan, would win the Nobel Peace Prize for Marshall.]

A CALL FOR CONTAINMENT

622. Once a given party line has been laid down on a given issue of current policy, the whole Soviet governmental machine, including the mechanism of diplomacy, moves inexorably along the prescribed path, like a persistent toy automobile wound up and headed in a given direction, stopping only when it meets with some unanswerable force. The individuals who are the components of this machine are unamenable to argument or reason which comes to them from outside sources. Their whole training has taught them to mistrust and discount the glib persuasiveness of the outside world. Like the white dog before the phonograph, they hear only the "master's voice." ("X" [George F. Kennan], "Sources of Soviet Conduct," *Foreign Affairs*, July 1947.)

623. Thus the Kremlin has no compunction about retreating in the face of superior force. And being under the compulsion of no timetable, it does not get panicky under the necessity for such retreat. Its political action is a fluid stream which moves constantly, wherever it is permitted to move, toward a given goal. Its main concern is to make sure that it has filled every nook and cranny available to it in the basin of world power. But if it finds unassailable barriers in its path, it accepts these philosophically and accommodates itself to them. The main thing is that there should always be pressure, unceasing constant pressure, toward the desired goal. (Ibid.)

624. In these circumstances it is clear that the main element of any United States policy toward the Soviet Union must be that of a long-term, patient but firm and vigilant containment of Russian expansive tendencies. (Ibid.)

DEFINING A GRINGO

625. In my childhood I lived in the cultural future of the United States. There were no gringos in southern Arizona or West Texas then. Although many people had blond hair and blue eyes and spoke English without a trace of the soft vowels and musical endings of sentences born on the border, there were no gringos. . . .

A gringo is one who cannot bear the dust of the desert or the cactus's thorny will to survive. A gringo cannot soften a vowel or countenance a jalapeno in his stew. A gringo is always in the process of getting diarrhea, or of having diarrhea, or recovering from diarrhea. Gringos drink directly from the bottle and eat tostadas with a fork. They address waiters as "Sir" and grandmothers as "Miss." The male of the species is always in search of a whorehouse, while the female looks for a live-in maid. (Earl Shorris, recollections of the Southwest, ca. late 1940s, from *Latinos: A Biography of the People*.)

AIRLIFT

626. We stay in Berlin, period. . . . We are in Berlin by the terms of the agreement, and the Russians have no right to get us out by either direct or indirect pressure. (President Harry S Truman, statement to top staff, White House, Washington, D.C., June 24, 1948, cited in *Truman*, by David McCullough.)

[On this day, Stalin had cut off all rail, water, and highway access to the American, British, and French zones of Berlin. The intention was to force the Western Allies out of Berlin. Truman instituted the Berlin airlift to provide food and fuel to Berlin. The Soviet blockade of Berlin would last for 321 days, during which more than 272,000 flights were made into Berlin, transporting 23 million tons of food, fuel, and other supplies.]

THE HISS–CHAMBERS AFFAIR

627. For a year I lived in hiding, sleeping by day and watching through the night with gun or revolver within easy reach. That was what underground Communism could do to one man in the peaceful United States in the year 1938.

I had some reason for supposing that the Communists might try to kill me. For a number of years I had myself served in the underground, chiefly in Washington, D.C. The heart of my report to the United States Government consisted of a description of the apparatus to which I was attached. It was an underground organization of the United States Communist Party. . . .

The purpose of this group at that time was not primarily espionage. Its original purpose was the Communist infiltration of the American Government, but espionage was certainly one of its eventual objectives. . . .

The head of the underground group at the time I knew it was Nathan Witt, an attorney for the National Labor Relations Board. Later, John Abt became the leader. Lee Pressman was also a member of this group, as was Alger Hiss, who, as a member of the State Department, later organized the conferences at Dumbarton Oaks, San Francisco, and the United States side of the Yalta Conference. [Eight men were named in all, including Donald Hiss, brother of Alger.] (Whittaker Chambers, statement before the House Committee on Un-American Activities, Washington, D.C., August 3, 1948.)

628. I do not know Mr. Chambers and so far as I am aware, have never laid eyes on him. (Alger Hiss, telegram to House committee, August 3, 1948.)

629. [Following a face-to-face confrontation with Chambers:]

I am now perfectly prepared to identify this man as [a person I knew as] George Crosley. . . . May I say for the record at this point, that I would like to invite Mr. Whittaker Chambers to make those same statements out of the presence of this committee without their being privileged for suit for libel. I challenge you to do it, and I hope you do it damned quickly. (Alger Hiss, statement to committee members, Hotel Commodore, New York, August 17, 1948.)

[Chambers repeated his accusations on *Meet the Press*. Hiss filed a libel suit, but before the end of the year he was indicted for perjury. There was a hung jury in the first trial, but Hiss was convicted in the second. He was sentenced to five years in prison.]

PILLS AND POLLS

630. Polls are like sleeping pills designed to lull the voters into sleeping on Election Day. You might call them "sleeping polls." (President Harry S Truman, campaign speech, fall 1948, cited in *Presidential Wit*, edited by Bill Adler.)

[During the election campaign of 1948, pollsters almost unanimously predicted that Governor Thomas E. Dewey of New York would defeat Truman. They proved wrong.]

FROM A PLAY

Willy Loman, an aging traveling salesman, has taken his own life. The scene is the cemetery. Charley, his best friend, speaks.

631. Nobody dast blame this man. You don't understand. Willy was a salesman. And for a salesman, there is no rock bottom to the life. He don't put a bolt to a nut, he don't tell you the law or give you medicine. He's a man way out there in the blue, riding on a smile and a shoeshine. And when they start not smiling back—that's an earthquake. And then you get yourself a couple of spots on your hat, and you're finished. Nobody dast blame this man. A salesman is got to dream, boy. It comes with the territory. (Arthur Miller, from the play *Death of a Salesman*, 1949.)

FROM A PARIS SPEECH

632. [America was built] on the backs of the white workers from Europe. . . . and on the backs of millions of blacks. . . . And we are resolved to share it equally among our children. And we shall not put up with any hysterical raving that urges us to make war on anyone. Our will to fight for peace is strong. We shall not make war on anyone. We shall not make war on the Soviet Union. (Paul Robeson, speech, Congress of the World Partisans of Peace, Paris, April 1949, cited in *Paul Robeson*, by Martin Bauml Duberman.)

FROM A NEW YORK CITY SPEECH

633. I defy any errand boys, Uncle Toms of the Negro people to challenge my Americanism, because by word and deed I challenge this vicious system to death; because I refuse to let my personal success as part of a fraction of one percent of the Negro people, to explain away the injustices to 14 million of my people; because with all the energy at my command, I fight for the right of Negro people and other oppressed, labor-driven Americans to have decent homes, decent jobs, and the dignity that belongs to every human being. (Paul Robeson, speech, New York City, June 19, 1949.)

RIOT AT A CONCERT

Paul Robeson had become a highly controversial figure because of remarks he had made that were interpreted as unpatriotic and pro-Soviet. He was supposed to give a concert in Peekskill, New York, on August 27, but it was called off when local demonstrators blocked access to the event and injured some of those trying to attend. The concert was rescheduled for September 4, with some of the left-wing labor unions volunteering to protect the concertgoers.

634. At 6:00 A.M. . . . the first union guards arrived to set up defense lines at the concert site at Hollow Brook Golf Course, three miles outside of Peekskill. The state police . . . set up a command post in a nearby area. Overhead a police helicopter circled. Four ambulances stood by. As some 20,000 concert-goers began to arrive at midday, a veterans protest parade . . . marched outside the grounds . . . yelling anti-Semitic and anti-black remarks and taunting the arrivals with shouted threats: . . . "You'll get in but you won't get out!" . . .

[When the concert ended] the crowd started home. Or tried to. As the line of buses and cars crawled along the steep road winding out of the hollow, it ran into a gauntlet of enraged locals. Some hurled rocks from the embankment; others stopped cars, dragged out the occupants, and beat them. The police did nothing to intervene. . . . Before long the scene was a nightmare of crashing rocks, flying glass, blood, and swerving cars.

Hundreds of the volunteer union guards were trapped on the hollow, surrounded by the stone-throwing mob and by a thousand state policemen who refused to let the union men return to their buses. . . .

By the time it was over, dozens of buses and cars had their windows smashed and been overturned, and 130 people were injured seriously enough to require immediate treatment. . . .

The grand jury [investigating the riots] concluded that the Communists had deliberately fomented "racial and religious hatred" . . . and at the same time insisted that the violence "was basically neither anti-Semitic nor anti-Negro in character. . . . The fundamental cause of resentment and the focus of hostility was Communism . . . and Communism alone." (Martin Bauml Duberman, from *Paul Robeson*, citing events of September 4, 1949.)

BIRTH OF "McCARTHYISM"

The word "McCarthyism" is defined in *Webster's Ninth New Collegiate Dictionary* as "a mid-20th century political attitude characterized chiefly by opposition to elements held to be subversive and by the use of tactics involving personal attacks on individuals by means of widely publicized indiscriminate allegations esp. on the basis of unsubstantiated charges." The term derives from the tactics of U.S. senator Joseph R. McCarthy, a Republican from Wisconsin. His campaign to expose Communist subversion began with the speech that follows.

635. Five years after a world war has been won, men's hearts should anticipate a long peace, and men's minds should be free from the heavy weight that comes from war. But this is not such a period—for this is not a period of peace. This is a time of the "cold war." This is a time when all the world is split into two vast, increasingly hostile camps—a time of a great armament race. . . .

The reason why we find ourselves in a position of impotency is not because our only powerful potential enemy has sent men to invade our shores, but rather because of the traitorous actions of those who have been treated so well by this Nation. It has not been the less fortunate or members of minority groups who have been selling this Nation out, but rather those who have had all the benefits that the wealthiest nation on earth has had to offer—the finest homes, the finest college education, and the finest jobs in Government we can give.

This is glaringly true in the State Department. There the bright young men who are born with silver spoons in their mouths are the ones who have been the worst. . . .

In my opinion the State Department, which is one of the most important government departments, is thoroughly infested with Communists.

I have in my hand 57 cases of individuals who would appear to be either card carrying members or certainty loyal to the Communist Party, but who nevertheless are still helping to shape our foreign policy.

[The foregoing paragraph is as it appears in the *Congressional Record*. The quote, as it was originally reported, was as follows: "I have here in my hand, a list of 205, a list of names that were made known to the Secretary of State as being members of the Communist Party and who nevertheless are still working and shaping policy in the State Department." The night after the Wheeling speech, McCarthy was interviewed on a radio station in Salt Lake City, where the number of names was reduced to 57.]

One thing to remember in discussing the Communists in our Government is that we are not dealing with spies who get 30 pieces of silver to steal the blueprints of a new weapon. We are dealing with a far more sinister type of activity because it permits the enemy to guide and shape our policy. . . .

This brings us down to the case of Alger Hiss who is important not as an individual any more, but rather because he is so representative of a group in the State Department. It is unnecessary to go over the sordid events showing how he sold out the Nation which had given him so much. Those are rather fresh in all of our minds. [Three months earlier, Hiss had been sentenced to five years' imprisonment for perjury.]

However, it should be remembered that the facts in regard to his connection with this international Communist spy ring were made known to the then Under Secretary of State [Adolf A.] Berle [Jr.] three days after Hitler and Stalin signed the Russo-German alliance pact [in August 1939]. At that time one Whittaker Chambers—who was also part of the spy ring—apparently decided that with Russia on Hitler's side he could no longer betray our Nation to Russia. He gave Under Secretary Berle—and this is all a matter of record—practically all, if not more, of the facts upon which the Hiss conviction was based.

Under Secretary Berle promptly contacted Dean Acheson and received word in return that Acheson (and I quote) "could vouch for Hiss absolutely"—at which time the matter was dropped. . . .

As you know, very recently the Secretary of State [Acheson] proclaimed his loyalty to a man guilty of what has always been considered as the most abominable of all crimes—of being a traitor to the people who gave him a position of great trust. The Secretary of State in attempting to justify this continued devotion to the man who sold out the Christian world to the atheistic world, referred to Christ's Sermon on the Mount as a justification and reason. . . .

He has lighted the spark which is resulting in a moral uprising and will end only when the entire sorry mess of twisted, warped thinkers are swept from the national scene so that we may have a new birth of national honesty and decency in Government. (Senator Joseph R. McCarthy, Speech, Ohio County Women's Republican Club, Wheeling, West Virginia, February 9, 1950, text from *Congressional Record*, 81st Congress, second session.)

[As the most feared man in Washington, McCarthy attacked those whom he considered subversive in government, the military, academe, and the media. His investigation of the army backfired. He was condemned by the Senate in 1954, and his influence came to an end.]

LIBERTY VERSUS SECURITY

636. Big Government denies the great fundamental that the primary purpose of all government is to preserve liberty. By asserting that security is the chief aim of our society, it seeks to turn our people to the lotus and away from the basic truth that without working and producing we perish. . . .

Big Government gradually destroys the mainspring of our society. It offers no incentives to those who must create the goods and services which provide the security. In the words of the ancient writer, it sings a siren song: "Cast in thy lot among us; let us have one purse." It levels all down and throttles the source of our strength which lies in the restless ambitions of the ten million centers of initiative in our individual business and on our farms. (Governor Thomas E. Dewey, lecture, Princeton University, Princeton, New Jersey, February 9, 1950.)

AID FOR SOUTH KOREA

637. In [South] Korea the Government forces, which were armed to prevent border raids and to preserve internal security, were attacked by invading forces from North Korea. The Security Council of the United Nations called upon the invading troops to cease hostilities and to withdraw to the 38th parallel [the border between Communist-controlled North Korea and South Korea]. This they have not done, but on the contrary have pressed the attack. The Security Council called upon all members of the United Nations to render every assistance to the United Nations in the execution of this resolution. In these circumstances I have ordered United States air and sea forces to give the [South] Korean Government troops cover and support.

The attack upon Korea makes it plain beyond all doubt that Communism has passed beyond the use of subversion to conquer independent nations and will now use armed invasion and war. (President Harry S Truman, statement, Washington, D.C., June 27, 1950.)

RESPONSE TO A PAN

638. I've just read your lousy review of [daughter] Margaret's concert. . . . It seems to me that you are a frustrated old man who wishes he could have been successful. . . .

Some day I hope to meet you. When that happens you'll need a new nose, a lot of beefsteak for black eyes, and perhaps a supporter below!

[Westbrook] Pegler, a gutter snipe, is a gentleman alongside you. I hope you'll accept that statement as a worse insult than a reflection on your ancestry. (President Harry S Truman, letter to music critic Paul Hume of the *Washington Post*, Washington, D.C., December 6, 1950.)

[It is reported that Truman, believing that his secretary would tear up the letter if he tried to mail it from the White House, waited until she left. He then canvassed the Executive Mansion for a stamp and dropped the letter in a mailbox on Pennsylvania Avenue. Hume thought that he was the butt of a practical joke and showed the letter to a friend on a rival newspaper—which broke the story.]

THE GUARDIANS

In his novel, Wouk tells the story of a "mutiny" on a U.S. Navy ship during World War II. In the midst of a crisis at sea, Captain Queeg had been placed on the sick list and relieved of his command by junior officers. Those officers are later court-martialed and are defended by Navy lawyer Barney Greenwald. Following their acquittal, Greenwald discusses Queeg and the role of American military professionals with some of the ship's officers.

639. "See, the Germans aren't kidding about the Jews. They're cooking us down to soap over there. They think we're vermin and should be 'sterminated and our corpses turned into something useful. . . . But I just can't cotton to the idea of my mom melted down into a bar of soap. . . .

"See, while I was studying law 'n old Keefer here was writing his play for the Theatre Guild, . . . all that time these birds we call regulars [professionals in the American military]—these stuffy, stupid Prussians, in the Navy and the Army— were manning guns. . . . [Captain Queeg] was standing guard on this fat, dumb and happy country of ours. Meantime me, I was advancing my little free non-Prussian life for dough. Of course, we figured in those days, only fools go into armed service. Bad pay, no millionaire future, and you can't call your mind or body your own. Not for sensitive intellectuals. So when all hell broke loose and the Germans started running out of soap and figured, well it's time to come over and melt down old Mrs. Greenwald—who's gonna stop them? Not her boy Barney. Can't stop a Nazi with a lawbook. So I dropped the lawbooks and ran to learn how to fly. . . . Meantime, and I took a year and a half before I was any good, who was keeping Mama out of the soap dish? Captain Queeg.

"Yes, even Queeg, poor sad guy, yes, and most of them not sad at all, fellows, a lot of them sharper boys than any of us, don't kid yourself, best men I've ever seen, you can't be good in the Army or Navy unless you're goddamn good. . . .

"Queeg deserved better at my hands. I owed him a favor, don't you see? He stopped Hermann Goering from washing his fat behind with my mom." (Herman Wouk, from his novel *The Caine Mutiny*, 1951.)

NO THIRD TERM

640. No person shall be elected to the office of the President more than twice, and no person who has held the office of President, or acted as President, for more than two years of a term in which some other person was elected President shall be elected to the office of the President more than once. (22nd Amendment, ratified February 27, 1951.)

RELIEVING A COMMANDER

641. You may ask: Why can't we take other steps to punish the aggressor [in Korea]? Why don't we assist Chinese Nationalist troops to land on the mainland of China? If we were to do these things we would be running a very grave risk of starting a general war. If that were to happen, we would have brought about the exact situation we are trying to prevent. . . . We would become entangled in a vast conflict on the continent of Asia and our task would become immeasurably more difficult all over the world. . . .

A number of events have made it evident that General MacArthur did not agree with that policy [to limit the war]. I have therefore considered it essential to relieve General MacArthur [as commander of United Nations forces in Korea] so that there would be no doubt or confusion as to the real purpose and aim of our policy. (President Harry S Truman, speech, April 11, 1951.)

NO SUBSTITUTE FOR VICTORY

642. Our victory [in Korea] was complete and our objectives within reach when Red China intervened with numerically superior ground forces. This created a new war. . . .

While no man in his right mind would advocate sending our ground forces into continental China and such was never given thought, the new situation did urgently demand a drastic revision of strategic planning. . . .

Apart from the military need as I saw it to neutralize the sanctuary protection given the enemy north of the Yalu, I felt that military necessity in the conduct of the war made mandatory:

1. The intensification of our economic blockade against China;
2. The imposition of a naval blockade against the China coast;
3. Removal of restrictions on air reconnaissance of China's coastal areas of Manchuria;
4. Removal of restrictions on the forces of the Republic of China on Formosa [Taiwan] with logistical support to contribute to their effective operations against the common enemy. . . .

In war there is no substitute for victory. (General Douglas MacArthur, address to Congress, Washington, D.C., April 19, 1951.)

CONVICTIONS UPHELD

643. It [the Smith Act] is directed at advocacy, not discussion. . . . Congress did not intend to eradicate the free discussion of political theories, to destroy the traditional rights of Americans to discuss and evaluate ideas without fear of governmental sanction. Rather Congress was concerned with the very kind of activity in which the evidence showed these petitioners engaged. . . . Their conspiracy to organize the Communist Party and to teach and advocate the overthrow of the Government of the United States by force and violence created a "clear and present danger" of an attempt to overthrow the Government by force and violence. They were properly and constitutionally convicted for violation of the Smith Act. (Chief Justice Fred M. Vinson, majority opinion, *Dennis v. United States*, June 4, 1951.)

[The conviction of 11 top leaders of the American Communist Party was upheld.]

LOOKING INTO THE FUTURE

644. We need faith as Americans have needed it in every crisis of history. The faith we need is the faith to do the things that should be done for the betterment of our people; not just some of our people, but all our people. We should not be afraid to speak of or advocate the "general welfare." Lincoln had no such fear and the Constitution says it is the fundamental purpose for which our Government is formed. We should not shy away from the term "civil liberties." The Constitution was not ratified until assurance had been given that they would be guaranteed in the Bill of Rights. . . . The term "social justice" is not an evil one. It comes to us from the Holy Bible. (Governor Earl Warren, Lincoln Day address, Boston, February 12, 1952.)

CONVENTIONS AND SMOKE-FILLED ROOMS

645. The national party conventions are, I believe, a vital part of the American political system. Smoke-filled rooms are indispensable to their successful operation. . . .

The main argument for the convention is simple. It works. During the last century it has brought before the country men of the caliber of Lincoln, Cleveland, McKinley, Bryan, Wilson, Hughes, Smith, Willkie, both Roosevelts, and others. The critics of the convention argue that such men were nominated despite the system rather than because of it. Is this really so?

The smoke-filled room is essential to the convention for it serves as the mechanism that allows party leaders to shift their choices toward a compromise candidate. Without such a mechanism there would be eternal deadlock. . . .

The only real alternative to the convention system is a nation-wide direct Presidential primary system. (James MacGregor Burns, "The Case for the Smoke-Filled Room," *The New York Times Magazine*, June 15, 1952.)

[The summer when this article appeared the Republican convention chose Dwight D. Eisenhower, and the Democratic convention chose Adlai E. Stevenson.]

CALL FOR LEADERSHIP

646. What counts now is not just what we are *against*, but what we are *for*. *Who* leads us is less important than *what* leads us—what convictions, what courage, what faith—win or lose. A man doesn't save a century, or a civilization, but a militant party wedded to a principle can.

So I hope our preoccupation here is not just with personalities but with objectives. . . .

What America needs and the world wants is not bombast, abuse and double talk, but a sober message of firm faith and confidence. . . . All the world is watching and listening. (Governor Adlai E. Stevenson, welcoming address, Democratic National Convention, Chicago, July 21, 1952.)

THE "CHECKERS" SPEECH

In the midst of the presidential campaign of 1952, a newspaper had charged that Senator Richard M. Nixon had a "secret fund" provided by his supporters. Nixon—Eisenhower's running mate—said that this money was purely for office expenses not otherwise covered. But it suggested corruption, and Nixon was being pressured to step down from the ticket. On the advice of Governor Thomas Dewey of New York, Nixon decided to tell his story to a nationwide television audience—and have them decide his fate.

647a. [Shortly before the telecast] I got an urgent call from Dewey. He told me that while he did not agree, a majority of Eisenhower's advisers had just met and wanted me to submit my resignation to Eisenhower at the end of the broadcast. He thought that I should say that while I felt I had done no wrong, I did not want my presence on the ticket to be a liability to the Eisenhower campaign. When he asked me what he should tell them I was going to do, I exploded and said I didn't have the slightest idea and they should listen to the broadcast. (Senator Richard M. Nixon, recollections of September 23, 1952, from *In the Arena, a Memoir of Victory, Defeat, and Renewal*.)

While preparing his speech, Nixon remembered Franklin Roosevelt's "Fala" speech in 1944, when Roosevelt "defended" his dog from Republican criticism.

647b. [A]fter rebutting, all of the false charges about receiving illegal gifts, I said that there was one gift I had received. Someone in Texas had sent us a little black-and-white cocker spaniel puppy. My daughters had named it Checkers. They liked the dog, and I said that regardless of what anyone said about it. I was going to keep it. [That reference is what gave the speech its name.] (Ibid.)

[The speech was a success. Nixon won the support of viewers, and he and Eisenhower would be elected in November.]

POLITICS AND TELEVISION

648. With a half-hour on a single television network running from $50,000 to $60,000, and even a 20-second spot announcement costing to $600, it . . . [was] necessary to divert funds from more traditional campaign investments, such as billboards, advertising and even, to some extent, travel. . . .

[T]here is a feeling in both radio-TV and political circles that television has not yet played, if indeed it ever will, the decisive campaign role that some enthusiasts predicted for it early in the year. . . .

The fireside type of television campaign presents a danger all its own. At first glance nothing could be more democratic than this direct contact between a candidate and his television audience, with no distracting scene stealers and no audience to sway the viewer with either partisan applause or catcalls. Perhaps it is the most satisfactory way of presenting a political argument, but if it is allowed to stand alone, without the wholesome questioning of the press or the chance of heckling, it can be an invitation to the demagogue. (Robert Bendiner, "How Much Has TV Changed Campaigning?" *The New York Times Magazine*, November 2, 1952.)

ON INVESTIGATING COMMUNISTS

649. I see no reason why congressional committees or others should not bring to the attention of the public the fact that men are Communists if they are Communists. I know of no civil rights infringed upon by such publicity, partic-

ularly fields infiltrated for the purpose of affecting public opinion, like the teaching profession, the movie and television field, the publishing field. But I see no
particular purpose in examining the views of a few individual professors if they
are not part of an organization promoting the spread of communism.

The question whether men should be dismissed from their jobs after the public
has been made aware of their connections is an entirely different problem, a
much more difficult one, and certainly depends very much on the particular case.

I see no reason why the Government should continue to employ people with
Communist sympathies. On the other hand, it seems to me doubtful whether
anybody ought to be fired from a job in a college if he is not using that job to
spread and teach doctrine intended to undermine and overthrow the Government of this country in favor of a Communist state. But those who are objecting
to investigation seem to me to be claiming a freedom that does not exist. They
not only want to express unorthodox opinions, but they want apparently to be
free from criticism for expressing unorthodox opinions. Certainly the people of
this country have a right to criticize Communists, and even criticize them to an
extent which might drive them from the positions where they are able to influence other people. . . .

I must say as a member of the board of trustees of a university, I would not
favor firing anybody for simply being a Communist, unless I was certain that he
was teaching communism or having some effect on the developments of the
thoughts of the students in that field. (Senator Robert A. Taft, speech, Chicago,
February 21, 1953, cited in *Readings for Republicans*, edited by Franklin L. Burdette.)

TAKING ON McCARTHY

650. The line between investigation and persecuting is a very fine one, and
the Junior Senator from Wisconsin [Joseph R. McCarthy] has stepped over it
repeatedly.. . . .

We will not be driven by fear into an age of unreason, if we dig deep in our
history and our doctrine; and remember that we are not descended from fearful
men. Not from men who feared to write, to speak, to associate, and to defend
causes that were for the moment unpopular.

This is no time for men who oppose Senator McCarthy's methods to keep
silent—or for those who approve. We *can* deny our heritage and our history but
we cannot escape responsibility for the result. . . .

The actions of the Junior Senator from Wisconsin have caused alarm and
dismay among our allies abroad and given considerable comfort to our enemies.

And whose fault is that? Not really his. He didn't create this situation of fear, he merely exploited it, and rather successfully.

Cassius was right. "The fault, dear Brutus, is not in our stars, but in ourselves." (Edward R. Murrow, *See It Now* telecast, CBS television network, March 9, 1954, cited in *Murrow: His Life and Times*, by Ann M. Sperber.)

16

Civil Rights Movement

The issue of civil rights goes back to the founding of the republic, with the addition of the Bill of Rights. But the modern civil rights movement begins in 1954 with the decision of the Supreme Court regarding racially segregated schools. A unanimous Court rules that "separate is inherently unequal." From that case would come demands from other groups for equal protection under the law.

It would not happen without a struggle—in the courts and in the streets. From Eisenhower, to Kennedy, to Johnson, the issue would grow, culminating in a Voting Rights Act.

The international issues evoked tense political drama about the Bay of Pigs, the Cuban missile crisis, and the problem of what to do in Southeast Asia.

SEPARATE IS NOT EQUAL

651. These cases come to us from the States of Kansas, South Carolina, Virginia, and Delaware. . . .

In each of the cases, minors of the Negro race, through their legal representatives, seek the aid of the courts in obtaining admission to the public schools of their community on a nonsegregated basis. In each instance, they had been denied admission to schools attended by white children under laws requiring or permitting segregation according to race. This segregation was alleged to deprive the plaintiffs of the equal protection of the laws under the 14th Amendment. In

Black students sit-in at a segregated lunch counter in Greensboro, North Carolina, 1960.
They waited to be served.

each of the cases other than the Delaware case, a three-judge federal district
court denied relief to the plaintiffs on the so-called "separate but equal" doctrine
announced by the Court in *Plessy v. Ferguson*. . . . Under that doctrine, equality
of treatment is accorded when the races are provided substantially equal facilities,
even though these facilities be separate. . . .

The plaintiffs contend that segregated public schools are not "equal" and cannot be made "equal," and that hence they are deprived of the equal protection
of the laws. . . .

Our decision . . . cannot turn on merely a comparison of these tangible factors
in the Negro and white schools involved in each of the cases. We must look
instead to the effect of segregation itself on public education.

In approaching this problem, we cannot turn the clock back to 1868 when
the [14th] Amendment was adopted or even to 1896 when *Plessy v. Ferguson*
was written. We must consider public education in the light of its full development and its present place in American life throughout the Nation. . . .

Today, education is perhaps the most important function of state and local
governments. Compulsory school attendance laws and the great expenditures for
education both demonstrate our recognition of the importance of education in

our democratic society. It is required in the performance of our most basic public responsibilities, even service in the armed forces. It is the very foundation of good citizenship. . . . In these ways, it is doubtful that any child may reasonably be expected to succeed in life if he is denied the opportunity of an education. Such an opportunity, where the state has undertaken to provide it, is a right which must be made available to all on equal terms. . . .

Does segregation of children in public schools solely on the basis of race, even though the physical facilities and other "tangible" factors may be equal, deprive the children of the minority group of equal educational opportunities? We believe that it does. . . .

To separate them from others of similar age and qualifications solely because of their race generates a feeling of inferiority as to their status in the community that may affect their hearts and minds in a way unlikely ever to be undone. The effect of the separation on their educational opportunities was well stated by a finding in the Kansas case by a court which nevertheless felt compelled to rule against the Negro plaintiffs:

"Segregation of white and colored children in public schools has a detrimental effect upon the colored children. The impact is greater when it has the sanction of the law; for the policy of separating the races is usually interpreted as denoting the inferiority of the negro group. A sense of inferiority affects the motivation of a child to learn. Segregation with the sanction of law, therefore, has a tendency to [retard] the educational and mental development of negro children and to deprive them of some of the benefits they would receive in a racially integrated school system." . . .

We conclude that in the field of public education the doctrine of "separate but equal" has no place. Separate educational facilities are inherently unequal. (Chief Justice Earl Warren, unanimous opinion, *Brown v. Board of Education of Topeka, Kansas*, May 17, 1954.)

PRELUDE TO A DOWNFALL

652. Until this moment, Senator [Joseph R. McCarthy], I think I never really gauged your cruelty or your recklessness. Little did I dream you could be so reckless to do an injury to that lad. It is true that he is still with Hale and Dorr [law firm]. It is true that he will continue to be with Hale and Dorr. It is, I regret to say, equally true that I fear he shall always bear a scar needlessly inflicted by you. If it were in my power to forgive you for your reckless cruelty I will do so. I like to think I am a gentleman, but your forgiveness will have to come from someone other than me. . . .

Let us not assassinate this lad further, Senator. You have done enough. Have you no sense of decency, sir, at long last? Have you left no sense of decency? If there is a God in heaven, it will do neither you nor your cause any good. (Joseph N. Welch, to Senator Joseph R. McCarthy during televised hearings of the Army-McCarthy investigation, Washington, D.C., June 9, 1954.)

[The investigation had to do with charges by McCarthy that members of the U.S. Army were carrying on Communist activities. The army responded that the heart of the matter was that McCarthy's investigators were trying to get special treatment for a former Mc-Carthy staff member, recently inducted into the army. Welch was counsel to the army during these hearings. McCarthy had just made accusations against a young associate at Welch's law firm. The preceding was Welch's immediate response. The confrontation, seen by millions on television, effectively marked the end of McCarthy's power in Washington. Before the end of the year, McCarthy was condemned by the Senate.]

WHY PEOPLE VOTE

653. People vote as they do for reasons related to every facet of human behavior. Education, occupation, income status, sex, age, race, nationality, religion, even regional differences are some of the standard items of classification against which the political scientist tests the issues of an election. Issues, in turn, may be grouped "anatomically" as pertaining to:

(1) The head, applying to voters who try to reason things out, to evaluate issues and candidates, and also to those who vote on the basis of their prejudices, acquired or hereditary;

(2) The heart, for those voters who respond emotionally;

(3) The pocketbook, whether full, empty or squeezed. (Louis H. Bean, "The Head, the Heart, or the Pocketbook?" *The New York Times Magazine*, October 31, 1954.)

ORIGIN OF "CATCH-22"

The setting of the novel is an Army Air Force base in the Mediterranean during World War II. Yossarian is an army pilot who does not want to fly combat anymore. He decides to plead that he is crazy and should be grounded. He goes to see Doc Daneeka.

654. "Can't you ground someone who's crazy?"

"Oh, sure. I have to. There's a rule saying I have to ground anyone who's crazy."

"Then why don't you ground me? I'm crazy. . . ."

[Yossarian gets nowhere and tries another approach.]

"Is Orr crazy?"

"He sure is. . . ."

"Can't you ground him?"

"I sure can. But first he has to ask me to. I have to. That's part of the rule."

"Then why doesn't he ask you to?"

"Because he's crazy," Doc Daneeka said. "He has to be crazy to keep flying combat missions after all the close calls he's had. Sure, I can ground Orr. But first he has to ask me to."

"That's all he has to do to be grounded?"

"That's all. Let him ask me."

"And then you can ground him?" Yossarian asked.

"No. Then I can't ground him."

"You mean there's a catch?" . . .

"Catch-22. Anyone who wants to get out of combat duty isn't really crazy."

There was only one catch and that was Catch-22, which specified that a concern for one's own safety in the face of dangers that were real and immediate was the process of a rational mind. Orr was crazy and could be grounded. All he had to do was ask, and as soon as he did, he could no longer be crazy and would have to fly more missions. Orr would be crazy to fly more missions and sane if he didn't, but if he was sane he had to fly them. If he flew them he was crazy and didn't have to, but if he didn't want to he was sane and had to. Yossarian was moved deeply by the absolute simplicity of this clause of Catch-22 and let out a respectful whistle.

"That's some catch, that Catch-22," he observed. (Joseph Heller, from his novel *Catch-22*, 1955.)

SOUNDING CRY OF A REVOLUTION

655. No. (Rosa Parks, refusing the order of a bus driver to leave her seat in the white section and move back to the Negro section, which had no vacant seats available, Cleveland Avenue Bus, Montgomery, Alabama, December 1, 1955.)

A MODEST PROPOSAL

666. 1. Negro bus riders be given courteous treatment.

2. All bus riders be seated on a first-come, first-serve basis; that Negroes would sit from the back toward the front, the white passengers from the front toward the back.

3. Negro drivers be hired on routes that served predominantly Negro sections. (Montgomery Improvement Association, original proposal by African American organization to end the bus boycott in Montgomery, Alabama, 1956, from *The Negro Revolt*, by Louis E. Lomax.)

MOVIE LINES

667.

> The flagon with the dragon has the pellet with the poison,
> The vessel with the pestle has the brew that is true. . . .
> Now the vessel with the pestle has the pellet with the poison,
> The chalice from the palace has the brew that is true.

(Mildred Natwick to Danny Kaye, *The Court Jester* [Paramount], 1956, routine by Sylvia Fine.)

[Natwick gives Kaye advice on how to survive a perilous toasting ceremony. This movie quote was selected to point up differences in past humor and what passes for humor in today's media.]

BRINKMANSHIP

668. The ability to get to the verge without getting into the war is the necessary art. If you try to run away from it, if you are scared to go to the brink, you are lost. (Secretary of State John Foster Dulles, quoted by James Shepley, in "How Dulles Averted War," *Life*, January 16, 1956.)

CARTOON

Man, wife, and child are walking toward a church in the distance. Two men, standing at a Montgomery, Alabama, bus stop, eye them angrily. One speaks.

669. Somebody from outside must have influenced them. (Herbert Block, *Washington Post*, February 28, 1956, from *Herblock's Special for Today*.)

DISSENT ON INTEGRATION

670. We regard the decision of the Supreme Court in the school cases as a clear abuse of judicial power. It climaxes a trend in the Federal Judiciary undertaking to legislate, in derogation of the authority of Congress, and to encroach upon the reserved rights of the States and the people.

The original Constitution does not mention education. Neither does the 14th Amendment nor any other amendment. . . .

[The original "separate but equal"] interpretation, restated time and again, became a part of the life of the people of many of the States and confirmed their habits, customs, traditions, and way of life. . . . It [the Supreme Court's current decision] is destroying the amenable relations between the white and black races that have been created through 90 years of patient effort by the good people of both races. It has planted hatred and suspicion where there has been heretofore friendship and understanding. (Southern Manifesto Statement by 19 U.S. senators and 81 representatives from the South, March 11, 1956, *Congressional Record*, 84th Congress, 2nd session.)

A UNIQUE INTEGRATION PLAN

Late in July 1956 the North Carolina legislature met in special session to amend the state constitution on education matters. The legislature voted to amend compulsory school attendance so that students would not be forced to attend a school with a child of another race. It provided for "Education Expense Grants" for use in private schools. With tongue planted firmly in cheek, journalist Harry Golden proposed his own integration plan.

671. The white and Negro stand at the same grocery and supermarket counters, deposit money at the same bank teller's window, pay phone and light bills to the same clerk; walk through the same dime and department stores, and stand at the same drugstore counters.

It is only when the Negro "sets" that the fur begins to fly. . . .

Now here is the GOLDEN VERTICAL NEGRO PLAN. Instead of all those complicated proposals, all the next session needs to do is pass one small amendment which would provide only desks in all the public schools of our state—no seats.

The desks would be those standing-up jobs, like the old-fashioned bookkeeping desks. Since no one in the South pays the slightest attention to a VERTICAL NEGRO, this will completely solve the problem. (Harry Golden, essay in *The Carolina Israelite*, 1956, from *Only in America*.)

ASSESSING THE UNITED NATIONS

---

672. [O]ur foreign policy is an American policy and is not and will not be tied as a tail to a United Nations kite. (Senator William F. Knowland, speech, Georgetown University, Washington, D.C., February 11, 1957.)

CARTOON

Two bureaucrats in a government office. One speaks.

673. Well, we certainly botched this job. What'll we stamp it—"secret" or "top secret"? (Herbert Block, *Washington Post*, March 13, 1957, from *Herblock's Special for Today*.)

DEFIANCE IN LITTLE ROCK

674. It will be a sad day for this country—both at home and abroad—if school children can safely attend their classes only under the protection of armed guards. (President Dwight D. Eisenhower, statement upon issuing proclamation, Newport, Rhode Island, September 23, 1957.)

[The proclamation called on those who were obstructing the integration of Central High School in Little Rock, Arkansas, to cease and desist their obstruction and to disperse. The proclamation came about after mobs blocked the entry of several black students into Central High. The day after the proclamation was issued, federal troops were sent to Little Rock to enforce the Court orders.]

CALLING FOR TROOPS

675. In that city [Little Rock], under the leadership of demagogic extremists, disorderly mobs have deliberately prevented the carrying out of proper orders from a federal court. Local authorities have not eliminated that violent opposition and, under the law, I yesterday issued a proclamation calling upon the mob to disperse. This morning the mob again gathered in front of the Central High school of Little Rock, obviously for the purpose of again preventing the carrying out of the court's order relating to the admission of Negro children to that school.

Whenever normal agencies prove inadequate to the task and it becomes necessary for the executive branch of the federal government to use its powers and authority to uphold federal courts, the President's responsibility is inescapable.

In accordance with that responsibility, I have today issued an Executive Order directing the use of troops under federal authority to aid in the execution of federal law at Little Rock, Arkansas. (President Dwight D. Eisenhower, address, Washington, D.C., September 25, 1957.)

THE FBI: HISTORIAN'S VIEW

676. Besides civil rights, another unwanted issue the [19]50s placed on [J. Edgar] Hoover's agenda was organized crime. Once again, he rejected suggestions that he modify his exclusive emphasis on domestic security. Hoover looked upon demands that the Bureau make a new commitment to organized crime investigation as an implicit challenge to his authority and competence, because he had been on record for years denying that organized crime even existed. This stand put him in an embarrassing position when, on November 14, 1957, New York State Police Sergeant Edgar L. Croswell discovered a conference of more than 60 Mafia dons in the upstate New York town of Apalachin. In the ensuing uproar, the question was asked why Hoover, with his secret sources of information, had not known about the Mafia while it grew to the extent revealed by the Apalachin conference. Hoover's critics pulled out the statements he had made over the years in which he denied the existence of any such national crime syndicate, thus making him out to be either a fool or deliberately obtuse. (There was even some muttering about corrupt bargains between Hoover and organized crime to keep out of each others' bailiwicks.) (Richard Gid Powers, historian, commenting on events following November 14, 1957, from *Secrecy and Power: The Life of J. Edgar Hoover.*)

MOVIE LINES

677. Well, nobody's perfect. (Joe E. Brown to Jack Lemmon, *Some Like It Hot* [United Artists], 1959, screenplay by Billy Wilder and I.A.L. Diamond.)

[Lemmon, who has been hiding out from gangsters, has just pulled off his wig and told Brown that he cannot marry him because he is a man. In 2000 *Some Like It Hot* was voted the outstanding film comedy of all time.]

NEED FOR HELP

678. [O]ur own national interests demand some help from us in sustaining in [South] Vietnam the morale, the economic progress, and the military strength necessary to its continued existence in freedom. (President Dwight D. Eisenhower, speech, Gettysburg, Pennsylvania, April 4, 1959.)

A NEW KIND OF PROTEST

Four black college students were discussing what they might do to demonstrate on behalf of civil rights. They thought that they might go down to the local F. W. Woolworth and try to get served at the "whites only" lunch counter rather than at the takeout. One finally made the decision.

679. We might as well go now. (Student, North Carolina Agricultural and Technical College, Greensboro, February 1, 1960, cited in *Parting of Waters: America in the King Years 1954–63* by Taylor Branch.)

[The four students were David Richmond, Franklin McCain, Ezell Blair Jr., and Joseph McNeil. They sat down at the counter, tried to order food, and were refused service. They remained sitting all day, without being served. Other students joined them later, and the idea spread across the segregated areas of America. The "sit-in" was born.]

IMPROVING SLUM SCHOOLS

680. The contrast in the money spent per pupil in wealthy suburban schools and in slum schools of the large cities challenges the concept of equality of opportunity in American public education. More money is needed in slum schools.

Social dynamite is building up in our large cities in the form of unemployed out-of-school youth, especially in the Negro slums. . . .

The schools should be given the responsibility for educational and vocational guidance of youth after they leave school until age 21. . . .

Increased attention ought to be paid in both slums and suburbs to developing meaningful courses for pupils with less than average abilities. . . . [C]onsideration should be given by every school and community to the expansion of work-study programs for slow students. . . .

Employment opportunities in the large cities must be promptly opened on a non-discriminatory basis. Because of the attitude of management and labor this can be done only through . . . federal funds.

The answer to improving Negro education in the large Northern cities is to spend more money and to upgrade Negro schools, many of which are in slums, rather than to effect token integration by transporting pupils across attendance lines. Fully integrated teaching staffs are a necessity as well.

More teachers and perhaps more pay for teachers are necessary for schools in the slums. . . . Special training programs for teachers in slum schools are needed.

No effort should be spared in slum areas to enlist the support of parents in the education of their children. To this end adult education programs should be improved and expanded.

Big cities need decentralized administration in order to bring the schools closer to the needs of the people in each neighborhood. . . .

Nonpolitical, honest school boards composed of high-minded citizens who can differentiate between policy-making and administration are essential. (James B. Conant, from *Slums and Suburbs: A Commentary on Schools in Metropolitan Areas,* 1961.)

A LEGAL TECHNIQUE

681. Every lawyer dreams of the ultimate electronic invention that could recapture from the airwaves the words spoken in the past. Then we would hear the original Sermon on the Mount, Shakespeare's sonnets read by him, Lincoln's Gettysburg Address, and other great words proven to be deathless in more than the symbolic sense. We could also be certain of what every witness said years before the trial. In the meantime there is a technique that serves almost as well. I shall call it the rule of probability. It tells me what facts to seek. It leads me to witnesses and documents which I did not know existed. It points out the vulnerable area of the hostile witness's testimony and suggests cross-examination. It is an all-potent-weapon in the contest for truth. (Louis Nizer, attorney, from *My Life in Court,* 1961.)

PSEUDO-EVENTS AND CELEBRITIES

682. A pseudo-event . . . is a happening that possesses the following characteristics:

1. It is not spontaneous, but comes about because someone has planned, planted, or incited it. . . .

2. It is planted primarily (not always exclusively) for the immediate purpose of being reported or reproduced. . . .

3. Its relation to the underlying reality of the situation is ambiguous. . . .

4. Usually it is intended to be a self-fulfilling prophecy. (Daniel J. Boorstin, from *The Image: A Guide to Pseudo-Events in America*, 1961.)

683. Two centuries ago when a great man appeared, people looked for God's purpose in him; today we look for his press agent. (Ibid.)

684. We can make a celebrity, but we can never make a hero. In a now-almost-forgotten sense, all heroes are self-made. (Ibid.)

685. Celebrity-worship and hero-worship should not be confused. Yet we confuse them every day, and by doing so we come dangerously close to depriving ourselves of all real models. We lose sight of the men and women who do not simply seem great because they are famous but who are famous because they are great. (Ibid.)

686. The celebrity is a person who is known for his well-knownness. (Ibid.)

SOUNDING A WARNING

687. This conjunction of an immense military establishment and a large arms industry is new in the American experience. . . . In the councils of government, we must guard against the acquisition of unwarranted influence, whether sought or unsought, by the military-industrial complex. The potential for the disastrous rise of misplaced power exists and will persist. (President Dwight D. Eisenhower, Farewell Address, Washington, D.C., January 17, 1961.)

CALL FOR SACRIFICE

688. Let every nation know, whether it wishes us well or ill, that we shall pay any price, bear any burden, meet any hardship, support any friend, oppose any foe to assure the survival and the success of liberty. (President John F. Kennedy, Inaugural Address, Washington, D.C., January 20, 1961.)

689. Let us never negotiate out of fear. But let us never fear to negotiate. (Ibid.)

690. Now the trumpet summons us again—not as a call to bear arms, though arms we need—not as a call to battle, though embattled we are—but a call to bear the burden of a long twilight struggle, year in and year out, "rejoicing in hope, patient in tribulation"—a struggle against the common enemies of man: tyranny, poverty, disease and war itself. . . .

In the long history of the world, only a few generations have been given the role of defending freedom in its hour of maximum danger. I do not shrink from this responsibility—I welcome it. (Ibid.)

691. And so, my fellow Americans, ask not what your country can do for you—ask what you can do for your country. (Ibid.)

VOTES FOR D.C.

---

692. The District constituting the seat of Government of the United States shall appoint . . . a number of electors of President and Vice President equal to the whole number of Senators and Representatives in Congress to which the District would be entitled if it were a State, but in no event more than the least populous State. . . . [T]hey shall be considered, for the purpose of the election of President and Vice President . . . and they shall meet in the District and perform such duties. (23rd Amendment, ratified March 29, 1961.)

TEN DAYS IN APRIL

---

693. [T]here will not be, under any conditions, an intervention in Cuba by the United States Armed Forces. This Government will do everything it possibly can, and I think it can meet its responsibilities, to make sure that there are no Americans involved in any actions inside Cuba. . . .

The basic issue in Cuba is not one between the United States and Cuba. It is between the Cubans themselves. (President John F. Kennedy, news conference, Washington, D.C., April 12, 1961.)

[Rumors had been flooding Washington that a force had been assembled in Florida to overthrow Cuban dictator Fidel Castro. Five days after this press conference, anti-Castro forces began an amphibious invasion of Cuba at the Bay of Pigs.]

694. You are under a serious misapprehension in regard to events in Cuba. For months there has been evidence and growing resistance to the Castro dictatorship. More than 100,000 refugees have recently fled from Cuba into neighboring countries. Their urgent hope is naturally to assist their fellow Cubans in their struggle for freedom. . . .

I have previously stated, and I repeat now, that the United States intends no military intervention in Cuba. In the event of any military intervention by any outside force we will immediately honor our obligations under the inter-American system to protect the hemisphere against external aggression. (President John F. Kennedy, message to Premier Nikita Khrushchev of the Soviet Union, April 18, 1961.)

[By April 20, the invaders were forced to surrender.]

695. We dare not fail to see the insidious nature of this new and deeper struggle. We dare not fail to grasp the new concepts, the tools, the new sense of urgency we will need to combat it—whether in Cuba or South Vietnam. (Address, President John F. Kennedy, American Society of Newspaper Editors, Washington, D.C., April 20, 1961.)

696. There's an old saying that victory has a hundred fathers and defeat is an orphan. (President John F. Kennedy, Press conference, Washington, D.C., April 21, 1961.)

[The invasion by Cuban exiles had been planned a full year earlier by the Central Intelligence Agency during the Eisenhower administration. Kennedy had gone along with it, anticipating an uprising in Cuba when the forces landed. There was no uprising, and the invasion force of 1,500 men was crushed. The captured prisoners were later ransomed for food and medicine.]

CHALLENGE

697. I believe that this nation should commit itself to achieving the goal, before this decade is out, of landing a man on the moon and returning him safely to the earth. (President John F. Kennedy, message to Congress, May 25, 1961.)

POISONING THE EARTH

698. If Darwin were alive today the insect world would delight and astound him with its impressive verification of his theories of the survival of the fittest. Under the stress of intensive chemical spraying the weaker members of the insect populations are being weeded out. . . . [O]nly the strong and fit remain to defy our efforts to control them. . . .

We stand now where two roads diverge . . . The road we have long been traveling is deceptively easy, a smooth super-highway. . . . , but at its end lies disaster. The other fork of the road . . . offers our last, our only chance to reach a destination that assures the preservation of our earth.

The choice . . . is ours. . . . If . . . we have concluded that we are being asked to take senseless and frightening risks, then we should no longer accept the counsel of those who tell us that we must fill our world with poisonous chemicals; we should look about and see what other course is open to us.

A truly extraordinary variety of alternatives to the chemical control of insects is available. . . .

As crude a weapon as the cave man's club, the chemical barrage has been hurled against the fabric of life—a fabric on the one hand delicate and destructible, on the other miraculously tough and resilient, and capable of striking back in unexpected ways. These extraordinary capacities of life have been ignored by the practitioners of chemical control. . . .

The "control of nature" is a phrase conceived in arrogance, born of the Neanderthal age of biology and philosophy, when it was supposed that nature exists for the convenience of man. . . .

It is our alarming misfortune that so primitive a science has armed itself with the most modern and terrible weapons, and that in turning them against the insects it has also turned them against the earth. (Rachel Carson, from *Silent Spring*, 1962.)

NUCLEAR CONFRONTATION

699. Within the past week, unmistakable evidence has established the fact that a series of offensive missile sites is now in preparation on that imprisoned island [Cuba]. The purpose of these bases can be none other than to provide a nuclear strike capability against the Western Hemisphere. . . .

The characteristics of these new missile sites indicate two distinct types of installations. Several of them include medium-range ballistic missiles, capable of carrying a nuclear warhead for a distance of more than a thousand nautical miles. Each of these missiles, in short, is capable of striking Washington, D.C., the Panama Canal, Cape Canaveral, Mexico City, or any other city in the southeastern part of the United States, in Central America, or in the Caribbean area. . . .

Additional sites not yet completed appear to be designed for intermediate-range ballistic missiles—capable of traveling more than twice as far—and thus capable of striking most of the major cities in the Western hemisphere, ranging as far north as Hudson Bay, Canada, and as far south as Lima, Peru. . . .

We will not prematurely or unnecessarily risk the costs of worldwide nuclear war in which even the fruits of victory would be ashes in our mouth—but neither will we shrink from that risk at any time it must be faced. Acting, therefore, in the defense of our own security and of the entire Western Hemisphere, and under the authority entrusted to me by the Constitution . . . I have directed that the following initial steps be taken immediately:

To halt this offensive buildup, a strict quarantine on all offensive military equipment under shipment to Cuba is being initiated. All ships of any kind bound for Cuba from whatever nation or port will, if found to contain cargoes of offensive weapons, be turned back. . . .

It shall be the policy of this nation to regard any nuclear missile launched from Cuba against any nation in the Western Hemisphere as an attack by the Soviet Union on the United States, requiring a full retaliatory response upon the Soviet Union. (President John F. Kennedy, televised address, Washington, D.C., October 22, 1962.)

[As the U.S. Navy began its blockade of Cuba, intensive negotiations went on between the president and Soviet premier Khrushchev. Two communications were conveyed by the Soviet leader, one conciliatory and the other more formal and tough. Kennedy decided to ignore the latter and concentrate on a compromise satisfactory to both sides. In the final agreement, Khrushchev removed his missiles from Cuba. The United States, on the other hand, agreed that it would not invade Cuba in the future and removed its own missiles from Turkey.]

PRESS CONFERENCE

700. You won't have Nixon to kick around anymore. Because, gentlemen, this is my last press conference. (Richard M. Nixon, press conference following his defeat in the California gubernatorial race, November 7, 1962.)

CONFLICTING ROLES

701. Over and over women heard in voices of tradition and Freudian sophistication that they could desire no greater destiny than to glory in their own femininity [and] to pity the neurotic, unfeminine, unhappy women who wanted to be poets or physicians or presidents. (Betty Friedan, from *The Feminine Mystique*, 1963.)

702. The glorification of the "woman's role," then, seems to be in proportion to society's reluctance to treat women as complete human beings; for the less real function that role has, the more it is decorated with meaningless details to conceal its emptiness. (Ibid.)

703. The problem that has no name—which is simply the fact that American women are kept from growing to their full human capacities—is taking a far greater toll on the physical and mental health of our country than any known disease. (Ibid.)

DEFIANCE

704. Segregation now, segregation tomorrow, segregation forever. (Governor George C. Wallace, Inaugural Address as governor, Montgomery, Alabama, January 14, 1963.)

A LETTER FROM JAIL

705. I am in Birmingham because injustice is here . . . I am cognizant of the interrelatedness of all communities and states. I cannot sit idly by in Atlanta and not be concerned about what happens in Birmingham. Injustice anywhere is a threat to justice everywhere. (Dr. Martin Luther King Jr., letter to fellow clergymen, Birmingham, Alabama, jail, April 16, 1963.)

[King had gone from Atlanta to Birmingham to take part in acts of civil disobedience to protest against segregation laws. He had been jailed and labeled an "outside agitator." A group of distinguished white clergymen had urged that the protests be ended and the matter left to the courts.]

PENALTY FOR REGISTERING TO VOTE

In January 1963, Fannie Lou Hamer became one of a handful of African Americans to register to vote in Sunflower County, Mississippi. She became active in voter education and attended a South Carolina workshop for that purpose in June of that year. This is what happened when she returned to Mississippi with others in her group.

706. Four of our group got off the bus to get food in the bus terminal. Two got off to use the washroom. . . .

I saw six people rush out, and I got off to see what was happening.

Miss Ann Ponder told me the chief of police and a state highway patrolman had ordered them out. . . .

I looked out of the [bus] window and they were putting the Negroes in a car. . . .

"You are under arrest. Get in the car." As I went to get in, he kicked me. In the car, they would ask me questions. When I started to answer, they would curse and tell me to hush, and call me awful names.

They carried me to the County jail. Later I heard Miss Ponder's voice and the sound of kicks. She was screaming awfully.

Then three white men came to my room. A state highway policeman asked me where I was from. . . .

They said they were going to make me wish I was dead. They had me lay down on my face, and they ordered two Negro prisoners to beat me with a blackjack. That was unbearable. It was leather, loaded with something.

The first prisoner beat me until he was exhausted. Then the second Negro began to beat. I have limp. I had polio when I was about six years old. I was holding my hands behind me to protect my weak side. I began to work my feet. The state highway patrolman ordered the other Negro to sit on my feet.

My dress pulled up and I tried to smooth it down. One of the policemen walked over and raised my dress as high as he could. They beat me until my body was hard, 'til I couldn't bend my fingers or get up when they told me to.

That's how I got this blood clot in my left eye—the sight's nearly gone, now. (Fannie Lou Hamer, Winona, Mississippi, events of June 9, 1963, testimony before Select Panel on Mississippi and Civil Rights, Washington, D.C., June 8, 1964.)

LIMITED TEST BAN

707. Yesterday a shaft of light cut into the darkness. Negotiations were concluded in Moscow on a treaty to ban all nuclear tests in the atmosphere, in outer space, and under water. For the first time, an agreement has been reached on bringing the forces of nuclear destruction under international control. . . .

The treaty initialed yesterday, therefore, is a limited treaty which permits continued underground testing and prohibits only those tests that we ourselves can police. It requires no control posts, no on-site inspection, no international body.

We should also understand that it has other limits as well. Any nation which signs the treaty will have an opportunity to withdraw . . . and no nation's right of self-defense will in any way be impaired. Nor does this treaty mean an end to the threat of nuclear war. It will not reduce nuclear stockpiles; it will not halt the production of nuclear weapons; it will not restrict their use in time of war.

Nevertheless, this limited treaty will radically reduce the nuclear testing which would otherwise be conducted on both sides; it will prohibit the United States, the United Kingdom, the Soviet Union, and all others who sign it, from engaging in the atmosphere tests which have so alarmed mankind, and it offers to all the world a welcome sign of hope. . . .

The important point is that efforts to seek new agreements will go forward. . . .

Let us make the most of this opportunity, to reduce tension, to slow down the perilous nuclear arms race, and to check the world's slide toward final annihilation. . . .

According to the ancient Chinese proverb, "A journey of a thousand miles must begin with a single step."

My fellow Americans, let us take that first step. Let us, if we can, step back from the shadows of war and seek out the way of peace. And if that journey is a thousand miles, or even more, let history record that we, in this land, at this time, took the first step. (President John F. Kennedy, televised address, Washington, D.C., July 26, 1963.)

[The treaty was formally signed by the foreign ministers in Moscow on August 5. It was ratified by the U.S. Senate on September 24 and went into effect on October 10, 1963.]

A DREAM ON THE MALL

708. I have a dream that one day this nation will rise up and live out the true meaning of its creed: "we hold these truths to be self-evident that all men are created equal." (Martin Luther King Jr., Freedom March on the Mall, Washington, D.C., August 28, 1963.)

709. I have a dream that my four little children will one day live in a nation where they will not be judged by the color of their skin, but by the content of their character. (Ibid.)

710. And when this happens—when we allow freedom to ring . . . we will be able to speed up that day when all of God's children—black men and white men; Jews and gentiles; Protestants and Catholics will be able to join hands and sing in the words of that old Negro spiritual: "Free at last, free at last. Thank God almighty, we are free at last!" (Ibid.)

SPEECH BY PROXY

711. We will not stop until the dogs stop biting us in the South and the rats stop biting us in the North. (James Farmer, civil rights activist, March on Washington ceremonies, Washington, D.C., August 28, 1963.)

[Because Farmer was in a southern jail for his civil rights activities, his speech was delivered in Washington by an aide, Floyd McKissick.]

SERVICE FOR AN ASSASSIN

712. Mrs. Oswald tells me that her son, Lee Harvey, was a good boy and that she loved him. And today, Lord, we commit his spirit to Your divine care. (Rev. Louis Saunders, Rose Hill Cemetery, Ft. Worth, Texas, November 1963, cited in *New York Times*, April 17, 1998.)

[Delivered when the scheduled ministers, fearing snipers, backed out.]

EDUCATION

713. I never learned hate at home, or shame. I had to go to school for that. (Dick Gregory, from his autobiography, *Nigger*, 1964.)

NO POLL TAX

714. The right of citizens of the United States to vote in any primary or other election for President or Vice President, or for Senator or Representative in Congress, shall not be denied or abridged by the failure to pay any poll tax or other tax. (24th Amendment, ratified January 23, 1964.)

MISSISSIPPI MYSTERY

715. That night [June 21, 1964] I discovered that a church had been burned in the county five days before. In reading an out-of-state newspaper, the New Orleans *Times-Picayune*, some friends and I came across an article dated Tuesday, June 16, which said that night riders struck Neshoba County, "when a Negro church was surrounded by armed white men, most of them masked. Three Negroes attending a church board meeting were beaten and chased away. A short time later the church went up in flames." At first it seemed impossible that a church could have been burned in the county five days before without any of us hearing a word about it. . . .

On Monday, I went to the *Neshoba Democrat* office to ask Jack Tannehill about the burning. He said, "Florence, you can't tell who burned that church. Do you know where the story came from? It came off the AP [Associated Press] wire service from New York."

"Yes, but was a church burned?" I asked.

"Well, yes, a church was burned—but—"

I said I understood some people were beaten.

"They *said* some were beaten. I went out there and talked to some of them and they didn't even know how many night riders were supposed to be there. Some said 30, some said 300." The editor told me that Mt. Zion was the church that was burned. . . .

I knew of no church burning in Mississippi before this and was especially puzzled that Mt. Zion Church had been burned. I knew people who lived in the community; it was an old, established one of Negro landowners who had the long-standing respect of the white community. . . .

Jack Tannehill then told me about the disappearance of three civil rights workers. (Florence Mars, Philadelphia, Mississippi, describing events of mid-June 1964, from *Witness in Philadelphia*, by Florence Mars with Lynn Eden.)

[The three missing civil rights workers were James Chaney, Andrew Goodman, and Michael Schwerner. They had come to Mississippi to help blacks register to vote. Arrested on speeding charges, they had been released late at night after paying fines. They had then "disappeared." After their bodies were discovered, the FBI investigated and found out what had happened. The three had been seized on the road by Klansmen—some of whom were police officers—and shot to death. In October 1967, seven men were convicted of conspiring to violate the civil rights of the murdered men and were sentenced to prison terms. Eight others were acquitted; three had mistrials. The trial had taken place in Mississippi, before a Mississippi judge and a Mississippi jury, and pursued by a Mississippi prosecutor.]

COMMISSION FINDINGS

716. The shots which killed President Kennedy and wounded Governor [John] Connally were fired from the sixth floor windows at the southeast corner of the Texas School Book Depository. . . .

The weight of the evidence indicates that there were three shots fired. . . .

The shots which killed President Kennedy and wounded Governor Connally were fired by Lee Harvey Oswald. . . .

The Commission has found no evidence that either Lee Harvey Oswald or Jack Ruby [who killed Oswald before he could be brought to trial] was part of any conspiracy, domestic or foreign, to assassinate President Kennedy. . . .

In its entire investigation the Commission has found no evidence of conspiracy, subversion, or disloyalty to the U.S. Government by any Federal, State, or local official.

On the basis of the evidence before the Commission it concludes that Oswald acted alone. (Warren Commission Report on the assassination of President Kennedy, September 27, 1964.)

[These were the key findings in the 888-page report. The commission was appointed by President Johnson shortly after the November 22, 1963, assassination. The panel, headed by Chief Justice Earl Warren, included six other distinguished Americans.]

CAMPAIGN WISECRACK

717. The trouble with our liberal friends is not that they are ignorant, but that they know so much that isn't so! (Governor Ronald Reagan, speech on behalf of presidential candidate Barry Goldwater, October 27, 1964.)

BEST-SELLER

718. *Unsafe at Any Speed.* (Ralph Nader, book title, 1965.)

[The book attacked the automobile industry for emphasizing profits at the expense of safety. What would follow: padded dashboards, passenger restraints, airbags, headrests, reinforced doors, new designs to check tire wear, elimination of sharp, protruding edges, and design changes on the placement of gasoline tanks.]

SHARING IN BLESSINGS

719. The promise of America is a simple promise: Every person shall share in the blessings of this land. And they shall share on the basis of their merits as a person. They shall not be judged by their color or by their beliefs, or by their religion, or by where they were born, or the neighborhood in which they live. (President Lyndon B. Johnson, press conference, Washington, D.C., March 10, 1965.)

ON VOTING RIGHTS

720. At times history and fate meet at a single time in a single place to shape a turning point in man's unending search for freedom. So it was at Lexington and Concord. So it was a century ago at Appomattox. So it was last week in Selma, Alabama.

There, long-suffering men and women peacefully protested the denial of their rights as Americans. Many were brutally assaulted. One good man, a man of God, was killed. . . .

There is no Negro problem. There is no Southern problem. There is no Northern problem. There is only an American problem. And we are met here tonight as Americans, not as Democrats or Republicans. We are met here as Americans to solve that problem.

This was the first nation in the history of the world to be founded with a purpose. The great phrases of that purpose still sound in every American heart, North and South: "All men are created equal"—"Government by consent of the governed"—"Give me liberty or give me death." Those are not just clever words. Those are not just empty theories. . . .

Those words are a promise to every citizen that he shall share in the dignity of man. . . . It says that he shall share in freedom, he shall choose his leaders, educate his children, provide for his family according to his ability and his merits as a human being.

To apply any other test—to deny a man his hopes because of his color or race, or his religion, or the place of his birth—is not only to do injustice, it is to deny America and to dishonor the dead who gave their lives for American freedom.

Our fathers believed that if this noble view of the rights of man was to flourish, it must be rooted in democracy. The most basic right of all was the right to choose your own leaders. The history of this country in large measure is the history of expansion of that right to all of our people. . . . Every American citizen must have an equal right to vote. . . .

Yet the harsh fact is that in many places in this country men and women are kept from voting simply because they are Negroes. . . .

Experience has clearly shown that the existing process of law cannot overcome systematic and ingenious discrimination. No law that we now have on the books—and I have helped to put three of them there—can ensure the right to vote when local officials are determined to deny it.

In such a case our duty must be clear to all of us. The Constitution says that no person shall be kept from voting because of his race or his color. We have all sworn an oath before God to support and to defend that Constitution. We must now act in obedience to that oath. . . .

I will send to Congress a law designed to eliminate illegal barriers to the right to vote. . . .

This bill will strike down restrictions to voting in all elections—Federal, State, and local—which have been used to deny Negroes the right to vote.

This bill will establish a simple, uniform standard which cannot be used however ingenious the effort to flout our Constitution.

It will provide for citizens to be registered by officials of the United States government if the state officials refuse to register them. (President Lyndon B. Johnson, address to Joint Session of Congress, Washington, D.C., March 15, 1965.)

CROSSROADS

721. I have a choice of things to do with my life. I think it is time to charge in head first. I want to start a peace movement. . . . The time is ripe and I feel I could do anything I want. . . .

I just feel that people are searching and groping for something real, something truthful—The movement will be nonviolent. It is terribly vague, but I see no harm in preparing yourself in spirit for something even when you are not sure exactly what it is. I have to be ready to sacrifice just about everything I have. Who can ever tell if he's ready to do that till the time comes. . . .

I must be ready not to die for something, but to live for it, which is really much harder. (Joan Baez, letter to her parents, 1965, quoted in *And a Voice to Sing With: A Memoir.*)

[The singing star would become involved in demonstrations for peace, civil rights, and antipoverty.]

PRESIDENTIAL PHILOSOPHY

722. You let these intellectuals get me the ideas [for domestic programs]. I'll worry about the politics. The trouble with the Democratic party is that all the intellectuals want to be politicians and all the politicians want to be intellectuals. (President Lyndon B. Johnson, statement to Joseph A. Califano Jr., 1965, quoted in *The Triumph & Tragedy of Lyndon Johnson: The White House Years*, by Joseph A. Califano Jr.)

723. It's not doing what is right that's hard for a President. It's knowing what is right. (Ibid.)

FARMWORKERS MEETING

724. You are here to discuss matter which is of extreme importance to yourselves, your families, and all the community. . . . A hundred and fifty-five years ago, in the state of Guanajuato in Mexico, a padre proclaimed the struggle for liberty. He was killed, but ten years later Mexico won its independence. . . . We Mexicans here in the United States, as well as all other farm laborers, are engaged in another struggle for the freedom and dignity which poverty denies us. But it must not be a violent struggle, even if violence is used against us. . . . The strike [against the grape growers] was begun by the Filipinos, but it is not exclusively for them. Tonight we must decide if we are to join our fellow workers in this great labor struggle. (Cesar Chavez, Farm Workers Association meeting, Our Lady of Guadalupe church hall, Delano, California, September 16, 1965, recorded by Eugene Nelson, cited in *Cesar Chavez: A Triumph of Spirit*, by Richard Griswold del Castillo and Richard A. Garcia.)

[The workers voted overwhelmingly to join the strike against the grape growers. Several years later, a boycott would be called against California table wine grapes. The strike would end in 1970 with a contract agreement.]

SWITCHING STRATEGIES

725. We been saying "Freedom" for six years. What we are going to start saying now is "Black Power"! (Stokely Carmichael, speech, following his 27th arrest for taking part in civil rights demonstrations, Greenwood, Mississippi, June 16, 1966.)

A CHANGE IN TACTICS

---

726. This is their message: The days of singing freedom songs and the days of combating bullets and billy clubs with love are over. . . . Man, the people are too busy getting ready to fight to bother with singing any more! . . .

Wasn't it only a month after the March on Washington that four children were killed in a church bombing in Birmingham? Whites could feel morally outraged, but they couldn't feel the futility, despair and anger that swept through The Nation within a nation—Black America. . . .

What was needed that Sunday was ol' John Brown to come riding into Birmingham as he had ridden into Lawrence, Kansas, burning every building that stood and killing every man, woman and child that ran from his onslaught. (Julius Lester, "The Angry Children of Malcolm X," from *Sing Out*, October/November 1966.)

POLITICAL MONOLOGUE

---

727. I am willing to let any objective historian look at my record. . . . FDR [Franklin D. Roosevelt] passed five major bills in the first 100 days. We passed 200 in the last two years. . . . There never has been an era in American history when so much has been done for so many in such a short time. . . . Several Presidents have passed education bills. I passed 18. . . . In medical care, we passed 24 bills—in all the years before they passed 17. . . . In conservation we have passed 20 major bills. . . . We are the only administration in history that has done anything about dirty water. . . . truth in packaging. . . . We must tell people what we have done. (President Lyndon B. Johnson, musing to staffers, Anchorage, Alaska, Presidential Daily Diary, November 2, 1966, cited in *The Triumph & Tragedy of Lyndon Johnson: The White House Years*, by Joseph A. Califano Jr.)

[Johnson had originally thought of campaigning for Democrats based on the record of the 89th Congress. Sensing Democratic losses, he decided not to do it. He felt that he would be blamed for any losses. In the 1966 off-year election, the Democrats lost 47 seats in the House and three in the Senate.]

WAR AND PEACE

The president called for continuation and expansion of his domestic programs. He then turned to the Vietnam War.

728. I wish I could report to you that the conflict is almost over. This I cannot do. We face more cost, more loss, and more agony. For the end is not yet. I cannot promise that it will come this year—or come next year. . . .

How long it will take I cannot prophesy. I only know that the will of the American people . . . is tonight being tested. (President Lyndon B. Johnson, State of the Union address, Washington, D.C., January 10, 1967.)

ON PRESIDENTIAL DISABILITY

729. In case of the removal of the President from office or of his death or resignation, the Vice President shall become President.

Whenever there is a vacancy in the office of the Vice President, the President shall nominate a Vice President who shall take office upon confirmation of a majority vote of both houses of Congress.

Whenever the President transmits to the President pro tempore of the Senate and the Speaker of the House of Representatives his written declaration that he is unable to discharge the powers and duties of his office, and until he transmits to them a written declaration to the contrary, such powers and duties shall be discharged by the Vice President as Acting President. (25th Amendment, ratified February 10, 1967.)

ASSESSING THE ENEMY

730. The real enemy of my people is right here. (Muhammad Ali, quoted in the *Daily Worker*, April 25, 1967.)

APPEAL FROM DETROIT

731. I hereby officially request the immediate deployment of federal troops. ... There is reasonable doubt that we can suppress the existing looting, arson and sniping without the assistance of federal troops. (Governor George Romney of Michigan, telegram to President Johnson, July 24, 1967.)

[Detroit was one of the American cities experiencing race riots during the summer of 1967. Other cities included Newark and Plainfield, New Jersey, New York, Birmingham, Rochester, and New Britain, Connecticut.]

SECURITY PROGRAM

732. [E]xpose, disrupt, misdirect, discredit, or otherwise neutralize the activities of black nationalist, hate-type organizations and groupings; their leadership, spokesman. ... [C]ounter their propensity for violence and civil disobedience. (Federal Bureau of Investigation memo to 23 field offices, August 25, 1967, cited in *Let Freedom Ring*, edited by Peter B. Levy.)

POLITICAL GAFFE

733. I just had the greatest brainwashing that anyone can get when you go over to Vietnam, not only by the generals, but also by the diplomatic corps over there, and they do a very thorough job. (Governor George Romney of Michigan, television interview, September 4, 1967.)

[Two years earlier, Romney had visited Vietnam and declared U.S. involvement "morally right and necessary." Now, in the television interview, he had called the same involvement "tragic." The interviewer pointed out the inconsistency, and Romney had explained himself as just quoted. The "brainwashing" comment virtually destroyed his chances for the Republican presidential nomination.]

CONFESSION AND CONTRITION

734. I became a rapist. . . . I started out by practicing on black girls in the ghetto—in the black ghetto where dark and vicious deeds appear not as aberrations or deviations from the norm, but as part of the sufficiency of the Evil of the day—and when I considered myself smooth enough, I crossed the tracks and sought out white prey. I did this consciously, deliberately, willingly, methodically. . . .

Rape was an insurrectionary act. It delighted me that I was defying and trampling upon the white man's law, upon his system of values, and that I was defiling his women—and this point, I believe, was the most satisfying to me because I was very resentful over the historical fact of how the white man has used the black woman. I felt I was getting revenge. (Eldridge Cleaver, *Soul on Ice*, 1968.)

735. I took a long look at myself and, for the first time in my life, admitted that I was wrong, that I had gone astray—astray not so much from the white man's law as from being human, civilized—for I could not approve the act of rape. Even though I had some insight into my own motivations, I did not feel justified. I lost my self-respect. My pride as a man dissolved and my whole fragile moral structure seemed to collapse, completely shattered.

It is why I started to write. To save myself. (Ibid.)

A REPORTER'S ANALYSIS

736. To say that we are mired in stalemate [in Vietnam] seems the only realistic, yet unsatisfactory, conclusion. . . .

[I]t is increasingly clear to this reporter that the only rational way out then will be to negotiate, not as victors, but as an honorable people who lived up to their pledge to defend democracy, and did the best they could. (Walter Cronkite, telecast, CBS-TV Network, February 27, 1968.)

SLOGAN

737.

Hey! Hey!
L.B.J.!
How many boys have you killed today?

(Slogan chanted by antiwar demonstrators outside the White House, 1968.)

KERNER COMMISSION REPORT

738. Our nation is moving toward two societies, one black, one white—separate and unequal. (Report of the National Advisory Commission on Civil Disorders, March 1, 1968.)

[The commission, set up by President Johnson, was headed by Illinois governor Otto Kerner. It investigated the 1967 riots in American Cities. The report is often identified as the Kerner Commission Report.]

REFUSAL

739. I shall not seek—and will not accept—the nomination of my party for another term as your President. (President Lyndon B. Johnson, speech, Washington, D.C., March 31, 1968.)

END TO A COLUMBIA SIT-IN

740a. On April 30, 1968, acting on an official complaint lodged by Columbia University President Grayson Kirk, members of the New York City Police Department effected the arrests of approximately 695 students and other persons who were trespassing in various buildings of the University complex and on the campus and refused to leave upon repeated requests of the University. . . . [B]ecause of the fact that force was used to effect the arrests, a number of injuries were sustained by the demonstrators (92) and by the police (17). (Interim report prepared by the first deputy commissioner of police events of April 30, 1968, cited in *Up against the Ivy Wall: A History of the Columbia Crisis*, by Jerry L. Avorn with members of the staff of the *Columbia Daily Spectator*.)

[The police report deals with the culmination of a weeklong series of demonstrations and occupation of university buildings by students and others. The report was issued on May 4, 1968. Updated statistics would set the arrests at 711 and the injured at 148.]

740b. In the emergency room of St. Luke's Hospital Robert Zevin, the radical economics instructor who had worked with the strikers, sat dazed, blood crusted on his cap and staining his face. Shenton and Morgenbesser were there too, the former with an injured shoulder, the latter with a slit scalp. Jack Miller, professor of chemistry, sat in a chair, waiting to help some of his colleagues, and saying, "You must realize we, the faculty, knew what the strike committee wanted, but it was insane. They wanted the University. You think I'm crazy but I'm not." Peter Kenen, the young pro-administration economics professor, also stood in St. Luke's emergency room, telling a student, "It had to come. You think Kirk enjoyed this? I wouldn't have wanted to be in his place in the last 40 hours." (Events of April 30, 1968, from ibid.)

[On August 23, 1968, Grayson Kirk announced his retirement.]

PREPARING FOR A DRAFT?

741. It became apparent to [his aide Larry] Temple at the ranch and me back at the West Wing of the White House that LBJ [President Johnson] hoped, and probably anticipated, that the [Democratic National] Convention delegates in Chicago would offer to draft him to be their party's candidate, a draft he intended to turn down but one that would validate his presidency in the eyes of fellow Democrats. (Joseph A. Califano Jr., special assistant to President Johnson for domestic affairs, recalling events of late August 1968, from *The Triumph & Tragedy of Lyndon Johnson: The White House Years*.)

CHICAGO CONFRONTATION

Late in August 1968 the Democrats met in Chicago to nominate a national ticket. Demonstrators came to protest the Vietnam War policies of President Lyndon Johnson. The resulting confrontation led to what was later dubbed "a police riot."

742. [A] part of the crowd was trapped in front of the Conrad Hilton and pressed hard against a big plate glass window of the Haymarket Lounge. A reporter who was sitting inside said, "Frightened men and women banged . . . against the window. A captain of the fire department inside told us to get back from the window, that it might get knocked in. As I backed away a few feet I could see a smudge of blood on the glass outside."

With a sickening crack, the window shattered, and screaming men and women tumbled through, some cut badly by the jagged glass. The police came after them.

"I was pushed through by the force of large numbers of people," one victim said. "I got a deep cut in my right leg, diagnosed later by [Senator] Eugene McCarthy's doctor as a severed artery. . . . I fell to the floor of the bar. There were 10 to 20 people who had come through. . . . I could not stand on the leg. It was bleeding profusely."

"A squad of policemen burst into the bar, clubbing all those who looked to them like demonstrators, at the same time screaming over and over, 'We've got to clear this area.' The police acted literally like mad dogs looking for objects to attack."

There is little doubt that during this whole period . . . lasting nearly 20 minutes, the preponderance of violence came from the police. It was not entirely a one-way battle, however. (Daniel Walker, chairman of the investigating committee, describing events of August 28, 1968, from *Rights in Conflict: The Violent Confrontation of Demonstrators and Police in the Parks and Streets of Chicago during the Democratic National Convention of 1968.*)

743. The whole world is watching! (Chant of the demonstrators in Chicago during confrontations with police.)

17

From Nixon to Reagan

It was a roller-coaster era. There were the elation of Americans on the moon and the shock of Watergate. It was the agony of My Lai and the horror of Kent State. It was relief at the end of the Vietnam War and the rage of American hostages being held in Iran. It was the end of a nightmare with a Ford pardon and the beginning of a human rights agenda with Carter. It was the optimism of Reagan and the lift that he gave to the American spirit.

The era also saw a continuation of civil rights with a new emphasis on women's issues, particularly the issue of rape.

HAVING A "PLIGHT"

744. One of the finest things about being an Indian is that people are always interested in you and your "plight." Other groups have difficulties, predicaments, quandaries, problems, or troubles. Traditionally we Indians have had a "plight." (Vine Deloria Jr., *Custer Died for Your Sins*, 1969.)

745. It has been said of missionaries that when they arrived they had only the Book and we had the land; now we have the Book and they have the land. (Ibid.)

Commander of the *Apollo 15* lunar module, explores the moon, July 1971.

A PLEA FOR CIVILITY

746. We cannot learn from one another until we stop shouting at one another—until we speak quietly enough so that our words can be heard as well as our voices. . . .

[W]e will set as our goal the decent order that makes progress possible and our lives secure. (President Richard M. Nixon, Inaugural Address, Washington, D.C., January 20, 1969.)

747. [O]ur destiny lies not in the stars but on earth itself, in our own hands and our own hearts. (Ibid.)

INCIDENT AT "PINKVILLE"

748. It was late in April, 1968 that I first heard of "Pinkville" and what allegedly happened there. . . . [I]n the following months I was to hear similar stories from such a wide variety of people that it became impossible for me to disbelieve that something rather dark and bloody did indeed occur sometime in March, 1968 in a village called "Pinkville" in the Republic of Vietnam. . . .

[P]fc "Butch" Gruver told me . . . the first of many reports I was to hear of "Pinkville."

"Charlie" Company . . . had been assigned to Task Force Barker in late February, 1968 to help conduct "search and destroy" operations on the Batangan Peninsula. . . .

Gruver said that Charlie Company had sustained casualties, primarily from bloody traps and enemy soldiers. It was located about six miles northeast of Quang Nhai city. . . . It was a notorious area and the men of Task Force Barker had a special name for it: they called it "Pinkville." One morning in the latter part of March, Task Force Barker moved out from its firebase headed for "Pinkville." Its mission: destroy the trouble spot and all of its inhabitants. . . .

The other two companies that made up the task force cordoned off the village so that "Charlie" Company could move through to destroy the structures and kill the inhabitants. Any villagers who ran from Charlie Company were stopped by the encircling companies. I asked "Butch" several times if all the people were killed. He said that he thought they were, men and women and children. . . .

It was so bad, Gruver said, that one of the men in his squad shot himself in the foot in order to be medivaced out of the area so that he would not have to participate in the slaughter. Although he had not seen it, Gruver had been told by people he considered trustworthy that one of the company's officers, 2nd Lieutenant Kally (this spelling may be incorrect) had rounded up several groups of villagers (each group consisting of a minimum of 20 persons of both sexes and all ages). According to the story, Kally then machine-gunned each group. (Ron Ridenhour, letter to the White House, the Pentagon, and 24 members of Congress, March 29, 1969.)

[The story broke in the press on November 16, 1969. "Pinkville" was the Vietnamese village of My Lai, where some 450 South Vietnamese were killed on March 16, 1968. "Kally" was Lieutenant William L. Calley Jr., who was later court-martialed. He was found guilty of the premeditated murder of at least 22 unarmed civilians.]

AUDIENCES

749. The fact that I'm not trying to win converts bugs some people, but I don't think an entertainer *can*. I've never known any white bigot to pay to see a black man, unless the black man was being hung. (Bill Cosby, interview, *Playboy*, May 1969.)

BOYCOTT

750. We, the striking grape workers of California, join on this International Boycott Day with the consumers across the continent in planning the steps that lie ahead on the road to our liberation. . . .

If this road we chart leads to the rights and freedoms we demand, if it leads to just wages, humane working conditions, protection from the misuse of pesticides, and to the fundamental right of collective bargaining; if it changes the social order that relegates us to the bottom reaches of society, then in our wake will follow thousands of American farm workers. (United Farm Workers boycott declaration, California, May 10, 1969, cited in *Latino Literacy*, by Frank de Varona.)

[At this point, the strike had been going on for four years. It would end in 1970 with a collective bargaining agreement.]

LUNAR LANDING

751. Tranquility Base here. The Eagle has landed. (Neil Armstrong, upon landing on the moon, July 20, 1969.)

752. That's one small step for a man, one giant leap for mankind. (On taking his first step upon the moon, ibid.)

TALKING TO THE MOON

753. Because of what you have done the heavens have become a part of man's world. (President Richard M. Nixon, speaking to the astronauts who have landed on the moon, July 20, 1969.)

ON JUSTICE AND PEACE

754. White folks don't want peace; they want quiet. The price you pay for peace is justice. Until there is justice, there will be no peace or quiet. (Jesse Jackson, interview, *Playboy*, November 1969.)

JOKE

755. If our forefathers thought that taxation without representation was bad, they should see what it's like *with* representation. (Contemporary joke, 1970s.)

BLACK AND FEMALE

756. Of my two "handicaps," being female put many more obstacles in my path than being black. (Shirley Chisholm, *Unbought and Unbossed*, 1970.)

757. Everyone else is represented in Washington by a rich and powerful lobby, it seems. But there is no lobby for the people. (Ibid.)

DREAM VERSUS NIGHTMARE

758. There is the America of the American dream, and there is the America of the American nightmare. I feel that I am a citizen of the American dream, that the revolutionary struggle of which I am a part is a struggle against the American nightmare, which is the present reality. It is the struggle to do away with this nightmare and to replace it with the American dream which should be the reality. (Eldridge Cleaver, conversation, 1970, cited in *Quotations in Black*, edited by Anita King.)

BURIED HISTORY

759. The United States, it has been said, has a history but not a tradition of domestic violence. A history, because violence has been frequent, voluminous, almost commonplace in our past. But not precisely a tradition, for two reasons: First, our violence lacks both an ideological and a geographical center; it lacks cohesion, it has been too various, diffuse, and spontaneous to be forged into a single, sustained, inveterate hatred shared by entire social classes. Second, we have a remarkable lack of memory where violence is concerned and have left most of our excesses a part of our buried history. (Richard Hofstadter, from *American Violence: A Documentary History*, edited by Richard Hofstadter and Michael Wallace, 1970.)

760. [M]ost American violence—and this also illuminates its relationship to state power—has been initiated with a "conservative" bias. It has been unleashed against abolitionists, Catholics, radicals, workers and labor organizers, Negroes, Orientals, and other ethnic or racial or ideological minorities, and has been used ostensibly to protect the American, the Southern, the white Protestant, or simply the established middle-class way of life and morals. A high proportion of our violent actions has thus come from the top dogs or the middle dogs. . . . This may help to explain why so little of it has been used against state authority, and why in turn it has been so easily and indulgently forgotten. . . .

Violence has now become, to a degree unprecedented in the United States, the outgrowth of forcible acts of dissidents and radicals who are expressing hostility to middle-class ways and to established power. (Ibid.)

NEWS FROM KENT STATE

On May 4, 1970, four students were killed and nine wounded by National Guardsmen on the campus of Kent State University in Ohio. A number of students had been protesting the incursion of American forces into Cambodia. It is uncertain how many of the casualties had been demonstrators and how many had been bystanders.

761. Arthur Krause was in a meeting at work when his secretary called him out to answer a telephone call from his brother, who lives in Cleveland. . . . [T]here had been trouble at Kent and the radio was reporting that Allison Krause had been killed. . . .

"Oh yes, Mrs. Krause," he [a spokesman at the hospital] said. "Allison arrived DOA." . . .

A friend drove them to Kent. . . .

After they had been taken to the morgue and identified the body, Dorothy Krause asked a doctor if he could determine whether the bullet that killed her daughter had come from a military weapon? The doctor said the bullet had fragmented. It broke into four pieces as it tore through the left lower lung, spleen, stomach, duodenum, liver and vena cava, the major vein leading to the heart. There was a large wound where the remainder of the bullet exited. The doctor told Dorothy Krause that the fragments were being sent to the laboratory to determine where it had come from. . . .

[A]t the hospital, reporters gathered around Arthur Krause and in his grief he talked:

"All I know is that my daughter is dead! I'm not on anybody's side. We were so glad we had two daughters so they could stay out of Vietnam. Now she's dead. What a waste. What a horrible waste."

His sorrow turned to anger as he lashed out at the National Guard:

"I'd like to know who the boys were who shot my daughter. I'd like to meet them. They're young, immature guys who joined the National Guard to stay out of Vietnam. . . . They've got a miserable job to do." . . .

A few weeks later the university sent them a check for $514. It was a refund of Allison's spring tuition. (Joe Eszterhas and Michael D. Roberts, from *Thirteen Seconds: Confrontation at Kent State*, events of May 4, 1970, and thereafter.)

[On May 14, two Jackson State College students were killed by state police during a campus antiwar demonstration in Jackson, Mississippi.]

VOTE AT 18

762. The right of citizens of the United States, who are 18 years or age or older, to vote shall not be denied or abridged by the United States or by any State on account of age. (26th Amendment, ratified July 1, 1971.)

RAPE, RACE, AND POWER

763. Rape is a weapon of terror and violence, aimed at keeping women subordinate to men and divided from each other. But it is more. It is also a symbol and manifestation of power aimed at the men of a subordinate group. The practice of symbolizing the conquest of another tribe or people, by making captives of their men and sexually abusing—that is raping or prostituting—their women as a means of humiliating the males of the conquered group, antedates history. . . .

The sexual exploitation of slave women by white men during and after slavery affirms the colonial nature of the oppression of black people in the United States. Black men, like all conquered foes, were symbolically castrated and effectively humiliated by being prevented from defending their wives and daughters from the sexual abuses of white men. The sexual exploitation of black women by white men is an essential feature of race-caste oppression in the United States and continued unabated until very recently, when the militancy of the black movement helped to redirect it. . . .

The dual function of rape as a means of sexual and caste oppression is no place more evident than in the death penalty statutes which reveal that rape, the very crime for which most white men escape punishment or are lightly punished, is the cause of more death penalty sentences if the rapist or alleged rapist is black. In the post–Civil War period and as late as the 1940s the accusation of rape against black men was the chief cause of lynchings. (Susan Griffin, "Rape: The All-American Crime," article in *Ramparts*, September 1971.)

ATTICA UPRISING

On September 9, 1971, inmates at Attica State Prison in New York overpowered guards, took hostages, and took over the prison. Over four days, there were talks aimed at ending the takeover. At the request of the convicts, a group of "observers" was invited to observe the negotiation sessions. The observers included government officials, reporters, clergymen, and organization leaders. Then came September 13.

764. Morning came gray and misty. At 6:30 A.M . . . , peering out of the windows . . . , the first observers awake saw through the slow drizzle the renewed preparations for an attack—men lining up, checking weapons, trying on gas masks. At 6:55, trying to find out what was happening, the observers learned that they were no longer allowed to see Commissioner [of Correctional Services Russell] Oswald. . . .

[Oswald appeals to the leaders of the uprising to turn over all hostages, unharmed, and help restore order. He asks for a reply "within the hour."]

On the floors of A- and C-blocks, officers were quietly assembling state police teams of marksmen qualified with the service's standard .270 rifle—a big-game weapon that fired an unjacketed, soft-lead, expanding bullet with sufficient accuracy to hit a five-inch target at 800 to 1,000 yards. Team members lay prone on the floors to stay out of sight of D-yard. . . .

A corrections official entered and said that the inmates had made no response to Oswald but had taken hostages to the roof of Times Square [a section of the prison], apparently for execution. . . .

It was 9:46 A.M. In his "command post," Russell Oswald heard a voice crackle on the police radio, "Jackpot One has made the drop." . . .

A choking cloud of CS gas [dropped by helicopter] fell abruptly over D-yard. On the roofs of A- and C-blocks the crouching riflemen were intently peering through their gas-mask eyeholes at the inmates on the catwalks, the riflemen were alert for any hint of "overt, hostile" action toward the hostages. . . .

[As the gas descended, inmates and hostages alike instinctively dropped to the ground. The movements might have been misinterpreted by the marksmen.]

A shot rang out from a troop post . . . a second . . . then a barrage, as the rifle units on the roofs and at the third-floor windows generally opened fire. (Tom Wicker, reporter for *New York Times*, recalling events of September 13, 1971, Attica State Prison, New York, from *A Time to Die*.)

[Wicker was one of the observers. The firing lasted about nine minutes. Ten hostages and

29 inmates were killed by the police gunfire; three hostages and 85 inmates were wounded. While in the hands of the inmates, two of the hostages had been seriously injured.]

INCIDENT AT THE WATERGATE

---

765. Five men, one of whom said he is a former employee of the Central Intelligence Agency, were arrested at 2:30 A.M. yesterday in what authorities described as an elaborate plot to bug the offices of the Democratic National Committee here. (Lead paragraph of news story, *Washington Post*, June 18, 1972.)

[This was the genesis of what became known as the Watergate affair, named for the complex that housed many business offices, including that of the Democratic National Committee. The attempted bugging would lead to investigations by journalists and Congress. Investigations would eventually uncover political dirty tricks, a break-in at a psychiatrist's office, an "enemies list" of journalists and politicians, money laundering, cover-up, bribery, and perjury. In the end would come impeachment hearings and the resignation of President Richard Nixon.]

ENTER "DEEP THROAT"

The Watergate affair unfolded largely as the result of the work of reporters Bob Woodward and Carl Bernstein of the *Washington Post*. A secret informant helped unravel the story.

766. Woodward had a source in the Executive Branch who had access to information at CRP [Committee to Re-elect the President] as well as at the White House. His identity was unknown to anyone else. He could be contacted only on very important occasions. Woodward had promised he would never identify him or his position to anyone. Further, he had agreed never to quote the man, even as an anonymous source. Their discussions would be only to confirm information that had been obtained elsewhere and to add some perspective.

In newspaper terminology, this meant the discussions were on "deep background." Woodward explained the arrangement to managing editor Howard Simons one day. He had taken to calling the source "my friend," but Simons dubbed him "Deep Throat," the title of a celebrated pornographic movie. The name stuck. (From *All the President's Men*, by Carl Bernstein and Bob Woodward, ca. July 1972.)

A DRAGNET INVESTIGATION?

---

767. The American Civil Liberties Union [ACLU] has received reports about the special measures being taken by several federal agencies, particularly the Federal Bureau of Investigation and the Immigration and Naturalization Service, against resident Arabs. Apparently, the purpose of these measures is to forestall acts of terrorism against Israeli citizens and American Jews.

While terrorist incidents abroad make clear that the government interests here are important, the measures reportedly being taken by the several federal agencies give the appearance of dragnet investigations based solely upon an individual's national origin. If that impression is accurate, they must be condemned as constitutionally impermissible insofar as they go beyond fair and respectful inquiries by law enforcement officers for the purpose of securing voluntary information about the planning or commission of crimes.

But the reports we have received suggest that federal officers are going beyond the limit of neutral inquiry, and are engaging in a visible course of investigation, interrogation and surveillance of members of a specific national group which has the effect of harassing and intimidating them. That in itself is to be condemned; beyond that, however, the law enforcement activities have generated the impression in the Arabic community that public statements of support for the Arabic position in the Arab–Israeli dispute will be reason enough for federal officers to take an official interest . . . [with] the effect of discouraging the expression of such views with the consequent impairment of rights protected . . . by the First Amendment. . . .

To single out any group on the basis of national origin, race, political beliefs or religion as a target for criminal investigation is objectionable from a Constitutional point of view and treads upon the presumption of innocence. (Aryeh Neier, executive director, American Civil Liberties Union, letter to Attorney General Richard Kleindienst, October 16, 1972.)

[The ACLU letter came about after the following had taken place. On September 5, 11 Israeli athletes were murdered by Arab guerrillas at the Munich Olympics. That same day, President Nixon said that security measures would be taken to prevent such incidents in the United States. On October 6, the *New York Times* had reported that federal agencies were screening people of Arab origin for possible links to terrorism.]

THE NEW ASSOCIATE

768. From the outset, there was little doubt that my experience of being an associate at a large [law] firm was going to be somewhat different from the experience of my male colleagues. When I came to New York for a day's worth of interviews with Skadden, Arps, Slate, Meagher & Flom, . . . I noticed that the interviewing attorneys were giggling at my resume. Finally I asked one of them what was so funny. He handed me his copy of my resume, bearing the notation of the partner who had come to my law school to recruit. "A terrific broad," the recruiting partner had written, "a real bomb-thrower!" (Peggy L. Kerr, recalling events of 1973, quoted in *Women Lawyers*, edited by Emily Couric.)

[In 1981 Kerr became the first female partner of the law firm.]

CALL FOR LESS GOVERNMENT

769. In our own lives, let each of us ask not just what will government do for me, but what can I do for myself? . . .

Just as building a structure of peace abroad has required turning away from old policies that have failed, so building a new era of progress at home requires turning away from old policies that have failed. . . .

That is why I offer no promises of a purely governmental solution for every problem. We have lived too long with that false promise. In trusting too much in government, we have asked of it more than it can deliver. This leads only to inflated expectations, to reduced individual effort and to a disappointment and frustration that erode confidence both in what government can do and in what people can do. Government must learn to take less from people so that people can do more for themselves. (President Richard M. Nixon, Second Inaugural Address, Washington, D.C., January 20, 1973.)

AN "INSPECTOR" CALLS

One of the most popular television series of the 1970s was *Columbo*. The detective series inspired columnist Art Buchwald to speculate on how the fictional sleuth might have solved the Watergate break-in case. Inspector Columbo introduces himself to President Nixon, explaining that he is looking into the matter on behalf of the Senate Investigating Committee.

770. "Say, this sure is a nice house you got here. How much does a place like this cost?" . . .

[Columbo admires the paintings and furnishings. Nixon says that he is having a private party for his staff and proceeds to introduce them.]

"This is my assistant, H. R. Haldeman; my legal aide, John Dean III; my former assistant, Charles Colson; the former Secretary of Commerce, Maurice Stans; and the former Attorney General, John Mitchell." . . .

[Columbo questions each on his whereabouts the night of the break-in. They were all somewhere else. The president offers Columbo a drink, and he asks for an orange juice. The butler brings it in. He is questioned by Columbo.]

"Where were you on the night of the break-in?"

"I was polishing the silver."

"You're lying. . . . You were at the Watergate. . . . This coaster that the orange juice was served on says 'Property of the Watergate Bar and Grill.' "

"My God," said H. R. Haldeman, "the butler did it."

"Why didn't we think of that?" John Dean III said. (Art Buchwald, from *I Never Danced at the White House*, a collection of columns by Art Buchwald, 1973.)

SPOTLIGHT ON THE CIA

---

771. "It is a multi-purpose, clandestine arm of power . . . more than an intelligence or counterintelligence organization. It is an instrument for subversion, manipulation and violence, for the secret intervention in the affairs of other countries." Allen Dulles wrote those words about the KGB in 1963 so that Americans would better understand the nature of the Soviet security service. His description was a correct one, but he could—just as accurately—have used the same terms to describe his own CIA. He did not, of course, because the U.S. leaders of Dulles' generation generally tried to impute the worst possible methods and motives to the forces of international communism, while casting the "defensive actions of the free world" as honest and democratic. Both sides, however, resorted to ruthless tactics. Neither was reluctant to employ trickery, deceit, or, in Dulles' phrase, "subversion, manipulation, and violence." They both operated clandestinely, concealing not so much from the "opposition" (they couldn't) as from their own peoples. Secrecy itself became a way of life, and one was unpatriotic or unmindful of the "national security." (Former CIA staffer Victor Mar-

chetti and former State Department staffer John D. Marks, 1974, from their book *The CIA and the Cult of Intelligence*.)

[This was one of the first critical books about the Central Intelligence Agency written by former insiders. Before publication of the book, a federal court ordered that the manuscript be reviewed by the CIA for security reasons. Some 339 passages were ordered to be deleted by the CIA. Of these, 168 were reinstated on appeal. Requests for additional restoration continued after the book went to press.]

STEPPING DOWN

772. Throughout the long and difficult period of Watergate, I have felt it was my duty to persevere, to make every possible effort to complete the term of office to which you elected me. In the past few days, however, it has become evident to me that I no longer have a strong enough political base in the Congress to justify continuing that effort.

As long as there was such a base, I felt strongly that it was necessary to see the constitutional process through to its conclusion; that to do otherwise would be unfaithful to the spirit of that deliberately difficult process and a dangerously destabilizing precedent for the future.

But with the disappearance of that base, I now believe that the constitutional purpose has been served and there is no longer a need for the process to be prolonged.

I would have preferred to carry through to the finish, whatever the personal agony it would have involved, and my family unanimously urged me to do so.

But the interest of the nation must always come before any personal considerations. From the discussions I have had with Congressional and other leaders, I have concluded that because of the Watergate matter, I might not have the support of the Congress that I would consider necessary to back the very difficult decisions and carry out the duties of the office in the way the interests of the nation would require.

I have never been a quitter.

To leave office before my term is completed is abhorrent to every instinct in my body. But as President, I must put the interest of America first.

America needs a full-time President and a full-time Congress, particularly at this time, with problems we face at home and abroad. To continue to fight through the months ahead for my personal vindication would almost totally absorb the time and attention of both the President and the Congress in a period when our entire focus should be on the great issues abroad and prosperity without inflation at home.

Therefore, I shall resign the Presidency, effective at noon tomorrow. . . .

I regret deeply any injuries that may have been done in the course of the events that led to this decision. I would say only that if some of my judgments were wrong—and some were wrong—they were made in what I believed at the time to be the best interest of the nation. (President Richard M. Nixon, address to the nation, White House, Washington, D.C., August 8, 1974.)

ADVICE

773. Always give your best, never get discouraged, never be petty. Always remember, others may hate you. Those who hate you don't win unless you hate them. And then you destroy yourself. (Former president Richard M. Nixon, address to White House staff following his resignation, August 9, 1974.)

SWEARING-IN

774. I feel it is my first duty to make an unprecedented compact with my countrymen. Not an inaugural address, not a fireside chat, not a compaign speech, just a little straight talk among friends. . . .

If you have not chosen me by secret ballot, neither have I gained office by any secret promises. I have not campaigned either for the Presidency or the Vice Presidency. I have not subscribed to any partisan platform. I am indebted to no man and only to one woman, my dear wife, as I begin this very difficult job.

I have not sought this enormous responsibility, but I will not shirk it. (President Gerald R. Ford, swearing-in ceremony, Washington, D.C., August 9, 1974.)

775. I believe that truth is the glue that holds government together, not only our government but civilization itself. That bond, though strained, is unbroken at home and abroad. (Ibid.)

776. My fellow Americans, our long national nightmare is over. Our Constitution works. Our great Republic is a government of laws and not of men. Here, the people rule. (Ibid.)

IDENTITY

777. I am only a Ford—not a Lincoln. (President Gerald R. Ford comment, Washington, D.C., August 1974.)

ON THE PARDON

778. I was very sure of what would happen if I let the charges against Nixon run their legal course. Months were sure to elapse between an indictment and trial. The entire process would no doubt require years: a minimum of two, a maximum of six. And Nixon would not spend time quietly in San Clemente. He would be fighting for his freedom, taking his cause to the people, and his constant struggle would have dominated the news. The story would overshadow everything else. No other issue could compare with the drama of a former President trying to stay out of jail. It would be virtually impossible for me to direct public attention to anything else. Passions on both sides would be aroused. A period of such prolonged vituperation and recrimination would be disastrous for the nation. America needed recovery, not revenge. The hate had to be drained and the healing begun. (President Gerald R. Ford, reflecting on his decision to pardon the former president, in September 1974, from *A Time to Heal.*)

[Much soul-searching—and searching for legal precedent—would be involved before the final decision would be made. Among the questions that had to be answered: Could a pardon be given before a person was indicted, or convicted, or jailed? Was an admission of guilt necessary? The answer was that a pardon before indictment was legal—with some kind of admission of guilt. The following is the nearest thing to an admission from the former president. Nevertheless, the pardon was granted.]

779. Looking back on what is still in my mind a complex and confusing maze of events, decisions, pressures and personalities, one thing I can see clearly now is that I was wrong in not acting more decisively and more forthrightly in dealing with Watergate, particularly when it reached the stage of judicial proceedings and grew from a political scandal into a national tragedy. . . .

That the way I tried to deal with Watergate was the wrong way is a burden I shall bear for every day of the life that is left to me.

I know that many fair-minded people believe that my motivations and actions in the Watergate affair were intentionally self-serving and illegal. I now understand how my own mistakes and misjudgments have contributed to that belief and seemed to support it. This burden is the heaviest one of all to bear. (Former president Richard M. Nixon, from his statement on the pardon, San Clemente, California, September 1974, ibid.)

WATERGATE COVER-UP SUMMATION

On June 17, 1972, five men broke into the offices of the Democratic National Committee headquarters at the Watergate complex in Washington, D.C. They were carrying wiretapping equipment, and one of them worked for the Committee to Re-Elect the President (Nixon). All quickly pleaded guilty to burglary charges. Journalists investigating the break-in uncovered a series of scandals that led to the White House. After large cash payments were made to the five "burglars," key White House figures were charged with obstruction of justice and lying to government investigators. Part of the government summation follows.

780. There has been some effort here to beguile you [members of the jury] by stating over and over again that this nearly half million dollars paid to the original Watergate defendants was attorney fees, family support, income replacement and bail. And so what is the big problem?

The Government agrees that the use to which this money was put was attorney fees, income replacement, family support and bail. But we say most emphatically . . . that that does not answer the question, that simply poses it. The question is, what was the motive or intent behind the payments?

One billion dollars, or one trillion dollars paid for family support, income replacement, and attorney fees, bail, is not an offense. It is fine if it is motivated purely by charitable or humanitarian purposes and nothing else. But one red cent paid to keep somebody from talking and divulging information to the appropriate authorities, whether it is a red cent for attorney fees or a red cent for a haircut, is obstruction of justice. . . .

As you have heard, the money was paid in absolute secrecy. Communications were made from public phones to phone booths. Code names were used and coded messages were sent. Cash, that non-fundable commodity, was always used. The bundles of cash were left in phone booths, in lockers in airports, on ledges in hotels, and in the dead of night in mail boxes out in Potomac, Maryland.

The drops of money were made, ladies and gentlemen, so that the persons delivering the money and the persons receiving the money never saw each other.

Doesn't that impress you as a rather extraordinary effort to conceal humanitarian or charitable impulses? On the other hand, these efforts were necessary if there was a conspiracy to keep people from talking. (James F. Neal, assistant prosecutor, summation to the jury, Washington, D.C., December 1974, cited in *The Right and the Power*, by Leon Jaworski.)

[On January 1, 1975, the following were convicted: John Mitchell, H. R. Haldeman, John Ehrlichman, and Robert Mardian. Acquitted was Kenneth Parkinson. Though other key officials had testified against the accused, the most damning evidence was the taped conversations between President Nixon and his advisers.]

THE VIEW FROM CONGRESS

781. The message was clear: get out, *fast.* (President Gerald R. Ford, summarizing his meeting with the Senate Foreign Relations Committee on the situation in Vietnam, April 14, 1975, from *A Time to Heal.*)

782. I will give you large sums for evacuation, but not one nickel for military aid. (Senator Jacob Javits, spoken to President Ford, ibid.)

[On April 18, South Vietnam President Thieu resigned and fled the country. The military situation disintegrated, and Communist forces swept into South Vietnam.]

EVACUATION

As the North Vietnamese moved closer to Saigon, American planes were used to evacuate South Vietnamese civilians. Evacuation was delayed until the firing let up.

783. The firing did cease, but we had a new problem to solve. Refugees were streaming out onto the airport's runways, and our planes couldn't land. The situation there was clearly out of control. The only option left was to remove the remaining Americans, and as many Vietnamese as possible, by helicopter from the roof of the U.S. embassy in Saigon. Choppers were standing by on the

decks of U.S. Navy ships steaming off the coast, and just before midnight I ordered the final evacuation. Over the next 16 hours we managed to rescue 6,500 U.S. and South Vietnamese personnel without sustaining significant casualties. (President Gerald R. Ford, recalling events of April 28–29, 1975, from *A Time to Heal*.)

THE MAYAQUEZ INCIDENT

784. In the wake of our humiliating retreat from Cambodia and South Vietnam . . . our allies around the world began to question our resolve. . . .

As long as I was President, I decided, the U.S. would not abandon its commitments overseas. We would not permit our setbacks to become a license for others to fish in troubled waters. Rhetoric alone, I knew, would not persuade anyone that America would stand firm. They would have to see proof of our resolve.

[On May 12, 1975, the American merchant ship S.S. *Mayaquez* is seized off the coast of Cambodia. President Ford stands ready to act decisively.] (President Gerald R. Ford, recalling events of May 12, 1975, from *A Time to Heal*.)

> As the National Security Council debates massive air strikes against Cambodia, a photographer stops shooting pictures to say what is on his mind.

785. Has anyone considered that this might be the act of a local Cambodian commander who has just taken it into his own hands to halt any ship that comes by? Has anyone stopped to think that he might not have gotten his orders from Phnom Penh? If that's what has happened, you know, you can blow the whole place away and it's not gonna make any difference. Everyone here has been talking about Cambodia as if it were a traditional government. Like France. We have trouble with France, we just pick up the telephone and call. We know who to talk to. But I was in Cambodia just two weeks ago and it's not that kind of government at all. We don't even know who the leadership is. Has anyone considered that? (David Kennerly, White House photographer, Cabinet Room, White House, May 15, 1975, ibid.)

[Believing that massive air strikes would be "overkill," Ford opts for limited "surgical" strikes against specific targets and orders the navy and marines to retake the ship and free the crew. The operations are successfully carried out.]

CARTOON

Series of six panels. The first five depict a succession of presidents. The final panel is Secretary of State Henry Kissinger.

786. Who lost Vietnam?
EISENHOWER: Not I. . . . I just sent money.
KENNEDY: Not I. . . . I just sent advisers.
JOHNSON: Not I. . . . I just followed Jack.
NIXON: Not I. . . . I just honored Jack and Lyndon's commitments.
FORD: Not I. . . . What was the question?
[Kissinger, pointing his finger directly at the reader:] Not I. . . . YOU lost Vietnam. . . . because you didn't trust your leaders. (Jules Feiffer, June 8, 1975, from *Man Bites Man: Two Decades of Satiric Art*, edited by Steven Heller.)

TELEPHONE CONVERSATION

787. Mr. President, I am going to make an announcement, and I want to tell you about it ahead of time. I am going to run for President. I trust we can have a good contest, and I hope that it won't be divisive. (Governor Ronald Reagan, telephone call to President Ford, November 19, 1975, from *A Time to Heal*, by Gerald R. Ford.)

788. Well, Governor, I'm very disappointed. I'm sorry you're getting into this. I believe I've done a good job and that I can be elected. Regardless of your good intentions, your bid is bound to be divisive. It will take a lot of money, a lot of effort, and it will leave a lot of scars. It won't be helpful, no matter which of us wins the nomination. (President Gerald R. Ford, responding to Governor Reagan, ibid.)

[Ford would win the Republican nomination but lose the election to Jimmy Carter.]

ON SEX AND POWER

789. [S]ome years ago at a conference on the female orgasm . . . I heard a bunch of balding, authoritative male experts decry the absence of female orgasm, and Masters and Johnson reported for the first time on the amazing results that could be achieved with mechanical devices. I shocked that conference by saying they might do more for sex—and the female orgasm—by considering the conditions of women's lives, as they affected her feelings about herself and men, than by promoting these mechanical contraptions to bring a twitch out of her.

In the years that followed, as women began to share their real feelings with each other, they expressed a mix of revulsion against and obsession with sex. . . . There were conferences and workshops on sexuality where women taught other women how to masturbate with vibrators so they wouldn't be dependent on men, or the human penis, at all. In *Fear of Flying*, Erica Jong had her heroine move from masochistic, rape-and-humiliation fantasies and sexual obsessions to the "zipless f——"—where she reduced the male to a dehumanized sex instrument, the Playboy Bunny in reverse. . . .

I don't think a thousand vibrators would make much difference . . . if the unequal power positions in real life weren't changed. The "zipless f——" was simply sexual revenge. The question is: How can we enjoy the true human differences of sex—male and female, . . . ? How can we evade the final fact that our humanity is *ours* as male and female if we are to truly realize ourselves? It was the *economic* imbalance, the power imbalance in the world that subverted sex, or made sex itself into a power game where no one could win.

Work and love, Freud said, are the two essentials of the human condition. (Betty Friedan, from *It Changed My Life: Writings on the Women's Movement*, 1976.)

APPEAL FOR HUMAN RIGHTS

790. We cannot look away when a government tortures its own people, or jails them for their beliefs, or denies minorities fair treatment or the right to emigrate or the right to worship. (Jimmy Carter, speech, Notre Dame, South Bend, Indiana, May 1976.)

[The subject would be one of the cornerstones of his administration. In his Inaugural Address the following January, Carter would state, "Our commitment to human rights must be absolute."]

WITHOUT BOAST OR
BELLIGERENCE

791. It is time for America to move and to speak, not with boasting and belligerence, but with a quiet strength—to depend in world affairs not merely on the size of an arsenal but on the nobility of ideas—and to govern at home not by confusion and crisis but with grace and imagination and common sense. (Jimmy Carter, acceptance speech, Democratic National Convention, New York City, July 13, 1976.)

POLITICAL GAFFE

On a campaign trip, a prominent Republican was asked why the Republican Party—the party of Lincoln—garnered so few votes from blacks. He answered with a "joke."

792. You know what the coloreds are interested in, don't you? A tight pussy, loose shoes, and a warm place to shit. (Earl Butz, secretary of agriculture, cited in late September 1976.)

[Most of the media did not carry the exact quote. A number of them used vague references to sexual habits and bathroom preferences. *Facts on File*, the news reference publication, did a quick poll among library subscribers—including parochial schools—to ask if the exact quote should be printed. The librarians said to go with it—and they did. Butz submitted his resignation to President Ford on October 4.]

EMPHASIS ON FAIRNESS

793. [The Panama Canal Treaties mark America's commitment] to the belief that fairness, and not force, should be at the heart of our dealings with the nations of the world. (President Jimmy Carter, speaking at the signing ceremony of the Panama Canal Treaties, Washington, D.C., September 7, 1977.)

[Negotiations for such treaties began as early as 1964, when anti-American riots in Panama had killed two dozen people. President Carter had appointed Ellsworth Bunker and Sol Linowitz to revive the negotiations, which resulted in two canal treaties. One turned over administration of the canal to Panama effective January 1, 2000. The other provided for joint U.S.–Panamanian defense of the canal. The U.S. Senate ratified the two treaties in March and April 1978 by identical 68–32 margins.]

RACIST FEMINISM?

794. It is a particular academic arrogance to assume any discussion of feminist theory in this time and in this place without examining our many differences, and without a significant input from poor women, black and third world women and lesbians. . . . What this says about the vision of this conference is sad, in a country where racism, sexism and homophobia are inseparable. . . .

Poor and third world women know there is a difference between the daily manifestations and dehumanizations of marital slavery and prostitution, because it is our daughters who line 42nd Street. The black panelists' observation about the effects of relative powerlessness and the differences of relationship between black women and men from white women and men illustrates some of our unique problems as black feminists. If white American feminist theory need not deal with the differences between us, and the resulting difference in aspects of our oppressions, then what do you do with the fact that the women who clean your houses and tend your children while you attend conferences on feminist theory are, for the most part, poor and third world women? What is the theory behind racist feminism? . . .

Why weren't other black women and third world women found to participate in this conference? (Audre Lorde, comments at "The Personal and the Political" Panel, Second Sex Conference, October 29, 1979, cited in *This Bridge Called My Back: Writings by Radical Women of Color*, edited by Cherrie Moraga and Gloria Anzaldúa.)

LABEL FOR A FISCAL PROGRAM

795. Voodoo economics. (George H. Bush, campaigning for the Republican presidential nomination, 1980, during Pennsylvania primary, cited in *George Bush: The Life of a Lone Star Yankee*, by Herbert S. Parmet.)

[Bush was characterizing the "supply-side" ideas advocated by his chief rival, Ronald Reagan. The program was intended to stimulate the economy and cut the deficit by means of tax cuts.]

RESCUE MISSION LAID OUT

796. On the evening of April 16, we met in the Situation Room for a thorough review of every aspect of the operation [to rescue Americans being held hostage at the American embassy in Tehran, Iran]. This session lasted two and a half hours, and I was particularly impressed with mission commanders Generals James B. Vaught and Philip C. Gast, and Colonel Charles Beckwith. These were the leaders who, working with the Joint Chiefs of Staff and the Secretary of Defense, would direct the mission and I authorized it to begin.

In their meticulous description of every facet of the operation, I received satisfactory answers to all my many questions. I informed the military leaders that they had my complete confidence and support, and I made it clear that there could be no interference from the White House while the mission was underway. However, I wanted to be kept constantly informed. Beginning that night, we were a team, realizing that all of us were responsible for the lives and safety of the captive Americans—and for the reputation of our military forces and nation. (President Jimmy Carter, the White House, Washington, D.C., recalling events of April 16, 1980, from *Keeping Faith: Memoirs of a President.*)

[The plan included using trucks to carry the rescue team to the embassy. Helicopters would pick up the rescuers and the hostages and fly them to an abandoned airstrip near Tehran. Finally, transport planes would carry everyone to freedom, while the helicopters would be left behind.]

MISSION ABORTED

797a. I think we have an abort situation. One helicopter at Desert One has hydraulic problem. We thus have less than the minimum six to go. . . . Request decision on mission termination from the President literally within minutes. (Harold Brown, secretary of defense, to Zbigniew Brzezinski, national security adviser, the White House, Washington, D.C., 4:45 P.M. [local time], April 24, 1980, from *Keeping Faith: Memoirs of a President*, by Jimmy Carter.)

[Speed was essential if the rescue operation was to be carried out in Iran at night. The president asked for recommendations by the two commanders—Vaught in Egypt and Beckwith in Iran. Both recommended termination of the mission.]

797b. Let's go with his recommendation. (President Jimmy Carter to Defense Secretary Harold Brown, 4:57 P.M. [local time], ibid.)

[Six helicopters were needed. Eight had been provided, but two came down short of the landing site because of a sandstorm. The mission was called off when a third helicopter developed hydraulic problems. But the worst was yet to come. In the darkness, one of the remaining helicopters crashed into one of the transports. Eight men were killed and five wounded. Carter went on the air to take full responsibility for the operation.]

AN ASTRONAUT'S LEGACY

---

798. [T]he people who make this world run, whose lives can be termed successful, whose names will go down in the history books, are not the cynics, the critics, or the armchair quarterbacks.

They are the adventurers, the explorers, and doers of this world. When they see a wrong or a problem, they do something about it. When they see a vacant place in our knowledge, they work to fill that void.

Rather than leaning back and criticizing how things are, they work to make things the way they should be. . . .

Every generation has the obligation to free men's minds for a look at new worlds. . . .

Your vision is not limited by what your eye can see, but by what your mind can imagine. Many things that you take for granted were considered unrealistic dreams by previous generations. If you accept these past accomplishments as commonplace, then think of the new horizons that you can explore.

From your vantage point, your education and imagination will carry you to places which you won't believe possible.

Make your life count—and the world will be a better place because you tried. (Ellison S. Onizuka, astronaut, address to the graduating class, Konawaena High School, Hawaii, 1980, cited in *Famous Asian Americans*, by Janet Nomura Morey and Wendy Dunn.)

[Ellison S. Onizuka and six fellow astronauts were killed on January 28, 1986, when the *Challenger* space shuttle exploded 73 seconds after liftoff.]

A TIME FOR STRENGTH

799. Adversaries large and small test our will and seek to confound our re-solve. But we are given [by the current administration] weakness when we need strength, vacillation when the times demand firmness. (Ronald Reagan, accep-tance speech following his nomination for president, Republican National Con-vention, Detroit, July 17, 1980.)

AN ELECTION IN THE BALANCE

800. This campaign is ours, but it's ours to throw away, too. . . . If [President Carter] does something with the hostages, or pulls something else out of the hat, as only an incumbent president can, we're in big trouble. (Reagan campaign aide, quoted in *The National Journal*, July 26, 1980.)

THE STOLEN BRIEFING BOOK

801. [W]hen I was preparing to have a debate with Ronald Reagan, my only debate, someone in the White House stole my book of briefings which described every question that I was going to ask or be asked and my answers to all the questions and my response to things that I thought Reagan might say. They gave it to [Washington reporter] George Will who used it to brief Reagan against me. (Former president Jimmy Carter, recalling events of the fall of 1980, interview with Robert Fulghum, on C-Span, December 19, 1996, cited in *Conversations with Carter*, edited by Don Richardson.)

[This statement by Carter was made in the context of forgiveness for the betrayal.]

FEMINISM DEFINED

802. Feminism is the political theory and practice to free *all* women: women of color, working-class women, poor women, physically challenged women, lesbians, old women, as well as white economically privileged heterosexual women. Anything less than this is not feminism, but merely female self-aggrandizement. (Barbara Smith, cited in *This Bridge Called My Back: Writings by Radical Women of Color*, edited by Cherrie Moraga and Gloria Anzaldúa, 1981.)

ON THE HOSTAGE RELEASE

On January 20, 1981, Ronald Reagan was sworn in as president. Minutes later, the American Embassy hostages were released and flown out of Iran. Years later, Carter is asked about reports that the Reagan team had been carrying on their own private negotiations with the Iranians.

803. The thing that I can certify is that when we tried to inform [key Reagan advisers] Alexander Haig and George Shultz . . . about what was going on with our negotiations to get the hostages released, they absolutely refused to accept any briefings. They did not want to be involved in anything that related to the hostages, even our efforts to get them freed. . . . "Don't involve us, we don't want to be informed, we don't want to be involved in any fashion." Obviously, when I was successful in getting the hostages released, Reagan was the one who welcomed them back . . . and making the statement that still kind of rubs me the wrong way, "Never under my administration, will any hostages be taken," as though he was responsible for getting them freed. . . . [H]e never had anything to do with it. (Former president Jimmy Carter, recalling events before, during, and after January 20, 1981, interview with Don Richardson, October 17, 1997, from *Conversations with Carter*, edited by Don Richardson.)

THE PRICE OF PEACE

804. To those neighbors and allies who share our freedom, we will strengthen our historic ties and assure them of our support and firm commitment. We will match loyalty with loyalty. . . . As for the enemies of freedom, those who are potential adversaries, they will be reminded that peace is the highest aspiration of the American people. We will negotiate for it, sacrifice for it; we will not surrender for it, now or ever. (President Ronald Reagan, Inaugural Address, Washington, D.C., January 20, 1981.)

A QUESTION OF TIMING

805a. I was in the [White House] Situation Room as the hours dragged on, until Iran formally accepted the terms exactly five minutes after Ronald Reagan was sworn in as President.

The curious timing of the release gave rise to rumors of a secret deal between the Republicans and the Iranians to delay the release of the hostages until after the presidential election. . . . I had refused to believe such rumors. . . .

The puzzle . . . kept gnawing away at the corner of my mind. . . . Part of its fascination was the sheer magnitude of the charge. . . .

If a deal had been made by Reagan's team, bartering the freedom and conceivably the safety of 52 Americans for political gain, the very legitimacy of the Reagan presidency was put into question. (Gary Sick, staff member of the National Security Council, recalling events of January 20, 1981, from *October Surprise: American Hostages in Iran and the Election of Ronald Reagan.*)

[In November 1979, some 52 staff members of the U.S. Embassy in Teheran had been seized and held hostage.]

805b. [T]he essence of the arrangement from the start was for Iran to hand the hostages over to the Republicans (rather than to Jimmy Carter) in return for some arms immediately (via Israel) plus the promise of future arms and political benefits once the Reagan administration came into office. . . .

Arms began flowing to Iran from well before the election, including a planeload of badly needed tires for Iran's U.S.-built jet fighters. . . .

The evidence strongly implies that individuals within the government worked actively with members of the Reagan–Bush campaign to influence the outcome of the 1980 election. Those allegations are exceptionally grave. If true, even in part, they suggest that there was an organized cabal among individuals inside and outside the elected government of the United States to concoct an alternative and private foreign policy with Israel and Iran without the knowledge or approval of the Carter administration. (Subsequent findings, ibid.)

AFTER THE SHOOTING

806. I forgot to duck. (President Ronald Reagan to his wife, Nancy, following his shooting by John Hinckley Jr., Washington, D.C., March 30, 1981.)

807. I hope you are all good Republicans. (To waiting doctors in the operating room, ibid.)

CARTOONISTS AND THEIR TARGETS

808. The success of any given political cartoon is predicated on an intelligent manipulation of symbols that are at the same time unique yet understandable to the widest possible audience. . . . [T]he personification of a personality or an issue into a broader representation is a necessary means for transmitting ideas, and cartoons have been a formidable medium for this communication. The drawings that reflect American socio-political concerns of the [19]60s and [19]70s epitomize the virtuosity of modern satiric art.

In his satiric swansong to the [Jimmy] Carter era, Jules Feiffer declared that the former President was a "cartoonist's nightmare." Although he was a prime physical candidate for caricature, Carter was an enigma, void of the necessary substance that makes a viable target. As Feiffer acutely points out, "while most leaders, throughout the ages, seemed larger than life, Carter was much, much smaller."

Predictably, without a proper handle, the resultant cartoons were often slapstick jabs rather than insightful comments. While Carter failed to be an inspiration, Richard Nixon was definitely the cartoonist's dream. A caricature of himself, he has earned a place in the iconographic hall of infamy alongside Napoleon, Boss Tweed, and Bismarck. Although he attempted to transform his physical persona through hair dyes and makeup, Nixon's neuroses, phobias, and other distinctive blemishes were exposed for all to see. Furthermore, he was easy to render; his five o'clock shadow, his widow's peak, his posture and gestures were eminently transformable into comic terms; he was Robert Grossman's Naked Emperor, Ed Sorel's Milhous I, and David Levine's Captain Queeg. (Steven Heller, from *Political Graphics: Art as a Weapon*, by Robert Philippe, 1982.)

[The political cartoons of the 1990s were far more strident and daring than those of earlier decades. Virtually anything went. In the midst of the Paula Jones sexual harassment lawsuit against President Clinton, one cartoonist depicted a police lineup. Five men are lined up facing Ms. Jones. Their trousers and undershorts have been dropped down to their ankles. She squints, points her finger, and says, "Third from the left."]

PEONAGE

---

809. Many thousands of illegal [Hispanic] immigrants find themselves living in what amounts to slavery. The law calls it "involuntary servitude." It occurs whenever a worker is forced, by whatever means, to stay at a job he does not want. If he is forced to work off a debt to his boss, his employer is guilty of "peonage." The size of the debt doesn't matter. It makes no difference whether the worker agreed to take the job in the first place. Nor does the boss have to hold the worker in chains or under lock and key. The threat of force is enough to make it slavery. Employers simply take advantage of the risky position of illegal immigrants.

The laws against peonage go back to the time right after the Civil War, when freed slaves were often forced to work by their former masters. The practice of peonage has continued to the present day. . . .

In Arkansas . . . a smuggler of aliens sold Mexican immigrants to farmers for $400 each. The farmers held back each Mexican's wages until the $400 was worked off, and then sold the aliens to other farmers for $400. The Mexican workers never got any cash—in essence, each farmer was getting free labor. Some Mexicans were forced to work for three or four farmers in a row and never made a penny the whole time they were in the United States. (Milton Meltzer, from *The Hispanic Americans*, 1982.)

A WITCH'S BREW

810. [The world is] plagued and besieged by subversion and a witch's brew of destabilization, terrorism and insurgency . . . fueled by Soviet arms, Cuban manpower and Libyan money. . . .

Beginning in 1974 and 1975, the Soviet Union undertook a new, much more aggressive strategy in the Third World . . . fully aware of the political climate in this country. . . .

It is much easier and much less expensive to support an insurgency than it is for us and our friends to resist one. It takes relatively few people and little support to disrupt the internal peace and economic stability of a small country. (William J. Casey, director of Central Intelligence, speech, Center for the Study of the Presidency, Washington, D.C., Mid-March 1982, cited in *Veil: The Secret Wars of the CIA, 1981–1987*, by Bob Woodward.)

PUERTO RICAN POLITICS

811. Certain political institutions have directly influenced some of the ways in which Puerto Rican politics developed in various cities. The Democratic party, for instance, inhibited the political growth of the Puerto Rican community. In control of the political machines in cities like New York, Chicago, and others, it refused to welcome Puerto Ricans as it did other ethnic groups. And when the machine bosses did try to control Puerto Rican voters, they did so paternalistically. This paternalism was evident in New York City before and after World War II; in Boston and other cities it has not yet fully flowered. The Republican party, except for a brief period during Mayor [John] Lindsay's tenure in New York City, also ignored Puerto Ricans as a potential source of electoral power. This posture generally discouraged Puerto Rican electoral activism.

The anti-poverty structure of the Great Society played an important role in Puerto Rican politics in the 1960s and 1970s. . . .

For many Puerto Rican activists the anti-poverty programs were the only available channels for political mobilization, and thus they were used exclusively to enter the electoral arena. But . . . these structures were also functional in discouraging independent and uncontrolled community activism, which could possibly lead to mobilization around systemic demands. (James Jennings, from *Puerto Rican Politics in Urban America*, edited by James Jennings and Monte Rivera, 1984.)

812. The development of a progressive electoral activism will determine some of the leadership and participatory patterns emerging in the Puerto Rican community. Increasingly leadership will be based on class—or at least socioeconomic—interests rather than ethnicity. This will affect black–Puerto Rican political relationships. Progressive elements in both communities will seek alliances based on calculations of common interests. Those seeking systemic change in the black community may develop partnerships with Puerto Rican activists with similar goals. (Ibid.)

RESPECTED, ABUSED, LIKED, HATED

813. What have I learned as state prosecutor?

I have learned that the law is not always right. The law is not always what it should be. To attempt to weave the law in a fair fashion through the human tragedies, emotions, and conflicts of a great and growing city [Miami] that has become the nation's melting pot—to achieve justice in the end—is what this job has been about.

I have also learned that my office is the common denominator of the criminal justice system in a jurisdiction of 26 different police agencies. I think it is our responsibility to look through the violence, gore, and fraud they deal with to understand why people commit crime, to look beyond the criminal justice system to other institutions that may have failed the criminal to see what can be done to prevent crime and to make the system better. . . .

What effect has my being a woman had? None, I would say. . . . I think I am respected, abused, liked, and hated in my role as a prosecutor, as a person, not as a woman. (Janet Reno, state attorney, Dade County, Florida, quoted in *Women Lawyers*, edited by Emily Couric, 1984.)

COACHES VERSUS TEACHERS

814. There is no accountability in the public school system—except for coaches. You know what happens to a losing coach. You fire him. A losing teacher can go on losing for 30 years and then go to glory. (H. Ross Perot, corporation executive, quoted in the *Dallas Morning News*, April 19, 1984.)

MESSAGE AT A MEMORIAL

815. Dad,

I came to visit you today. I haven't ever felt so close to you before. I never got a chance to know you but I love you very much. There isn't a day go by Mom doesn't think of you. Me and Gladene are always thinking of you too. You're gone from us now but we'll be together again one day. You'll never be forgotten, you still live in every one of us. I'm really proud to be your son, I hope I can be as good a man as you were. I love you Dad and I'll be back to see you if it's the last thing I ever do. (Carwain L. Herrington, USN, letter, Washington, D.C., undated, from *Shrapnel in the Heart: Letters and Remembrances from the Vietnam Veterans Memorial*, by Laura Palmer.)

CITIZENS, POLITICIANS, AND TIME

Many former residents of Centralia, Pennsylvania, believe that the disaster began with a landfill fire on May 27, 1962. They feel that that fire was never completely extinguished and set off a coal mine fire that burned underground for more than 20 years. During that period, individual citizens—later, citizens' groups—complained of deadly gases and other dangers that threatened lives and property. Many government agencies at all levels were called upon to solve the problem. Many solutions were offered. By 1983 residents had been moved out of the danger area and relocated.

816. A[n] important though less obvious lesson of Centralia was that citizens have the power to force government to heed their will, if . . . they have the courage and determination to use that power. Lois Gibbs, who organized her neighbors in the Love Canal area of Niagara Falls, New York, to fight for government relocation of families endangered by toxic waste there in the late 1970s, believed that was the central lesson to be drawn from Centralia, Love Canal and the toxic waste disaster at Times Beach, Missouri, in the early 1980s. "You can't fight it scientifically and you can't fight it legally," she said.

After her own relocation from Love Canal, Lois Gibbs helped the Citizens Clearinghouse for Hazardous Waste. . . . The group disseminates information about toxic waste and helps citizens around the country organize to fight for government cleanup of toxic waste sites. Mrs. Gibbs . . . worked with . . . Concerned Citizens against the Centralia Mine Fire and Centralia Homeowners Association. Centralia was not a toxic waste site, but it had many of the same problems as Love Canal and Times Beach.

"You've got to go out and talk to your neighbors, and you've got to fight it with an organized political front," Mrs. Gibbs said. "That's probably the hardest thing for people to accept. Nothing's ever, ever going to move until they go after elected officials with the issue."

It was a lesson the citizens of Centralia learned too late to save their community. Concerned Citizens organized in 1981, but by then the fire had burned for 19 years and was probably too large and too close to populated areas to bring under control without destroying a major portion of the village. (David Dekok, from *Unseen Danger: A Tragedy of People, Government, and the Centralia Mine Fire,* 1986.)

VIETNAMESE BOAT PERSON

---

817. Although we lived in a small village south of Saigon, my father was considered [by the Communist authorities to be] friendly to the Americans. . . . My mother's brother found us in 1986. He had a little money from the black market in Saigon and a small boat. We left Vietnam on his boat. . . .

It was dangerous on the ocean in this little boat. There were 23 people. The Thai pirates captured us on our third week out. I do not wish to tell you all that happened to us. I will say that I was beaten and raped and no longer wished to live when our ordeal was over. My father and two brothers were thrown overboard. We never saw them again. My mother, youngest brother, and baby sister and I survived, as did my uncle and his wife and three of their children. Everyone else was lost. Our only luck this trip was to not be put into a detention camp when we reached Hong Kong. My uncle knew people from an American missionary church who were to sponsor us. We left quickly for San Francisco.

Life was very difficult when we got there. All nine of us . . . shared a one-bedroom apartment. (Kim Thi Linh, recalling events of 1986 during her escape from Vietnam, quoted in *Vietnamese Americans,* by Alexander Bandon.)

[She was 14 at the time.]

IRAN-CONTRA AFFAIR

818. I think I figured out a way to provide some funds to the *contras* out of the Iranian project. (Lieutenant Colonel Oliver North, National Security Council staff, to Vice Admiral John Poindexter, late January 1986, from Poindexter deposition to the Joint Select Committee of Congress, cited in *Perilous Statecraft: An Insider's Account of the Iran-Contra Affair*, by Michael A. Ledeen.)

[The *contras* were insurgents fighting to overthrow the Sandinista regime in Nicaragua. The Iranian project was to sell Iran weapons and spare parts. Iran would also use its influence to have American hostages released in Beirut, Lebanon. The idea attributed to North was to sell the Iranians weapons at a profit and use the proceeds to help fund the *contras*.]

819. I thought about it. I felt that it was in terms of supporting and implementing the President's policy, that it was entirely consistent.

The President really never changed his policy with regard to supporting the *contras*. . . . I knew that it would be a controversial issue. . . . I felt I had the authority to approve Colonel North's request. I also felt that it was, as I said, consistent with the President's policy; and that if I asked him, I felt confident that he would approve it.

But because it was controversial, and I obviously knew that it would cause a ruckus if it were exposed, I decided to insulate the President from the decision and give him some deniability, and so I decided . . . at that point not to tell the President. (Vice Admiral John Poindexter, national security adviser to President Reagan, recalling the preceding conversation, ibid.)

[Though scholars may debate whether President Reagan knew about this arrangement in advance, few doubt the involvement of CIA director William Casey. During congressional hearings in 1987, it was revealed that in 1984 Casey had asked North about the creation of an "off-the-shelf, self-sustaining, stand-alone entity." It could conduct covert operations without congressional approval, funding, or oversight.]

ROLE OF SDI

820. SDI [the Strategic Defense Initiative] is the key to a world without nuclear weapons. (President Ronald Reagan, address to the nation return, from his meeting with General Secretary Gorbachev, Washington, D.C., October 13, 1986.)

ON CONTROLS, TESTS, AND COSMETICS

821. Control mechanisms are in place in this country that are extremely efficient. . . . They are so efficient, they don't need police in jackboots walking down the street, knocking on your door at three in the morning . . . [because] the most efficient control systems are the ones where the people who are the victims are also the enforcers of the control systems. (Ralph Nader, speech, Harvard University, Cambridge, Massachusetts, March 3, 1987, cited in *Courtroom Crusaders*, by Mark Litwak.)

822. Multiple-choice [standardized testing] tracks you from kindergarten all the way to the licenses you get in the professional and occupational arena. Now most students say to themselves, "I will accept that standard of measurement. I will take cram courses. I'm not interested in what this measures. . . . I'm just interested in scoring, because that's the way up." As a result, educational curriculum in high school is tailored to these multiple-choice tests. Experiences that don't get you a reward on these tests get you a low status, a low priority. . . . These tests do not measure the most important aspects of your personality, your chances for success in life.

It's a system of control. (Ibid.)

823. Who sets the standard of personal beauty in our country? The cosmetic companies and the fashion magazines. They set it. So that they can generate proper anxieties in your mind, proper deteriorations of self-esteem, so you can then crave for the products that will diminish the gap between you and Revlon and you and *Vogue* and you and *Playboy*'s ads. . . .

Millions of people put this stuff on their hair, on their eyes, on their skin, on their nails without asking: "What are these toxic chemicals? How many are carcinogens?" . . . There are plenty. How many are getting into the bloodstream, through the perms and the hair dyes? What about the millions of people who work in the beauty salons and are exposed to this stuff eight hours a day? . . .

For what? In order to meet an externally imposed standard of increasing centralization, commercialization, and exploitation. . . .

Now you may think that's trivial. Try reading some of the letters of teenagers on the verge of nervous breakdowns because they don't think they appear the right way. (Ibid.)

CHALLENGE

824. General Secretary Gorbachev, if you seek peace, if you seek prosperity for the Soviet Union and Eastern Europe, if you seek liberalization: Come here to this [Brandenburg] gate! Mr. Gorbachev, tear down this wall! (President Ronald Reagan, speech at the Berlin Wall, which then separated East and West Berlin, June 12, 1987.)

FALL GUY

In the summer of 1987, the Joint Select Committee of Congress held hearings related to the Iran-Contra affair. In short, arms had been sold to Iran in return for using its influence to free American hostages being held in Beirut. Profits from that sale were used to fund the *contras* in Nicaragua. This was all being done without the knowledge or approval of Congress. The following are brief excerpts from testimony by Lieutenant Colonel Oliver North, formerly of the National Security Council. He is questioned by Arthur Liman, counsel for the committee.

825. NORTH: The actions that I took, all of them, to include the use of residual funds from the sale of arms to Iran to support the Nicaraguan resistance and other activities were approved. All of them.

LIMAN: And is it also so that for some months you had been telling friends . . . that you were going to be the fall guy?

NORTH: I may well have told Mr. Owen and perhaps others that if this whole thing came down to creating a political controversy, or embarrassment . . . that I would be the person who would be dismissed or reassigned or fired or blamed or fingered or whatever one wants to use as a description. That I was willing to serve in that capacity. All of that assumed that this was not going to be a matter of criminal behavior, but rather one of deniability for the White House, for the Administration, or whatever, for political purposes. And when I say "political purposes" I'm speaking not only domestic, but the international ramifications. That is one of the essences of plausible deniability in a covert operation.

LIMAN: Are you saying, Colonel, that you were prepared to take the rap for political purposes, but not for criminal purposes?

NORTH: Precisely. (Testimony before Joint Select Committee of Congress, Washington, D.C., July 9, 1987, from *Taking the Stand: Testimony of Lieutenant-Colonel Oliver L. North.*)

826. [Liman questions North about a discussion that he had with the attorney general about the affair.]

LIMAN: Well, who were you protecting?

NORTH: What do you mean, who was I protecting? I was protecting the lives and the safety of the people who were engaged in the operation.

LIMAN: Well, explain to us how telling the Attorney General of the United States that [CIA] Director [William] Casey approved a diversion [of funds] would jeopardize lives, other than, perhaps, put him in jeopardy of this kind of investigation that you've been through?

NORTH: I don't know, other than the fact that this investigation could indeed result in lives being put in jeopardy.

(Ibid.)

827. NORTH: My recollection is that [in the fall of 1986] Director Casey agreed with my assessment that the time had come for someone . . . to take the hit or the fall. He, quite frankly, did not think that I was senior enough to do that, and suggested that—I am trying to recall—but suggested that it was probably going to go up the line, or something like that.

LIMAN: Did he suggest who else could take the hit?

NORTH: He suggested that it might be Admiral Poindexter [national security adviser to the president]. . . .

LIMAN: So, Casey . . . as I understand it discussed with you the fact that it just might not be credible for you to take the hit and that it might have to be Admiral Poindexter?

NORTH: Words to that effect.

LIMAN: Did he discuss anyone else who might have to take the hit?

NORTH: No but he was concerned that the President not be damaged, and I shared that belief. (Ibid.)

[North was later convicted for his part in the Iran-Contra affair. The conviction was overturned on appeal, as he had been granted immunity by the congressional committee.]

CONVERSATIONS

828. "Edgar, I hear you're moving to Gables by the Sea. Even if I had all the money in the world, I wouldn't move there. No more dominoes at your place.

That city has an ordinance against dominoes and colored underwear. For me, moving there is like living in a Listerine bottle, too disinfected, lifeless." (Roberto G. Fernandez, from his novel *Raining Backwards*, 1988.)

829. "Excuse me, young man, my hearing is not too good, but did I hear you say you are going to call your building Kennedy Towers?"

"Do you realize what that name means to us?"

"Sure, the name of one of our Presidents."

"Do you realize he sold us into slavery?"

"He's dead, Mr. Gonzalez. Give the man a break!"

"One death is nothing compared to the calvary of a whole people. You are too young to remember, but he never made good what he promised us at the Orange Bowl!"

"We are lost, Pepe. We have plowed in the sea!" (Ibid.)

830. WILL THE LAST AMERICAN TO LEAVE MIAMI PLEASE BRING THE FLAG (Quotation, without attribution, immediately preceding the novel, ibid.)

"QUIET RIOTS"

---

831. There are "quiet riots" in all of America's central cities: unemployment, poverty, social disorganization, segregation, family disintegration, housing and school deterioration, and crime are worse now [than in 1968, when the Kerner Commission report warned of "two societies, one black, one white—separate and unequal"]. These "quiet riots" are not as alarming as the violent riots of 20 years ago, or as noticeable to outsiders. But they are even more destructive of human life. National security requires renewed human investment if we are to be a stable and secure society of self-esteem. We have the means. We must summon the will. (Fred R. Harris and Roger W. Wilkins, from *Quiet Riots*, 1988.)

STUDENT ACTIVISM

---

832. It never went away.

It may have subsided, and it certainly changed, reflecting changing times and circumstances, but progressive student political activism never really stopped after the much-heralded anti-Vietnam War era.

College students of the late 1980s live in a different universe than their older brothers and sisters (or parents). How they view the world, and how they choose to act in it, stems from factors and influences college students a generation ago did not encounter. Those who dismiss today's politically active college students as "throwbacks" or "nostalgia freaks" or "escapists from reality" would do well to acquaint themselves with these differences.

Social relationships between men and women, between students of different racial, ethnic, economic and geographic backgrounds, between heterosexual and homosexual students, between students and non-students—all these interactions both complicate the atmosphere on the campus, and make that campus a test area for future encounters. Co-ed living arrangements place students of all kinds in close proximity with one another, forcing them to confront hidden prejudices and feelings of superiority or inferiority, often with dramatic results. Students understand that the personal is political.

Colleges today teach more and more non-traditional students—those older than 22, those who are married or divorced, have children, have a full-time job, are seeking to change careers; those who are not able-bodied, those for whom English is a second language. And women students play a larger role in the political life of a campus than ever before. This remarkable diversity provides a demanding political mix as well. . . .

[T]he issues students are working on: South Africa, Central America, the role of the CIA, the War Machine, the Economy, Racism, Women's issues, Gay, Lesbian and Bisexual Rights, and Student Empowerment. (Tony Vellela, from *New Voices: Student Activism in the '80s and '90s*, 1988.)

18

New World Order—and Disorder

This chapter might easily have been entitled "From Bush to Bush." Under President George H. Bush, Soviet Communism collapsed, and a "New World Order" was envisioned.

In the eighth month of his presidency, George W. Bush faced the disorder of terrorism on a massive, unprecedented scale.

From Bush to Bush, here is how the events unfolded:

As Soviet Communism expired, those European nations formerly under Soviet domination were free to map out their own futures.

The Soviet collapse meant new challenges for the United States in other parts of the world.

When Iraq invaded Kuwait and threatened Saudi Arabia, the United States organized an international coalition to oppose Iraqi aggression.

When "ethnic cleansing" led to genocide in parts of a disintegrating Yugoslavia, the United States joined with its NATO allies in stopping the atrocities.

There were domestic challenges, as well. For only the second time in American history, a president was impeached—and acquitted.

The 2000 census revealed profound changes among America's 281,000,000 people. The population was getting older, more Hispanic, and more Asian. What political, social, and economic changes might come about in the new century?

The presidential election of 2000 resulted in a virtual tie and a sharply divided electorate.

Then, on September 11, 2001, everything changed. That "New World Order" became a world of disorder—and that great divide in America vanished in a matter of minutes. It became a unity not seen in America since the Japanese attacked Pearl Harbor 60 years earlier.

On Sept 11, 2001, targets in the United States were hit by terrorists who had hijacked passenger planes. They crashed two planes into the World Trade Center towers (above) in New York City. A third suicide plane was crashed into the Pentagon outside Washington, D.C. A fourth hijacked plane crashed in Pennsylvania when passengers put up a fight against their captors. Thousands perished.

Terrorists crashed hijacked passenger planes into the World Trade Center in New York and the Pentagon outside Washington, D.C. Many thousands lay dead, including hundreds of police officers, fire-fighters, and rescue workers. A brand new kind of warfare confronted not just America, but the civilized world. In the wake of the terrorist attacks, there was bipartisan support in Congress for President George W. Bush to do whatever was necessary to punish the terrorist leaders and those who harbor them.

After September 11, 2001, there was a universal call among Americans for action against the cruel, crafty, faceless enemy who lay in wait to commit new atrocities.

The American mood in the days immediately following the new "day of infamy" was reminiscent of the days following December 7, 1941, when Japan attacked Pearl Harbor.

At that time, an apocryphal story swept the country. It reflected both a recognition of terrible losses and the desire for retaliation. The story went like this:

A man was passing a sandlot baseball field and stopped to watch the game. He yelled to the third-baseman, "Who's ahead?"

"They are," the kid said.

"What's the score?"

"Twenty-six to nothing," the kid said.

"Twenty-six to nothing!" the man said. "Aren't you worried?"

"Nah," the kid said, "We ain't had our turn at bat yet."

TAX PLEDGE

833. The Congress will push me to raise taxes, and I'll say no. And they'll push, and I'll say no. And they'll push again, and I'll say to them, "Read my lips: no new taxes." (Vice President George H. Bush acceptance speech following his nomination for president, Republican National Convention, New Orleans, August 18, 1988.)

[This campaign promise was enthusiastically received by the Republican delegates, as well as by many in the television audience. During his term as president, Bush would agree to a tax hike. When he ran for reelection in 1992, Bush was assailed by political opponents for breaking his pledge, and he was defeated.]

ASIANS IN AMERICA

834. In Palolo Valley on the island of Oahu, Hawaii, where I lived as a child, my neighbors had names like Hamamoto, Kauhane, Wong, and Camara. . . .

After graduation from high school, I attended a college in a midwestern town where I found myself invited to "dinners for foreign students" sponsored by local churches and clubs like the Rotary. I politely tried to explain to my kind hosts that I was not a "foreign student." My fellow students and even my professors would ask me how long I had been in America and where I had learned to speak English. In this country, I would reply. And sometimes I would add: "I was born in America, and my family has been here for three generations." (Ronald Takaki, from *Strangers from a Different Shore: A History of Asian Americans*, 1989.)

835. Today Asian Americans belong to the fastest-growing ethnic minority group in the United States. In percentage, they are increasing more rapidly than Hispanics. . . . The target of immigration exclusion laws in the 19th and early 20th centuries, Asians have recently been coming again to America. . . . Currently half of all immigrants entering annually are Asian. (Ibid.)

KINDER AND GENTLER

836. [M]ake kinder the face of the Nation and gentler the face of the world. (President George H. Bush, Inaugural Address, Washington, D.C., January 20, 1989.)

837. Are we enthralled with material things, less appreciative of the nobility of work and sacrifice. My friends we are not the sum of our possessions. They are not the measure of our lives. (Ibid.)

838. The old solution, the old way [to solve people's problems] was to think that public money alone could end these problems. But we have learned that that was not so. And in any case our funds are low. We have a deficit to bring down. (Ibid.)

ASSESSING MEXICAN FIELD HANDS

839. It's difficult to get other people to do this work. . . . [P]hysically it's very hard. It's very hot, about 100 degrees plus every day. You sweat a lot, you're bent over a lot, it's boring, monotonous, doing the same process over and over and over for hours and hours. . . . You'll get some white people out there and they just won't come back the next day. . . .

When I was in Mexico, the guys I knew from California weren't doing anything. They didn't want to work for my friend who was growing there because they were only going to make three dollars a day. Well, why should they when they can go back to California and make that in an hour? . . .

I've been lucky. I've never had a raid [by the immigration authorities]. But if I did have a raid at a crucial period it would be devastating. Especially with the new fine. . . . Everybody is going to hire only documented workers, or apparently documented workers. . . . It's a little more difficult now, but you can get a license or state ID, like, no problem. So it's not going to be that hard to get around the new law. It's just that I can't knowingly hire illegal aliens. (Robert Bascom [pseudonym], seed grower, Sacramento, California, quoted in *Mexican Voices/American Dreams*, by Marilyn P. Davis, 1990.)

A MEXICAN VIEW OF AMERICA

840. Streets of gold: that is the vision they carry setting out from their villages heading to *el norte*. There are wonderful tales about the other side: the hood jobs, the beauty, the *gringas*, how someone got their papers. And the treasures! People bring back televisions, VCRs, and these new microwaves that cook dinner in less than a minute! Many an afternoon has been spent with *compañeros* and tequila going over and over those stories, stories the younger generation are raised on.

No one ever has a realistic view of the United States before arriving, and it can never live up to their expectations, either as a place or in the possibility of fulfilling their dreams. After a short while, many immigrants see past their fantasies [and] adjust their expectations. (Anthropologist Marilyn P. Davis, from *Mexican Voices/American Dreams: An Oral History of Mexican Immigration to the United States*, 1990.)

TELEVISION AND POLITICS

841. A candidate who would dare discuss the pros and cons of a vital piece of legislation instead of doling out one-liners and applause lines prepared by his media consultants is destined for oblivion.

In the television age, style not only takes precedence over substance but threatens to completely eclipse it. Thirty-second sound bites are more influential than carefully thought-out thirty-minute speeches. (Richard M. Nixon, from *In the Arena, a Memoir of Victory, Defeat, and Renewal*, 1990.)

NEW PHRASE FOR A NEW PHASE

842. Time and again in this century, the political map of the world was transformed. And in each instance, a new world order came about through the advent of a new tyrant, or the outbreak of a bloody global war, or its end. Now the world has undergone another upheaval, but this time, there's no war. We've seen a bold Soviet leader initiate daring reforms. . . . We've seen both the Berlin Wall and the Romanian dictatorship tumble into ruins. And I think it's fair to say that the day of the dictator is over.

Victor Hugo said that no army can match the might of an idea whose time has come. In the Revolution of '89, an idea overcame armies and tanks, and that idea is democracy. (President George H. Bush, speech, fund-raising dinner for gubernatorial candidate Pete Wilson, San Francisco, February 28, 1990.)

[According to the Bush Presidential Library, this is his earliest use of the phrase "new world order."]

WAR IN THE PERSIAN GULF

On August 1, 1990, Iraq invaded Kuwait, a potential threat to Saudi Arabia. President Bush weighed his response.

843. While I was prepared to deal with this crisis unilaterally if necessary, I wanted the United Nations involved as part of our first response, starting with a strong condemnation of Iraq's attack on a fellow member. Decisive U.N. action would be important in rallying international opposition to the invasion and reversing it. . . . it was keenly aware that this would be the first post–Cold War test of the Security Council in crisis. (President George H. Bush, recalling events of August 1, 1990, from *A World Transformed*, by George Bush and Brent Scowcroft.)

[Within twenty-four hours of the invasion, the United Nations (UN) Security Council voted 14–0 to condemn the invasion, demanded withdrawal of Iraqi troops, and called for negotiations to settle any dispute between Iraq and Kuwait.]

ASSESSMENT

844. The sooner we can get an invitation from the Saudis [for U.S. military forces] the better. I believe the Iraqis would think twice before engaging us. We can get our air power in quickly. We can handle the Iraqi Air Force. We also have some naval forces that can be augmented. Ground forces can be introduced over the course of a month. All this would draw down our ability to act anywhere else in the world. The ultimate size of the force would be a hundred thousand men. (General Colin Powell, chairman, Joint Chiefs of Staff, National Security Council meeting, Camp David, August 4, 1990, quoted in *A World Transformed*, by George Bush and Brent Scowcroft.)

[The United States would first build up a force in Saudi Arabia. Then it would try, through diplomatic efforts and economic sanctions, to get Iraq to withdraw from Kuwait. According to Scowcroft, it would not be until October that President Bush would conclude that Iraq would have to be driven out by force.]

CONGRESS LOOKS AT WAR-MAKING

845. Debate on the use of force was intensifying, but it would be inaccurate to say it developed into a struggle with Congress over policy in the Gulf as a whole. The issues were narrower; there was general agreement about the need to resist Iraqi aggression. Congress itself had passed resolutions soundly condemning the invasion [of Kuwait] and supporting the Administration's over-all policy up to this point. But the increase in troops [sent to Saudi Arabia] brought subsidiary issues to the fore. Should force be used or should sanctions continue to be the main weapon against Saddam [Hussein]? And, if military action was to be considered, who—the President or the Congress—had the authority to order it? . . .

While the Constitution provides that only Congress may declare war, it does not withhold authority from the President to use force as a tool of foreign policy. (Brent Scowcroft, national security adviser, recalling events of mid-November 1990, from A World Transformed, by George Bush and Brent Scowcroft.)

LOBBYING THE SECURITY COUNCIL

846. In the midst of this careful diplomacy, former President Carter wrote the members of the Security Council asking them not to support the resolution [giving Iraq a deadline to withdraw from Kuwait or face force]. He argued that the costs in human life and the economic consequences, not to mention the permanent destabilization of the Middle East, were too high and unnecessary, "unless all peaceful resolution efforts are first exhausted." He called for the U.N. to mandate a "good faith" negotiation with the Iraqi leaders to consider their concerns, and to ask the Arabs to try to work out a peaceful solution, "without any restraint on their agenda." It was an unbelievable letter, asking the other members of the council to vote against his own country. . . .

It seemed to me that if there was ever a violation of the Logan Act prohibiting diplomacy by private citizens, this was it. President Bush was furious at this interference in the conduct of his foreign policy and the deliberate attempt to undermine it, but told me just to let it drop. (Brent Scowcroft, national security adviser, recalling events of late November 1990, from A World Transformed, by George Bush and Brent Scowcroft.)

[On November 29, 1990, the UN Security Council approved the resolution. It set January 15, 1991, for Iraq to comply.]

COMMENT ON GULF WAR

847. Look how good we feel. Why do we feel good? Because the big gorilla whipped a midget. (H. Ross Perot, corporation executive, comment, *Larry King Live* television show, Cable Network News, March 19, 1991.)

ON MEMBERS OF CONGRESS

848. These people work for you and me, but they don't act like our servants. Close the [free] barber shop, the gym, the parking lot. Make them pay for it. Ground every airplane for Federal officials except Air Force One. Let 'em fly commercial, get in line, wait three hours, get their baggage lost. We're going broke, and they're flying around in our airplanes. (H. Ross Perot, corporation executive, quoted in the *New York Times*, November 5, 1991.)

ASSESSING THE GULF WAR

849. Here are my answers to . . . questions I am most often asked. . . .
Why didn't we go all the way to Baghdad and "finish the job"?
It should be clearly understood that the option of going all the way to Baghdad was never considered. Despite all the so-called experts who . . . are now criticizing that "decision," at the time the war ended there was not a single head of state, diplomat, Middle East expert, or military leader who, as far as I am aware, advocated continuing the war and seizing Baghdad. The United Nations resolutions that provided the legal basis for our military operations in the gulf were clear in their intent: kick the Iraqi military force out of Kuwait. We had authority to take whatever actions were necessary to accomplish that mission, including attacks into Iraq; but we had no authority to invade Iraq for the purpose of capturing the entire country or its capital. . . . I am certain that had we taken all of Iraq . . . we would still be there, and we, not the United Nations, would be bearing the costs of that occupation. . . .

Since Saddam is still alive and in control in Iraq, wasn't the whole war fought for nothing?

[C]onsider what would have happened if Saddam had been allowed to succeed with his aggression—if the Gulf War hadn't been fought.

First he would now control all the oil from Kuwait and perhaps from the entire Arabian Peninsula. . . .

Instead, a defanged Saddam has been forced to retreat behind his own borders. His nuclear, biological, and chemical military capabilities have been destroyed and will stay that way if we can figure out how to prevent him from getting them in the future the same way he got them in the past—from unscrupulous firms, both western and eastern, more interested in the corporate bottom line than in world peace. (General H. Norman Schwarzkopf, from *It Doesn't Take a Hero*, with Peter Petre, 1992.)

[In 1991 Schwarzkopf led a multinational coalition that drove Iraqi military forces out of Kuwait.]

EARTH IN THE BALANCE

---

850. Life is always motion and change. Fueled by the fruits of sun, soil, water and air, we are constantly growing and creating, destroying and dying, nurturing and organizing. And as we change, the world changes with us. The human community grows ever larger and more complex, and in doing so demands ever more from the natural world. Every day, we reach deeper into the storehouse of the earth's resources, put more of these resources to use, and generate more waste of every kind in the process. Change begets change, then feeds on its own momentum until finally the entire globe seems to be accelerating toward some kind of profound transformation. (Senator Albert Gore Jr., from *Earth in the Balance: Ecology and the Human Spirit*, 1992.)

851. Increasingly, people feel anxious about the accumulation of dramatic changes that portend ever-larger "avalanches" cascading down the slopes of culture and society, uprooting institutions like the family and burying values like those that have always nurtured our concern for the future. The actions of any isolated group now reverberate throughout the entire world, but we seem unable to bridge the chasms that divide us from one another. Is our civilization stuck in conflict between isolated nations, religions, tribes, and political systems—divided by gender and race and language? And now that we have developed the capacity to affect the environment on a global scale, can we also be mature enough to care for the earth as a whole? (Ibid.)

852. For civilization as a whole, the faith that is so essential to restore the balance now missing in our relationship to the earth is the faith that we do have a future. We can believe in that future, and work to achieve it and preserve it, or we can whirl blindly on, behaving as if one day there will be no children to inherit our legacy. The choice is ours; the earth is in the balance. (Ibid.)

PUERTO RICANS IN NEW YORK

853. Life in New York City is full of famous woes. Everyone in the city is afflicted with dreaming and gossip. Nothing private endures; the truth has no purchase on what is known; everything is made to fit the expectations of the market. No more cruel or democratic place exists or was ever imagined.

The tragedy of the Puerto Ricans began the moment they chose New York. It condemned them to live as the objects of invention even as it set them to furious dreaming. They ceased to be who they were. They became words and music. In Puerto Rico they had been conquered by force of arms and politics; in the new city they fell victim to disappointment and the *Daily News*. (Earl Shorris, from *Latinos: A Biography of the People*, 1992.)

REMEMBERING COLUMBUS

854. For many people around the world, [1992] will be a year to celebrate the accomplishments of a man who was a product of an emerging industrial society, and his discovery of what was to him an unknown hemisphere. This land, however, was not only inhabited when Columbus arrived, but also shared and cultivated by ethnically diverse peoples who had prospered in every region of these vast "new" lands for many thousands of years. . . .

It is estimated that more than ten million people, the ancestors of present-day Indian tribes, inhabited North America when Columbus arrived. It is difficult to comprehend the magnitude of the atrocities—intentional, neglectful, or accidental—perpetrated on Indian people by the conquering culture, and later by the very government that assumed responsibility for their protection. By 1900, the Indian population had dwindled because of imported disease, slavery, forced relocation, and outright genocide, to an estimated 100,000. (Ben Nighthorse

Campbell, "Reflections on the Quincentenary," in *Journal of Legal Commentary,* spring 1992.)

THE FEDERAL DEFICIT

---

855. The chief financial officer of a publicly owned corporation would be sent to prison if he kept books like our government.

We cannot continue to tolerate this. The average citizen works five months a year just to pay his taxes. Forty-two percent of his income goes to taxes. All the personal income taxes collected west of the Mississippi are needed just to pay the interest on the national debt. That's kind of depressing, isn't it?

The total national debt was only $1 trillion in 1980 when President Reagan took office. It is now $4 trillion. Maybe it was voodoo economics. Whatever it was, we are now in deep voodoo. (H. Ross Perot, speech, National Press Club, Washington, D.C., March 18, 1992.)

[Perot had announced earlier in the year that if he got on the ballot of all 50 states, he would run as an independent candidate for president. He ran as a third-party candidate in 1992 and 1996 but was unsuccessful.]

RAISING CONGRESSIONAL
SALARIES

---

856. No law, varying the compensation for the services of the Senators and Representatives, shall take effect, until an election of Representatives shall have intervened. (27th Amendment, ratified May 7, 1992.)

ON INDIAN ART

---

857. It seems to me that the guiding set of esthetics in Indian art is inextricably tied to a shared concept of nature and a belief that life exists in things others might see as inanimate. (W. Richard West Jr., quoted in the *New York Times*, September 13, 1992.)

FIGHTING FOR LOST CAUSES

858. Many of the cases I've handled over the last 25 years could be called "lost causes" because the defendants, often out of synch with mainstream society, stood very little chance of being acquitted and were, in the words of Clarence Darrow, "life's damned." They may be members of a minority or another oppressed group. They may have radical political views. They may have committed other crimes. They may be hated by almost everyone.

Throughout our history, we have had government-manufactured villains, such as Communists, terrorists, labor-union leaders, mobsters, black militants, Islamic fundamentalists, or whatever group was out of favor at the time. In order to support official terrorism, like the shooting down of union members and Black Panthers, or the beating of antiwar and civil rights demonstrators, the government makes its enemies into monsters so that it can get away with murder and the public says no more than "What does it matter? They were only criminal syndicalists, union people, or organized crime figures, or terrorists."

In the past, for example, striking union workers were considered enemies of the people because a labor union on strike was committing a crime called criminal syndicalism. At different times throughout our history, our enemies have been anarchists, pacifists, Japanese-Americans, or suffragettes. Today our enemies of choice are alleged terrorists, particularly those with Arabic names. But organized-crime figures run a close second.

Ironically, some groups that were yesterday's villains are today's heroes. Who would have imagined, for example, when we fought Japan during World War II—and even imprisoned Japanese-Americans in concentration camps in this country—that today we would seek Japan's business and its money? (William M. Kunstler, from *My Life as a Radical Lawyer*, with Sheila Isenberg, 1994.)

ON MANIFEST DESTINY

859. It is my observation that we are suffering from the attitudes that come from the Christian doctrine of manifest destiny—that one people will rule the world. Inherent in this is the idea that a chosen people have a divine right—nay mission—to dominate the world. (Oren R. Lyons, commencement address, Syracuse University, Syracuse, New York, 1993.)

860. By killing the salmon in their spawning grounds, by clear cutting the forests without reseeding, by polluting fresh water that all life needs for survival, you have broken the great cycles of regeneration, the fundamental law of natural life. . . . The law that is absolute and merciless. The law that provides life endlessly if we abide, and the law that destroys in exact ratio to transgressions that challenge it. (Ibid.)

ENIGMAS

861. Today, a generation raised in the shadows of the Cold War assumes new responsibilities in a world warmed by the sunshine of freedom—but threatened, still, by ancient hatreds and new plagues.

Raised in unrivaled prosperity, we inherit an economy that is still the world's strongest, but is weakened by business failures, stagnant wages, increasing inequality, and deep divisions among our own people.

We must invest more in our people, in their jobs and in their future—and at the same time cut our massive debt.

Let us put aside personal advantage so that we can feel the pain and see the promise of America.

Today, as an old order passes, the new world is more free but less stable. (President Bill Clinton, Inaugural Address, Washington, D.C., January 20, 1993.)

GAYS IN THE MILITARY

During the 1992 presidential campaign, Bill Clinton had promised to lift the ban on gays and lesbians in the military. The issue came up in his first week in office. A meeting was held in the White House with the Joint Chiefs of Staff.

862. Yes, he was commander in chief, but Clinton's formal powers were bound by the fact that he was a new President, elected with only 43 percent of the vote, who had never served in the military and stood accused of dodging the draft.

Presidential power . . . is the power to persuade, but the chiefs weren't here to be persuaded. . . . Their message was clear: Keeping this promise will cost you the military. Fight us, and you will lose—and it won't be pretty. . . .

One by one, the chiefs made that point to Clinton in measured but uncompromising tones. . . .

Colin Powell was the most effective. He . . . laid down a marker: The armed forces under Clinton's command were in "exquisite" shape, he said. We shouldn't do anything to put that at risk. We'd never had full civil rights in the military, and it would be impossible to maintain morale if gay and straight soldiers were integrated.

The President . . . said he intended to keep his commitment, making the irrefutable point that gays and lesbians had served—and were serving—in the military both honorably and well. The only question . . . is whether they should have to live a lie. . . .

I was proud of his argument, but I also knew that we had no cards to play. If we didn't work out a compromise with the chiefs, they would sabotage us on the Hill. . . .

That's all we needed: the top military brass led by Colin Powell, lined up in a row in direct confrontation with a new President who, they said, was sacrificing national security for the sake of a campaign pledge to a special interest—all live on CNN.

Impassioned testimony from the highest-ranking black man in America denying the parallels between skin color and sexual orientation would trump our strongest civil rights argument for ending the ban. (George Stephanopoulus, White House aide, recalling events of January 25, 1993, from *All Too Human: A Political Education*.)

[A compromise would be announced on July 19, 1993. The policy would be "don't ask, don't tell, don't pursue." Individuals would not be questioned about their sexual orientation, and gays would not reveal it.]

THE MAFIA: HISTORICAL VIEW

863. For most of the 20th century, what has been called the "Mafia," "Cosa Nostra," or simply "organized crime" seemed as inevitable as increased taxes. Some Mafia chieftains even attained widespread public notoriety and were treated like folk heroes. . . . People who understood power and the "the way things worked" . . . recognized organized crime as a key player in politics, vice, and legitimate industry ranging from shipping and trucking to garbage disposal and the garment industry.

Despite, or perhaps because of, its power and pervasiveness . . . Cosa Nostra faced relatively little opposition from law enforcement. . . . Remarkably, until well into the 1960s the FBI, under . . . J. Edgar Hoover, disputed the very existence of an American Mafia.

Congressional attention to organized crime dates back to the Kefauver Committee hearings in 1951 and the McClellan Committee hearings in 1957. The Department of Justice began to focus on organized crime during Robert Kennedy's tenure as attorney general in the early 1960s. He sponsored anti-racketeering legislation. . . . By the end of the decade Congress had passed the Organized Crime Control Act; Title III provided a comprehensive regimen for electronic surveillance by federal, state, and local police. After Hoover's departure from the FBI in 1972, that agency began to devote significant resources to organized-crime control. Various successes [occurred] throughout the 1960s and 1970s, but there can be no mistaking the proliferation of achievements beginning in the late 1970s.

From approximately 1978, the federal government mounted an extraordinary effort to eradicate Cosa Nostra. Utilizing extensive electronic surveillance, undercover government agents, and mob turncoats, the FBI, the federal Organized Crime Strike Force, and the United States attorneys' offices initiated a steady stream of intensive investigations and produced a regular flow of Cosa Nostra prosecutions throughout the country. (James B. Jacobs, director of the Center for Research in Crime and Justice, from *Busting the Mob: United States v. Cosa Nostra*, with Christopher Panarella and Jay Worthington, 1994.)

[Between 1981 and 1992 there were prosecutions in New York City, New Orleans, Denver, Chicago, Kansas City, Los Angeles, Boston, Pittston, Pennsylvania, Philadelphia, Cleveland, St. Louis, Buffalo, Providence, and the state of New Jersey.]

LESSONS OF VIETNAM

864. We misjudged then—as we have since—the geopolitical intentions of our adversaries. . . . [A]nd we exaggerated the dangers to the United States of their actions.

We viewed the people and leaders of South Vietnam in terms of our own experience. We saw in them a thirst for—and a determination to fight for—freedom and democracy. . . .

We underestimated the power of nationalism to motivate . . . the North Vietnamese and Vietcong to fight and die for their beliefs and values. . . .

Our misjudgments of friend and foe alike reflected our profound ignorance of the history, culture, and politics of the people in the area. . . .

We failed then—as we have since—to recognize the limitations of modern, high-technology military equipment, forces, and doctrine in confronting unconventional, highly motivated people's movements. . . .

We failed to draw Congress and the American people into a full and frank discussion and debate . . . of a large-scale U.S. military involvement. . . .

After the action got under way and unanticipated events forced us off our planned course . . . we did not explain fully what was happening and why. . . .

We did not hold to the principle that U.S. military action—other than in response to direct threats to our own security—should be carried out only in conjunction with multinational forces. . . .

We failed to recognize that in international affairs, as in other aspects of life, there may be problems for which there are no immediate solutions. . . .

Underlying many of these errors lay our failure to organize the top echelons of the executive branch to deal effectively with the extraordinarily complex range of political and military issues, involving the great risks and costs—including, above all else, loss of life—associated with the application of military force under substantial constraints over a long period of time. (Robert S. McNamara, *In Retrospect: The Tragedy and Lessons of Vietnam*, with Brian VanDeMark, 1995.)

ON ROMANCE AND IDENTITY

865. At the start of every semester, in September or in January, I walk into my classes and I fall in love again. Most of the time, I am loved back. I enjoy it. I encourage it. I thrive on it. Teaching is romance. I'm a successful teacher to the extent that I can get my students to fall for me. There's no learning without love, no knowledge without passion, and for students to feel passionately about the material, they need to feel passionately about me. In a deep sense, I *am* the material. Whether we are reading *Don Quijote* or 19th century Spanish fiction or modern Spanish-American poetry, I am still the conduit for the emotions and ideas and attitudes of the authors and texts under discussion. My job is to make Cervantes or Galdos or Neruda speak to my class. I give them a face and a voice. I am medium and ventriloquist. (Gustavo Perez Firmat, from *Next Year in Cuba: A Cuban's Coming-of-Age in America*, 1995.)

866. In Spanish the word for country is *país*, while the word for fatherland is *patria*. For . . . me, Cuba remains my *patria* but the United States has become our

país. . . . When I assert that Cuba is my *patria*, I'm telling you where I come from. (Ibid.)

THE IMPORTANCE OF EDUCATION

---

867. Yes, the world is unfair; there is racism and discrimination. . . . Don't feel so sorry for yourself. . . . Education is the great equalizer. . . . The better you do in school, the better it is for your future. . . . Education is your ticket out of where you want to leave. (Geraldo Rivera, advice to young minorities, March 1995, quoted in *Famous People of Hispanic Heritage*, by Barbara J. Marvis.)

THE IMPORTANCE OF DIFFERENCES

---

868. I try to understand other people's points of view. On one hand, we are really all the same, but on the other, we all have our differences. We were all brought up differently depending on our family circumstances and where we're from, but we must understand other people's backgrounds and differences. Basically, we are all one family. (Federico Pena, April 1995, quoted in *Famous People of Hispanic Heritage*, by Barbara J. Marvis.)

SUMMATION

---

869. Your verdict will go far beyond the walls [of this courtroom]. Your verdict talks about justice in America and it talks about the police and whether they should be above the law. . . . There's [someone] in your background . . . that helps you understand that this is wrong. . . . Maybe you're the right people at the right time, at the right place to say, "No more—we're not going to have this." (Johnnie Cochran Jr., defense attorney, summation in the O. J. Simpson murder case, Los Angeles, September 27–28, 1995, cited in *Without a Doubt*, by Marcia Clark.)

[The jury, composed mainly of African Americans, found Simpson not guilty of murdering his former wife and her friend.]

BATTLE LINES

870. There is a great battle raging in America today. The cause of the hostility is one the nation's founders could never have imagined: gay rights. On one side of the battlefield are religious conservatives who believe they are taking a last stand against moral decline; on the other, gays and lesbians who believe that they are fighting for the basic civil liberties guaranteed by the Constitution. After years of skirmishes, two groups that had been largely unknown to the public and noticed by the press seem suddenly to be everywhere, locked in combat. That combat promises to be part of the political landscape for years to come. . . .

Some of the controversies have taken place at the highest levels of government, most notably in the showdown over gays in the military. Other battles have been local, such as the antigay ballot measures in Oregon, Colorado, and Idaho. Each of the local fights is part of the enormous war over the place of gays in American society. . . .

Religious conservatives and gay activists have become perfect enemies, propelling each other's movement and affecting the politics of the country as a whole. (John Gallagher and Chris Bull, *Perfect Enemies: The Religious Right, the Gay Movement, and the Politics of the 1990s*, 1996.)

GOING, COMING, OR STAYING?

871. Those intrigued by the community of Cuban exiles and Cuban Americans in south Florida frequently ask what will happen in Miami once there is a change of the guard in Cuba. Will the emigres return to their homeland? Or will thousands more Cubans immigrate to the United States? The answer is yes—to both questions. . . .

The numbers are difficult to predict: a poll conducted in 1993 by Florida International University revealed that 29 percent of Cuban-born heads of households wanted to return to live permanently in Cuba, while a similar poll conducted in 1990 showed that only 14 percent would actually return. Among those born or raised in the United States, the percentages are probably much lower. . . . As several interviewees told me, "Why uproot yourself twice in one lifetime? The first time was hard enough. . . ."

For Cubans who grew up in the U.S., "returning" to Cuba would be akin to moving to a foreign country notwithstanding the culture they claim to share with those on the island. The emigres most likely to return will be the elderly, eager to spend their remaining years in their homeland. Also likely to return are those who feel alienated in the U.S., and have found it impossible to adapt. (Maria Christina Garcia, from *Havana USA: Cuban Exiles and Cuban Americans in South Florida, 1959–1994,* 1996.)

LATINO PAST, PRESENT, FUTURE

872. Today there are some 25 million Latinos in America, according to the U.S. Census Bureau—nearly 10 percent of the population. Immigrants from the Caribbean, Central America, and Mexico have swelled the numbers of Hispanics in the United States, and will continue to do so. It is predicted that by the year 2050 the Hispanic population will increase to 81 million and make up more than a fifth of this country's population. A group this large, soon expected to pass African Americans as America's largest minority group, has to be considered a serious player in American society. (Frank de Varona, from *Latino Literacy: The Complete Guide to Our Hispanic History and Culture,* 1996.)

873. [I]t is hardly novel to observe that the official history of our country has, as always, been written by the "victors"—the dominant Anglo-Saxon, Protestant culture. Most Americans consider their history an English march from east to west. Spain, for centuries a prosperous and powerful Catholic monarchy, aroused significant envy in Protestant northern Europe, culminating in the promotion of the anti-Spanish Black Legend by these powers. By this distorted account, the Spanish experience in the Americas was an unmitigated record of rape and plunder that decimated the native populations and left nothing of value behind when it was over. . . .

At any rate, anti-Catholicism held on as one of the United States' most powerful prejudices until well into the current century. (Ibid.)

AMERICAN DIPLOMATIC TRADITIONS

874. OUR OLD TESTAMENT
1. Liberty, or Exceptionalism (so called)
2. Unilateralism, or Isolationism (so called)
3. The American System, or Monroe Doctrine (so called)
4. Expansionism, or Manifest Destiny (so called)
   OUR NEW TESTAMENT
5. Progressive Imperialism
6. Wilsonianism, or Liberal Internationalism (so called)
7. Containment
8. Global Meliorism. . . .
The biblical metaphor is meant to suggest that the leaders who founded and led the United States throughout the 19th century imagined the nation as a sort of New Israel destined to fill a rich Promised Land and enjoy the blessings of liberty, so long as its people kept the commandments of their Old Testament canon. Chief among those commandments was "Thou shalt not have truck with foreigners even for the purpose of converting them." (Walter A. McDougall, *Promised Land, Crusader State: The American Encounter with the World since 1776*, 1997.)

IDENTITY

875. I love them [the Three Kings rather than Santa Claus] because they are in my tradition, in my blood and, above all, because I was a poor child.

[Diaz also pointed out that one of the kings was dark-skinned, while Santa was not only white but dressed in heavy winter clothing.]

(Abelarado Diaz Alfaro, writer, article in *Cultura*, magazine of the Institute of Puerto Rican Culture, cited in the *New York Times*, July 26, 1999.)

WAR CRIMES AND RESPONSIBILITY

876. The war in the Balkans began in Slovenia and Bosnia in 1991. In a small Croatian city called Vukovar the pernicious character of the conflict became manifest early on. But it was the fighting in Bosnia the following year that administered a particular shock to the international system, demonstrating that Europeans were still thoroughly capable of inflicting on one another the kind of vile abuses Westerners with short memories had come to expect only of distant Third World lands. Bosnia also stripped the veneer of relevance from post-war institutions designed to promote prosperity and peace, among them the European Union and the United Nations. Indeed, the international [war crimes] tribunal for Bosnia was the UN's only successful assertion of moral authority—and even the implementation of that decision was woefully tardy.

Ultimately the United States, acting through NATO, summoned the will to put an end to the war in Bosnia. Had it not done so, NATO would have joined the list of international institutions with self-inflicted wounds from the war. Moreover, if NATO troops leave Bosnia without apprehending the principal indicted war criminals and turning them over to the proper authorities for prosecution, its mission may yet be judged a failure.

Of course, NATO is no substitute for the civilian institutions needed to prevent future Bosnias. It remains unclear whether new international peacemaking or peacekeeping institutions will emerge, or whether significant efforts will be made to reform those that failed to stop the war. So far, the only bodies to emerge are the [war crimes] tribunals, and they are still being tested. The heart says civilized men and women with respect for the rule of law cannot permit these kinds of crimes to happen again. The mind, sadly, sends a different message. (Aryeh Neier, from *War Crimes: Brutality, Genocide, Terror, and the Struggle for Justice*, 1990.)

DENIAL

877. I am going to say this again. I did not have sexual relations with that woman, Miss Lewinsky. I never told anybody to lie, not a single time—never. These allegations are false. (President Bill Clinton, speech, the White House, Washington, D.C., January 26, 1998.)

[Monica Lewinsky had been an intern working in the White House. President Clinton did not believe that oral sex constituted "sexual relations." His denials before a grand jury would lead to his impeachment.]

ON EXPANDING NATO

878. I think it is the beginning of a new cold war. I think the Russians will gradually react quite adversely and it will affect their policies. I think it is a tragic mistake. There was no reason to this whatsoever. No one was threatening anybody else. This expansion would make the Founding Fathers of this country turn over in their graves. We have signed up to protect a whole series of countries, even though we have neither the resources nor the intention to do so in any serious way. (George F. Kennan, commenting on a U.S. Senate vote approving NATO expansion to include Poland, the Czech Republic, and Hungary, quoted in Thomas Friedman's column, the *New York Times*, May 2, 1998.)

EXPLANATION

879. In a deposition in January [in a sexual harassment suit brought by Paula Jones], I was asked questions about my relationship with Monica Lewinsky. While my answers were legally accurate, I did not volunteer information. Indeed I did have a relationship with Ms. Lewinsky that was not appropriate. In fact, it was wrong. It constituted a critical lapse of judgment and a personal failure on my part for which I am sorry and completely responsible. (President Bill Clinton, speech, the White House, Washington, D.C., August 17, 1998.)

CHARGE

880. The Office of the Independent Counsel . . . hereby submits substantial and credible information that President William Jefferson Clinton committed acts that may constitute grounds for an impeachment. (Kenneth Starr, independent counsel, report to the House of Representatives, September 9, 1998.)

IMPEACHMENT

---

881. Resolved that William Jefferson Clinton, President of the United States, is impeached for high crimes and misdemeanors, and that the following articles of impeachment be exhibited to the United States Senate. . . .

[The president was accused of perjury and obstruction of justice, specifically, that he had lied to a grand jury and had encouraged others to lie in a civil rights action brought against him.]

Wherefore, William Jefferson Clinton, by such conduct, warrants impeachment and trial, and removal from office and disqualification to hold and enjoy any office of honor, trust or profit under the United States. (House of Representatives, resolution of impeachment, Washington, D.C., December 19, 1998.)

[The president was impeached by the House of Representatives. All the House Republicans but five voted to impeach; all the Democrats but five had voted against impeachment. A trial took place in the Senate beginning January 7, 1999. On February 12 the president was acquitted by the Senate on the perjury charge, 55 to 45. On the charge of obstruction of justice, the vote was 50 to acquit and 50 to convict. The necessary two-thirds vote for conviction thus failed by a wide margin.]

FROM A CAMPAIGN BIO

---

882. [A] gap of hope is found in the poverty of our inner cities, where neighborhoods have become urban war zones, a world of barred windows and gang violence and failed schools, a world of shattered glass and shattered dreams. But the gap of hope is also found in the large but sometimes empty houses of our affluent suburbs, where young people turn to drugs or alcohol or sex in a failed search for something they are missing. We see glimpses of this hopelessness in schoolyards where children inexplicably, tragically, horrifically murder other children. And we worry about our national soul.

This gap of hope threatens the very fabric of America. I worry that we are being divided into two nations, separate and unequal: one nation with the tools and confidence to seek the American dream; another nation that is being left behind. We risk becoming two societies: one that reads and one that can't, one that dreams and one that doesn't. Some think they can protect themselves through willful apathy. Some put up big fences and live in gated communities. Some close the shutters, turn on the television, and withdraw. (Governor George W. Bush, from *A Charge to Keep*, 1999.)

883. I reject the thinking of those who would lump Americans into different groups based on characteristics such as skin color or ethnic heritage or economic circumstances. Group thought pits people against one another. (Ibid.)

884. During the more than half century of my life, we have seen an unprecedented decay in our American culture, a decay that has eroded the foundation of our collective values and moral standard of conduct: "If it feels good, do it" and "If you've got a problem, blame somebody else." (Ibid.)

885. Compassionate conservatism is neither soft nor fuzzy. It is clear and compelling. It focuses not on good intentions but on good results. (Ibid.)

PREDICTION FOR CENTURY 21

886. The unique 20th-century creation, the corporation, is not going to survive in the next century. . . .

In business, you are becoming bored, because we know so much. When I came in, nobody knew the routine and that made it exciting. . . .

The 20th century was the century of business. The next century is going to be the century of the social sector. (Peter F. Drucker, interview, Claremont, California, quoted in *the New York Times*, November 14, 1999.)

PREDICTIONS FOR THE YEAR 3000

887. An Encyclopedia of Lost Practices

Like dueling and taking snuff, many of our cherished passions and diversions will baffle people in the year 3000. . . .

The Saturday Night Date. . . .
The Cigarette. . . .
The Book. . . .
Talk Radio. . . .
Reproductive Sex. . . .
The Elvis Phenomenon. . . .
The New York Times. . . . (*The New York Times Magazine,* "The Times Capsule for the Year 3000," December 5, 1999.)

[In separate articles, individual writers explain what each one of these diversions was all about.]

POLICE TACTICS

888. Years ago, when we were sent in to investigate the report of gunfire in progress, we would charge in and try to stop the shooting. In recent years—with all the police casualties and problems with complaints of excessive police force—we would show up in the patrol car and wait until the shooting stopped. That would usually mean that someone was dead and the shooter was still around. Then we would get out of the car and investigate. (Retired police officer, New York City Police Department, January 2000.)

O TEMPORA! O MORES!

889. It took something like this to make the Miss America pageant look good to me. At least with the Miss America pageant you get scholarship money and the guarantee of a year-long run. It perpetuates some very limited stereotypes that men are success objects and women are sex objects. (Patricia Ireland, president, National Organization for Women, commenting on the television program *Who Wants to Marry a Multimillionaire?* quoted in the *New York Times,* February 17, 2000.)

[On the program, young women competed for the privilege of marrying a man whom they had never met but who was a multimillionaire. The wedding took place at the end of the show, following the signing of a prenuptial agreement.]

ACCEPTANCE BY BUSH

---

890. We will confront the hard issues—threats to our national security, threats to our health and retirement security—before the challenges of our time become crises for our children.

And we will extend the promise of prosperity to every forgotten corner of this country. To every man and woman, a chance to succeed. To every child, a chance to learn. To every family, a chance to live with dignity and hope.

For eight years, the Clinton–Gore administration has coasted through prosperity.

And the path of least resistance is always downhill.

But America's way is the rising road. This nation is daring and decent and ready for change.

Our current president embodied the potential of a generation. So many talents. So much charm. Such great skill. But, in the end, to what end? . . .

This administration had its chance. They have not led. We will. . . .

We will strengthen Social Security and Medicare. . . .

On education, too many American children are segregated into schools without standards, shuffled from grade-to-grade because of their age, regardless of their knowledge.

This is discrimination, pure and simple, the soft bigotry of low expectations.

And our nation should treat it like other forms of discrimination. We should end it. . . .

[T]hose who spend your tax dollars must be held accountable.

When a school district receives federal funds to teach poor children, we expect them to learn. And if they don't, parents should get the money to make a different choice. . . .

The world needs America's strength and America's armed forces need better equipment, better training and better pay.

We will give our military the means to keep the peace, and we will give it one thing more, a commander in chief who respects men and women in uniform, and a commander in chief who earns their respect. . . .

We must help protect our children, in our schools and streets, by finally and strictly enforcing our nation's gun laws. . . .

I will lead our nation toward a culture that values life, the life of the elderly and the sick, the life of the young, and the life of the unborn. (Governor George W. Bush of Texas, Republican nominee for president, acceptance speech, Republican National Convention, Philadelphia, August 3, 2000.)

COMMENTARY

891. Only in America can you turn to a Jew for your hail-Mary pass. (William Safire, columnist, the *New York Times*, August 10, 2000.)

[Commenting on the decision by Vice President Albert Gore Jr. to select Senator Joseph Lieberman, an Orthodox Jew, as his running mate in 2000. Lieberman had been the first Democrat to attack President Clinton on the floor of the Senate for his misconduct with a White House intern. Political observers thought the choice would help separate Gore from scandals associated with the president.]

ACCEPTANCE BY GORE

892. Together, let's make sure that our prosperity enriches not just the few, but all working families. Let's invest in health care, education, a secure retirement and middle-class tax cuts. . . .

[M]y focus is on working families; people trying to make house payments and car payments, working overtime to save for college and do right by their kids. Whether you are in a suburb, or an inner-city, whether you raise crops or drive hogs and cattle on a farm, drive a big rig on the interstate or drive e-commerce on the Internet, whether you're starting out to raise your own family or getting ready to retire after a lifetime of hard work.

So often, powerful forces and powerful interests stand in your way, and the odds seemed stacked against you, even as you do what's right for you and your family. . . .

To all the families in America who have to struggle to afford the right education and the skyrocketing cost of prescription drugs, I want you to know this: I've taken on the powerful forces. And as president I'll stand up to them, and I'll stand up for you. . . .

I stand here tonight as my own man. . . .

It's time to take the medical decisions away from the H.M.O.'s and insurance companies and give them back to the doctors, the nurses, and the health care professionals.

So this is not just an election between my opponents and me. It's about our people, our families, and our future and whether forces standing in your way will keep you from having a better life. . . .

If you entrust me with the presidency, I will put our democracy back in your hands, and get all the special interest money—all of it—out of our democracy, by enacting campaign finance reform. . . .

We will move toward universal health coverage, step by step, starting with all children. . . .

I will not go along with any plan that would drain taxpayer money away from our public schools and give it to private schools in the form of vouchers. . . .

I will protect and defend a woman's right to choose. The last thing this country needs is a Supreme Court that overturns *Roe v. Wade.* . . .

Do not rest where we are, or retreat. Do all we can to make America all it can become. (Vice President Albert Gore Jr., Democratic nominee for president, acceptance speech, Los Angeles, August 17, 2000.)

BUSH–GORE ELECTION OF 2000

The presidential election of 2000 took place on November 7, but it took five weeks before a candidate was declared president. On election night, the Democratic candidate, Vice President Albert Gore Jr., held the lead in the popular vote. But the electoral vote hung in the balance. The key state was Florida, which had 25 electoral votes. If he won the state, it was enough to give Texas governor George W. Bush, a Republican, the presidency.

The situation was complicated by the fact that George's brother, Jeb, was governor of Florida. What is more, the Florida secretary of state, responsible for certifying election results, was cochairman of the state's George W. Bush campaign.

The vote was so close that, out of 6 million votes, only a few hundred separated the two candidates. There were complaints of confusing ballots, of ballots not registering on the machines, of absentee ballots from overseas without the required postmarks, of voters with registration cards being denied the vote, of illegal changes made on absentee ballot applications.

Because of the closeness of the vote, there was an automatic machine recount, which was won by Bush. The secretary of state certified him the winner. Gore asked for recounts by hand in areas of his greatest strength or, if Bush wished, in the entire state. Bush turned down the idea, and the battle went to the courts.

Over a five-week period, the lawyers went from circuit court to state supreme court to federal district court and finally to the U.S. Supreme Court itself.

As the time for certifying electors for the electoral college came closer, leaders of the Florida legislature, which was Republican, announced that it would choose its own slate of electors. A special session of the legislature was called to do exactly that.

Meanwhile, the Florida Supreme Court, in a 4–3 vote, ordered a manual recount in a number of counties. The Bush team appealed that decision to the U.S. Supreme Court.

Late in the evening of December 12, the highest court in the land ruled 5–4 that any further hand recounting must end. The following day, Gore conceded. What follows are very brief segments of the majority and dissenting opinions, plus news stories that followed.

MAJORITY OPINION

893. The petition [by Bush] presents the following questions: whether the Florida Supreme Court established new standards for resolving presidential election contests . . . , [through] the use of standardless manual recounts violates the equal protection and due process clauses. With respect to the equal protection question, we find a violation of the equal protection clause.

The closeness of this election, and the multitude of legal challenges which have followed in its wake, have brought into sharp focus a common, if heretofore unnoticed, phenomenon.

Nationwide statistics reveal that an estimated 2 percent of ballots cast do not register a vote for president for whatever reason, including deliberately choosing no candidate at all or some voter error, such as voting for two candidates or insufficiently marking a ballot. In certifying election results, the votes eligible for inclusion in the certification are the votes meeting the properly established legal requirements.

This case has shown that punch-card balloting machines can produce an unfortunate number of ballots which are not punched in a clean, complete way by the voter. After the current counting, it is likely legislative bodies nationwide will examine ways to improve the mechanisms and machinery for voting. . . .

[The U.S. Supreme Court discusses some of the ballot problems.] In some cases a piece of the card—a chad—is hanging, say by two corners. In other cases there is no separation at all, just an indentation. The Florida Supreme Court has ordered that the intent of the voter be discerned from such ballots. For purposes of resolving the equal protection challenge, it is not necessary to decide whether the Florida Supreme Court had the authority under the legislative scheme for resolving election disputes to define what a legal vote is and to mandate a manual recount implementing that definition. The recount mechanisms implemented in response to the decisions of the Florida Supreme Court do not satisfy the minimum requirement for non-arbitrary treatment of voters necessary to secure the fundamental right. Florida's basic command for the count of legally cast votes is to consider the "intent of the voter." This is unobjectionable as an abstract position and a starting principle. The problem inheres in the absence of specific standards to ensure its equal application. The formation of uniform rules to determine intent based on these recurring circumstances is practicable and, we conclude, necessary.

The law does not refrain from searching for the intent of the actor in a multitude of circumstances, and in some cases the general command to ascertain intent is not susceptible to much further refinement. In this instance, however, the question is not whether to believe a witness but how to interpret the marks or holes or scratches on an inanimate object, a piece of cardboard or paper which, it is said, might not have registered as a vote during the machine count. The factfinder confronts a thing, not a person. The search for intent can be confined by specific rules designed to ensure uniform treatment. The want of those rules here has led to unequal evaluation of ballots in various respects. . . . The standards for accepting or rejecting contested ballots might vary not only from county to county but indeed within a single county from one recount team to another.. . . .

[T]here is no recount procedure in place under the [Florida] State Supreme Court's order that comports with minimal constitutional standards. Because it is evident that any recount seeking to meet the Dec. 12 date will be unconstitutional . . . we reverse the judgment of the Supreme Court of Florida ordering a recount to proceed. (From the majority opinion, *Bush v. Gore*, December 12, 2000.)

[There were two votes by the Court. By 7–2, the justices agreed that there were constitutional problems with the manual recount ordered by the Florida Supreme Court. The key vote, however, was 5–4 ordering an end to recounting.]

DISSENTING VIEWS

894. Time will one day heal the wound to that confidence, that will be inflicted by today's decision. One thing, however, is certain. Although we may never know with complete certainty, the identity of the winner of this year's presidential election, the identity of the loser is perfectly clear. It is the nation's confidence in the judge as an impartial guardian of the rule of law. (Associate Justice John Paul Stevens, dissent, *Bush v. Gore*, December 12, 2000.)

895. The Florida Supreme Court thought that the recount could be completed on time, and, within hours, the Florida Circuit Court was moving in an orderly fashion to meet the deadline. This court improvidently entered a stay [ending the recount]. As a result, we will never know whether the recount could have been completed. . . .

[T]here are two sides to the opinion's argument that the Florida Supreme Court "virtually eliminated the [Florida] secretary [of state]'s discretion."

The Florida statute in question was amended in 1999 to provide that the "grounds for contesting an election" include "rejection of a number of legal votes sufficient to . . . place in doubt the result of the election." And the parties have argued about the proper meaning of the statute's term "legal vote." The secretary [of state] has claimed that the "legal vote" is a vote "properly executed in accordance with the instructions provided to all registered voters." On that interpretation, punch-card ballots for which the machines cannot register a vote are not "legal" votes. The Florida Supreme Court did not accept her definition. But it had a reason. Its reason was that a different provision of Florida election laws (a provision that addresses damaged or defective ballots) says that no vote shall be disregarded "if there is a clear indication of the intent of the voter as determined by the canvassing board" (adding that ballots should not "be counted" if it is impossible to determine the elector's choice"). (Associate Justice Steven Breyer, dissent, *Bush v. Gore*, December 12, 2000.)

896. In sum, the [U.S. Supreme] court's conclusion that a constitutionally adequate recount is impractical is a prophecy the court's own judgment will not allow to be tested. Such an untested prophecy should not decide the Presidency of the United States. (Associate Justice Ruth Bader Ginsburg, dissent, *Bush v. Gore*, December 12, 2000.)

CONCESSION

897. Just moments ago I spoke with George W. Bush and congratulated him on becoming the 43rd President of the United States. . . .

I offered to meet with him as soon as possible so that we can start to heal the divisions in the campaign and the contest through which we've just passed. . . .

I say to President-elect Bush that what remains of partisan rancor must now be put aside, and may God bless his stewardship of this country.

Neither he nor I anticipated this long and difficult road. Certainly neither of us wanted it to happen. Yet it came, and now it has ended, resolved as it must be resolved, through the honored institutions of our democracy. . . .

Now the U.S. Supreme Court has spoken. Let there be no doubt, while I strongly disagree with the court's decision, I accept it. I accept the finality of this outcome, which will be ratified next Monday in the Electoral College. And tonight, for the sake of our unity as a people and the strength of our democracy, I offer my concession.

I also accept my responsibility, which I will discharge unconditionally, to honor the new President-elect and do everything possible to help him bring Americans together in fulfillment of the great vision that our Declaration of Independence defines and that our Constitution affirms and defends. (Vice President Albert Gore Jr., television address to the nation, December 13, 2000.)

JOURNALISTS' ANALYSIS

898. "The Bush strategy was fight everything everywhere all the time," said John D. C. Newton, a Tallahassee lawyer who worked on Mr. Gore's legal team here. "There were deadlines, and they were short, and as long as they kept fighting, the official record said they were ahead."

Mr. [James A.] Baker and his team of lawyers arrived within two hours after the polls had closed, plunging immediately into a tumultuous and anxious environment. The Texas Governor's lead over Mr. Gore had dropped to 327 votes as the state's 67 counties conducted a mandatory post-election machine recount. And Mr. Gore had quickly moved to seize the political advantage, pressing for a more thorough count of the votes. . . .

Mr. Baker and his aides moved into the state party headquarters . . . and seized on the goal that would govern their decisions in the courts and the political arena:

To block a recount. The overriding concern, one senior Bush aide said, was that any tally putting Mr. Gore even fleetingly in the lead, especially since the vice president was carrying the popular vote nationwide, would be politically devastating for Mr. Bush. (Adam Nagourney and David Barstow, from "G.O.P.'s Depth Outdid Gore's Team in Florida," the *New York Times*, December 22, 2000.)

POSTSCRIPT TO AN ELECTION

899. [The election of 2000] tested our constitutional system in ways it has never been tested before. The Florida state courts, the lower federal courts and the Supreme Court of the United States became involved in a way that one hopes will seldom, if ever, be necessary in the future. (Chief Justice William Rehnquist, annual report to Congress, cited in the *New York Times*, January 1, 2001.)

CLINTON FAREWELL

900. In all the work I have done as president, every decision I have made, every executive action I have taken, every bill I have proposed and signed, I've tried to give all Americans the tools and conditions to build a future of our dreams in a good society with a strong economy, a cleaner environment and a freer, safer, more prosperous world. . . .

I have sought to give America a new kind of government, more modern, more effective, full of ideas and policies appropriate to this new time, always putting people first, always focusing on the future. . . .

If we choose wisely, we can pay down the debt, deal with the retirement of the baby-boomers, invest more in our future and provide tax relief. . . .

We must remember that America can not lead in the world unless here at home we weave the threads of our coat of many colors into the fabric of one America. As we become ever more diverse, we must work harder to unite around our common values and common humanity. . . .

I'll leave the presidency more idealistic, more full of hope, than the day I arrived and more confident than ever that America's best days lie ahead. (President Bill Clinton, Farewell Address, Washington, D.C., January 19, 2001.)

BUSH INAUGURAL

---

901. Through much of the last century, America's faith in freedom and democracy was a rock in a raging sea. Now it is a seed upon the wind, taking root in many nations. . . .

Today we affirm a new commitment to live out our nation's promise through civility, courage, compassion, and character. . . .

Together, we will reclaim America's schools, before ignorance and apathy claim more young lives. We will reform Social Security and Medicare, sparing our children from struggles we have the power to prevent.

We will reduce taxes, to recover the momentum of our economy and reward the effort and enterprise of working Americans. We will build our defenses beyond challenge, lest weakness invite challenge.

We will confront weapons of mass destruction, so that a new century is spared new horrors. . . .

I will live and lead by these principles: to pursue the public interest with courage, to speak for greater justice and compassion, to call for responsibility, and try to live it as well. In all these ways, I will bring the values of our history to the care of our times. . . .

I ask you to be citizens. Citizens, not spectators. Citizens, not subjects. Responsible citizens, building communities of service and a nation of character.

Americans are generous and strong and decent, not because we believe in ourselves, but because we hold beliefs beyond ourselves. When this spirit of citizenship is missing, no government program can replace it. When this spirit is present, no wrong can stand against it. (President George W. Bush, Inaugural Address, Washington, D.C., January 20, 2001.)

TERRORISTS STRIKE AMERICA

902. Hijackers rammed jetliners into each of New York's World Trade Center towers yesterday, toppling both in a hellish storm of ash, glass, smoke, and leaping victims, while a third jetliner crashed into the Pentagon in Virginia. There was no official count, but President Bush said thousands had perished, and in the immediate aftermath, the calamity was already being ranked the worst and most audacious terror attack in American history. (Serge Schmemann, recounting events of the morning of September 11, 2001, the *New York Times*, September 12, 2001.)

PRESIDENT ASSAILS ATTACKS

903. Today our fellow citizens, our way of life, our very freedom, came under attack in a series of deliberate and deadly terrorist acts. The victims were in airplanes or in their offices: secretaries, businessmen and women, military and federal workers, moms and dads, friends and neighbors. Thousands of lives were suddenly ended by evil, despicable acts of terror.

The pictures of airplanes flying into buildings, fires burning, huge structures collapsing, have filled us with disbelief, terrible sadness and a quiet, unyielding anger.

These acts of mass murder were intended to frighten our nation into chaos and retreat. But they have failed. Our country is strong. A great people has been moved to defend a great nation. . . .

The search is under way for those who are behind these evil acts. . . . We will make no distinction between the terrorists who committed these acts and those who harbored them. (President George W. Bush, address to the nation, Washington, D.C., evening of September 11, 2001.)

HOW MANY CASUALTIES?

904. More than any of us can bear. (Mayor Rudolph Giuliani, New York City, September 12, 2001, responding to a query about estimated casualties at the World Trade Center.)

"ACTS OF WAR"

905. The deliberate and deadly attacks, which were carried out yesterday against our country were more than acts of terror. They were acts of war. This will require our country to unite in steadfast determination and resolve.

Freedom and democracy are under attack.

The American people need to know we're facing a different enemy than we have ever faced. This enemy hides in shadows and has no regard for human life. This is an enemy who preys on innocent and unsuspecting people, then runs for cover. But it won't be able to run for cover forever. This is an enemy that tries to hide, but it won't be able to hide forever. This is an enemy that thinks its harbors are safe, but they won't be safe forever. (President George W. Bush, address to the nation, Washington, D.C., September 12, 2001.)

CONGRESS ACTS

906. JOINT RESOLUTION

To authorize the use of United States armed forces against those responsible for the recent attacks launched against the United States.

That the President is authorized to use all necessary and appropriate force against those nations, organizations, or persons he determines planned, authorized, committed, or aided the terrorist attacks that occurred on September 11 2001, or harbored such organizations or persons, in order to prevent any future acts of international terrorism against the United States by such nations, organizations, or persons. (Joint Resolution, approved by Congress, September 14, 2001.)

END OF AN ERA

907. This is the end: the end of an era, the era of our invulnerability. We will recover physically and even psychologically, but nothing will ever be quite the same again. A barrier has been irrevocably breached: a barrier against the world outside. (Ronald Steel, Professor of International Relations, University of Southern California, Op-Ed column, the *New York Times*, September 14, 2001.)

AMONG THE DEAD

908. The marriage proposal was famous in the Resta family. John Resta already had a reputation as a hopeless romantic, relatives said, but in this one he outdid even himself.

Mr. Resta and his wife, Sylvia SanPio Resta, had traveled to Florida several times, and there she found a seafood restaurant that she adored. So on the day he was to propose, he took the day off work. He had a meal—lobster and other dishes—and menus flown into New York City from the restaurant. He rented a tuxedo, a top hat, and a cane, and spent the day setting up their apartment in Bayside, Queens, with candles, a fancy tablecloth, and flowers.

Needless to say, the answer was yes, and they were married in the summer of 2000.

When the two—both traders for Carr Futures—were killed in the September 11th terrorist attack, she was seven months pregnant. (From "Portraits of Grief," the *New York Times*, October 28, 2001.)

[The *Times* planned to run a series of brief biographical descriptions of every single individual killed or missing and presumed dead in the September 11th attacks.]

Biographical Sketches

John Adams (1735–1826) was the first vice president and second president of the United States. He served on the small committee that drafted the Declaration of Independence. As a young lawyer, he defended the British soldiers accused of the Boston Massacre.

John Quincy Adams (1767–1848) was the sixth president. The son of President John Adams, he was elected to the U.S. Senate before he became president. After he left the White House, he was elected to the House of Representatives.

Samuel Adams (1722–1803) was a leading figure in the fight for American independence from Great Britain. Historians believe that Adams gave the signal for the Boston Tea Party.

Jane Addams (1860–1935) created Hull House in Chicago—a community center then known as a settlement house. It provided education and recreation for the poor. During her lifetime she campaigned against child labor and for voting rights for women and world peace. She was awarded the Nobel Peace Prize in 1931.

Louisa May Alcott (1832–1888) was the author of *Little Women* and other books for young readers. During the Civil War, she was a volunteer in a Union army hospital in Washington.

Horatio Alger Jr. (1832–1899) wrote a series of novels about poor boys who become successful because they are honest and hardworking. His most famous series: *Ragged Dick*, *Luck and Pluck*, and *Tattered Tom*.

Muhammad Ali (1942–   ) was the heavyweight boxing champion of the world several times. Originally known as Cassius Clay, he was once stripped of his title when he refused to be drafted to fight in the Vietnam War.

William Allen (1803–1879) was a U.S. senator during the debate over the northern boundary of the Oregon Territory.

John Peter Altgeld (1847–1902) was governor of Illinois from 1893 to 1897. During his brief stint he pardoned some of those convicted in the Haymarket Square bombing. He also protested the use of federal troops in Illinois during the Pullman strike of 1894.

American Horse (1840–1908) was a Sioux Indian who witnessed the massacre at Wounded Knee, South Dakota, in 1890.

John W. Anderson (1906–?) was an organizer and activist for the United Automobile Workers from its inception in the depths of the Great Depression until his retirement.

Robert Anderson (1805–1871) commanded Fort Sumter in Charleston harbor, South Carolina. In April 1861, at the outbreak of the Civil War, he was ordered to surrender the Union fort to the Confederacy. Running out of food and munitions, he was forced to surrender after a crushing enemy bombardment.

Susan B. Anthony (1820–1906) was an advocate for the abolition of slavery, for temperance, and for woman's rights.

Benedict Arnold (1741–1801) was a general during the American Revolution. He served with great gallantry in a number of battles but became disillusioned and bitter by what he felt was unfair treatment. He sold out to the enemy and attempted to turn over West Point to the British. The plot was uncovered. Arnold fled behind British lines and fought against his countrymen. After the war, he settled in England.

Neil Armstrong (1930–) was the first human to walk on the surface of the moon.

Joan Baez (1941–) is a popular singing star who became a political activist.

Sullivan Ballou (mid-19th century) was a major in the Second Rhode Island Volunteers of the Union army during the Civil War. He was killed in the Battle of Bull Run.

Benjamin Banneker (1731–1806) was an African American who helped design the city of Washington, D.C.

David Barstow (late 20th to early 21st century) was a *New York Times* reporter who covered the Florida recount controversy at the end of the 2000 presidential campaign.

Robert Bascom (mid-to late 20th century) is the pseudonym of an American seed grower who makes extensive use of Mexican farm labor in California.

Katharine Lee Bates (1859–1929) was the poet who wrote "America the Beautiful."

Mary S. Battey (mid-19th century) taught newly freed slaves in Georgia following the Civil War.

Edward Fitzgerald Beale (mid-19th century) carried out exploratory trips in the West using camels. These trips were made at the behest of the War Department.

Louis H. Bean (mid-20th century) wrote extensively on politics and how to predict elections.

Charles A. Beard (1874–1948) was a university professor, historian, and political scientist. He wrote numerous books and articles. Among his works are *An Economic Interpretation of the Constitution* and *President Roosevelt and the Coming of the War: 1941*.

Barnard E. Bee (mid-19th century) was a Confederate general.

Robert Bendiner (mid-20th century) was a freelancer who wrote many articles on the subject of American politics.

Henry Bibb (mid-19th century) was a runaway slave who wrote a book about his adventures.

Clara K. Bishara (early 20th century) was a Syrian American who was interested in encouraging the younger generation to learn the Arabic language.

Herbert Block (1909–2001) was an editorial cartoonist for the *Washington Post*.

Daniel J. Boorstin (1914–1984) is a prizewinning historian who has served as librarian of Congress.

William Bradford (1590–1657) was one of the Pilgrim leaders who came over on the *Mayflower*. In 1621 he was elected governor of the Plymouth Colony. He wrote a history of the early colony.

Solomon Bradley (1836–1863) was a former slave who fought for the Union during the Civil War.

Richard Bradley (early 18th century) was the attorney general of New York under royal Governor William Cosby. As such, Bradley prosecuted John Peter Zenger on charges of libeling Cosby.

Anne Bradstreet (mid-17th century) was a New England housewife and poet.

Stephen Breyer (1938–) was named an associate justice of the U.S. Supreme Court by President Clinton in 1994.

Harold Brown (1927–) was secretary of defense in the administration of President Carter.

John Brown (1800–1859) was an abolitionist who led a raid on Harper's Ferry, Virginia, in 1859. He intended to free slaves. An armed conflict broke out, and several people were killed. Brown was captured, tried for treason, and hanged.

William Jennings Bryan (1860–1925) was the Democratic nominee for president three times in the late 19th and early 20th centuries. He was secretary of state for several years in President Wilson's cabinet.

James Buchanan (1791–1868) was the 16th president. At the close of his term—following the election of 1860—southern states seceded from the Union and formed the Confederacy.

Art Buchwald (1925–) is one of the great satirists of the 20th century. His targets: the high and the mighty, the haughty, the pretentious. Collections of his newspaper columns have appeared in a number of books.

Chris Bull (late-20th century) has written extensively on gay issues. He is the coauthor of *Perfect Enemies*.

Samuel D. Burchard (1812–1891) was a clergyman. He earned a footnote in history by swaying an election with a remark equating the Democratic Party with "rum, Romanism, and rebellion."

James MacGregor Burns (1927–) is a university professor, political scientist, and author. He is probably best known for *The Lion and the Fox*, a study of Franklin D. Roosevelt.

George H. Bush (1924–) was the U.S. representative to the United Nations, director of the Central Intelligence Agency, vice president, and 41st president of the United States. During his term of office he championed Desert Storm, the military operation to drive Iraqi forces from Kuwait.

George W. Bush (1946–) was elected 43rd president in the election of 2000. Though he trailed in the popular vote, he won the electoral vote following a five-week recount dispute in Florida. The son of former president George H. Bush, he had served as governor of Texas before becoming president.

Earl Butz (1909–) was the secretary of agriculture in the cabinet of President Ford.

Richard E. Byrd (1888–1957) was a U.S. Navy pilot who became an Antarctic explorer. Admiral Byrd was the first man to fly over both the North and South Poles.

John C. Calhoun (1782–1850) served under two presidents as vice president, another as secretary of state, and still another as secretary of war. He was the first vice president to resign the office. As a U.S. senator from South Carolina, he was a strong advocate of states' rights.

Joseph A. Califano Jr. (1931–) was President Lyndon Johnson's special assistant for domestic affairs. He also served as secretary of health, education and welfare during the Carter administration. He has written a number of books on social and political issues.

Ben Nighthorse Campbell (1933–) was elected to the U.S. Senate in 1992. A Cheyenne, he represents the state of Colorado.

Stokely Carmichael (1941–1998) was an African American civil rights leader. In the early 1960s, he called for strengthening civil rights for blacks. In 1966 he took on a more activist approach, calling for "black power."

Andrew Carnegie (1835–1919) is probably the most extraordinary example of the American success story. Born in Scotland, he came to America with his poverty-stricken family. From the humblest of beginnings, he worked his way up to become the dominant steel producer in the United States. Upon his retirement, he devoted himself to philanthropic works, endowing foundations and libraries.

Dale Carnegie (1880–1958) was a lecturer on the general theme of self-improvement. He put several of his lecturers into one book, calling it *How to Win Friends and Influence People*. It was hugely successful.

Rachel Carson (1907–1964) was a marine biologist and author. Her series of articles in *The New Yorker* became the best-selling book *Silent Spring*. It inspired scores of environmental movements around the world.

Jimmy Carter (1924–   ) was the 39th president of the United States, succeeding Gerald Ford. The former naval officer and Georgia governor served one term and was succeeded by Ronald Reagan.

William J. Casey (1913–1987) was on the staff of the Office of Strategic Services during World War II, campaign manager for Ronald Reagan in 1980, and director of the Central Intelligence Agency from 1981 to 1987.

Whittaker Chambers (1901–1961) was a writer who joined the American Communist Party, took part in its underground activities, and then fled from it. In the late 1940s he denounced the secret group, leading to the disgrace and imprisonment of Alger Hiss.

Cesar Chavez (1927–1993) organized farmworkers in California in the mid-1960s.

Chief Joseph (1840–1904) was leader of the Nez Perce tribe. To avoid being confined to a reservation, he fled with his people in an attempt to reach the Canadian border. Thirty miles short of his destination, he was forced to surrender.

Shirley Chisholm (1924–   ) was elected to Congress in 1968. An African American, she represented a district in Brooklyn, New York.

Francis P. Church (1839–1906) wrote the famous editorial "Yes, Virginia, There Is a Santa Claus."

Walter Van Tilburg Clark (1909–1971) was the novelist who wrote *The Ox-Bow Incident*.

Henry Clay (1777–1852) represented Kentucky in the U.S. Senate. He ran unsuccessfully for president several times. His statesmanship in working out the Compromise of 1850 prevented secession and civil war at that time. It led to his title as "the Great Compromiser" and "the Great Peacemaker."

Eldridge Cleaver (1935–1998) was a leader of the radical Black Panther Party in the late 1960s. His book *Soul on Ice* told of black rage during the civil rights revolution.

Bill Clinton (1946–   ) was 42nd president of the United States. He defeated George H. Bush for reelection in 1992. In 1998 he was impeached by the House of Representatives, charged with perjury and obstruction of justice. In a virtual party-line vote, the Senate failed to convict him.

Cochise (?–1874) was an Apache chief who carried on a guerrilla campaign against the white man for 10 years in Arizona. He surrendered in 1871 and was confined to a reservation until his death.

Johnnie Cochran Jr. (1937–   ) is a lawyer. He is probably best known as the attorney who successfully defended O. J. Simpson in a double-murder case.

Ralph Coghlan (early to mid-20th century) was a reporter and editorial writer. He worked for the *Louisville Courier-Journal* and the *St. Louis Post-Dispatch*.

Christopher Columbus (1451–1506) was an Italian navigator who believed that he could reach Cathay and India by sailing west. Ferdinand and Isabella of Spain financed his voyages. On October 12, 1492, he landed on what he thought was an island off India but was actually an island of the New World.

James B. Conant (1893–1978) was an educator, chemist, and statesman. The onetime president of Harvard wrote a number of books on American education.

Conassatego (18th century) was an Iroquois chief.

Calvin Coolidge (1872–1933) was 30th president, succeeding to the office on the death of Warren G. Harding. He was elected to another term on his own. Coolidge had been a Massachusetts political figure who made his name as governor by breaking a Boston police strike.

James Fenimore Cooper (1789–1851) was a novelist whose *Leatherstocking Tales* were enormously popular during the middle of the 19th century. These were a series of books about the frontier, including *The Last of the Mohicans, The Deerslayer*, and others.

Bill Cosby (1937–) is an African American comedian who started as a stand-up comic and became one of the world's most successful television personalities.

Stephen Crane (1871–1900) was a novelist and war correspondent. He is most famous for *The Red Badge of Courage*, a realistic novel of men in battle during the Civil War. He covered the Spanish-American War as a correspondent.

George Creel (1876–1953) was a journalist who was selected by President Wilson to head the Committee on Public Information during World War I. The committee included the secretaries of state, war, and navy. Its news releases, pamphlets, posters, and movies were intended to provide public support for the U.S. war effort.

J. Hector St. John Crevecoeur (1735–1813) was a Frenchman who first traveled through, and then settled in, America from 1754 to 1780. His observations on life in America appeared in *Letters from an American Farmer*, published in 1782.

Charles Crocker (mid- to late 19th century) was superintendent of the Central Pacific Railroad during the building of the Transcontinental Railroad.

Walter Cronkite (1916–) was a journalist. He became a radio correspondent for CBS and anchorman for the CBS-TV evening news program. In the latter post, he was said to be the most trusted man in America.

William Cummings (1903–1944) was a military chaplain stationed in the Philippines during World War II.

Robert E. Cushman (late 19th to mid-20th century) was a professor of government at several universities. He wrote extensively on legal issues. His best-known work was *Leading Constitutional Decisions*.

Clarence Darrow (1857–1938) was an attorney. An opponent of capital punishment, he defended Loeb and Leopold during their murder trial. He also defended John Scopes' right to teach the theory of evolution.

David Davis (1815–1886) was appointed to the Supreme Court by President Lincoln in 1862. He wrote the opinion in the *Milligan* case involving civil rights in wartime.

Jefferson Davis (1808–1889) was president of the Confederate States of America. On February 18, 1861, he became provisional president. On February 22, 1862, he was inaugurated president in Richmond, Virginia. Before that, he had been a U.S. congressman, senator, and secretary of war in the Franklin Pierce administration. Captured after the Civil War, he was charged with treason, but the charges were dropped.

Marilyn P. Davis (mid- to late 20th century) is an anthropologist who has studied Mexican life in both Mexico and the United States.

Matthew L. Davis (late 18th to mid-19th century) was a close friend of Aaron Burr. He was a witness at the duel in which Burr killed Hamilton.

David Dekok (mid-to late 20th century) is a prizewinning journalist who covered the Centralia (Pennsylvania) coal mine fire disaster.

Vine Deloria Jr. (1939–) is a standing Rock Sioux who has written extensively on the problems of Native American Indians. He is a professor of law at the University of Colorado, Boulder.

J. Harve Dew (mid-to late 19th century) was a Confederate soldier. He was with the 9th Virginia Cavalry.

Thomas E. Dewey (1902–1971) was governor of New York state. He was twice the Republican candidate for president, but he lost in 1944 to Franklin Roosevelt and in 1948 to Harry Truman.

J. L. DeWitt (20th century) was a lieutenant general in the U.S. Army. He was in charge of the Japanese American relocation in northern California during World War II.

Abelardo Diaz Alfaro (1917–1999) wrote short stories about Puerto Rican life.

Anna Dickinson (mid-19th century) was a writer and lecturer.

Emily Dickinson (1830–1886) was a poet.

William J. Donovan (1883–1959) organized the Office of Strategic Services during World War II. After the war it became the Central Intelligence Agency. Donovan was an officer in the Rainbow Division during World War I.

John Dos Passos (1896–1970) was a writer and newspaperman. He wrote many novels, the most famous of which became the trilogy in *U.S.A.*

Stephen A. Douglas (1813–1861) was a U.S. senator from Illinois. In 1858 he took part in a series of debates with Lincoln on the slavery issue. Douglas was a Democratic nominee for president against Lincoln in 1860. A split in the Democratic Party led to the election of Lincoln.

Frederick Douglass (1817–1895) was a former slave who became one of the nation's most ardent abolitionists. He was also a writer, orator, and government official.

Peter F. Drucker (1909–) has written extensively on the corporation, business, and management techniques. An Austrian by birth, he came to the United States in 1937.

Martin Baum Duberman (mid- to late 20th century) is a professor of history at Lehman College of the City University of New York.

W.E.B. Du Bois (1868–1963) was an African American educator, scholar, and founder of the National Association for the Advancement of Colored People.

John Foster Dulles (1888–1959) was secretary of state in the administration of President Eisenhower. At different times in this post, he advocated several different policies toward the Soviet Union, ranging from "massive retaliation," to "liberation," to "brinkmanship."

Finley Peter Dunne (1867–1936) was the political satirist of his day. He invented "Mr. Dooley," a character whose commentaries in Irish dialect cut through the pretensions of the rich and powerful.

Charles A. Eastman (1858–1939) was a Santee Sioux, one of the first American Indians to obtain his M.D. degree. His books about Sioux life became best-sellers.

Albert Einstein (1879–1955) was a German-born mathematician and physicist who fled his country to settle in America. He convinced President Roosevelt to launch the program to develop an atomic bomb.

Dwight D. Eisenhower (1890–1969) commanded Allied forces in Europe during World War II. Following the war, he was twice elected president.

Elizabeth I (1533–1603) was queen of England from 1558 to 1603.

Ralph Waldo Emerson (1803–1882) was a poet and essayist.

Joe Eszterhas (1945–   ) is a journalist who has written stories on My Lai and Kent State.

Donald M. Fairfax (mid- to late 19th century) was executive officer of the USS *San Jacinto*. During the Civil War, he was directly involved in the forced removal of Confederate commissioners Mason and Slidell from the British ship *Trent*.

James Farmer (1920–1999) was a key African American civil rights leader during the 1950s and 1960s. He founded the Congress of Racial Equality.

David G. Farragut (1801–1870) was a Union admiral during the Civil War. His most famous exploit was forcing entry into Mobile Bay, Alabama.

Jules Feiffer (1929–   ) is a satirical cartoonist.

Roberto G. Fernandez (mid- to late 20th century) is a novelist and satirist of the Cuban American community in Miami. He was born in Cuba and came to the United States in 1961. He teaches Hispanic literature at Florida State University, Tallahassee.

Millard Fillmore (1800–1874) became 13th president on the death of Zachary Taylor.

Paul Finkelman (mid- to late 20th century) holds the John F. Seiberling Chair of Constitutional Law at the University of Akron.

Gustavo Perez Firmat (1949–   ) was born in Cuba and came to the United States when he was 11. A poet, writer, and scholar, he is a professor of Spanish at Duke University.

John T. Flynn (late 19th to mid-20th century) was an author, lecturer, and journalist. He was managing editor of the *New York Globe*.

Gerald R. Ford (1913–   ) was a member of Congress before he was named by Richard Nixon to replace Vice President Spiro Agnew, who had resigned in disgrace. When Nixon resigned in 1974, Ford was sworn in as 38th president.

Henry Ford (1863–1947) revolutionized the automobile industry by mass-producing cars on an assembly-line basis. During World War I he tried, unsuccessfully, to have neutral countries mediate a peace among the major belligerents.

Stephen Foster (1826–1864) composed the songs "My Old Kentucky Home," "Beautiful Dreamer," "Swanee River," "Old Folks at Home," and others.

The Four Bears (?–1837) was chief of the Mandans. He and many members of his tribe caught smallpox from the whites.

Benjamin Franklin (1706–1790) was a writer, philosopher, diplomat, scientist, inventor, and political figure. He was the only person to sign the four basic documents of American government: the Albany Plan of Union, the Declaration of Independence, the Articles of Confederation, and the Constitution of the United States.

Betty Friedan (1921–   ) was a leader of the American feminist movement. She helped found the National Organization for Women and wrote *The Feminine Mystique*.

John Gallagher (late 20th century) was a correspondent for the gay publication *The Advocate*. He is the coauthor of *Perfect Enemies*.

Maria Cristina Garcia (late 20th century) is assistant professor of history at Texas A&M University.

James A. Garfield (1831–1881) was the 20th president. He was assassinated by a disappointed office-seeker his first year in office.

William Lloyd Garrison (1805–1879) was an abolitionist who started the newspaper the *Liberator* and organized the Anti-Slavery Society prior to the Civil War.

Marcus Garvey (1887–1940) founded the Universal Negro Improvement Association in the 1920s.

Horatio Gates (1728–1806) came to America as an English officer to fight in the French and Indian War. He settled in Virginia and then took a command in the Continental Army, winning victory at Saratoga.

Henry George (1839–1897) was a writer and editor who championed the poor during the period of industrial growth in America.

Ruth Bader Ginsburg (1933–   ) was named associate justice of the U.S. Supreme Court by President Clinton in 1994.

Rudolph Giuliani (1944–   ) served as mayor of New York City during the World Trade Center attacks on September 11, 2001.

George Glieg (late 18th to mid-19th century) was a British army officer who witnessed the burning of Washington during the War of 1812.

Harry Golden (1902–1981) was editor, publisher, and essaylist of the monthly *The Carolina Israelite*. Many of his essays were compiled into full-length books.

Samuel Gompers (1850–1924) was born in Great Britain. He came to the United States and became a labor leader, heading the American Federation of Labor.

Albert Gore Jr. (1948–   ) was defeated for president by George W. Bush in the election of 2000. Gore won the popular vote by half a million votes but lost in the electoral college. The issue was resolved by the U.S. Supreme Court, which ended a recount in Florida. Gore had been vice president under Clinton for eight years, a former U.S. senator, and a member of Congress.

Ulysses S. Grant (1822–1885) was the outstanding Union general during the Civil War. Later he became the 18th president.

Dick Gregory (1932–   ) was among the first African American stand-up comics. Much of his humor dealt with the ironies of race in America.

Susan Griffin (mid- to late 20th century) has written on the role of rape as an aspect of power.

John Gunther (1901–1970) was an American journalist who wrote a popular series of books on national and international affairs. They included *Inside Europe, Inside Asia, Inside Latin America,* and *Inside U.S.A.*

Hy Haas (1915–2000) was a sergeant in the U.S. Army during World War II. He landed on Omaha Beach on D-Day.

Masse Hadjo (late 19th century) was a Sioux who wrote about the Ghost Dance.

William Ivy Hair (mid- to late 20th century) is a professor of history at Georgia College, Milledgeville, Georgia. He is the author of several books on Louisiana history and politics.

Fannie Lou Hamer (1917–1977) was an African American woman who paid a heavy price for registering to vote in Mississippi. She began by losing her job and was later brutally beaten by the Mississippi police. She helped form the Mississippi Freedom Democratic Party and tried, unsuccessfully, to unseat the regular Democratic delegates from Mississippi at the 1964 Democratic convention.

Alexander Hamilton (1755–1804) fought hard to have the Constitution adopted. He was Washington's first secretary of the treasury. Hamilton fought a duel with Aaron Burr, who ended his life.

Andrew Hamilton (early 18th century) was a Philadelphia lawyer who came to New York to defend John Peter Zenger on charges of libeling the governor of New York. He successfully defended Zenger, winning a major victory for freedom of the press.

Cornelia Hancock (mid- to late 19th century) was a volunteer nurse during the Civil War.

James G. Harbord (1866–1947) was chief of staff to General John J. Pershing during World War I. As a major general, he led the Second Division at Soissons.

Warren G. Harding (1865–1923) was the 29th president. During his administration the Teapot Dome scandal broke. He died in office and was succeeded by Calvin Coolidge.

Robert G. Harper (1765–1825) was a South Carolina congressman.

Fred R. Harris (1930–   ) was a U.S. senator from Oklahoma, a member of the Kerner Commission, and a professor of political science at the University of New Mexico.

Joel Chandler Harris (1848–1908) wrote the Uncle Remus stories. He apparently heard them as a child living on a Georgia plantation.

William Henry Harrison (1773–1841) was a soldier, secretary of the Northwest Territory, and minister to Colombia. He was elected ninth president but died a month after his inauguration.

Frank A. Haskell (mid-19th century) was a Union general during the Civil War.

Nathaniel Hawthorne (1804–1864) was a novelist and short story writer. His best-known works are *The Scarlet Letter* and *The House of the Seven Gables*. Less-known is that he wrote a campaign biography for Franklin Pierce.

John Hay (1838–1905) was a private secretary to, and biographer of, Lincoln. Later he became secretary of state under Presidents William McKinley and Theodore Roosevelt.

Ira Hayes (1922–1955) was a Pima Indian who became known worldwide as one of the U.S. Marines who raised the flag over Iwo Jima during World War II. The famous photograph by Joe Rosenthal put Hayes into an uncomfortable spotlight. After the war, he became a drifter, dying of alcoholism and exposure.

Rutherford B. Hayes (1822–1893) was the 19th president. Before that he had served as governor of Ohio. He won the presidency upon the decision of an electoral commission that awarded him disputed electoral votes from several southern states. Reconstruction ended during his term of office.

William Randolph Hearst (1863–1951) was a newspaper publisher. His sensationalism and what became known as "yellow journalism" helped bring about the Spanish-American War. He served briefly in Congress and ran unsuccessful campaigns for mayor of New York City and governor of New York state.

Joseph Heller (1923–   ) authored the best-selling novel *Catch-22*.

Steven Heller (mid- to late 20th century) is art director of *The New York Times Book Review*.

Patrick Henry (1736–1799) was a leading political figure in the days prior to the American Revolution. He later became governor of Virginia.

Carwain L. Herrington (mid- to late 20th century) left a touching letter letter to his dead father at the Vietnam Veterans Memorial in Washington.

Joe Hill (1879–1915) was Swedish immigrant Joseph Hillson, who came to the United States and joined the labor movement. He was a member of the Industrial Workers of the World and wrote labor songs. Following a controversial Utah trial, he was convicted of murder and executed. He is considered a labor martyr.

Alger Hiss (1904–1996) was a high State Department official who was accused of being a Communist agent by Whittaker Chambers. The resulting congressional investigation led to the downfall of Hiss and the political rise of Congressman Richard Nixon.

Laura Z. Hobson (1900–1986) was a novelist. Her book on anti-Semitism, *Gentleman's Agreement*, became a best-seller and a highly successful motion picture.

Richard Hofstadter (1916–   ) was De Witt Clinton Professor of History at Columbia

University. His books on American history and politics were widely acclaimed. Two received Pulitzer Prizes.

James Hogg (1851–1906) was governor of Texas from 1891 to 1895. He fought against the special interests in Texas—especially the railroads—and vigorously supported public respect for the law.

Oliver Wendell Holmes Jr. (1841–1935) was an associate justice of the U.S. Supreme Court.

Oliver Wendell Holmes Sr. (1809–1894) was not only a poet and essayist but a doctor and Harvard professor.

Herbert Hoover (1874–1964) was the 31st president. He took office in 1929, the year of the stock market crash that set off the Great Depression. Earlier in his career had he served as food administrator in Europe after World War I and as secretary of commerce.

Elbert Hubbard (1856–1915) was a writer. His magazine article "A Message to Garcia" made him world-famous. Hubbard died on the *Lusitania*, which was sunk by a German U-boat during World War I.

Henry Hudson (?–1611) was an English navigator who was hired by the Dutch East India Company to find a Northwest Passage to the Orient. During several voyages to the New World, he became the first European to discover the Hudson River and Hudson Bay. On his last voyage, his crew mutinied and set him adrift in Hudson Bay. He was never seen again.

Harriot K. Hunt (1805–1875) was a female doctor who tried to attend lectures at Harvard Medical School.

Daniel Inouye (1924–) is a U.S. senator representing Hawaii. During World War II, he lost an arm fighting in the Japanese American 442nd Combat Team. After the war, he became a lawyer, entered politics, and became the first Japanese American to be elected to the House of Representatives. Later, he won election to the Senate. In 2000, more than half a century after World War II ended, he was awarded the Congressional Medal of Honor for his heroism.

Patricia Ireland (1945–) is president of the National Organization for Women.

Washington Irving (1783–1859) was an essayist, biographer, and historian. He also wrote a series of short stories about the New York area. His best-known works include *Rip Van Winkle*, *The Legend of Sleepy Hollow*, and the satirical *Knickerbocker's History of New York*.

Andrew Jackson (1767–1845) was the hero of the Battle of New Orleans at the close of the War of 1812. Later he became the seventh president of the United States, opposing the idea that any state could nullify a federal law.

Helen Hunt Jackson (1830–1885) was a poet, essayist, and novelist. Her novel *Ramona* and her tract *A Century of Dishonor* portrayed the plight of the American Indian.

Jesse Jackson (1941–) is an African American clergyman and civil rights advocate. He has campaigned for the presidential nomination on the Democratic ticket.

Thomas (Stonewall) Jackson (1824–1863) was one of the top generals in the Confederate army. He died of wounds after he was accidentally shot by his own men during the Battle of Chancellorsville.

James B. Jacobs (mid- to late 20th century) is professor of law and director of the Center for Research in Crime and Justice at New York University.

Jacob Javits (1904–1986) was a Republican U.S. senator, representing the state of New York.

Thomas Jefferson (1743–1826) was the author of the Declaration of Independence.

Third president of the United States, he arranged the purchase of the Louisiana Territory from Napoleon in 1803.

James Jennings (mid- to late 20th century) was associate professor of political science and dean of the College of Public and Community Service at the University of Massachusetts in Boston when he edited *Puerto Rican Politics in Urban America*.

Isaac Jogues (1607–1646) was a Jesuit missionary who came from France to convert American Indians. At one point, he was taken prisoner by the Iroquois, from whom he escaped. Several years later, when he returned to continue his work, he was slain.

Andrew Johnson (1808–1875) succeeded to the presidency after Lincoln's assassination. Johnson had major problems with both Congress and Lincoln's cabinet. He was impeached by the House of Representatives, but the Senate failed to convict and remove him from office by a single vote.

Lyndon B. Johnson (1908–1973) was the 36th president. The vice president under Kennedy, Johnson became president following Kennedy's assassination. Johnson's "Great Society" domestic programs were over-shadowed by his escalation of the Vietnam war.

Leon W. Johnson (1904–1997) was one of five American servicemen to win the Congressional Medal of Honor for heroism during the attack on the Ploesti oil fields of Romania during World War II.

John Paul Jones (1747–1792) was born in Scotland. He went to sea at the age of 12 and became first mate at 19. He came to America as the Revolution was breaking out and was given a warship to harass British shipping.

Helen Keller (1880–1968) overcame deafness and blindness to become a renowned writer, lecturer, and humanitarian.

George Wilkins Kendall (mid-19th century) was a correspondent for the *New Orleans Picayune*. His dispatches on the Mexican-American War often portrayed the exploits of young officers who would play major roles in the Civil War.

George F. Kennan (1904–   ) was a U.S. Foreign Service officer during and after World War II. He is best known as the "anonymous" author of a 1945 article advocating containment of the Soviet Union.

John F. Kennedy (1917–1963) was the youngest man to be elected president. Following Eisenhower in office, he symbolized the change in power from one generation to the next. He failed in the abortive attempt to invade Cuba and overthrow Castro but faced down the Soviet Union during the Cuban missile crisis. He was assassinated on November 22, 1963. His civil rights proposals would be pushed through Congress by his successor, Lyndon B. Johnson.

David Kennerly (mid-to late 20th century) took pictures for *Time* magazine before he became the White House photographer.

Otto Kerner (1908–1976) was governor of Illinois. He headed the National Advisory Commission on Civil Disorders, which issued its report in 1968.

K. Austin Kerr (mid-to late 20th century) was professor of history at Ohio State University.

Peggy L. Kerr (1946–   ) was the first woman to become a partner at the law firm of Skadden, Arps, Slate, Meagher & Flom.

Francis Scott Key (1779–1843) was a lawyer. He wrote "The Star-Spangled Banner" during the War of 1812.

Joyce Kilmer (1886–1918) was the poet best known for "Trees." He was killed in action in France during World War I.

Ernest J. King (1878–1956) was U.S. chief of naval operations during World War II.

Martin Luther King Jr. (1929–1968) was a clergyman who inspired the civil rights movement in the 1960s. An African American, he led the March on Washington in August 1963. An advocate of nonviolent protest, he was awarded the Nobel Peace Prize. His assassination in 1968 set off riots throughout the United States.

King Philip (1620–1676) was a Wampanoag chief who led his people against Massachusetts colonists in King Philip's War. He died in battle.

Barbara S. Kraft (mid-to late 20th century) is an author and editor.

William M. Kunstler (1919–1997) was a lawyer who specialized in defending radical individuals and groups.

Fiorello La Guardia (1882–1947) was a congressman and mayor of the city of New York. After World War II, he headed the United Nations Relief and Rehabilitation Administration. This agency was set up to help feed a starving Europe.

Jack Lait (1883–1954) was a journalist who became editor of the *New York Daily Mirror*.

James Lawrence (1781–1813) was a naval commander during the War of 1812. Mortally wounded in battle, he urged his crew not to give up the ship.

Emma Lazarus (1849–1887) was the poet who composed the inscription at the base of the Statue of Liberty.

David D. Lee (1948–) wrote the biography of World War I hero Alvin C. York.

Richard Henry Lee (1732–1794) proposed the resolution on independence during the Second Continental Congress.

Robert E. Lee (1807–1870) commanded the Confederate army during the Civil War. A brilliant strategist and former superintendent of the U.S. Military Academy at West Point, he had turned down Lincoln's offer to command the Union forces.

Max Lerner (1902–1992) wrote and lectured on political and social issues through much of the 20th century.

Julius Lester (mid-to late 20th century) was a civil rights activist, with specific concern for African Americans.

Meriwether Lewis (1774–1809) explored the newly purchased Louisiana Territory—and sought a Northwest Passage to the Pacific Ocean—for President Thomas Jefferson.

Sinclair Lewis (1885–1951) was a novelist. His works include *Main Street, Babbitt, Arrowsmith, Dodsworth, Elmer Gantry*, and *It Can't Happen Here*. The latter dealt with the possibility of a fascist America. His *Kingsblood Royal* dealt with a man's discovery that he has black blood.

Arthur Liman (1932–) was counsel to the congressional committee investigating the Iran-Contra affair in 1987.

Abraham Lincoln (1809–1865) was the president who issued the Emancipation Proclamation during the Civil War. He was assassinated shortly after his second inauguration.

Charles A. Lindbergh Jr. (1902–1974) became a hero overnight when he flew solo across the Atlantic—the first person to do so. He was a prominent isolationist prior to Pearl Harbor.

Kim Thi Linn (1972–) was a refugee from Vietnam when she came to the United States in 1986.

Little Crow (1803?–1863) was a Santee Sioux chief. He signed a treaty with the whites in 1851 and conferred with officials in Washington in 1858. At one point he had to defend himself against charges by some braves that he was disloyal. In 1862 he took part in the Sioux uprising.

Henry Cabot Lodge (1850–1924) was chairman of the Senate Foreign Relations Committee at the time the Versailles Treaty and the League of Nations were coming up for approval. He attached a number of reservations to the treaty. It failed to win two-thirds of the Senate.

Jack London (1876–1916) wrote novels and short stories. Much of his work takes place in Alaska around the time of the gold rush. His novels include *Call of the Wild* and *The Sea Wolf*.

Breckinridge Long (1881–1958) was the State Department official in charge of visas and immigration during most of World War II.

Henry Wadsworth Longfellow (1807–1882) was a poet who wrote about Americana, including *Paul Revere's Ride* and *The Village Blacksmith*.

James Longstreet (1821–1904) was a Confederate general who took part in many Civil War battles.

Audre Lorde (mid- to late-20th century) is a feminist author. She was born in New York City of West Indian parents.

Louis L. Ludlow (early- to mid-20th century) was an Indiana congressman. In the late 1930s he tried to have a resolution passed by Congress to have wars declared by popular vote, except in cases of attack.

Oscar R. Luhring (mid-20th century) was a judge of the Supreme Court of the District of Columbia.

Oren R. Lyons (1930–   ) is associate professor of American studies at the State University of New York at Buffalo. He is a chief of the Turtle Clan of the Onondaga Nation.

Douglas MacArthur (1880–1964) was in charge of Allied forces in the Southwest Pacific during World War II. After the war, he ruled over a defeated Japan, leading it into a democratic society. When the Korean War broke out, MacArthur wanted to expand the war into Communist China. This was contrary to American policy, and he was relieved of his command by President Truman.

Horace Mann (1796–1859) was a leading figure in developing the American public school. He was a lawyer, legislator, and, finally, secretary of the Massachusetts Board of Education.

Victor Marchetti (mid-20th century) was a member of the CIA for 14 years. He became executive assistant to the deputy director. He coauthored *The CIA and the Cult of Intelligence* with John D. Marks.

Edwin Markham (1825–1940) was a poet whose work reflected his feelings for the downtrodden.

John D. Marks (mid-20th century) was an analyst with the State Department. He and Victor Marchetti wrote a a critical book on the Central Intelligence Agency in 1974.

Don Marquis (1878–1937) was the pen name of Donald Robert Perry. The humorist was a columnist for the *New York Sun* and *New York Tribune*. He created the characters archy and mehitabel.

Florence Mars (mid-20th century) lived in Neshoba County, Mississippi, before, during, and after three civil rights workers were murdered. Her roots in the community go way back. She has eight great-grandparents who are buried in the country.

Charles Marshall (mid-19th century) was a colonel in the Confederate army. Aide-de-camp to General Robert E. Lee, Marshall witnessed the surrender at Appomattox Court House.

George C. Marshall (1880–1959) was army chief of staff during World War II. After the war, he served in various capacities in the Truman cabinet, including secretary of defense and secretary of state. His Marshall Plan for the recovery of postwar Europe won him the Nobel Peace Prize.

John Marshall (1755–1835) was the third chief justice of the United States. He was the first, however, to establish the principle of judicial review—determining the constitutionality of laws and official acts.

Thurgood Marshall (1908–1993) was an African American and great-grandson of a slave. He attended segregated public schools and graduated from Howard University Law School. He joined the NAACP Legal Defense Fund, argued successfully for school desegregation, and was appointed an associate justice of the Supreme Court by President Lyndon Johnson. An outspoken liberal on the Court, he was succeeded by Clarence Thomas.

George Mason (1725–1792) drafted Virginia's Declaration of Rights in May 1776. It was one of the models drawn on by Jefferson when he wrote the Declaration of Independence. It was also used in drafting the Bill of Rights—the first 10 amendments to the Constitution.

Cotton Mather (1663–1728) was a Boston clergyman who condemned witchcraft.

Bill Mauldin (1921–   ) was an army cartoonist during World War II. His grim humor appeared in the army newspaper *Stars and Stripes* and was also distributed through United Features Syndicate. After the war he continued drawing editorial cartoons.

Anthony McAuliffe (1898–1975) commanded the 101st Airborne Division during World War II. During the Battle of the Bulge, his refusal to surrender the Belgian town of Bastogne prevented an American military disaster.

Lee McCardell (early to mid-20th century) was a reporter for the *Baltimore Evening Sun*.

Joseph R. McCarthy (1909–1957) was a U.S. senator who conducted a series of investigations to uncover Communist subversives. His tactics resulted in the word "McCarthyism" being added to the English language. He was formally condemned by the Senate in December 1954.

Walter A. McDougall (late 20th century) is a professor of history and of international affairs at the University of Pennsylvania. He is also the editor in chief of *Orbis, a Journal of World Affairs*.

William McKinley (1843–1901) was president during the Spanish-American War. Elected in 1896 and reelected in 1900, he was assassinated in 1901. Vice President Theodore Roosevelt succeeded him.

Robert S. McNamara (1916–   ) was secretary of defense under Presidents Kennedy and Johnson. He served during most of the Vietnam War. He has headed the Ford Motor Company and the World Bank.

Joseph Medill (mid-19th century) was editor of the *Chicago Tribune*.

Milton Meltzer (mid- to late 20th century) is a social historian and biographer. He was written about ethnic groups in the United States as well as issues in American and world history.

H. L. Mencken (1880–1956) was a social critic, magazine editor, and Baltimore journalist. His comments on American life and morals—sometimes witty, sometimes acerbic—amused and outraged readers for nearly half a century.

Meninock (late 19th to early 20th century) was a Yakima chief who fought for Indian fishing rights in the state of Washington. In 1915 he was found guilty of violating the state's salmon fishing code.

Arthur Miller (1915–   ) is a playwright and novelist. His plays include *All My sons, Death of a Salesman, The Crucible*, and *A View from the Bridge*.

Margaret Mitchell (1900–1949) was the author of *Gone with the Wind*.

James Monroe (1754–1831) was the fifth president of the United States. His doctrine forbade further European colonization on the American continents.

Clement Clarke Moore (1779–1863) was a scholar who taught literature at the General Theological Seminary in New York City. He is best known as the author of "A Visit from St. Nicholas."

Samuel Eliot Morison (1887–1976) was a professor of history, historian, and biographer. He is responsible for a wide range of historical works, receiving Pulitzer Prizes for biographies of Christopher Columbus and John Paul Jones. He also wrote a history of the United States, a history of World War II, and the multivolume *History of the United States Naval Operations in World War II.*

Samuel F. B. Morse (1791–1872) is best known as the inventor of the telegraph and developer of the Morse code. He was also a portrait artist. Less well known was his opposition to further immigration into the United States.

Nathaniel Morton (early to mid-17th century) was secretary of the Massachusetts Bay Colony. He is a major source of the case of Roger Williams, who chose banishment rather than compromise on matters of personal conscience.

Lucretia Mott (1795–1880) was an early fighter on behalf of equal rights for women.

Edward R. Murrow (1908–1965) was a radio and television journalist. Just before the outbreak of World War II, he set up the CBS news staff in Europe. Murrow broadcast from London and told radio listeners of the London blitz. After the war he became a television journalist. His *See It Now* telecasts on national and international issues are considered classics.

Gunnar Myrdal (1898–1987) was the Swedish sociologist and economist who wrote *An American Dilemma*, a study of race relations in the United States.

Ralph Nader (1934–   ) is a lawyer and an advocate for consumer protection. His 1965 book, *Unsafe at Any Speed*, exposed the auto industry as more interested in sales than safety. Harassed by agents of General Motors, he sued for invasion of privacy. His victory enabled him to establish a series of public interest agencies. His staffers were dubbed "Nader's Raiders" by the press. In 1996 and 2000 he ran for president on the Green Party ticket.

Adam Nagourney (late 20th to early 21st century) was a *New York Times* reporter who covered the Florida recount controversy at the end of the 2000 presidential campaign.

Ruby Nakfoor (mid-20th century) was a Syrian American high school student who felt that the Arabic language could not be passed on to the younger generation without active parental support.

James F. Neal (mid-20th century) was an assistant prosecutor handling the Watergate cases.

Aryeh Neier (1937–   ) heads the Soros Foundation. Formerly, he directed the American Civil Liberties Union and Human Rights Watch.

William Neville (mid-19th to early 20th century) was a member of Congress representing a Nebraska district. A Civil War veteran and former judge, he was the last Populist member of Congress.

Chester W. Nimitz (1885–1966) was an admiral who took charge of the U.S. Pacific Fleet after the attack on Pearl Harbor.

Richard M. Nixon (1913–1994) was a congressman, a senator, and vice president of the United States before his election to the presidency in 1968. Following the Watergate scandals, he resigned from the office in 1974. During his term of office, he established closer ties with the People's Republic of China.

Louis Nizer (1902–1994) was an attorney who handled many famous clients. He argued Quentin Reynolds' libel suit against Westbrook Pegler, the Billy Rose divorce case, and many others.

Oliver North (1943–   ) was a lieutenant colonel in the U.S. Marine Corps. A member of President Reagan's National Security Council, he played a major role in the Iran-Contra affair. It was a plan to provide arms for the Iranians and funds for the *contras* in Nicaragua.

Solomon Northrup (mid-19th century) was a slave for 12 years and wrote a book about it.

J. D. O'Connell (mid-19th century) was a former Louisiana state senator who witnessed the New Orleans race riot of 1866.

James H. O'Neill (mid-20th century) was an Army chaplain in World War II. During the Battle of the Bulge, he composed a prayer for good weather at the request of General George Patton.

Ellison S. Onizuka (1946–1986) was the first Asian American astronaut to travel in space. He was one of the crew who perished in the *Challenger* disaster.

J. Robert Oppenheimer (1904–1967) was in charge of the Manhattan Project, which developed the first atomic bomb during World War II. After the war, he opposed development of the hydrogen bomb.

John L. O'Sullivan (mid-19th century) was editor of the *Democratic Review* and the *New York News*. It was in the *Review* that the phrase "Manifest Destiny" was introduced.

William Tyler Page (1868–1942) wrote *the American's Creed* in 1917. For most of his life he worked in some capacity for the House of Representatives.

Robert Treat Paine (mid-18th century) was the chief prosecuting attorney in the case against the British soldiers charged in the Boston Massacre.

Thomas Paine (1737–1809) was a pamphleteer. His *Common Sense* was an early advocate of independence for the American colonies.

Rosa Parks (1913–   ) was the African American woman who refused to move to the back of a Montgomery, Alabama, bus—and changed history.

George S. Patton Jr. (1885–1945) commanded American armies in North Africa, Sicily, France, Belgium, and Germany during World War II. Probably his greatest military achievement was to relieve the garrison at Bastogne, Belgium, during the Battle of the Bulge.

John Howard Payne (1791–1852) was the poet and playwright who wrote "Home, Sweet Home." He also acted on New York and London stages.

Richard Pearson (18th century) was born in Britain. He was captain of the English ship *Serapis* during the American Revolution. It was defeated in battle by the *Bon Homme Richard* under John Paul Jones.

Federico Pena (1947–   ) was a civil rights lawyer who became mayor of Denver and secretary of transportation in the Clinton cabinet.

William Penn (1644–1718) was an English Quaker who founded Pennsylvania.

Pauline Cuoio Pepe (1892–?) was a sewing machine operator at the Triangle Shirtwaist Company in 1911. She survived the devastating fire at the factory, which took 147 lives.

H. Ross Perot (1930–   ) is a successful corporate executive. He ran for president on third-party tickets in 1992 and 1996, losing both times. His major issues were a burgeoning federal deficit and campaign finance reform.

Oliver H. Perry (1785–1819) won the great naval Battle of Lake Erie during the War of 1812.

John J. Pershing (1860–1948) headed the American Expeditionary Forces in Europe during World War I. Later he became army chief of staff. Earlier in his career he fought Indians, took part in the Spanish-American War, and saw service in the Philippines and along the Mexican border.

George Washington Plunkitt (late 19th to early 20th century) was a Tammany Hall political figure. He served in the New York state Senate and as a Democratic Party district leader.

Edgar Allan Poe (1809–1849) was a poet and short story writer. He is regarded as the father of the modern detective story, and each year "Edgars" are awarded for outstanding mystery stories.

John Poindexter (1936–) was national security adviser for President Reagan in 1986. He played a key role in the Iran-Contra affair.

James K. Polk (1795–1849) was the 11th president. He served during the Mexican War.

Marco Polo (1254–1324) was the Venetian traveler whose visits to the Far East aroused European interest in that part of the world. Specifically, it led to Columbus' attempt to reach China and India by sailing west and going around the world.

Richard Gid Powers (mid-to late 20th century) is a professor of history at the City University of New York's College of Staten Island. In addition to his biography of J. Edgar Hoover, he has written of the FBI's image in American culture.

Israel Putnam (1718–1790) fought at the Battle of "Bunker Hill" (Breed's Hill) during the American Revolution.

Ernie Pyle (1900–1945) was a World War II correspondent who covered both Europe and the Pacific. He was killed by a Japanese sniper on a small island off Okinawa.

A. Philip Randolph (1889–1979) was a union leader and civil rights activist. An African American, he led the Brotherhood of Sleeping Car Porters and campaigned tirelessly for the rights of all Americans.

Ronald Reagan (1911–) was a Hollywood film star who turned to politics. He first beame governor of California. After a few unsuccessful attempts to get the Republican nomination, he was nominated for president in 1980. He defeated President Jimmy Carter in 1980 and Walter Mondale in 1984.

Red Cloud (1822–1909) was a medicine man who became a war chief of the Oglala Sioux. When white men broke treaties and began settling on his hunting grounds, Red Cloud warred against them. In 1868 he agreed to make peace.

Red Iron (mid-19th century) was a Dakota tribal chief.

Red Jacket (1758?–1830) was a Seneca chief. He received his name from the jacket that he wore fighting on the British side during the American Revolution.

William Rehnquist (1924–) was appointed chief justice of the United States by President Reagan in 1986.

Frederic Remington (1861–1909) was an artist, sculptor, and illustrator. He is most famous for his paintings and sculptures on themes of the American West.

Robert V. Remini (1921–) is a professor of history and research professor of humanities at the University of Illinois, Chicago. He has written numerous biographies. Works on Andrew Jackson won the National Book Award in 1985 and the Carl Sandburg Award in 1989.

Janet Reno (1938–) was attorney general in the Clinton administration. Previously, she had been state attorney in Dade County, Florida.

Eddie Rickenbacker (1890–1973) was one of the America's outstanding air aces of World War I. He later became a commercial airline executive.

Ron Ridenhour (mid-to late 20th century) was an American soldier during the Vietnam War. When he heard accounts of what was later known as the My Lai massacre, he wrote to the appropriate authorities in Washington.

Geraldo Rivera (1943–) is a television personality and talk show host. He began his career as a lawyer, later turning to investigative journalism.

Michael D. Roberts (1940–) is a journalist who has covered stories on Kent State, Washington, Vietnam, and the Middle East.

Paul Robeson (1898–1976) was a college scholar and athlete who became a professional actor and singer. An African American, he was a civil rights activist.

Will Rogers (1879–1935) was a Cherokee who became the most famous humorist of his time. He was a star of stage, screen, and radio and wrote a popular newspaper column.

George Romney (1907–1995) was governor of Michigan during the Detroit race riots of 1967. Later he became a candidate for the Republican nomination for president.

Franklin D. Roosevelt (1882–1945) led the United States through the Great Depression and World War II. His New Deal revolutionized the role of government in America and led to the rise of a strong middle class. He was elected to the presidency four times, a unique political achievement that will never be duplicated.

Theodore Roosevelt (1858–1919) had been assistant secretary of the navy in the McKinley administration. When McKinley ran for reelection, Roosevelt was his running mate. He became president when McKinley was assassinated. He pushed through the construction of the Panama Canal. In 1912 he ran on a third-party ticket, drawing off Republican support from President Taft. This resulted in the election of Wilson.

William H. Russell (mid-19th century) was an English journalist who covered the Civil War for the *London Times*.

William Safire (1929–) is a columnist for the *New York Times*. He had served in the Nixon White House as a speechwriter.

Louis Saunders (1910–1998) was the minister who presided at the burial of Lee Harvey Oswald, accused slayer of President Kennedy.

Arthur M. Schlesinger Jr. (1917–) is a historian. His works include *The Age of Jackson* (for which he won a Pulitzer Prize), *The Age of Roosevelt* (on the New Deal), *A Thousand Days* (on the Kennedy administration, which also won a Pulitzer), and *Robert Kennedy and His Times*.

Serge Schmemann (mid- to late-20th century) is a reporter for the *New York Times*.

H. Norman Schwarzkopf (1934–) was the general in charge of a United Nations coalition that ousted Iraqi forces from Kuwait in 1991.

John T. Scopes (1900–1970) was a high school biology teacher. In 1925 he was convicted in Tennessee for teaching the theory of evolution.

Brent Scowcroft (mid- to late 20th century) was national security adviser for Presidents Ford and Bush.

Eleanor Cohen Seixas (1839–?) lived in Columbia, South Carolina, during its occupation by Union forces.

William T. Sherman (1820–1891) was a Union general during the Civil War. His taking of Atlanta and the march to the sea that followed were a major defeat for the Confederacy.

Earl Shorris (1936–) is a novelist, essayist, and reviewer.

Gary Sick (mid- to late 20th century) was a staff member of the National Security Council for Presidents Ford, Carter, and Reagan. Before that, he had been a U.S. naval analyst. During the Iran hostage crisis of 1979–1981, he was a key White House aide on the problem.

Upton Sinclair (1878–1968) was the muckraking author of *The Jungle*, an exposé of the meatpacking industry at the beginning of the 20th century. The novel led to passage of the Pure Food and Drug Act of 1906. In 1934, using the slogan "End Poverty in California," he ran unsuccessfully for governor of that state.

Sitting Bull (1834–1890) was a Hunkpapa Lakota chief. His forces, under Crazy Horse, defeated General George Custer at the Little Big Horn. Afterward, Sitting Bull and his people fled to Canada. On his return, he was placed on a reservation. There he died in a melee when police came to arrest him.

Barbara Smith (1946–) is a writer and activist. She is a black feminist and lesbian.

Luther Standing Bear (1868–1939) was a chief of the Oglala Sioux. His books on Indian life are considered classics.

Leland Stanford (1824–1893) is best known as the man who, as president of the Central Pacific Railroad Company, drove the last spike to link the Transcontinental Railroad. He also was governor of California, a U.S. senator, and founder of Stanford University.

Joseph Stansbury (mid- to late 18th century) was Benedict Arnold's emissary to Sir Henry Clinton, the British commander.

Charles E. Stanton (1859–1933) was a colonel in the U.S. Army during World War I. He delivered the famous line "Lafayette, we are here."

Kenneth Starr (1946–) was special counsel appointed to investigate allegations regarding Bill and Hillary Clinton. He recommended that Congress impeach the president. Clinton was impeached in the House, but a vote to remove him from office failed in the Senate.

Ronald Steel (1931–) is Professor of International Relations at the University of Southern California.

Lincoln Steffens (1866–1936) was a journalist. He was one of a group of writers who were labeled "muckrakers" for exposing political corruption in American cities.

John Steinbeck (1902–1968) was a novelist who wrote about the downtrodden. His works include *The Grapes of Wrath, In Dubious Battle,* and *Of Mice and Men.* During the course of his career, he won both a Pulitzer Prize and the Nobel Prize in literature.

George Stephanopoulos (1961–) was a senior adviser for President Clinton.

John Paul Stevens (1920–) was named associate justice of the U.S. Supreme Court by President Ford in 1975.

Sarah Christie Stevens (1844–1920) was a Minnesota farm wife. She dabbled in politics long before it was considered appropriate for women to do so.

Thaddeus Stevens (1792–1868) was an abolitionist before the Civil War who became a prominent member of the House of Representatives. One of the Radical Republicans, he supported measures to punish former Confederate states following the Civil War. He was chairman of the Joint Committee on Reconstruction and led the unsuccessful fight to remove President Andrew Johnson from office.

Adlai E. Stevenson (1900–1965) was governor of Illinois. He was twice nominated for president by the Democratic Party. Both times he ran against Dwight D. Eisenhower—and both times he lost. During the Kennedy administration he served as U.S. ambassador to the United Nations.

Henry L. Stimson (1867–1950) served as secretary of state in the Hoover administration and secretary of war in the cabinet of Franklin Roosevelt.

Harriet Beecher Stowe (1811–1896) was the author of *Uncle Tom's Cabin*, a novel about slave life in the South before the Civil War.

Edward Streeter (1891–?) was a writer. He is best known for *Dere Mable*, a series of fictional letters from an army recruit to his girl back home.

Peter Stuyvesant (1610–1672) was the Dutch governor of New Netherland from 1647 until its surrender to the British in 1664. The following year, he returned to Holland to deliver his final report as governor. Then he came back to America, where he lived out his life in what was then called New York.

William Graham Sumner (1840–1910) was a professor of sociology at Yale University.

Sweet Medicine (pre-Columbus) is described by scholars as a "cultural hero" of the Cheyenne who may have been based on a real person. Predictions attributed to him were apparently passed down in the oral tradition from one generation to the next.

Robert A. Taft (1889–1953) was a U.S. senator from Ohio. The son of President William Howard Taft, he was unsuccessful in getting the Republican nomination for president.

William Howard Taft (1857–1930) was the 27th president, succeeding Theodore Roosevelt. He served from 1909 to 1913, beaten for reelection because Teddy Roosevelt ran on a third-party ticket and split the Republican vote. President Harding later appointed him chief justice of the United States.

Roger B. Taney (1777–1864) was chief justice of the United States whose Court ruled in the *Dred Scott* case. Key points of the decision: Dred Scott, born a slave, had not become free merely by having lived in free territory; Scott had no rights as a citizen; the Missouri Compromise was unconstitutional because it deprived slave owners of their property rights.

Zachary Taylor (1784–1850) was the 12th president. Prior to that he had been an army officer who had great success during the Mexican War. He died during his term of office and was succeeded by Millard Fillmore.

Tecumseh (1768–1813) was a Shawnee chief who tried to unite Indiana tribes in the Ohio Valley and negotiate with Governor William Henry Harrison. The negotiations failed, and Tecumseh fought on the side of the British during the War of 1812.

James Thacher (mid-18th to mid-19th century) was an American army surgeon during the American Revolution.

Henry David Thoreau (1817–1862) was a philosopher and writer. In *Walden Pond*, he wrote of his experiences living alone in the woods for two years. In *Civil Disobedience*, he expressed his misgivings about the role of government.

James Thurber (1894–1961) was a humorist. His essays, short stories, and cartoons first appeared in *The New Yorker*. He was cowriter, with Eliott Nugent, of the 1940 play *The Male Animal*.

James Townsley (mid-19th century) witnessed the "Potawatomie Massacre" in Kansas. He was arrested after the killings but was never tried.

William B. Travis (1809–1836) fought for Texas independence from Mexico. He led the garrison at the Alamo, where he died with his men.

Rupert Trimmingham (mid- to late-20th century) was a corporal in the U.S. Army during World War II. An African American, he protested the Jim Crow restrictions while in the service.

Harry S Truman (1884–1972) was a U.S. senator who became Franklin Roosevelt's running mate in 1944. Upon Roosevelt's death, Truman was sworn in as president. He made the decision to drop the atomic bomb on Japan, initiated the European Recovery

Program, which became the Marshall Plan, set up the North Atlantic Treaty Organization to contain the Soviet Union, used an airlift to thwart the Russian blockade of Berlin, supported South Korea, which had been invaded by the Communist North, and fired General Douglas MacArthur for disobeying orders.

Sojourner Truth (1797–1883) was born a slave. She became free when New York state emancipated all its slaves in 1827. An antislavery speaker before the Civil War, she became a staunch supporter of women's rights afterward.

Harriet Tubman (1821–1913) was a former slave who led 300 fugitives to Canada via the Underground Railroad. Because of her work, she was often referred to as the Moses of her people.

Barbara W. Tuchman (1912–1989) was a historian. Her books included *The Guns of August, The Zimmerman Telegram, Stilwell and the American Experience in China,* and *The March of Folly.*

Frederick Jackson Turner (1861–1932) was a historian who advanced the theory about the importance of the western frontier in American history.

Nat Turner (1800–1831) was a slave who led a slave insurrection in Virginia in August 1831. A preacher, he believed that he had been divinely inspired to free the slaves. He was captured and executed.

Mark Twain (1835–1910) was the pseudonym of Samuel Langhorne Clemens, a novelist, satirist, and political observer. His works include *The Adventures of Tom Sawyer, Huckleberry Finn, Pudd'nhead Wilson,* and *A Connecticut Yankee in King Arthur's Court.*

Frank E. Vandiver (1925–) is a historian and biographer.

Emily Field Van Tassel (mid- to late 20th century) is visiting associate professor of law at Case Western Reserve University.

Bartolomeo Vanzetti (1888–1927) was born in Italy. He came to the United States and became an anarchist. He and Nicola Sacco were charged with murdering two men during a robbery. Though they were convicted and executed, their guilt is questioned to this day.

Frank de Varona (mid- to late 20th century) was born in Cuba. He is the region superintendent of schools in Dade County, Florida. He wrote the textbook *Hispanics in the United States.*

Tony Vellela (late 20th century) is a journalist and author. He has written for the *Christian Science Monitor, Rolling Stone,* the Bell-McClure Newspaper Syndicate, and others.

Comte de Vergennes (1717–1787) was the French foreign minister who negotiated the Treaty of Alliance between the United States and France during the American Revolution.

Fred M. Vinson (1890–1953) was chief justice of the United States from 1946 to 1953. Before that, he had been a member of Congress, a justice on the Court of Appeals, and secretary of the treasury.

Jonathan Wainwright (1883–1953) was the general forced to surrender Corregidor and the other fortified islands of Manila Bay during World War II. After the war, he was awarded the Congressional Medal of Honor.

Daniel Walker (mid-20th century) waw a lawyer who conducted an investigation of the riots during the Democratic National Convention in Chicago in 1968.

George C. Wallace (1919–1998) was a four-term governor of Alabama who ran unsuccessfully for president. An avowed segregationist, he won millions of votes from disaffected Democrats in the North. During the presidential campaign of 1972 he was badly wounded in an assassination attempt. Later in his life, he softened his stand on the issue of integration.

Artemus Ward (1834–1867) was the pen name of Charles Farrar Browne. A lecturer and newspaper columnist, he wrote many satirical pieces during the Civil War.

Samuel R. Ward (mid-19th century) was an African American who published *The Impartial Citizen*.

Earl Warren (1891–1974) was chief justice of the United States from 1953 to 1969. During that time, civil rights in America were expanded through many of his Court's decisions. Prior to joining the bench, he had been governor of California.

Joseph Warren (1741–1775) was a New England patriot who sent Paul Revere off on his midnight ride to warn the Minute Men that the British were coming. He died at the Battle of Breed's Hill (mistakenly called the Battle of Bunker Hill).

Booker T. Washington (1856–1915) was a former slave who became a prominent educator and founder of Tuskegee Institute.

George Washington (1732–1799) was the hero of the American Revolution. After the war, he presided over the constitutional convention in Philadelphia and became first president of the United States.

Daniel Webster (1782–1852) was a powerful orator who served in the House of Representatives and the U.S. Senate and as secretary of state for three presidents.

Joseph N. Welch (1890–1960) was a lawyer. He represented the U.S. Army in its confrontation with Senator Joseph R. McCarthy. A televised tongue-lashing by Welch destroyed the power of the Wisconsin senator.

W. Richard West Jr. (1943–   ), a Cheyenne, is director of the Smithsonian National Museum of the American Indian in Washington.

Wetatonmi (mid-19th century) was a Nez Perce. She and other members of the tribe fled with Chief Joseph toward Canada to escape life on a reservation. They were trapped just miles short of their goal. Her husband, brother of Chief Joseph, was killed in the battle.

Phillis Wheatley (1753?–1784) was born in West Africa. She was seized as a child and transported to America as a slave. She became a noted poetess, and her work was published both in England and in America.

Burton K. Wheeler (1882–1975) was a U.S. senator who vigorously opposed American entry into World War II.

Horace White (mid-19th century) was a reporter for the *Chicago Tribune*. He covered the Lincoln–Douglas debates and other political stories for that newspaper.

John White (late 16th century) was the leader of the English colony at Roanoke Island, Virginia. In 1587 he returned to England for badly needed provisions. He left behind not only his wife and children but his brand-new granddaughter, Virginia Dare, first English child born in America. His return to Roanoke was delayed by threats of the Spanish Armada. When he returned in 1590, he found the settlement deserted and in ruins.

William Allen White (1868–1944) was the editor of the *Emporia (Kansas) Gazette*. He also wrote novels, biographies, and essays.

Walt Whitman (1819–1892) was a poet and essayist. His works include *Leaves of Grass*, "When Lilacs Last in the Dooryard Bloomed," and "Song of the Open Road."

John Greenleaf Whittier (1807–1892) was a poet and author. Before the Civil War, he wrote extensively on the abolition of slavery.

Tom Wicker (1926–   ) was a journalist and author. He held numerous editorial posts with the *New York Times*.

Roger W. Wilkins (mid- to late 20th century) was assistant U.S. attorney general in the Lyndon Johnson administration. He has been involved in editorial projects with the *Washington Post* and the *New York Times*.

Wendell L. Willkie (1892–1944) was the Republican candidate who opposed Franklin Roosevelt for the presidency in 1940.

Woodrow Wilson (1856–1924) was president during World War I. He failed to get Senate approval for American participation in the League of Nations.

Walter Winchell (1891–1972) was one of the most influential newspaper columnists of the 1940s. Inventor of the gossip column, he was also a radio commentator.

Albert Wolff (1903–1998) was a federal agent. He was part of the Elliot Ness anti-bootlegging squad during Prohibition. The group had the reputation of being "untouchable," that is, incapable of being bribed.

Robert E. Wood (1879–1969) head of Sears, Roebuck, founded the America First Committee to keep America out of World War II.

Herman Wouk (1915–) is a novelist. His works include *The Caine Mutiny, The Winds of War,* and *War and Remembrance.*

Wovoka (1858–1932) was a Paiute medicine man. He had a vision about a time when Indian lands would be returned and the buffalo would come back. This would come about through a Ghost Dance, to be performed by the Indians.

Jonathan J. Wright (mid-19th century) was one of some 70 black delegates to the South Carolina constitutional convention of 1868. Wright, a lawyer, later became a justice of the state's supreme court.

Orville Wright (1871–1948) and his brother Wilbur (1867–1912) built and flew the first machine that could fly under its own power.

Richard Wright (1908–1960) was an African American who wrote about how white society dealt with blacks in America.

Israel Zangwill (1864–1926) was a British playwright and novelist.

Arthur Zimmermann (1864–1940) was German foreign secretary during several years of World War I. His intercepted telegram calling for an alliance with Mexico against the United States helped bring the United States into the war.

Chronology

Following are some important events in American history. A chronology of the entire American presidency appears separately.

ca. 35,000 B.C.: First Asians cross the land bridge from Siberia to North America.

ca. 10,000 to 8,000 B.C.: Many Native American tribes hunt, fish, and grow crops in areas now part of the United States.

ca. A.D. 1000: Viking Leif Ericson explores East Coast of North America.

ca. 1298: Marco Polo dictates his memoirs, telling of his travels and of the vast riches of the Far East.

1492: Seeking a sea route to the Far East by sailing west, Columbus lands on a North American island. Believing that he has reached India, he calls the inhabitants "Indians."

1507: Geographer Martin Waldseemuller calls the new land "America."

1513: Ponce de Leon explores Florida.

1522: Juan Sebastian del Cano, one of Magellan's captains, ends first circumnavigation of the world. Magellan had been killed in the Philippines.

1541: Coronado, seeking fabled lost cities of gold, discovers the Grand Canyon. De Soto discovers the Mississippi River.

1585: English colony established on Roanoke Island, North Carolina.

1607: English establish settlement at Jamestown, Virginia.

1613: Dutch fur traders set up a post on Manhattan Island.

1619: First Africans brought to English America. They come by Dutch ship to Jamestown, Virginia, as indentured servants.

1620: Pilgrims arrive at Plymouth, Massachusetts.

1626: Peter Minuit buys Manhattan Island and founds New Amsterdam.

1664: Duke of York seizes New Amsterdam from Dutch and changes name to New York.

1692: Witchcraft trials in Salem, Massachusetts. Twenty executed.

1712: Slave revolt in New York.

1735: John Peter Zenger, acquitted of libel, establishes truth as an absolute defense.

1756–1763: French and Indian War. Called the Seven Years' War in Europe, it ends with France's surrendering Canada to the English.

1764–1767: English Parliament passes series of laws taxing American colonists.

1770: Boston Massacre.

1773: Boston Tea Party. British shut port of Boston until tea is paid for.

1775: Paul Revere's ride. Shots fired at Lexington and Concord. American Revolution begins.

1776: Declaration of Independence adopted in Philadelphia.

1777: Americans defeat British at Saratoga, New York.

1778: United States signs treaty of alliance with France.

1781: Cornwallis surrenders British army at Yorktown, Virginia.

1783: Treaty of Paris. U.S. independence recognized.

1787: Delegates meeting in Philadelphia to amend Articles of Confederation decide to scrap it and write new Constitution.

1789: George Washington chosen first president of the United States, John Adams first vice president.

1801: John Marshall named chief justice of the United States by President John Adams.

1803: Chief Justice Marshall's Supreme Court, for the first time, rules that an act of Congress is unconstitutional. President Jefferson arranges purchase of Louisiana Territory from Napoleon.

1804: Lewis and Clark explore Louisiana Territory and proceed to the Pacific in search of a Northwest Passage.

1812: War of 1812, between United States and Britain, begins.

1814: British capture and burn Washington, D.C. Francis Scott Key writes "Star-Spangled Banner" during British bombardment of Ft. McHenry, Baltimore. Treaty of Ghent officially ends war.

1815: Battle of New Orleans takes place before the news arrives that war is over.

1820: Missouri Compromise. Initial boundaries are set by Congress for extension of slavery.

1823: President Monroe states doctrine that United States opposes any further European colonization in the Americas.

1831: The *Liberator*, an abolitionist newspaper, launched by William Lloyd Garrison. Nat Turner slave rebellion in Virginia.

1836: Mexicans storm the Alamo.

1845: United States annexes Texas.

1846: Mexican War.

1848: Mexico cedes to United States territories in California, Texas, and the New Mexico area. Gold discovered in California.

1850: Congress passes Compromise of 1850, setting rules for slavery extension and limitation in newly acquired territories.

1852: Harriet Beecher Stowe publishes *Uncle Tom's Cabin*.

1857: Chief Justice Taney issues *Dred Scott* decision. Congress had no right to ban slavery from any territory.

1859: John Brown leads raid on Harper's Ferry, Virginia. Brown is tried for treason and hanged.

1860: Following Lincoln's election, South Carolina secedes from the Union.

1861: After withdrawing from Union, 11 southern states form Confederacy. Firing on Fort Sumter sets off Civil War. Union troops defeated at Bull Run, Virginia.

1863: Lincoln issues Emancipation Proclamation. Union wins battle of Gettysburg, Pennsylvania. Draft riots in New York City.

1865: Lee surrenders to Grant at Appomattox Court House, Virginia. Lincoln assassinated. Slavery abolished by 13th Amendment to the Constitution.

1867: United States buys Alaska from Russia.

1868: President Andrew Johnson impeached by the House of Representatives. Senate fails to convict by a single vote.

1869: Transcontinental Railroad completed.

1871: Great Chicago fire.

1876: Custer and his command are annihilated at the Little Big Horn.

1877: Rutherford B. Hayes declared winner of disputed electoral votes and is declared president. Last federal troops withdrawn from the South, ending Reconstruction.

1881: President Garfield shot by a disappointed office-seeker.

1886: Haymarket bombing in Chicago.

1889: Oklahoma land rush.

1890: Indians massacred at Wounded Knee, South Dakota.

1896: Supreme Court rules that separate facilities for blacks are legal if they are equal.

1898: Spanish-American War. United States to be ceded the Philippines and Puerto Rico by Spain.

1901: President McKinley assassinated.

1903: Panama revolts from Colombia. United States makes treaty with Panama to build canal.

1906: San Francisco earthquake.

1914: Panama Canal opens. World War I breaks out in Europe.

1917: United States declares war on Germany.

1919: Boston police strike.

1925: John Scopes convicted for teaching evolution.

1927: Lindbergh flies Atlantic solo. Sacco and Vanzetti executed.

1929: Stock market crash sets off Great Depression.

1932: Bonus marchers routed in Washington, D.C.

1933: Franklin Roosevelt sworn in as president. New Deal begins.

1937: Roosevelt recommends adding members to Supreme Court. Proposal fails.

1939: World War II breaks out in Europe.

1941: Lend-Lease Act, approving arms sales to Britain, approved by Congress. Japanese attack Pearl Harbor, bringing United States into war.

1942: Philippines falls as Japanese take Bataan and Corregidor. U.S. military evacuate Japanese Americans from West Coast. They are put in relocation camps. U.S. Navy victorious over Japanese in Battle of Midway.

1943: Following victories in North Africa, United States and Britain invade Italy.

1944: Allies invade Normandy. Battle of the Bulge.

1945: President Roosevelt dies. Nazi Germany surrenders. Atomic bombs dropped on Japan, forcing Japanese surrender.

1948: Truman wins presidency in stunning upset.

1950: Alger Hiss, who had denied Communist spy charges, convicted of perjury. United States sends troops to South Korea to prevent takeover by Communist North.

1951: Senator Estes Kefauver conducts televised hearings on organized crime.

1953: Rosenbergs executed for wartime espionage on behalf of Soviet Union.

1954: Army-McCarthy hearings on television. Supreme Court rules unanimously that school segregation is unconstitutional.

1960: Nixon debates Kennedy in first televised presidential debates.

1961: U.S.-backed Cuban exiles land at Bay of Pigs but fail in attempt to overthrow Castro. Alan Shepard Jr. first American launched into space.

1962: Cuban missile crisis. At U.S. insistence, Soviet Union withdraws atomic missiles from Cuba.

1963: President Kennedy assassinated by Lee Harvey Oswald, who is himself killed by Jack Ruby.

1964: President Johnson signs Medicare into law and pushes War on Poverty.

1965: United States steps up aid to South Vietnam. Malcolm X assassinated. Voting Rights Act signed into law by President Johnson.

1966: U.S. participation in Vietnam War continues to expand.

1967: African Americans riot and burn ghetto areas of Detroit and Newark, New Jersey.

1968: Ghetto riots sweep across America following assassination of Dr. Martin Luther King Jr. Robert Kennedy assassinated. Protesters and police clash, disrupting Democratic National Convention in Chicago.

1969: Neil Armstrong first human to walk on the moon.

1970: Students at Kent State and Jackson State are slain during anti–Vietnam War demonstrations.

1971: Voting age lowered to 18 by constitutional amendment.

1972: Break-in at the Democratic National Committee headquarters at the Watergate complex by operatives working for the White House. Subsequent investigations by the press and Congress will destroy the Nixon presidency.

1973: Vice President Spiro Agnew resigns after pleading no contest to tax evasion charges.

1974: Facing impeachment, Nixon resigns. He is pardoned by President Ford.

1975: Vietnam War ends. North Vietnamese occupy all of South Vietnam as Americans are evacuated.

1978: President Carter negotiates, and Senate approves, Panama Canal treaties to turn over canal operations to Panamanians on December 31, 1999.

1979: Iranian mobs seize American hostages from U.S. Embassy in Tehran.

1980: U.S. attempt to rescue American hostages fails, Following negotiations, they are released in January 1981, when Carter is no longer president.

1981: President Reagan fires air traffic controllers for illegal strike.

1986: Six astronauts and observer teacher die as space shuttle *Challenger* blows up on launching.

1987: Senate investigates Iran-Contra affair, in which arms were sold to Iran and the profits used to finance Contra activities in Central America.

1989: President Bush orders invasion of Panama to arrest Manuel Noriegha for drug smuggling.

1990: President Bush sends U.S. forces to Saudi Arabia to protect it from invasion by Iraq.

1991: United States and allied forces liberate Kuwait and invade Iraq in Operation Desert Storm.

1993: Car bomb goes off in parking garage under World Trade Center, New York.

1993: President Clinton sets "don't ask, don't tell, don't pursue" policy on gays in the military.

1994: Independent counsel appointed to investigate the Whitewater case—an Arkansas land deal that had failed during Bill Clinton's term as governor. In 2000 the counsel concludes that there is no credible evidence on which either Bill or Hillary Clinton can be charged. Health care plan drafted under chairmanship of Hillary Rodham Clinton dies. "Contract with America" helps Republicans win control of both Houses of Congress in fall election.

1995: Truck bomb destroys a federal building in Oklahoma City and kills 168. United States joins other NATO forces to end "ethnic cleansing" in Bosnia. Some 20,000 American troops involved.

1996: Line-item veto is passed by Congress and approved by the president. It is ruled unconstitutional by the Supreme Court.

1998: President Clinton impeached by House of Representatives.

1999: U.S. Senate acquits Clinton.

2000: Governor George W. Bush of Texas is elected president, following 5–4 decision by U.S. Supreme Court denying recount in Florida. Vice President Albert Gore Jr. concedes. Gore won the popular vote, but Bush victory in Florida gives him the electoral vote majority.

2001: Terrorists strike at the World Trade Center in New York City and the Pentagon in Virginia. Thousands are killed or missing after the blasts. President George W. Bush declares the attacks acts of war.

THE AMERICAN PRESIDENCY: 1789–2001

President	Party	Born	Died	Years Served
George Washington	Federalist	1732	1799	1789–1797
John Adams	Federalist	1735	1826	1797–1801
Thomas Jefferson	Democratic-Republican	1743	1826	1801–1809
James Madison	Democratic-Republican	1751	1836	1809–1817
James Monroe	Democratic-Republican	1758	1831	1817–1825

John Quincy Adams	Democratic-Republican	1767	1848	1825–1829
Andrew Jackson	Democratic	1767	1845	1829–1837
Martin Van Buren	Democratic	1782	1862	1837–1841
William Henry Harrison	Whig	1773	1841	1841
John Tyler*	Whig	1790	1862	1841–1845
James K. Polk	Democratic	1795	1849	1845–1849
Zachary Taylor	Whig	1784	1850	1849–1850
Millard Fillmore*	Whig	1800	1874	1850–1853
Franklin Pierce	Democratic	1804	1869	1853–1857
James Buchanan	Democratic	1791	1868	1857–1861
Abraham Lincoln	Republican	1809	1865	1861–1865
Andrew Johnson*	Democratic	1808	1875	1865–1869
Ulysses S. Grant	Republican	1822	1885	1869–1877
Rutherford B. Hayes	Republican	1822	1893	1877–1881
James A. Garfield	Republican	1831	1881	1881
Chester Alan Arthur*	Republican	1830	1886	1881–1885
Grover Cleveland	Democratic	1837	1908	1885–1889
Benjamin Harrison	Republican	1833	1901	1889–1893
Grover Cleveland	Democratic	1837	1908	1893–1897
William McKinley	Republican	1843	1901	1897–1901
Theodore Roosevelt*	Republican	1858	1919	1901–1909
William Howard Taft	Republican	1857	1930	1909–1913
Woodrow Wilson	Democratic	1856	1924	1913–1921
Warren G. Harding	Republican	1865	1923	1921–1923
Calvin Coolidge*	Republican	1872	1933	1923–1929
Herbert Hoover	Republican	1874	1964	1929–1933
Franklin D. Roosevelt	Democratic	1882	1945	1933–1945
Harry S Truman*	Democratic	1884	1972	1945–1953
Dwight D. Eisenhower	Republican	1890	1969	1953–1961
John F. Kennedy	Democratic	1917	1963	1961–1963
Lyndon B. Johnson*	Democratic	1908	1973	1963–1969
Richard M. Nixon	Republican	1913	1994	1969–1974
Gerald R. Ford**	Republican	1913		1974–1977
Jimmy Carter	Democratic	1924		1977–1981
Ronald Reagan	Republican	1911		1981–1989
George H. Bush	Republican	1924		1989–1993

| Bill Clinton | Democratic | 1946 | 1993–2001 |
| George W. Bush | Republican | 1946 | 2001– |

*Assumed office on death of president.
**Assumed office following resignation of president.

Bibliography

Adams, Charles Francis, ed. *The Works of John Adams, Second President of the United States.* Boston: Little, Brown, 1854.

Adams, Joey. *Joey Adams Encyclopedia of Humor.* Indianapolis: Bobbs-Merrill, 1968.

Addams, Jane. *Twenty Years at Hull-House.* Phillips, Publishing Co., 1910. Reprinted by New American Library, 1961.

Adler, Bill, ed. *Presidential Wit.* New York: Trident Press, 1966.

Alcott, Louisa May. *Little Women.* Boston: Roberts Brothers, 1868–1869.

Alger, Horatio, Jr. *Ragged Dick.* New York: Collier Books, 1962. (Originally published in 1867.)

Andrews, Wayne, ed., *Concise Dictionary of American History.* New York: Charles Scribner's Sons, 1962.

Angle, Paul M., ed. *The Lincoln Reader.* New Brunswick, NJ: Rutgers University Press, 1947.

Angle, Paul M., ed. *The American Reader.* Chicago: Rand McNally, 1954.

Aptheker, Herbert, ed. *A Documentary History of the Negro People in the United States.* New York: Citadel Press, 1951.

Atkinson, Brooks, ed. *The Complete Essays and Other Writings of Ralph Waldo Emerson.* New York: Modern Library, 1950.

Avorn, Jerry L., with members of the staff of the *Columbia Daily Spectator.* *Up against the Ivy Wall: A History of the Columbia Crisis.* New York: Atheneum, 1969.

Baez, Joan. *And a Voice to Sing With: A Memoir.* New York: A Plume Book, New American Library, 1987.

Bandon, Alexander. *Vietnamese Americans.* New York: New Discovery Books, Macmillan, 1994.

Banneker, Benjamin. *Banneker's Almanac.* 1796.

Barck, Oscar Theodore, Jr., ed. *American in the World: Twentieth-Century History in Documents.* Cleveland, OH: World, 1961.

Bartlett, John, and Beck, Emily Morison, eds. *Familiar Quotations.* 15th ed. Boston: Little, Brown, 1980.

Battles and Leaders of the Civil War. New York: Century, 1884.

Beard, Charles A. *An Economic Interpretation of the Constitution of the United States.* New Brunswick, NJ: Transaction, 1998. (Originally published in 1913.)

Benet, William Rose, ed. *Benet's Reader's Encyclopedia.* New York: Harper and Row, 1987.

Benet, William Rose, and Cousins, Norman, ed. *The Poetry of Freedom.* New York: Modern Library, 1948.

Berger, Josef, and Berger, Dorothy, eds. *Diary of America.* New York: Simon and Schuster, 1957.

Bernstein, Carl, and Woodward, Bob. *All the President's Men.* New York: Simon and Schuster, 1974.

The Best from Yank, *the Army Weekly.* Selected by the editors of *Yank.* New York: E. P. Dutton, 1945.

Bibb, Henry. *Narrative of the Life and Adventures of Henry Bibb, an American Slave.* New York: 1849.

Blassingame, John W., ed. *Slave Testimony.* Baton Rouge: Louisiana State University Press, 1977.

Block, Herbert. *Herblock's Special for Today.* New York: Simon and Schuster, 1958.

Boorstin, Daniel J. *The Image: A Guide to Pseudo-Events in America.* New York: Atheneum, 1961.

Bourne, Peter G. *Jimmy Carter: A Comprehensive Biography from Plains to Postpresidency.* New York: Lisa Drew/Scribner, 1997.

Bradford, William. *History of the Plymouth Plantation.* New York: Charles Scribner's Sons, 1908.

Branch, Taylor. *Parting of Waters: America in the King Years, 1954–63.* New York: Simon and Schuster, 1988.

Brereton, Lewis H. *The Brereton Diaries.* New York: William Morrow, 1946.

A Brief Narrative of the Case and Tryal of John Peter Zenger of the New York Weekly Journal. New York: 1738.

Brockway, Wallace, and Winer, Bart Keith, eds. *Homespun America.* New York: Simon and Schuster, 1959.

Brown, Anthony Cave. *The Last Hero: William J. Donovan.* New York: Times Books, 1982.

Brown, Dee. *Bury My Heart at Wounded Knee.* New York: Holt, Rinehart, and Winston, 1971.

Brown, Stuart Gerry, ed. *We Hold These Truths.* New York: Harper and Brothers, 1941.

Buchwald, Art. *I Never Danced at the White House.* New York: G. P. Putnam's Sons, 1973.

Buell, Thomas B. *Master of Sea Power: A Biography of Fleet Admiral Ernest J. King.* Boston: Little, Brown, 1980.

Burdette, Franklin L., ed. *Readings for Republicans.* New York: Oceana, 1960.

Bureau of Indian Affairs. *Famous Indians, a Collection of Short Biographies.* Washington, DC: 1975.

Bush, George H., and Scowcroft, Brent. *A World Transformed.* New York: Alfred A. Knopf, 1998.

Bush, George W. *A Charge to Keep.* New York: William Morrow, 1999.

Butcher, Harry C. *My Three Years with Eisenhower.* New York: Simon and Schuster, 1946.

Byrd, Richard E. *Alone.* New York: G. P. Putnam's Sons, 1938.

Califano, Joseph A., Jr. *The Triumph & Tragedy of Lyndon Johnson: The White House Years.* New York: Simon and Schuster, 1991.

Carnegie, Andrew. *The Gospel of Wealth.* New York: 1900.

Carnegie, Dale. *How to Win Friends and Influence People*. New York: Simon and Schuster, 1936.

Carroll, Andrew, ed. *Letters of a Nation: A Collection of Extraordinary American Letters*. New York: Kodansha America, 1997.

Carson, Rachel. *Silent Spring*. Boston: Houghton Mifflin, 1962.

Carter, Jimmy. *Keeping Faith: Memoirs of a President*. New York: Bantam Books, 1982.

Castell, Ron, ed. *The Blockbuster Guide to Movies and Videos*. New York: Dell, 1995.

Castillo, Richard Griswold del, and Garcia, Richard A. *Cesar Chavez: A Triumph of Spirit*. Norman: University of Oklahoma Press, 1995.

Chisholm, Shirley. *Unbought and Unbossed*. Boston: Houghton Mifflin, 1970.

Chiu, Tony, ed. *Ross Perot: In His Own Words*. New York: Warner Books, 1992.

Christensen, A. N., and Kirkpatrick, E. M. *The People, Politics, and the Politician*. New York: Henry Holt, 1941.

Clanton, Gene. *Populism: The Humane Preference in America, 1890–1900*. Boston: Twayne, 1991.

Clark, Marcia. *Without a Doubt*. New York: Viking Penguin, 1997.

Clark, Walter Van Tilburg. *The Ox-Bow Incident*. New York: New American Library, 1960. (Originally published in 1940.)

Cleaver, Eldridge. *Soul on Ice*. New York: McGraw-Hill, 1968.

Clemens, Samuel Langhorne, Howells, William Dean, and Clark, Charles Hopkins, eds. *Mark Twain's Library of Humor*. New York: Charles L. Webster, 1888. Reprinted by Bonanza Books.

Cochran, Thomas C., advis. ed., and Andrews, Wayne, ed. *Concise Dictionary of American History*. New York: Charles Scribner's Sons, 1961.

Cohen, Steven, ed. *Vietnam: Anthology and Guide to a Television History*. New York: Alfred A. Knopf, 1983.

Colbert, David, ed. *Eyewitness to America*. New York: Pantheon Books, 1997.

Commager, Henry Steele, ed. *The Blue and the Gray: The Story of the Civil War as Told by Participants*. New York: Bobbs-Merrill, 1950.

Commager, Henry Steele, ed. *Documents of American History*. 6th edition. New York: Appleton-Century-Crofts, 1958.

Commager, Henry Steele, and Morris, Richard B., eds. *The Spirit of Seventy-Six: The Story of the American Revolution as Told by Participants*. 2 vols. New York: Bobbs-Merrill, 1958.

Conant, James B. *Slums and Suburbs: A Commentary on Schools in Metropolitan Areas*. New York: McGraw-Hill, 1961.

Cooke, Jacob E., ed. *The Federalist*. Hanover, NH: University Press of New England, 1982.

Coolidge, Calvin. *Autobiography of Calvin Coolidge*. New York: Cosmopolitan Book Corporation, 1929.

Cooper, James Fenimore. *The Last of the Mohicans*. New York: Oxford University Press, 1993. This edition reprinted the text established by James Sappenfield and E. N. Feltskog for *The Writings of James Fenimore Cooper*, published by the State University of New York Press. (Originally published in 1826.)

Cotner, Robert C., ed. *Addresses and State Papers of James Stephen Hogg*. Austin: University of Texas Press, 1951.

Couric, Emily, ed. *Women Lawyers*. New York: Law and Business/Harcourt Brace Jovanovich, 1984.

Crane, Stephen. *The Red Badge of Courage*. Appleton, 1895. Reprinted by Pocket Books, New York, 1972.

Creel, George. *Rebel at Large*. New York: 1947.

Crevecoeur, J. Hector St. John. *Letters from an American Farmer*. Gloucester, MA: Peter Smith, 1968. (Originally published in London in 1782.)

Darrow, Clarence. *The Story of My Life*. New York: Charles Scribner's Sons, 1932.

Davis, Marilyn P. *Mexican Voices/American Dreams: An Oral History of Mexican Immigration to the United States*. New York: Henry Holt, 1990.

Davis, Matthew L. *Memoirs of Aaron Burr*. New York: Da Capo Press, 1971. (Originally published in 1837.)

Davis, William C. *Jefferson Davis: The Man and His Hour*. New York: HarperCollins, 1991.

Dekok, David. *Unseen Danger: A Tragedy of People, Government, and the Centralia Mine Fire*. Philadelphia: University of Pennsylvania Press, 1986.

Deloria, Vine, Jr. *Custer Died for Your Sins*. New York: Macmillan, 1969.

Dickinson, Anna. *What Answer?* Boston: Ticknor and Fields, 1868.

Dos Passos, John. *U.S.A.* Boston: Houghton Mifflin, 1940.

Douglass, Frederick. *Life and Times of Frederick Douglass*. From *Frederick Douglass Biographies*. New York: Literary Classics of the United States, 1994. (Originally published in 1881.)

Drake, Samuel G. *Biography and History of the Indians of North America*. 3rd edition. Perkins and Hillard, Gray, 1834.

Duberman, Martin Baum, *Paul Robeson*. New York: Alfred A. Knopf, 1988.

Du Bois, W.E.B. *The Souls of Black Folk*. New York: Fawcett, 1961. (Originally published in 1903.)

Dunne, Finley Peter. *Observations by Mr. Dooley*. New York: 1902.

Eastman, Charles A. *From the Deep Woods to Civilization*. Boston: Little, Brown, 1916.

Eastman, Charles A. *Indian Heroes and Great Chieftains*. Boston: Little, Brown, 1918.

Eszterhas, Joe, and Roberts, Michael D. *Thirteen Seconds: Confrontation at Kent State*. New York: Dodd, Mead, 1970.

Feingold, Henry L. *The Politics of Rescue: The Roosevelt Administration and the Holocaust, 1938–1945*. New Brunswick, NJ: Rutgers University Press, 1970.

Fernandez, Roberto G. *Raining Backwards*. Houston, TX: Arte Publico Press, 1988.

Ferrell, Robert H., ed. *The Autobiography of Harry S Truman*. Boulder: Colorado Associated University Press, 1980.

Findling, John E. *Dictionary of American Diplomatic History*. Westport, CT: Greenwood Press, 1980.

Firmat, Gustavo Perez. *Next Year in Cuba: A Cuban's Coming-of-Age in America*. New York: Bantam Doubleday Dell, 1995.

Fleming, Walter L. *Documentary History of Reconstruction*. 2 vols. New York: 1950.

Foote, Henry Stuart. *Texas and the Texans*. Philadelphia, 1841.

Ford, Gerald R. *A Time to Heal*. New York: Harper and Row, 1979.

Franklin, Benjamin. *Poor Richard's Almanac*. Published between 1732 and 1757. Reprinted by Spencer Press.

Franklin, Benjamin. *Autobiography of Benjamin Franklin*. (Original manuscript published in 1790; complete text published in 1868.) Reprinted by Spencer Press.

Franklin, Penelope, ed. *Private Pages: Diaries of American Women, 1830s–1970s*. New York: Ballantine Books, 1986.

Freidel, Frank. *The Splendid Little War*. Boston: Little, Brown, 1958.

Friedan, Betty. *The Feminine Mystique*. New York: Dell Publishing Co., 1984. (Originally published in 1964.)

Friedan, Betty. *It Changed My Life: Writings on the Women's Movement*. New York: Random House, 1976.

Frost, Elizabeth. *The Bully Pulpit*. New York: Facts on File, 1988.

Gallagher, John, and Bull, Chris. *Perfect Enemies: The Religious Right, the Gay Movement, and the Politics of the 1990s*. New York: Crown, 1996.

Garcia, Maria Cristina. *Havana USA: Cuban Exiles and Cuban Americans in South Florida, 1959–1994*. Berkeley/Los Angeles: University of California Press, 1996.

Garvey, Marcus. *Philosophy and Opinions*. Dover, MA: Majority Press, 1986. (Originally published in 1923.)

Geddes, Donald Porter, ed. *Franklin Delano Roosevelt: A Memorial*. New York: Pocket Books, 1945.

George, Henry. *Progress and Poverty*. New York: W. J. Black, 1942. (Originally published in 1879.)

Glieg, George Robert. *The Campaigns of the British Army at Washington and New Orleans*. London: 1821.

Golden, Harry. *Only in America*. Cleveland: World, 1958.

Gompers, Samuel. *Seventy Years of Life and Labor*. New York: 1925.

Gore, Al [Jr.]. *Earth in the Balance: Ecology and the Human Spirit*. Boston: Houghton Mifflin, 1992.

Graf, LeRoy P., Haskins, Ralph, and Bergeron, Paul H., eds. *The Papers of Andrew Johnson*. Knoxville: University of Tennessee Press, 1967.

Gray, Thomas R., ed. *The Confessions of Nat Turner*. Baltimore, 1831.

Gregory, Dick. *Nigger*, New York: Dutton, 1964.

Gunther, John. *Inside U.S.A.* New York: Harper and Brothers, 1947.

Hair, William Ivy. *The Kingfish and His Realm: The Life and Times of Huey P. Long*. Baton Rouge: Louisiana State University Press, 1991.

Hakluyt, Richard. *The Principal Navigations, Voyages, Traffiques, and Discoveries of the English Nation*. Edinburgh: 1889.

Harbord, James G. *The American Army in France, 1917–1919*. Boston: Little, Brown, 1936.

Harris, Fred R., and Wilkins, Roger W., eds. *Quiet Riots*. New York: Pantheon Books, 1988.

Haskell, Frank A. *The Battle of Gettysburg*. Wisconsin History Commission Reports, No. 1, 1908.

Haun, Harry. *The Movie Quote Book*. New York: Lippincott and Crowell, 1980.

Hawthorne, Nathaniel. *The Scarlet Letter*. Columbus, OH: Charles E. Merrill, 1969. Text is that of the Centenary Edition of the Works of Nathaniel Hawthorne, published by Ohio State University Press. (Originally published in 1850.)

Heller, Joseph. *Catch-22*. New York: Simon and Schuster. Special edition 1994. (Originally published in 1955.)

Heller, Steven, ed. *Man Bites Man: Two Decades of Satiric Art*. New York: A and W, 1981.

Herrmann, Dorothy. *Helen Keller: A Life*. New York: Alfred A. Knopf, 1998.

Herwig, Holger H., and Heyman, Neil M. *Biographical Dictionary of World War I*. Westport, CT: Greenwood Press, 1982.

Hobson, Laura Z. *Gentleman's Agreement*. New York: Simon and Schuster, 1947.

Hofstadter, Richard, and Wallace, Michael, eds. *American Violence: A Documentary History*. New York: Alfred A. Knopf, 1970.

Hollander, John, ed. *American Poetry: The Nineteenth Century*. 2 vols. New York: Literary Classics of the United States, 1993.

Holli, Melvin G., and Jones, Peter d'A. *Biographical Dictionary of American Mayors, 1820–1980: Big City Mayors*. Westport, CT: Greenwood Press, 1981.

Holliday, Robert Cortes, ed. *Joyce Kilmer*. Vol. 1. Port Washington, NY: Kennikat Press, 1918.

Hoover, Herbert. *Public Papers of the Presidents*. 4 vols. Washington, DC: U.S. Government Printing Office, 1977.

Howard, Oliver O. *My Life and Experiences among Our Hostile Indians*. Worthington, 1907.

Hubbard, Elbert. *A Message to Garcia*. New York: Franklin Watts, 1962. (Original essay published in 1899.)

Humfreville, J. Leo. *Twenty Years among Our Savage Indians*. Hartford, 1897.

Hunt, Harriot K. *Glances and Glimpses, or Fifty Years Social, including Twenty Years Professional Life*. Boston: John P. Jewett, 1856.

Hunter, John D. *Memoirs of a Captivity among the Indians of North America*. London: 1924.

Irving, Washington. *Knickerbocker's History of New York*. Edited by Anne Carroll Moore. Garden City, NY: Doubleday, Doran, 1928. (Originally published in 1809.)

Irving, Washington. *Stories of the Hudson*. Harrison, NY: Harbor Hill Books, 1984. (Collection originally published in 1849.)

Jackson, Donald, ed. *Letters of the Lewis and Clark Expedition: With Related Documents, 1783–1854*. Urbana: University of Illinois Press, 1962.

Jackson, Helen Hunt. *A Century of Dishonor*. Boston: Little, Brown, 1913. (Originally published in 1881.)

Jacobs, James B., with Panarella, Christopher, and Worthington, Jay. *Busting the Mob: United States v. Cosa Nostra*. New York: New York University Press, 1994.

Jameson, J. Franklin, ed. *Narratives of New Netherland: 1609–1664*. New York: Barnes and Noble, 1937. (Originally published in 1909.)

Jaquette, Henrietta, ed. *South after Gettysburg: Letters of Cornelia Hancock from the Army of the Potomac, 1863–1865*. Philadelphia: University of Pennsylvania Press, 1937.

Jaworski, Leon. *The Right and the Power: The Prosecution of Watergate*. New York: Readers Digest Press, distributed by Thomas Y. Crowell, 1976.

Jennings, James, and Rivera, Monte, eds. *Puerto Rican Politics in Urban America*. Westport, CT: Greenwood Press, 1984.

Jensen, Merrill, ed. *American Colonial Documents to 1776*. Oxford University Press, 1955.

Kasdin, Steven J., ed. *The Collected Jack London*. New York: Dorsey Press, 1991.

Keegan, John. *The First World War*. New York: Alfred A. Knopf, 1998.

Keller, Albert C., and Davie, Maurice R., eds. *Essays of William Graham Sumner*. 2 vols. New Haven, CT: 1934.

Kelly, Fred C. *The Wright Brothers*. New York: Farrar, Straus, and Young, 1950.

Kendrick, Alexander. *Prime Time: The Life of Edward R. Murrow*. Boston: Little, Brown, 1969.

Kerr, K. Austin. *Organized for Prohibition: A New History of the Anti-Saloon League*. New Haven, CT: Yale University Press, 1985.

King, Anita, ed. *Quotations in Black*. Westport, CT: Greenwood Press, 1981.

Kirkpatrick, Evron M., and Kirkpatrick, Jeanne J., eds. *Elections—U.S.A.: A Selection of Articles from The New York Times Magazine*. New York: Henry Holt, 1956.

Kisseloff, Jeff. *You Must Remember This*. New York: Harcourt Brace Jovanovich, 1989.

Klingberg, Frank W., ed. *A History of the United States: From 1865 to the Present.* Cleveland: World, 1962.

Kraft, Barbara S. *The Peace Ship: Henry Ford's Pacifist Adventure in the First World War.* New York: Macmillan, 1978.

Kuebler, Harold W., ed. *The Treasury of Science Fiction Classics.* Garden City, NY: Hanover House, 1954.

Kull, Irving S., and Kull, Nell M. *A Chronological Encyclopedia of American History.* New York: Popular Library, 1969.

Kunstler, William M. *The Case for Courage.* New York: William Morrow, 1962.

Kunstler, William M., with Isenberg, Sheila. *My Life as a Radical Lawyer.* New York: Carol, 1994.

Lamon, Ward Hill. *Recollections of Abraham Lincoln, 1847–1865.* Chicago: A. C. McClurg, 1895.

Langer, Howard J., ed. *American Indian Quotations.* Westport, CT: Greenwood Press, 1996.

Langer, Howard J., ed. *World War II: An Encyclopedia of Quotations.* Westport, CT: Greenwood Press, 1999.

Ledeen, Michael A. *Perilous Statecraft: An Insider's Account of the Iran-Contra Affair.* New York: Charles Scribner's Sons, 1988.

Lee, David D. *Sergeant York: An American Hero.* Lexington: University of Kentucky Press, 1985.

Lee, Robert E. [Jr.]. *Recollections and Letters of General Robert E. Lee.* New York: Doubleday, Page, 1904.

Lerner, Gerda. *The Female Experience: An American Documentary.* Indianapolis: Bobbs-Merrill, 1977.

Lerner, Max. *Ideas Are Weapons.* New York: Viking Press, 1939.

Levy, Peter B., ed. *Let Freedom Ring: A Documentary History of the Modern Civil Rights Movement.* Westport, CT: Praeger, 1992.

Lewis, Sinclair. *Babbitt.* New York: Harcourt Brace Jovanovich, 1922. Reprinted by New American Library, 1961.

Lindbergh, Charles A., Jr. *We.* New York: G. P. Putnam's Sons, 1927.

Litwack, Leon P. *Been in the Storm So Long: The Aftermath of Slavery.* New York: Alfred A. Knopf, 1979.

Litwak, Mark. *Courtroom Crusaders.* New York: William Morrow, 1989.

Lomask, Milton. *Aaron Burr: The Conspiracy and Years of Exile, 1805–1836.* New York: Farrar, Straus, and Giroux, 1982.

Lomax, John A., and Lomax, Alan. *American Ballads and Folk Songs.* New York: Macmillan, 1934.

Lomax, Louis E. *The Negro Revolt.* New York: New American Library, 1964.

Longstreet, James. *From Manassas to Appomattox: Memoirs of the Civil War in America.* Revised. Philadelphia: J. B. Lippincott, 1903.

Lynd, Alice, and Lynd, Staughton, eds. *Rank and File: Personal Histories by Working-Class Organizers.* Boston: Beacon Press, 1973.

Macdonald, Dwight. *Memoirs of a Revolutionist.* New York: Farrar, Straus, and Cudahy, 1957.

Mann, Arthur. *Branch Rickey: American in Action.* Boston: Houghton Mifflin, 1957.

Mann, Horace. *Report of the Massachusetts Board of Education.* Boston: Dutton & Wentworth, 1838–1849.

Marchetti, Victor, and Marks, John D. *The CIA and the Cult of Intelligence*. New York: Dell, 1975. (Originally published by Knopf in 1974.)

Marquis, Don. *archy and mehitabel*. New York: Doubleday, Doran, 1927.

Mars, Florence, with the assistance of Eden, Lynn. *Witness in Philadelphia*. Baton Rouge: Louisiana State University Press 1977.

Marshall, S.L.A. *American Heritage History of World War I*. New York: American Heritage/Bonanza Books, 1982.

Marvis, Barbara J. *Famous People of Hispanic Heritage*. Vol. 1. Childs, MD: Mitchell Lane Publishers, 1996.

Matthiessen, Peter. *In the Spirit of Crazy Horse*. New York: Viking, 1983.

Mauldin, Bill. *Up Front*. New York: Henry Holt, 1945.

Mauldin, Bill. *Back Home*. New York: William Sloane Associates, 1947.

Maurice, Frederick, ed. *An Aide-de-Camp of Lee, Being the Papers of Colonel Charles Marshall*. Boston: Little, Brown, 1927.

McCullough, David. *Truman*. New York: Simon and Schuster, 1992.

McDougall, Walter A. *Promised Land, Crusader State: The American Encounter with the World since 1776*. Boston: Houghton Mifflin, 1997.

McNamara, Robert S., with VanDeMark, Brian. *In Retrospect: The Tragedy and Lessons of Vietnam*. New York: Times Books, a division of Random House, 1995.

McWhorter, Lucullus V. *Hear Me My Chiefs!* Caldwell, ID 1952.

Mehdi, Beverlee Turner, ed. *The Arabs in America, 1492–1977*. Dobbs Ferry, NY: Oceana, 1978.

Meltzer, Milton. *The Hispanic Americans*. New York: Thomas Y. Crowell, 1982.

Melville, Herman. *Redburn, White-Jacket, Moby-Dick*. New York: Literary Classics of the United States, 1983. (*Moby-Dick* originally published in 1851.)

Metzker, Isaac, ed. *A Bintel Brief: Sixty Years of Letters from the Lower East Side to the Jewish Daily Forward*. Garden City, NY: Doubleday, 1971.

Miller, Arthur. *Death of a Salesman*. New York: Penguin Putnam, 1998. (Play originally produced in 1949.)

Mitchell, Margaret. *Gone With the Wind*. New York: Macmillan, 1936.

Moore, Frank, ed. *The Diary of the American Revolution: 1775–1781*. New York: 1860.

Moore, Frank, ed. *The Rebellion Record*. New York: 1871.

Moraga, Cherrie, and Anzaldúa, Gloria. *This Bridge Called My Back: Writings by Radical Women of Color*. Watertown, MA: Persephone Press, 1981.

Morey, Janet Nomura, and Dunn, Wendy. *Famous Asian Americans*. New York: Cobblehill Books, Dutton, Penguin Books USA, 1992.

Morison, Samuel Eliot. *Admiral of the Ocean Sea*. Boston: Little, Brown, 1942.

Morison, Samuel Eliot. *The Intellectual Life of Colonial New England*. Ithaca, NY: Cornell University Press, 1960.

Morris, Richard B., and Morris, Jeffrey B., eds. *Encyclopedia of American History*. 6th edition. New York: Harper and Row, 1982.

Moynihan, Ruth Barnes, Russett, Cynthia, and Crumpacker, Laurie. *Second to None: A Documentary History of American Women*. 2 vols. Lincoln: University of Nebraska Press, 1993.

Myrdal, Gunnar. *An American Dilemma: The Negro Problem and Modern Democracy*. New York: Harper and Row, 1944.

Nader, Ralph. *Unsafe at Any Speed*. New York: Grossman, 1965.

Neier, Aryeh. *War Crimes: Brutality, Genocide, Terror, and the Struggle for Justice*. New York: Random House, 1998.

Nevins, Allan, ed. *Polk: The Diary of a President*. London: Longmans, Green, 1929.

Newton, Joseph Fort. *Lincoln and Herndon*. Cedar Rapids: Torch Press, 1910.

Nichols, David, ed. *Ernie's War: The Best of Ernie Pyle's World War II Dispatches*. New York: Random House, 1986.

Niles, H. *Principles and Acts of the Revolution*. 1822.

Nixon, Richard M. *In the Arena, a Memoir of Victory, Defeat, and Renewal*. New York: Simon and Schuster, 1990.

Nizer, Louis. *My Life in Court*. Garden City, NY: Doubleday, 1961.

Northrup, Solomon. *Twelve Years a Slave*. Buffalo, NY: 1853.

O'Gorman, Angie, ed. *The Universe Bends toward Justice: A Reader on Christian Nonviolence in the U.S.* Philadelphia: New Society, 1990.

Palmer, Laura. *Letters and Remembrances from the Vietnam Veterans Memorial*. New York: Random House, 1987.

Parmet, Herbert S. *George Bush: The Life of a Lone Star Yankee*. New York: Lisa Drew/Scribner, 1997.

Peare, Catherine Owens. *William Penn*. Philadelphia: Lippincott, 1957.

The People Shall Judge: Readings in the Formation of American Policy. Chicago: University of Chicago Press, 1949.

Peoples Bicentennial Commission. *Voices of the American Revolution*. New York: Bantam, 1975.

Pershing, John J. *My Experiences in the World War*. 2 vols. New York: Frederick A. Stokes, 1931.

Philippe, Robert. *Political Graphics; Art as a Weapon*. New York: Abbeville Press, 1982.

Pogue, Forrest C., ed. *George C. Marshall: Organizer of Victory*. New York: Viking, 1973.

Powderly, T. V. *Thirty Years of Labor*. Excelsior, 1889.

Powers, Richard Gid. *Secrecy and Power: The Life of J. Edgar Hoover*. New York: Free Press, a division of Macmillan, 1987.

Pringle, Henry F. *Theodore Roosevelt: A Biography*. Revised edition. New York: Harcourt, Brace, and World, 1956.

Rachlis, Eugene. *They came to Kill: The Story of Eight Nazi Saboteurs in America*. New York: Random House, 1961.

Randall, James G. *Lincoln the President, Springfield to Gettysburg*. New York: Dodd, Mead, 1945.

Reed, Edward, ed. *Readings for Democrats*. New York: Oceana, 1960.

Remini, Robert V. *Henry Clay: Statesman for the Union*. New York: W. W. Norton, 1991.

Report of the Warren Commission on the Assassination of President Kennedy. New York: Bantam Books, 1964.

Richardson, Don, ed. *Conversations with Carter*. Boulder, Co: Lynne Rienner, 1998.

Rickenbacker, Eddie V. *Fighting the Flying Circus*. Edited by Arch Whitehouse. Garden City, NY: Doubleday, 1965. (Previous copyright: 1919.)

Rights in Conflict: The Violent Confrontation of Demonstrators and Police in the Parks and Streets of Chicago during the Democratic National Convention of 1968. New York: Dutton, 1968.

Riordon, William L. *Plunkitt of Tammany Hall*. New York: McClure, Phillips, 1905.

Robinson, Charles. *The Kansas Conflict*. 1892.

Rodgers, Marion Elizabeth, ed. *The Impossible H. L. Mencken: A Selection of His Best Newspaper Stories*. New York: Doubleday, 1991.

Romulo, Carlos P. *I Saw the Fall of the Philippines*. Garden City, NY: Doubleday, Doran, 1942.

Roosevelt, Theodore. *The New Nationalism*. New York 1910.

Rosenstiel, Annette. *Red & White: Indian Views of the White Man*. New York: Universe Books, 1983.

Rush, Richard. *Occasional Productions: Political, Diplomatic, and Miscellaneous*. Philadelphia: J. B. Lippincott, 1860.

Russell, William H. *My Diary North and South*. London: Bradbury and Evans, 1863.

Ryan, Halford, ed. *The Inaugural Addresses of 20th Century American Presidents*. Westport, CT: Praeger, 1993.

Schapsmeier, Edward L., and Schapsmeier, Frederick H. *Political Parties and Civic Action Groups*. Westport, CT: Greenwood Press, 1981.

Schechter, Stephen L., ed. *Roots of the Republic: American Founding Documents Interpreted*. Madison, WI: Madison House, 1990.

Schickel, Richard. *D. W. Griffith: An American Life*. New York: Simon and Schuster, 1984.

Schlesinger, Arthur M., Jr. *The Age of Jackson*. Boston: Little, Brown, 1953. (Originally published in 1945.)

Schoenbrun, David. *Triumph in Paris: The Exploits of Benjamin Franklin*. New York: Harper and Row, 1976.

Schwarzkopf, H. Norman, with Petre, Peter. *It Doesn't Take a Hero*. New York: Bantam Books, 1992.

Sherman, William T. *Memoirs of General William T. Sherman*. New York: D. Appleton, 1875.

Shorris, Earl. *Latinos: A Biography of the People*. New York: W. W. Norton, 1992.

Sick, Gary. *October Surprise: American Hostages in Iran and the Election of Ronald Reagan*. New York: Times Books/Random House, 1991.

Sifakis, Carl. *Encyclopedia of American Crime*. New York: Facts on File, 1982.

Simpson, Brooks D. *The Reconstruction Presidents*. Lawrence: University Press of Kansas, 1998.

Sinclair, Upton. *The Jungle*. New York: New American Library, 1960. (Originally published in 1906.)

Smith, John David. *Black Voices from Reconstruction*. Brookfield, CT: Millbrook Press, 1996.

Snyder, Louis L., and Morris, Richard B., eds. *A Treasury of Great Reporting*. 2nd edition. New York: Simon and Schuster, 1962.

Sorensen, Theodore C., ed. *Let the Word Go Forth: The Speeches, Statements, and Writings of John F. Kennedy*. New York: Delacorte Press, 1988.

Spanish Explorers in the Southern United States. New York: 1907.

Sperber, Ann M. *Murrow: His Life and Times*. New York: Freundlich Books, 1986.

Standing Bear, Chief. *Land of the Spotted Eagle*. Boston: Houghton Mifflin, 1933.

Stands in Timber, John, and Liberty, Margot. *Cheyenne Memories*. New Haven, CT: Yale University Press, 1967.

Stanton, Elizabeth Cady, Anthony, Susan B., and Gage, Matilda Joslyn, eds. *The History of Woman Suffrage*. 1881.

Steffens, Lincoln. *Autobiography*. New York: Harcourt, Brace, 1931.

Steinbeck, John. *The Grapes of Wrath*. New York: Viking Press, 1939.

Stephanopoulus, George. *All Too Human: A Political Education*. Boston: Little, Brown, 1999.

Stevenson, William. *A Man Called Intrepid*. New York: Harcourt Brace Jovanovich, 1976.

Storing, Herbert J., ed. *The Complete Anti-Federalist*. Chicago: University of Chicago Press, 1981.

Stowe, Harriet Beecher. *Uncle Tom's Cabin*. Everyman's Library, 1909. (Originally published in 1852.)

Streeter, Edward. *Dere Mable*. New York: Dodd, Mead, 1918, 1941.

Swanberg, W. A. *Citizen Hearst: A Biography of William Randolph Hearst*. New York: Charles Scribner's Sons, 1961.

Takaki, Ronald. *Strangers from a Different Shore: A History of Asian Americans*. Boston: Little, Brown, 1989.

Taking the Stand: The Testimony of Lieutenant-Colonel Oliver L. North. New York: Pocket Books, 1987.

Thacher, James. *Military Journal of the American Revolutionary War, 1775 to 1783*. Hartford, CT: Silas Andrus and Son, 1854.

Thatcher, B. B. *Indian Biography*. New York, 1845.

Thomas Jefferson: Writings. Notes and text selections by Merrill D. Peterson. New York: Library of America, 1984.

Thoreau, Henry David. *The Wariorum Walden and The Wariorum Civil Disobedience*. New York: Pocket Books, 1968. (Originally published in 1849.)

Thurber, James. *The Thurber Carnival*. New York: Dell, 1962.

Torres-Saillant, Silvlio, and Hernandez, Ramona. *The Dominican Americans*. Westport, CT: Greenwood Press, 1998.

Trefousse, Hans L. *Anddrew Johnson: A Biography*. New York: Norton, 1989.

Tuchman, Barbara. *The Zimmermann Telegram*. New York: Macmillan, 1958.

Tuchman, Barbara W. *Stilwell and the American Experience in China, 1911–45*. New York: Macmillan, 1970.

Turner, Frederick Jackson. *The Frontier in American History*. New York: Holt, 1950.

Twain, Mark. *The Adventures of Huckleberry Finn*. Charles L. Webster, 1885. Reprinted by New York: Random House, 1996.

Twain, Mark. *Pudd'nhead Wilson*. Reprinted by Bantam, 1959. (Originally published in *Century* magazine, 1893–1894.)

Van Doren, Carl. *Secret History of the American Revolution*. New York: Viking Press, 1968. (Originally published in 1941.)

Vandiver, Frank E. *Black Jack: The Life and Times of John J. Pershing*. 2 vols. College Station: Texas A&M University Press, 1977.

Van Tassel, Emily Field, and Finkelman, Paul. *Impeachable Offenses: A Documentary History from 1787 to the Present*. Washington, DC: Congressional Quarterly, 1999.

Varona, Frank de. *Latino Literacy: The Complete Guide to Our Hispanic History and Culture*. New York: A Round Stone Press Book, Henry Holt, 1996.

Vellela, Tony. *New Voices: Student Activism in the '80s and '90s*. Boston: South End Press, 1988.

The War of the Rebellion: Official Records of the Union and Confederate Armies. Series I. Washington, D.C., 1880.

Werstein, Irving. *The Great Struggle: Labor in America*. New York: Charles Scribner's Sons, 1965.

White, E. B., and White, Katharine S., eds. *A Subtreasury of American Humor*. New York: Coward-McCann, 1941.

White, William Allen. *The Autobiography of William Allen White*. New York: Macmillan, 1946.

Wicker, Tom. *A Time to Die*. New York: Quadrangle/A New York Times Book, 1975.

Williams, Charles R. *The Diary and Letters of Rutherford B. Hayes*. Columbus, OH: 1914.

Willkie, Wendell L. *One World*. New York: Simon and Schuster, 1943.

Winchell, Walter. *Winchell Exclusive: Things That Happened to Me—and Me to Them*. Upper Saddle River, NJ: Prentice-Hall, 1975.

Woodward, Bob. *Veil: The Secret Wars of the CIA, 1981–1987*. New York: Simon and Schuster, 1987.

World Almanac and Book of Facts 2000. Mahwah, NJ: Primedia Reference, 1999.

Wouk, Herman. *The Caine Mutiny*. Garden City, NY: Doubleday, 1951.

Wright, Richard. *Black Boy: A Record of a Childhood and Youth*. New York: Perennial Library, 1966. (Originally published in 1945.)

Zeligs, Meyer A. *Friendship and Fratricide: An Analysis of Whittaker Chambers and Alger Hiss*. New York: Viking Press, 1967.

Index

All the numbers in the index refer to quotation numbers, *not* page numbers. When a number appears *in italics* after an individual's name, it refers to a specific quotation by that individual. Numbers in roman type may refer to subject matter, an individual spoken to or about, an important location, or a reference in an editorial note accompanying the quotation.

About the Editor

HOWARD J. LANGER is currently a freelance writer. He has worked as a journalist, magazine editor, textbook editor, marketing director, and director of publications. His other books include *American Indian Quotations* (Greenwood, 1996), *The History of the Holocaust: A Chronology of Quotations* (1997), and *World War II: An Encyclopedia of Quotations* (Greenwood, 1999).